The Teacher's Role in Implementing Cooperative
Learning in the Classroom

COMPUTER-SUPPORTED COLLABORATIVE LEARNING

VOLUME 7

The *Computer-Supported Collaborative Learning Book Series* is for people working in the CSCL field. The scope of the series extends to 'collaborative learning' in its broadest sense; the term is used for situations ranging from two individuals performing a task together, during a short period of time, to groups of 200 students following the same course and interacting via electronic mail. This variety also concerns the computational tools used in learning: elaborated graphical whiteboards support peer interaction, while more rudimentary text-based discussion forums are used for large group interaction. The series will integrate issues related to CSCL such as collaborative problem solving, collaborative learning without computers, negotiation patterns outside collaborative tasks, and many other relevant topics. It will also cover computational issues such as models, algorithms or architectures which support innovative functions relevant to CSCL systems.

The edited volumes and monographs to be published in this series offer authors who have carried out interesting research work the opportunity to integrate various pieces of their recent work into a larger framework.

The titles published in this series are listed at the end of this volume.

R. M. Gillies • A. F. Ashman • J. Terwel
(Editors)

The Teacher's Role in Implementing Cooperative Learning in the Classroom

Springer

MT

Robyn M. Gillies
University of Queensland
Brisbane, Qld 4072
Australia
r.gillies@uq.edu.au

Adrian F. Ashman
University of Queensland
Brisbane, Qld 4072
Australia
adrian.ashman@uq.edu.au

Jan Terwel
Vrije University
1081 BT Amsterdam
the Netherlands
j.terwel@psy.vu.nl

Series Editor:

Pierre Dillenbourg
Swiss Federal Institute of Technology
Lausanne, CH-1015
Switzerland

ISBN 978-0-387-70891-1   e-ISBN 978-0-387-70892-8

Library of Congress Control Number: 2007920037

Printed on acid-free paper.

9 8 7 6 5 4 3 2 1

springer.com

9/9/09

Contents

Contributors

Adrian F. Ashman is a professor of special education in the School of Education at The University of Queensland, Brisbane, Australia. He has a 30-year history of publication in the education, psychology, and disability field and is known internationally for his work in the application of cognitive psychology to regular and special education contexts. He is a Fellow of the American Psychological Association and of the International Association for the Scientific Study of Intellectual Disability. He has published 20 books and major monographs and more than 150 research articles and book chapters, many on cooperative learning. In 2003, he co-edited with Gillies *Cooperative learning: The Social and Intellectual Outcomes of Learning in Groups* (RoutledgeFalmer). Contact: adrian.ashman@uq.edu.au

Ed Baines is a researcher based in the School of Psychology and Human Development at the Institute of Education, University of London. His main research interest is in children's interactions with peers in the classroom and in informal contexts such as at break time and outside school. Contact: E.Baines@ioe.ac.uk

Peter Blatchford is professor in psychology and education in the School of Psychology and Human Development at the Institute of Education, University of London. His research interests include social developmental processes in school settings, educational effects of class size differences and pupil adult ratios, improving the effectiveness of pupil groups in classrooms, grouping practices in primary and secondary schools, and peer relations and friendships and playground games and activities. He has published widely in such leading international journals as *The American Educational Research Journal*, *Learning and Instruction*, *The International Journal of Educational Research*, *The British Journal of Educational Research*, and *The British Journal of Educational Psychology*. Contact: P.Blatchford@ioe.ac.uk

Marieke Fakkert received her master's degree in educational pedagogy at the Vrije University Amsterdam, The Netherlands. She followed an internship within the PhD project of Fleur Prinsen and looked at the learning processes of the students in that particular CSCL setting. The outcomes resulted in her master thesis and a contribution to the chapter described in this handbook. She currently works as a curriculum designer at the Dutch National Police Academy. Contact: mcfakkert@gmail.com.

Robyn M. Gillies is an associate professor in the School of Education at the University of Queensland, Brisbane, Australia. She has worked extensively in schools to help teachers establish cooperative learning experiences in their classrooms. The results of this research have been published in many leading international journals including *The Journal of Educational Psychology*, *The Journal of Special Education*, *The International Journal of Educational Research*, *Learning and Instruction*, *The British Journal of Educational Psychology*, and in 2003 she co-edited *Cooperative learning: The Social and Intellectual Outcomes of Learning in Groups* (RoutledgeFalmer). Contact: r.gillies@uq.edu.au

Rachel Hertz-Lazarowitz is a professor in the Faculty of Education at Haifa University, Israel. Her research interests include classroom instruction and interaction, school-wide change, school–family–community partnerships, friendship development, and Arab and Jews coexistence. She has published widely in such leading international journals as *The Journal of Social and Personal Relationships*, *The Elementary School Journal*, *Merrill-Palmer Quarterly*, *Psychology in the Schools*, *Contemporary Educational Psychology*, *International Journal of Behavioral Development*, and *The Journal of Educational Psychology*. In 1992, she co-edited *Interaction in Cooperative Groups: The Theoretical Anatomy of Group Learning*. New York and London: Cambridge University Press. Contact: rachelhl@construct.haifa.ac.il

Anne A. Huber is an assistant professor at the University of Education at Weingarten. Her research subjects are the development, implementation, and evaluation of cooperative learning methods. Her particular interests are in how to support cooperative learning processes effectively and in how to implement cooperative learning in school and adult education. Contact: huber.anne@web.de

Günter L. Huber is a retired professor of educational psychology at the University of Tübingen, Germany, and was chair of the Department of Educational Psychology at the Institute of Educational Science. Among his publications are books and training materials on cooperative learning and teaching/learning problems, interindividual differences, and software for the analysis of qualitative data. Contact: huber.paedpsy@uni-tuebingen.de

David W. Johnson is arguably one of the leading international scholars and researchers on cooperative learning. He and his brother, Roger Johnson, are the proponents of the working together approach to using cooperative learning in schools. They are prolific writers and, over the last 30 years, have published several hundred articles and numerous books and book chapters on their approach to cooperative learning. Contact: johns009@tc.umn.edu

Roger T. Johnson is a professor in the Department of Curriculum and Instruction with an emphasis in Science Education at the University of Minnesota. He is an authority on inquiry teaching and has worked at the national level in science education in the USA and the UK. Together with David W. Johnson, he is the co-director of the Cooperative Learning Center at the University of Minnesota which conducts research and training nationally and internationally on changing the structure of classrooms and schools to a more cooperative environment at the University of Minnesota. Contact: johns009@tc.umn.edu

Alison King is professor emerita of educational psychology, California State University San Marcos and visiting professor of University of California Irvine. Her research has a dual focus: self-regulated learning (*Cognitive Strategies and Metacognition*) and socio-cognitive learning (*Socio-Cognitive Learning Strategies, Peer-Mediated Learning, Peer Tutoring, Questioning and Answering Processes in Thinking and Problem Solving*). In particular she is interested in processes involved in mediation of children's thinking and learning by teacher/caregivers, peers, and parents or other significant adult family members. Contact: aking@csusm.edu

Peter Kutnick is a professor of psychology and education at King's College London (University of London), United Kingdom. His research interests include understanding social pedagogy in classroom group work, grouping practices in pre-schools, primary and secondary schools, and peer relationships and friend-ships. He has published widely in such leading international journals as *The International Journal of Educational Research, The British Educational Research Journal, Educational Research, The British Journal of Educational Psychology*, and *The Social Psychology of Education*. He has also written and edited a number of books concerning children's social development and schooling. Contact: Peter.Kutnick@kcl.ac.uk

Rachel A. Lotan is an associate professor in the School of Education at Stanford University, California where she is involved in researching issues in *Access and Equity, Bilingual Education/ESL, Small Group Instruction and Interaction, Sociology of Education, Sociology of the Classroom*, and *Teacher Education and Certification*. Contact: rlotan@stanford.edu

Fleur Prinsen is a researcher at the Department of Education at the Vrije University Amsterdam in the Netherlands. She is currently conducting research on computer supported collaborative learning (CSCSL) for her doctoral degree. She received a masters degree in educational psychology at the University of Leiden with her thesis on learning styles and text comprehension. She has also taught several master classes at the University of Leiden and an online master's course on CSCL, as visiting lecturer at the University of Oulu, Finland. After her PhD, she intends to pursue a research career studying inclusion of all students in computer-supported collaborative learning. Contact: fr.prinsen@psy.vu.nl or frprinsen@gmail.com

John A. Ross is professor of curriculum, teaching, and learning at the Ontario Institute for Studies in Education at the University of Toronto. He has worked with teachers in one of OISE/UT's field centers for thirty years, designing, implementing, and evaluating curriculum, as well as teaching in the graduate studies program. His research focuses on student assessment, especially in cooperative learning contexts, school improvement, and program evaluation. Contact: jross@oise. utoronto.ca

Robert J. Stevens is an associate professor of educational psychology at Pennsylvania State University. He has written extensively on cooperative learning and its affect on children's literacy during the elementary and middle-years of schooling. His work has been published in such a leading international journals at *The American Educational Research Journal*, *The Elementary School Journal*, *The Journal of Educational Psychology*, *Reading Research Quarterly*, and *Teaching and Teacher Education*. Contact: rjs15@psu.edu

Jan Terwel is professor emeritus of education at the Vrije University Amsterdam in the Netherlands. His main contributions have been to curriculum studies, grouping in education, learning in cooperative groups and individual differences, especially in primary and secondary mathematics education. He is the author of numerous articles and book chapters, and co-editor with Decker Walker from Stanford University of *Curriculum as a Shaping Force* (2004). Until February 2006, he chaired the Department of Education in the Faculty of Psychology and Education and was director of the research program "Strategic Learning in the Curriculum." He was visiting professor at the School of Education, Stanford University, California in the US and visiting professor at the School of Education, University of Queensland, Australia. He currently participates in several PhD research projects as supervisor at the Department of Education of the Vrije University Amsterdam. Contact: J.Terwel@psy.vu.nl

Monique Volman is a professor of education in the Institute for Teacher Education and the Department of Education, in the Faculty of Education and Psychology at the Vrije Universiteit Amsterdam. She has published many articles in international journals and is the author of several books. Her areas of specialization are educational technology, social competence, and social and cultural differences between students. Contact: mll.volman@psy.vu.nl

Noreen M. Webb is a professor of social research methodology in the Graduate School of Education and Information Studies at the University of California, Los Angeles. Her research interests include classroom processes related to learning outcomes, small-group problem solving, achievement testing in mathematics and science, aptitude-treatment interaction research, and generalizability theory. She has published widely in many leading international journals including *Learning and Cognition*, *The Journal of Educational Psychology*, *The International Journal of Educational Research*, *The American Educational Research Journal*, and *Applied Measurement in Education*. Contact: webb@ucla.edu

The Teacher's Role in Implementing Cooperative Learning in the Classroom: An Introduction

Robyn M. Gillies, Adrian F. Ashman, and Jan Terwel

Peer-mediated learning is well recognised as a pedagogical practice that promotes learning, higher level thinking, and prosocial behaviour in students from pre-school to college. Children and adolescents learn from each other in a vast range of formal and informal settings. These include casual social meetings with friends, at skateboard parks, and even on the beach or ski slope. In formal settings, young people are often required to work and learn together and, indeed, small and large group sessions are common in all educational environments from preschool to tertiary education.

Peer-mediation has been the cornerstone of a range of instructional technologies that includes cooperative learning, peer collaboration, and peer-tutoring known under several labels (e.g., Classwide Peer-tutoring, Peer-Assisted Learning Strategies). The developers and advocates of these and many other peer-mediated learning programs argued that by working together, students have many opportunities to learn and develop a greater understanding of others with diverse social, interpersonal, adjustment, and learning needs (Shachar, 2003; Stevahn & King 2005).

This book is predominantly about cooperative learning that was developed by many scholars and researchers in the past four decades. Among the most important researchers we mention, David Johnson and Roger Johnson, Robert Slavin, Elizabeth Cohen and Noreen Webb. It is the apparent success of this approach (see Johnson & Johnson 1989) that led Slavin (1999) to suggest that it is one of the greatest educational innovations of recent times.

The most successful and influential approaches are not simply techniques to present the same old content in a different manner but have their roots in one of the Grand Theories on human development, teaching, and learning. The Johnsons explicitly mention Deutsch as a great inspiration in formulating their interdependence theory on cooperative learning. Cohen's work is firmly rooted in sociological theories and especially focused on social status. The work of Webb has been inspired by socio-cognitive theories on interaction and learning, originally developed by Piaget and Vygotsky while the research conducted by Slavin has been inspired by motivational theories, which apparently have their roots in behaviourism and management theories.

All authors of the subsequent chapters in this book are directly or more indirectly inspired by these Grand Theories or Schools for Thought (Bruer 1993) and stand on the shoulders of the already mentioned initiators of the cooperative learning movement in the last four decades. However, recent developments in social and cognitive theories, for example, socio-constructivism, on how knowledge is collaboratively constructed and the revolution in information technology have largely influenced theory and practice of cooperative learning as can be seen in, for example, computer supported collaborative learning (CSCL).

Although initial research on cooperative learning focused on the social and educational benefits, research over the last two decades has examined the factors that mediate and moderate learning that occurs when students participate in small groups. Included in this research are studies that have examined the role that students play in mediating each other's learning through to those that examine the types of help they provide, the quality of that help (see Ross & Cousins 1995; Terwel et al. 2001; Webb 1992), and the conditions required for successful helping to occur (Webb & Mastergeorge 2003). Other studies have examined how teachers can train students to use specific cognitive and metacognitive questioning strategies to facilitate discussion, thinking, and learning during cooperative group work (see King 1997; O'Donnell 1999; Palincsar & Herrenkohl 1999). More recently, the focus has moved to the role of teachers' discourse during cooperative learning and its affect on the quality of group discussions and the learning achieved (see Gillies 2004; Hertz-Lazarowitz & Shachar 1990) and meta-analytic studies that have examined collections of studies to gauge the extent of the effects of cooperative versus other teaching-learning configurations (see e.g., Johnson & Johnson 2002; Neber et al. 2001).

Despite the well-documented benefits of cooperative learning, implementing this pedagogical practice in classrooms, or indeed any of the structured peer-mediation programs, is a challenge that many teachers find difficult to accomplish (Cohen, 1994). Difficulties may occur because teachers often do not have a clear understanding about how to establish effective cooperative groups, the research and theoretical perspectives that have informed this approach, and how they can translate this information into practical classrooms applications.

Teachers' reluctance to embrace cooperative learning may also be due to the lack of time to learn about peer-mediated approaches, because of the challenge they perceive it might poses to their control of the learning process, the demands it places on classroom organisational changes, or the professional commitments that is required to sustain their efforts (Cohen et al. 2004). There is no doubt that getting cooperative learning up and running in a classroom requires a commitment to embedding the procedures into the curricula and in implementing, monitoring, and evaluating it.

The teacher's role in implementing cooperative learning in the classroom provides a comprehensive overview of these issues. In many chapters there are clear guidelines and discussion about how cooperative learning practices can be embedded into classroom curricula. This volume also provides an overview of the major research and theoretical perspectives that underpin the development of cooperative learning, outlines how specific small group experiences can promote interaction, thinking and learning, discusses key roles teachers play in promoting student discourse, and demonstrates how interaction style among students and teachers is crucial in facilitating discussion, problem-solving, and learning.

An Overview of the Chapters

The book is organised into three sections with the first section (Chap. 1–3) presenting both the research and theoretical perspectives that underpin successful small group work, including examples of how class teachers can implement cooperative learning. The second section (Chap. 4–9) highlights different ways in which teachers can structure group interactions among students to promote discourse and learning. The final section (Chap. 10–12) focuses on how students can be taught different cognitive and metacognitive skills to enhance discussions in small groups. The key roles teachers play in implementing this pedagogical practice and in promoting thinking and learning is a theme that is highlighted throughout the book.

In the Chapter 1, *Social Interdependence Theory and Cooperative Learning: The Teacher's Role*, Johnson and Johnson draw on their extensive experience in both the research and practical aspects of cooperative learning to draw out the factors that lead to success in academic tasks. They first provide a brief historical overview of the theoretical underpinnings of cooperative learning and then highlight the key role social interdependence plays in establishing a group structure that motivates group members to work together, build quality relationships, and actively support each other's learning. The outcomes of successful cooperative experiences lead to higher level reasoning and problem-solving, greater effort to achieve, enhanced relationships among group members, and improved psychological health.

In Chapter 2, *Beyond the classroom and into the community: The role of the teacher in expanding the pedagogy of cooperation*, Hertz-Lazarowitz argues that cooperative learning now has the potential to change teachers from conducting 'a set of cooperative learning methods' to implementing a 'cooperative learning critical pedagogy' that is part of the critical pedagogies that aim to change the nature of schooling and society. Based on research and theorizing since 1979 up until the present, this chapter presents four developmental elements that have contributed to a cooperative learning critical pedagogy. These involve: first, teachers' thinking on cooperative learning as a set of methods; second, teachers' perceptions and attitudes related to this approach to teaching and learning; third, teachers' instructional behaviours in the cooperative classroom and beyond, and finally, the restructuring of cooperative learning as a critical pedagogy. Hertz-Lazarowitz proposes that more theory on 'cooperative learning pedagogy' is needed so teachers can be empowered to use it effectively to create an impact on teaching and society.

The following chapter by Baines, Blatchford and Kutnick reviews the research on grouping students, the central premise being that all children in classrooms will be seated in some form of group. The authors argue, however, that this is only the starting point for a social pedagogic understanding of how classroom contexts may promote or inhibit learning. There is substantial evidence that seating pupils in groups is unlikely to relate to the learning purpose or intention of many lessons. The first challenge, the authors propose, is for teachers and researchers to understand how student groups are currently used in primary and secondary schools and how the use of groups may relate to classroom learning. The authors discuss two studies that they undertook that map group size and composition found in classrooms against intended learning tasks, patterns of group interaction and the role of the teacher. Findings of their research using Social Pedagogic Research into Groupwork (SPRinG) show that learning within groups is often limited due to their composition and that learning potential is often mismatched with pedagogic intent. The second challenge is determining how group work can be made more effective in classrooms. Here the chapter draws upon another study that shows how a relational approach to training for group working and committed teachers can support advanced cognitive knowledge, motivation and social development in children. Social pedagogic implications are drawn from these studies, noting the need for group training and involvement of teachers.

King in her chapter, *Structuring peer interaction to promote higher-order thinking and complex learning in cooperating groups,* argues that a major challenge in implementing cooperative learning approaches is to stimulate higher-level thinking and learning. She argues that higher-level learning requires learners to go beyond mere review of information or retrieval of previously-acquired knowledge to engage in thinking analytically about that knowledge, relating it to what they already know, and using that knowledge to construct new knowledge, solve new problems, and address new issues. A number of research studies have documented a direct relationship between the level of the verbal interaction within cooperating groups and the level of thinking and achievement of group members. Examination of the verbal interaction within these groups reveals specific ways in which learning is mediated by that interaction itself. Based on these findings King developed a form of cooperative learning called Guided Reciprocal Peer Questioning to structure group interaction to promote higher-order thinking and learning. The approach is inquiry-based and is characterized by sequenced question-asking and answering with a direct focus on metacognition and the roles of mediation and modelling. It has been used effectively with groups in a number of classroom contexts ranging from fourth graders to graduate students in a variety of subject areas. The theoretical underpinnings of this approach are also presented as are research findings from several studies.

In Chapter 5, *Cooperative learning and literacy instruction in middle level education*, Stevens argues that early adolescence is a time of important developmental changes as students become more capable of handling complex tasks, develop more independence, and become increasingly peer focused. Despite this, typical middle level instruction does not adequately match the developmental growth of the students, often focusing on didactic instruction and low-level skills. Research has documented the impact of this developmental mismatch contributing to a decline in student achievement and motivation resulting in lower attendance, achievement, and attachment. This chapter describes a cooperative learning approach based upon a teaching-learning approach that emphasizes Tasks, Autonomy, Recognition, Resources, Grouping, Evaluation, and Time (called the TARRGET model). Stevens describes the implementation of the model in a Student Team Reading and Writing Program that guided teachers in the redevelopment of their literacy program to be more developmentally responsive to the needs and abilities of early adolescents in urban middle schools. To address some of the structural and curricular issues described above, the teachers implemented a cooperative learning approach to an integrated reading and language arts program. The instructional elements the teachers used included: cooperative learning classroom processes; high interest reading materials; explicit instruction in reading comprehension strategies; integrated reading, writing, and language arts instruction; and a writing process approach to language arts.

The chapter describes the teachers' implementation of these instructional methods with students in a large urban school district and the impact it had on students' discourse and achievement. The chapter highlights the potential teachers have to use cooperative learning to increase student learning by making instruction more engaging and responsive to the nature of early adolescence.

In the following chapter, Huber and Huber discuss structuring group interaction to promote thinking and learning during small group discussions among high school students. The authors argue that teaching and learning in the upper grades of high school often presents contradictory classroom experiences to students. On the one hand students have learned to adapt to traditional teacher-centered learning while on the other, they are expected to self-regulate their learning processes. Along with these experiences different preferences for learning situations and individual roles in these situations develop. Indicators for these effects of classroom experiences are those episodes in small group interactions in classrooms, which are characterized by activities of mutual teaching and learning.

This chapter describes typical findings from recent studies in Jigsaw groups that show that 'experts' for a specific part of the common learning content achieve significantly more in their domain of expertise than teammates who are supposed to learn from them. In expert groups the discussions usually promote cognitive elaboration, while in many Jigsaw groups the authors observed less discussions, questions, and explanations, but expert-centered teaching.

Structuring group interaction by learning scripts and integrating small group discussions in a 'sandwich' style of teacher-centered activities, group discussions, and individual learning has shown to counter-balance dysfunctional distributions of roles in classroom processes. A sandwich model of cooperative teaching/learning in the upper grades of high school is described and results from two evaluation studies are presented and discussed. The chapter concludes with a summary of the findings and makes recommendations both for teachers and researchers who study group processes in classrooms.

In Chapter 7, *Feedback and reflection to promote student participation in computer supported collaborative learning: A multiple case study*, Prinsen, Terwel, Volman, and Fakkert review and examine what is known in the literature about differences in participation and learning outcomes of students differing in gender, ability, pre-knowledge and social-ethnic background when working in a CSCL environment. The authors argue that if there are differences between these student categories and their participation in CSCL environments then more attention should be paid to ways of including these students that lead to enhanced learning outcomes. This chapter also offers a critique on the way researchers report on the design of learning environments in their research. In order to address this concern, that authors approach CSCL as an ICT-application, in which the computer is used for communicative and collaborative ends. The chapter begins with a short summary of research into the differences in ICT and computer mediated communication. In the following sections the differences in participation, in the quality of participation, and in the outcomes of CSCL are discussed. The chapter concludes with a look into the future in which some possible avenues for research on CSCL are explored.

In his chapter, *School and inclusive practices,* Ashman, looks at some of the implications of peer support for students with diverse learning needs. Ashman takes a broad view of peer-mediated teaching and learning approaches as most forms (e.g., cooperative learning, peer-tutoring, peer-assisted learning strategies) have been used in special education and inclusive education settings. He draws attention to nexus between inclusive education and peer-mediated learning approaches where both are directed toward pedagogical efficiencies aimed at improving the learning of all students.

While there is a large research database relating to peer-mediated approaches for students with diverse learning needs, the literature is far from conclusive about their successes. Ashman reviews studies that have focused on students with intellectual disabilities, behavioural and social-emotional difficulties, and also gifted and high-achieving students.

In *Developing language and mastering content in heterogeneous classrooms,* Lotan describes the classroom conditions that support development in English as well as mastery of social studies content in mainstream, academically and linguistically heterogeneous middle schools. Lotan reports on a study where she found that the language designations attributed to transitional students by the school underestimated their linguistic and academic capacities as indicated by their performances in the classroom. Students from different language proficiency levels benefited similarly from the intellectually rigorous curriculum and from the quality of interactions with peers during cooperative group work. Lotan proposes that teachers need to rethink linguistic segregation and ensure access to challenging and grade-appropriate curricula and instruction for all students. These findings make theoretical, methodological, and practical contributions to the field of teaching and learning in heterogeneous classrooms where teachers need to accommodate children with diverse needs.

Theoretically, the emphasis on the linguistically rich and academically rigorous social context that leads students to use English to interact in the classroom and to demonstrate subject matter knowledge adds to a greater understanding of second language acquisition at the secondary level. Methodologically, exploring the quality and quantity of interaction at the cooperative, small group level and its relationship to second language growth and mastery of content by individual students reflects the theoretical stance while practically, from the findings, Lotan presents teachers with a model of effective research-based practice that expands their repertoire of strategies for teaching in heterogeneous classrooms.

In the following chapter, *Teacher Practices and Small-Group Dynamics in Cooperative Learning Classrooms,* Webb draws attention to the role collaborative peer learning environments have received due to the potential they hold for improving learning and achievement. Webb notes that students can learn from each other in many ways, for example, by giving and receiving help, sharing knowledge, building on each others' ideas, recognizing and resolving contradictions between their own and other students' perspectives, observing others' strategies, and internalizing problem-solving processes and strategies that emerge during group discussions. This chapter focuses on students' helping behaviour within small groups, specifically the exchanging of explanations about the content being learned. The purpose of the chapter is to summarize research about the helping processes that have been found to predict learning outcomes in peer-directed small groups and the classroom conditions that bring about effective helping behaviour.

The chapter is organized in four parts. The first part briefly reviews the theoretical bases underlying the benefits of different kinds of help. These include perspectives of Piaget, Vygotsky, and motivational theories. The second part reviews the kinds of helping processes found to predict student learning outcomes. These include help-seeking and help-giving behaviour of students within groups. The third part explores how the evolution of dynamics in groups may promote or hinder productive helping processes, with special attention given to the roles and responsibilities of students in help-seeking or help-giving roles. The fourth part describes features of the classroom context that influence group dynamics in classrooms. These features include teacher behaviour, task structure and content, and classroom reward and recognition structure.

In Chapter 11, *Explanation Giving and Receiving in Cooperative Learning Groups*, Ross proposes that students who more frequently give explanations to their peers are more likely to learn from small group discussions than students who offer explanations less frequently. Ross argues that the effect of explanation giving on learning is more powerful than other types of information exchange. This finding has been consistently demonstrated in observations of naturally occurring groups as well as in studies of formally structured cooperative learning groups. The instructional challenges posed by these research findings are: explanation giving is rare even when teachers ask students to explain their solutions; usually only upper ability students offer explanations of their thinking, meaning that the students who could most benefit from this powerful learning strategy are least likely to engage in it; asking for an explanation usually does not contribute to the learning of the explanation seeker; and the quality of explanations provided by even the most able students tends to be poor.

Ross describes practical classroom strategies for improving the quality and frequency of explanations in cooperative learning groups. These strategies have been assessed in observational studies that link student behaviour to achievement outcomes. The most promising instructional techniques involve teaching students how to generate explanations within the context of specific subjects, such as mathematics.

In the final chapter, *Teachers' and students' verbal behaviours during cooperative learning*, Gillies proposes that teachers play a critical role in promoting interactions among students and involving them in the learning process. Yet, while much is known about how teachers can promote discourse among students and how students, in turn, help each other, little is know about teachers' verbal behaviours during cooperative learning. This chapter builds on research undertaken by Hertz-Lazarowitz and Shachar that identified the differences in teachers' verbal behaviours during cooperative and whole-class instruction. It does this by discussing two studies undertaken by the author that examined the difference in teachers' verbal behaviours during cooperative and small-group instruction in high school classes and the additive benefits derived from training teachers to use specific communication skills to enhance children's thinking and learning during cooperative learning in elementary classes.

The chapter also discusses how students model many of the verbal behaviours their teachers use in their own discourse with each other and how this promotes students' verbal reasoning and learning. Finally, the theoretical implications of the role teachers play in the social construction of knowledge, both at the interpersonal and personal level, are discussed with particular emphasis on specific strategies teachers use to scaffold and challenge students' learning.

References

Bruer, J. T. (1993). Schools for Thought: A Science of Learning in the Classroom. Cambridge, Mass: MIT Press.

Cohen, E. (1994). Restructuring the classroom: Conditions for productive small groups. Review of Educational Research, 64, 1–35.

Cohen, E. G., Brody, C. M., & Sapon-Shevin, M. (2004). Teaching Cooperative Learning. The Challenge for Teacher Education. New York: State University of New York.

Gillies, R. (2004). The effects of communication training on teachers' and students' verbal behaviours during cooperative learning. International Journal of Educational Research, 41, 257–279.

Hertz-Lazarowitz, R. & Shachar, H. (1990). Teachers' verbal behaviour in cooperative and whole-class instruction. In S. Sharan (Ed.), Cooperative Learning: Theory and Research (pp. 77–94). New York: Praeger.

Johnson, D. & Johnson, R. (1989). Cooperation and Competition: Theory and Research. Edina, Minnesota: Interaction Book Company.

Johnson, D. & Johnson, R. (2002). Learning together and alone: Overview and meta-analysis. Asia Pacific Journal of Education, 22, 95–105.

King, A. (1997). Ask to think-tel why: A model of transactive peer tutoring for scaffolding higher level complex learning. Educational Psychologist, 32, 221–235.

Neber, H., Finsterwalk, M., & Urban, N. (2001). Cooperative learning with gifted and high-achieving students: A review and meta-analyses of 12 studies. High Ability Studies, 12, 199–214.

O'Donnell, A. (1999). Structuring dyadic interaction through scripted cooperation. In A. O'Donnell & A. King (Eds.), Cognitive Perspectives on Peer Learning (pp. 179–196). Mahwah, NJ: Lawrence Erlbaum.

Palincsar, A. & Herrenkohl, L. (1999). Designing collaborative contexts: lessons from three research programs. In A. O'Donnell & A. King (Eds.), Cognitive Perspectives on Peer Learning (pp. 151–177). Mahwah, NJ: Lawrence Erlbaum.

Ross, J. & Cousins, J. (1995). Giving and receiving explanations in cooperative learning groups. The Alberta Journal of Educational Research, 41, 103–121.

Shachar, H. (2003). Who gains what from cooperative learning: An overview of eight studies. In R. Gillies & A. Ashman (Eds.), Cooperative Learning: The Social and Intellectual Outcomes of Learning in Groups (pp. 103–118). London: Routledge.

Slavin, R. (1999). Comprehensive approaches to cooperative learning. Theory into Practice, 38, 74–79.

Stevahn, L. & King, J. (2005). Managing conflict constructively. Evaluation: The International Journal of Theory, Research and Practice, 11, 415–427.

Terwel, J., Gillies, R., van den Eden, P., & Hoek, D. (2001). Cooperative learning processes of students: A longitudinal multilevel perspective. British Journal of Educational Psychology, 71, 619–645.

Webb, N. (1992). Testing a theoretical model of student interaction and learning in small groups. In R. Hertz-Lazarowitz & N. Miller (Eds.), Interaction in Cooperative Groups (pp. 102–119). Cambridge, UK: Cambridge University Press.

Webb, N. & Mastergeorge, A. (2003). Promoting effective helping in peer-directed groups. International Journal of Educational Research, 39, 73–97.

Chapter 1
Social Interdependence Theory and Cooperative Learning: The Teacher's Role

David W. Johnson and Roger T. Johnson

Abstract Teachers who wish to use cooperative learning effectively will wish to base their classroom practices on theory validated by research. To do so, they must first understand the nature of social interdependence (that is, cooperative, competitive, and individualistic efforts). Second, teachers need to understand that social interdependence theory is validated by hundreds of research studies indicating that cooperation, compared to competitive and individualistic efforts, tends to result in greater achievement, more positive relationships, and greater psychological health. Third, teachers need to understand the five basic elements that make cooperation work: positive interdependence, individual accountability, promotive interaction, appropriate use of social skills, and group processing. Finally, teachers need to understand the flexibility and many faces of cooperative learning, such as formal cooperative learning, informal cooperative learning, and cooperative base groups.

1.1 Introduction

In the mid-1960s, cooperative learning was relatively unknown and largely ignored by educators. Elementary, secondary, and university teaching was dominated by competitive and individualistic learning. Cultural resistance to cooperative learning was based on social Darwinism, with its premise that students must be taught to survive in a "dog-eat-dog" world, and the myth of "rugged individualism" underlying the use of individualistic learning. While competition dominated educational thought, it was being challenged by individualistic learning largely based on B. F. Skinner's work on programmed learning and behavioral modification. Educational practices and thought, however, have changed. Cooperative learning is now an accepted and often the preferred instructional procedure at all levels of education. Cooperative learning is presently used in schools and universities in every part of the world, in every subject area, and with every age student. It is difficult to find a text on instructional methods, a teacher's journal, or instructional materials that do not discuss cooperative learning. Materials on cooperative learning have been translated into dozens of languages. Cooperative learning is one of the success stories of both psychology and education.

One of the most distinctive characteristics of cooperative learning is the close relationship among theory, research, and practice. The relationship between theory and research is as follows (Johnson 2003). Theory identifies, clarifies, and defines the phenomena of interest and their relationships with each other. Research validates or disconfirms the theory, that is, theory specifies the conditions under which the theory is valid. Practice is guided by the validated theory, that is, the theory is operationalized into practical procedures. The implementation of the procedures reveals shortcomings of the theory, thus leading to a revised theory, a new set of validating studies, and more refined practical procedures. This interaction among theory, research, and practice is not only necessary for scientific progress, but also for more effective behavior in applied situations.

Social interdependence theory underlies some of the most widely used cooperative learning procedures (Johnson & Johnson 2002). Social interdependence theory has been validated by hundreds of research studies (Johnson & Johnson 1974, 1989, 2005), a significant proportion of which has focused on the conditions under which cooperation may be effectively implemented. (commonly referred to as "the five basic elements" of cooperation). Practical procedures have been operationalized from social interdependence theory at the classroom (i.e., the teacher's role in structuring cooperative learning) and school (i.e., leading the cooperative school) levels (Johnson & Johnson 1999, 1994). This relationship among theory, research, and practice makes cooperative learning somewhat unique. In this chapter, these connections will be delineated. First, social interdependence theory will be reviewed. Second, the research validating the theory will be summarized. Third, the five basic elements needed to understand the dynamics of cooperation and operationalize the teacher's role will be discussed. Finally, the three types of cooperative learning and the ways the five basic elements are structured in cooperative situations will be presented.

1.2   Social Interdependence Theory

*Achievement is a **we** thing, not a **me** thing,*
always the product of many heads and hands.
J. W. Atkinson (1964)

In the 1930s and 1940s Lewin (1935, 1948) proposed that a person's behavior is motivated by states of tension that arise as desired goals are perceived and that it is this tension that motivates actions aimed at achieving the desired goals. One of Lewin's students, Deutsch (1949a, 1962) extended Lewin's notions to the relationship among the goals of two or more individuals. In doing so, he developed social interdependence theory.

Social interdependence exists when the accomplishment of each individual's goals is affected by the actions of others (Deutsch 1949a, 1962; Johnson 1970, 2003; Johnson & Johnson 1989, 2005) (see Fig. 1.1). There are two types of social interdependence, positive (cooperation) and negative (competition). *Positive interdependence* exists when individuals perceive that they can reach their goals if and only if the other individuals with whom they are cooperatively linked also reach their goals. They therefore promote each other's efforts to achieve the goals. *Negative interdependence* exists when individuals perceive that they can obtain

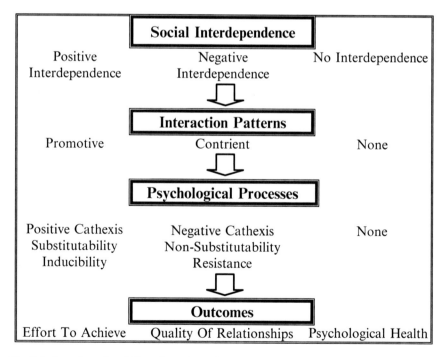

Fig. 1.1 Overview of social interdependence theory

their goals if and only if the other individuals with whom they are competitively linked fail to obtain their goals. They therefore obstruct each other's efforts to achieve the goals. *No interdependence* results in a situation in which individuals perceive that they can reach their goal regardless of whether other individuals in the situation attain or do not attain their goals. Each type of interdependence results in certain psychological processes.

1.2.1 Psychological Processes

The psychological processes created by positive interdependence include *substitutability* (i.e., the degree to which actions of one person substitute for the actions of another person), *inducibility* (i.e., openness to being influenced and to influencing others), and *positive cathexis* (i.e., investment of positive psychological energy in objects outside of oneself) (Deutsch 1949a, 1962). These processes explain how self-interest is expanded to joint interest and how new goals and motives are created in cooperative situations. Self-interest becomes expanded to mutual interest through: (a) other people's actions substituting for one's own; (b) an emotional investment in achieving goals that benefit others as well as oneself and generalizes to caring and committed relationships with those who are working for the same purposes and goals, and; (c) an openness to being influenced by and influencing others so that joint efforts are more effective. Demonstrating the transition from self-interest to mutual interest is perhaps one of the most important aspects of social interdependence theory.

Negative interdependence creates the psychological processes of *nonsubstitutability* (i.e., the actions of one person do not substitute for the actions of another person), *negative cathexis* (i.e., investment of negative psychological energy in objects outside of oneself), and resistance to being influenced by others. Thus, self-interest is strengthened and the motives to win and avoid losing are strengthened.

No interdependence detaches a person from others, thereby creating nonsubstitutability, cathexis only to one's own actions, and no inducibility or resistance. Thus, self-interest and the motive to succeed are maintained.

1.2.2 Interaction Patterns

The basic premise of social interdependence theory is that the way in which interdependence is structured determines how individuals interact and the interaction pattern determines the outcomes of the situation (Deutsch 1949a, 1962; Johnson 1970, 2003; Johnson & Johnson 1974, 1989, 2005). Positive interdependence results in promotive interaction, negative interdependence results in oppositional or contrient interaction, and no interdependence results in the absence of interaction. *Promotive interaction* may be defined as individuals encouraging and facilitating each other's efforts to complete tasks, achieve, or produce in order to reach the group's goals. It consists of a number of variables, including mutual help and assistance, exchange of needed resources, effective communication, mutual influence, trust, and constructive management of conflict. *Oppositional interaction* may be defined as individuals discouraging and obstructing each other's efforts to complete tasks, achieve, or produce in order to reach their goals; individuals focus both on increasing their own productivity and on preventing any other person from producing more than they do. It consists of such variables as obstruction of each other's goal achievement efforts, tactics of threat and coercion, ineffective and misleading communication, distrust, and striving to win in conflicts. *No inter-action* may be defined as individuals acting independently without any interchange with each other while they work to achieve their goals; individuals focus only on increasing their own productivity and achievement and ignore as irrelevant the efforts of others.

1.3   The Validating Research

1.3.1   Amount and Characteristics of Research

The study of cooperative, competitive, and individualistic efforts is commonly recognized as one of the oldest fields of research in social psychology. In the late 1800s Triplett (1898) in the United States, Turner (1889, cited in Trippett, 1898) in England, and Mayer (1903) in Germany conducted a series of studies on the factors associated with competitive performance. Since then over 750 studies have been conducted on the relative merits of cooperative, competitive, and individualistic efforts and the conditions under which each is appropriate. This is one of the largest bodies of research within psychology and education and it provides sufficient empirical research to test social interdependence theory's propositions.

An extensive literature search was conducted aimed at identifying all the available studies from published and nonpublished sources. Seven-hundred-fifty-four studies contained enough data to compute an effect size (there are many studies from which an effect size could not be computed). The characteristics of the studies are as follows (see Table 1.1). Many of the research studies have high internal validity, being carefully conducted by skilled investigators under highly controlled laboratory (31%) and field (65%) settings. When rated on the variables of random assignment to conditions, clarity of control conditions, control of the experimenter effect, control of the curriculum effect (same materials used in all conditions), and verification of the successful implementation of the independent variable, 51% of the studies met these criteria.

The research on social interdependence has an external validity and a generalizability rarely found in the social sciences. The more variations in places, people, and procedures the research can withstand and still yield the same findings, the

Table 1.1 General characteristics of studies

Characteristic	Number	Percent
Unknown	3	0.4
1900–1909	0	0
1910–1919	1	0.1
1920–1929	7	0.9
1930–1939	6	0.8
1940–1949	5	0.7
1950–1959	25	3.3
1960–1969	80	10.6
1970–1979	183	24.3
1980–1989	285	37.8
1990–1999	138	18.3
2000–2009	21	2.8
Unknown	4	0.5
No random assignment	280	37.1
Randomly assigned subjects	328	43.5
Randomly assigned groups, subject unit of analysis	98	13.0
Randomly assigned groups, group unit of analysis	44	5.8
Unknown	4	0.5
Ages 3–4	8	1.1
Ages 5–9	85	11.2
Ages 10–12	182	24.1
Ages 13–15	106	14.1
Ages 16–18	55	7.3
Ages 19–22	278	36.9
Ages 23+	34	4.5
Unknown	4	0.5
Journal article	578	76.7
Book	5	0.7
M.A. theses	11	1.5
Ph.D. dissertations	75	9.9
Technical report	59	7.8
Unpublished	22	2.9
Unknown	27	3.6
Laboratory	234	31.0
Field	490	65.0
Clinical	3	0.4
Unknown	46	6.1
1 session	216	28.6
2–9 sessions	150	19.9
10–19 sessions	98	13.0
20–29 sessions	57	7.6
30–39 sessions	53	7.0
40–49 sessions	44	5.8
50–59 sessions	18	2.4
60–69 sessions	18	2.4
70–79 sessions	6	0.8

(continued)

Table 1.1 (continued)

Characteristic	Number	Percent
80–89 sessions	8	1.1
90–99 sessions	37	4.9
100+ sessions	3	0.4
Unknown	27	5
Homogeneous	145	21
Mixed gender groups	552	74
Total	*754*	*100*

Only studies giving enough data so that effect sizes could be computed are included in this table

Source: Johnson & Johnson (2003). *Cooperative, competitive, and individualistic efforts: An update of the research*. Research Report, Cooperative Learning Center, University of Minnesota. Reprinted with permission.

more externally valid the conclusions. The research has been conducted over 12 decades by many different researchers with markedly different theoretical and practical orientations working in different settings. A wide variety of research tasks, ways of structuring social interdependence, and measures of the dependent variables have been used. Participants in the studies varied from ages three to post-college adults and have come from different economic classes and cultural backgrounds. The studies were conducted with different durations, lasting from one session to 100 sessions or more. Research on social interdependence has been conducted in numerous cultures in North America (with Caucasian, Black-American, Native-American, and Hispanic populations) and countries from North, Central, and South America, Europe, the Middle East, Asia, the Pacific Rim, and Africa. The research on social interdependence includes both theoretical and demonstration studies conducted in educational, business, and social service organizations. The diversity of these studies gives social interdependence theory wide generalizability and considerable external validity.

Promotive, oppositional, and no interaction have differential effects on the outcomes of the situation (see Johnson & Johnson 1989, 1999, 2005). The research has focused on numerous outcomes, which may be subsumed within the broad and interrelated categories of effort to achieve, quality of relationships, and psychological health (Johnson 2003; Johnson & Johnson 1989, 2005) (see Table 1.2 and Fig. 1.2). Figure 1.2 shows the relationships among the outcomes.

1.3.2 Effort to Achieve

From Table 1.2 it may be seen that cooperation promotes considerable greater effort to achieve than do competitive or individualistic efforts. Effort exerted to achieve includes such variables as achievement and productivity, long-term retention, on-task behavior, use of higher-level reasoning strategies, generation of new ideas and solutions, transfer of what is learned within one situation to another, intrinsic motiva-

Table 1.2 Mean effect sizes for impact of social interdependence on dependent variables

Dependent variable	Cooperative vs. competitive	Cooperative vs. individualistic	Competitive vs. individualistic
Achievement	0.67	0.64	0.30
Interpersonal attraction	0.67	0.60	0.08
Social support	0.62	0.70	−0.13
Self-esteem	0.58	0.44	−0.23
Time on task	0.76	1.17	0.64
Attitudes toward task	0.57	0.42	0.15
Quality of reasoning	0.93	0.97	0.13
Perspective-taking	0.61	0.44	−0.13
High Quality Studies			
Achievement	0.88	0.61	0.07
Interpersonal attraction	0.82	0.62	0.27
Social support	0.83	0.72	−0.13
Self-esteem	0.67	0.45	−0.25

Source: Johnson & Johnson (1989). *Cooperation and competition: Theory and research.* Edina, MN: Interaction Book Company. Reprinted with permission.

tion, achievement motivation, continuing motivation to learn, and positive attitudes toward learning and school. Overall, cooperation tends to promote higher achievement than competitive or individualistic efforts (effect-sizes = 0.67 and 0.64 respectively). The impact of cooperative learning on achievement means that if schools wish to prepare students to take proficiency tests to meet local and state standards, the use of cooperative learning should dominate instructional practice.

An important aspect of school life is engagement in learning. One indication of engagement in learning is time on task. Cooperators spent considerably more time on task than did competitors (effect size = 0.76) or students working individualistically (effect size = 1.17). In addition, students working cooperatively tended to be more involved in activities and tasks, attach greater importance to success, and engage in more on-task behavior and less apathetic, off-task, disruptive behaviors. Finally, cooperative experiences, compared with competitive and individualistic ones, have been found to promote more positive attitudes toward the task and the experience of working on the task (effect-sizes = 0.57 and 0.42 respectively).

1.3.3 Quality of Relationships

Quality of relationships includes such variables as interpersonal attraction, liking, cohesion, esprit-de-corps, and social support. The degree of emotional bonding that exists among students has a profound effect on students' behavior. The more positive the relationships among students and between students and faculty, the lower the absenteeism and dropout rates and the greater the commitment to group goals, feelings of personal responsibility to the group, willingness to take on difficult

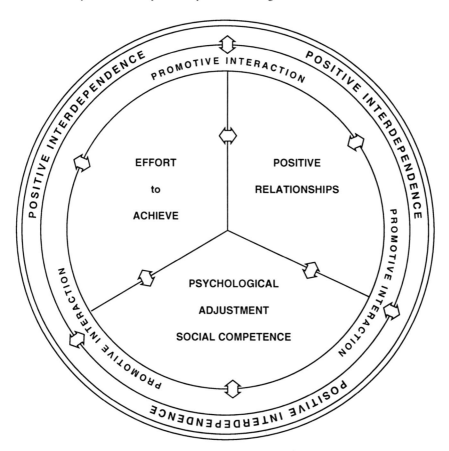

Fig. 1.2 Outcomes of cooperative learning
Source: Johnson & Johnson (1989). *Cooperation and competition: Theory and research.* Edina, MN: Interaction Book Company. Reprinted with permission.

tasks, motivation and persistence in working toward goal achievement, satisfaction and morale, willingness to endure pain and frustration on behalf of the group, willingness to defend the group against external criticism or attack, willingness to listen to and be influenced by colleagues, commitment to each other's professional growth and success, and productivity (Johnson & Johnson 2006).

There are over 175 studies that have investigated the relative impact of cooperative, competitive, and individualistic efforts on quality of relationships and another 106 studies on social support (Johnson 2003; Johnson & Johnson 1989, 2005). As Table 1.2 shows, cooperation generally promotes greater interpersonal attraction among individuals than does competitive or individualistic efforts (effect sizes = 0.67 and 0.60 respectively). Cooperative experiences tend to promote greater social support than does competitive (effect-size = 0.62) or individualistic (effect-size = 0.70) efforts. Stronger effects are found for peer support than for superior (teacher) support. The high-quality studies tend to have even more powerful effects.

It is difficult to overemphasize the importance of these research results. Friends are a developmental advantage (see Johnson 2003; Johnson & Johnson 1989, 2005). There is a close association between antisocial behavior and rejection by the normal peer group. Rejected children tend to be deficient in a number of social-cognitive skills, including peer group entry, perception of peer group norms, response to provocation, and interpretation of prosocial interactions. Among children referred to child guidance clinics, 30–75% (depending on age) are reported by their parents to experience peer difficulties. Moreover, children referred for psychological treatment have fewer friends and less contact with them than non-referred children, their friendships are significantly less stable over time, and their understanding of the reciprocities and intimacies involved in friendships is less mature. Peer group acceptance and friendships may be built through the extensive use of cooperative learning.

1.3.4 Psychological Health

Montagu (1966) was fond of saying that with few exceptions the solitary animal in any species is an abnormal creature. Similarly, Horney (1937) stated that the neurotic individual is someone who is inappropriately competitive and, therefore, unable to cooperate with others. Montagu and Horney recognized that the essence of psychological health is the ability to develop and maintain cooperative relationships. More specifically, *psychological health* is the ability (cognitive capacities, motivational orientations, and social skills) to build, maintain, and appropriately modify interdependent relationships with others to succeed in achieving goals (Johnson 2003; Johnson & Johnson 1989, 2005). People who are unable to do so often: (a) become depressed, anxious, frustrated, and lonely; (b) tend to feel afraid, inadequate, helpless, hopeless, and isolated; and (c) rigidly cling to unproductive and ineffective ways of coping with adversity.

With our students and colleagues, we have conducted a series of studies relating cooperative, competitive, and individualistic efforts and attitudes to various indices of psychological health (see Johnson 2003; Johnson & Johnson 1989, 2005). The samples studied included middle-class junior-high students, middle-class high school seniors, high-school age juvenile prisoners, adult prisoners, Olympic ice-hockey players, adult step-couples, and business executives in China. The diversity of the samples studied and the variety of measures of psychological health provide considerable generalizability of the results of the studies. A strong relationship was found between cooperativeness and psychological health, a mixed picture was found with competitiveness and psychological health, and a strong relationship was found between an individualistic orientation and psychological pathology.

Finally, there is evidence that cooperation promotes more frequent use of higher level reasoning strategies than do competitive (effect size = 0.93) or individualistic (effect size = 0.97) efforts. Similarly, cooperation tends to promote more accurate perspective taking than do competitive (effect size = 0.61) or individualistic (effect size = 0.44) efforts. Thus, the more cooperative learning experiences students are involved in, the more mature their cognitive and moral decision making and the more they will tend to take other people's perspectives in account when making decisions.

1.4   The Basic Elements

Social interdependence theory provides a foundation for cooperative learning. In operationalizing the teacher's role, however, the variables mediating the effectiveness of cooperative learning needed some clarification. This led to the expansion of positive interdependence to include individual and group accountability. It also lead to the expansion of promotive interaction into actions that facilitate goal accomplishment, appropriate use of social skills, and group processing. Thus, in creating cooperative learning lessons, the teacher has to structure positive interdependence, individual accountability, promotive interaction, the appropriate use of social skills, and group processing. In this section each of these basic elements of cooperation will be discussed. In the following section, the way they are operationalized into the teacher's role will be explained.

1.4.1   Positive Interdependence

Positive and negative interdependence were defined by Lewin and Deutsch as resulting from mutual goals. A number of researchers demonstrated, however, that positive and negative interdependence may be structured through complementary roles (Thomas 1957), group contingencies (Skinner 1968), and dividing information into separate pieces (Aronson et al. 1978). Various researchers and practitioners have structured interdependence in other ways, such as divisions of labor, mutual identity, in environmental spaces, and simulations involving fantasy situations (Johnson & Johnson 1992). Given the different ways in which positive and negative interdependence may be structured, Johnson & Johnson (1989, 2005) divided them into three categories: outcome, means, and boundary (see Fig. 1.3). First, when persons are in a cooperative or competitive situation, they are oriented toward a desired outcome, that is, a goal or reward. Goals can be real or imaginary (such as surviving on a desert island). Second, the means through which the mutual outcomes are to be accomplished specify the actions required on the part of group members. Means interdependence includes resource, role, and task interdependence (which are overlapping and not independent from each other). Third, the boundaries existing among individuals and groups can define who is interdependent with whom. Koffka (1935) pointed out that abrupt discontinuity produces segregating forces between the parts of a visual field that it separates, as well as unifying forces within the separated parts. Based on this principle of perceptual organization

Positive Interdependence	⇔	Promotive Interaction	⇔	Outcomes
Outcome Interdependence		Enhancing Other's Success		Effort To Achieve
Goal		Providing Mutual Help and Assistance		Achievement
Reward / Celebration		Exchanging Needed Resources		Long-Term Retention
Means Interdependence		Giving Accurate Mutual Feedback		Higher-Level Reasoning
Role		Challenging Each Other's Conclusions		Intrinsic Motivation
Resource		Advocating Effort To Achieve		On-Task Behavior
Task		Engaging in Mutual Influence		Positive Relationships
Boundary Interdependence		Engaging in Trusting And Trustworthy Behavior		Cohesion
Environmental		Being Motivated for Mutual Benefit		Liking For Each Other
Identity		Having a Moderate Level of Arousal		Heterogeneity
Outside Enemy		Engaging in More Accurate Perspective Taking		Academic Support
		Exploring Different Points Of View		Personal Support
Accountability				Psychological Health
Group		Teamwork And Taskwork Skills		Psychological Adjustment
Individual				Social Competencies
		Processing: Individual, Group		Self-Esteem
				Shared Identity
				Coping With Stress

Fig. 1.3 Social interdependence theory

(Koffka 1935; Wertheimer 1923), boundary interdependence may exist based on abrupt discontinuities among individuals that segregate individuals into separate groups. The discontinuity may be created by environmental factors (different parts of the room or different rooms), similarity (all seated together or wearing the same color shirt), proximity (seated together), past history together, expectations of being grouped together, and differentiation from other competing groups. Boundary interdependence thus includes outside enemy (i.e., negative interdependence with another group), identity (which binds them together as an entity), and environmental (such as a specific work area) interdependence (which are overlapping and not independent from each other).

A series of research studies was conducted to clarify the impact of positive interdependence on productivity and achievement. First, it is necessary to demonstrate that positive interdependence has effects greater than group membership or interpersonal interaction. There is evidence that group membership in and of itself does not seem sufficient to produce higher achievement and productivity–positive interdependence is also required (Hwong et al. 1993). Knowing that one's performance affects the success of groupmates seems to create "responsibility forces" that increase one's efforts to achieve. There is also evidence that interpersonal interaction is insufficient to increase productivity–positive interdependence is also required (Lew et al. 1986a, 1986b; Mesch et al. 1986, 1988). Individuals achieved higher under positive goal interdependence than when they worked individualistically but had the opportunity to interact with classmates. When positive interdependence is clearly perceived, individuals realize that their efforts are required in order for the group to succeed so that it is not possible to get a "free-ride" (Kerr 1983) and they have a unique contribution to make to the group's efforts. When members of a group see their efforts as dispensable for the group's success, they may reduce their efforts (Kerr 1983; Kerr & Bruun 1983; Sweeney 1973); when group members perceive their potential contribution to the group as being unique, they increase their efforts (Harkins & Petty 1982).

Given the impact of positive interdependence above and beyond group membership and interpersonal interaction, a number of studies have been conducted contrasting the impact of various ways of inducing positive interdependence. The studies have found:

1. Positive goal interdependence promotes higher achievement and greater productivity than does resource interdependence (Johnson et al. 1991).
2. Positive goal and reward interdependence tend to be additive; while positive goal interdependence is sufficient to produce higher achievement and productivity than do individualistic efforts, the combination of goal and reward interdependence tends to increase achievement more than goal interdependence alone or individualistic efforts (Johnson et al. 1990; Lew et al. 1986a, b; Mesch et al. 1986, 1988; Ortiz et al. 1996).
3. Resource interdependence by itself may decrease achievement and productivity compared with individualistic efforts (Johnson et al. 1990; Ortiz et al. 1996). That is, when individuals need the resources of other group members but do not

share common goals, the emphasis tends to be on obtaining resources from others without sharing one's own resources with them. The result tends to be an interference with each other's productivity.

4. Both working to achieve a reward and working to avoid the loss of a reward produced higher achievement than did individualistic efforts (Frank 1984). There is no significant difference between the working to achieve a reward and working to avoid a loss.

5. Positive interdependence does more than simply motivate individuals to try harder, it facilitates the development of new insights and discoveries through promotive interaction (Gabbert et al. 1986; Johnson & Johnson 1981; Johnson et al. 1980; Skon et al. 1981). Members of cooperative groups use higher level reasoning strategies more frequently than do individuals working individualistically or competitively.

6. The more complex the procedures involved in interdependence, the longer it will take group members to reach their full levels of productivity (Ortiz et al. 1996). The more complex the teamwork procedures, the more members have to attend to teamwork and the less time they have to attend to taskwork. Once the teamwork procedures are mastered, however, members concentrate on taskwork and outperform individuals working alone.

7. Studies on identity interdependence involving social dilemmas have found that when individuals define themselves in terms of their group membership, they are more willing to take less from common resources and to contribute more toward the public good (Brewer & Kramer 1986; De Cremer & Van Kijk, in press; De Cremer & Van Vjugt 1999; Kramer & Brewer 1984).

1.4.2   Individual Accountability and Personal Responsibility

Positive interdependence is posited to create "responsibility forces" that increase group members' feelings of responsibility and accountability for: (a) completing one's share of the work and; (b) facilitating the work of other group members. When a person's performance affects the outcomes of collaborators, the person feels responsible for their welfare as well as his or her own (Matsui et al. 1987). Failing oneself is bad, but failing others as well as oneself is worse. The shared responsibility created by positive interdependence adds the concept of "ought" to group members' motivation—one ought to do one's part, pull one's weight, contribute, and satisfy peer norms (Johnson 2003; Johnson & Johnson 1989, 2005). Such feelings of responsibility increase a person's motivation to perform well.

Responsibility forces are increased when there is group and individual accountability. *Group accountability* exists when the overall performance of the group is assessed and the results are given back to all group members to compare against a standard of performance. *Individual accountability* exists when the performance of each individual member is assessed, the results given back to the individual and the group to compare against a standard of performance, and the member is held responsible by groupmates for contributing his or her fair share to the group's success. Hooper et al. (1989) found that cooperation resulted in higher achievement when individual accountability was structured than when it was not. Archer-Kath et al. (1994) found that by increasing individual accountability perceived interdependence among group members may also be increased.

The lack of individual accountability may reduce feelings of personal responsibility. Members may reduce their contributions to goal achievement when the group works on tasks where it is difficult to identify members' contributions, when there is an increased likelihood of redundant efforts, when there is a lack of group cohesiveness, and when there is lessened responsibility for the final outcome (Harkins & Petty 1982; Ingham et al. 1974; Kerr & Bruun 1981; Latane et al. 1979; Moede 1927; Petty et al. 1977; Williams 1981; Williams et al. 1981). If, however, there is high individual accountability and it is clear how much effort each member is contributing, if redundant efforts are avoided, if every member is responsible for the final outcome, and if the group is cohesive, then the social loafing effect vanishes.

Generally, as the group gets larger and larger, members are less likely to see their own personal contribution to the group as being important to the group's chances of success (Kerr 1989; Olson 1965). Social loafing, therefore, increases as the size of the group increases. The smaller the size of the group, furthermore, the greater the individual accountability (Messick & Brewer 1983). Morgan et al. (1970) found that team performance actually improved when one team member was missing from five-person teams, perhaps because members believed that their contributions were more necessary. As group size increases, individual team members tend to communicate less frequently, which may reduce the amount of information utilized in arriving at a decision (Gerard et al. 1965; Indik 1965). As group size increases so does the likelihood individuals may alter their statements to conform to the perceived beliefs of the overall team (Gerard et al. 1965; Rosenberg 1961). Finally, Morgan et al. (1970) found that team performance actually improved when one team member was missing from five-person teams, perhaps because members believed that their contributions were more necessary.

1.4.3 Promotive Interaction

Positive interdependence results in individuals promoting each other's productivity and achievement. *Promotive interaction* occurs as individuals encourage and facilitate each other's efforts to accomplish the group's goals. While positive interdependence directly affects outcomes, its main influence may be fostering promotive interaction among individuals that in turn influences outcomes. Individuals focus both on being productive and on promoting the productivity of their groupmates. Promotive interaction is characterized by individuals (Johnson & Johnson 1999):

1. Providing each other with efficient and effective help and assistance (e.g., Johnson & Johnson 1981, 1982, 1984; Rosenbaum et al. 1980; Webb & Cullian 1983).
2. Exchanging needed resources such as information and materials and processing information more efficiently and effectively (e.g., Crawford & Haaland 1972; Johnson 1974; Laughlin & McGlynn 1967).
3. Providing each other with feedback in order to improve the subsequent performance of their assigned tasks and responsibilities (Pittman et al. 1980; Ryan 1982).
4. Challenging each other's conclusions and reasoning in order to promote higher quality decision making and greater insight into the problems being considered (e.g., Johnson & Johnson 1979, 2007).
5. Advocating the exertion of effort to achieve mutual goals (e.g., Wicklund & Brehm 1976).
6. Influencing each other's efforts to achieve the group's goals (e.g., Crombag 1966; Deutsch 1949b; Johnson et al. 1985; Raven & Eachus 1963).
7. Acting in trusting and trustworthy ways (e.g., Deutsch 1958, 1960, 1962; Johnson 1974; Johnson & Noonan 1972).
8. Being motivated to strive for mutual benefit (Deutsch 1949b; Johnson 2003; Johnson & Johnson 1989, 2005).
9. Having a moderate level of arousal characterized by low anxiety and stress (e.g., Blau 1954; Haines & McKeachie 1967; Naught & Newman 1966).
10. Taking the perspectives of others more accurately than individuals engaged in competitive or individualistic efforts (effect sizes of 0.61 and 0.44 respectively, [see Table 1.2]) and thus able to explore different points of view (Johnson & Johnson 1989).

1.4.4 Appropriate Use of Social Skills

Interpersonal and small group skills form the basic nexus among individuals, and if individuals are to work together productively and cope with the stresses and strains of doing so, they must have a modicum of these skills. Group members must have or be taught the interpersonal and small group skills needed for high quality cooperation and be motivated to use them. To coordinate efforts to achieve mutual goals participants must: (a) get to know and trust each other; (b) communicate accurately and unambiguously; (c) accept and support each other; and (d) resolve conflicts constructively (Johnson 2006; Johnson & Johnson 2006). Especially when groups function on a long-term basis and engage in complex, free exploratory activities over a prolonged period, the interpersonal and small group skills of the members may greatly influence the level of members' achievement and productivity.

In their studies on the long-term implementation of cooperative teams, Lew and Mesch (Lew et al. 1986a, b; Mesch et al. 1986, 1993) found that the combination of positive goal interdependence, a contingency for high performance by all group members, and a social skills contingency, promoted the highest achievement and productivity. Archer-Kath et al. (1994) found that giving participants individual feedback on how frequently they engaged in targeted social skills was more effective in increasing participants' achievement than was group feedback. Thus, the more socially skillful participants are, the more social skills are taught and rewarded, and the more individual feedback participants receive on their use of the skills, the higher tends to be the achievement and productivity in cooperative groups.

Not only do social skills promote higher achievement, they contribute to building more positive relationships among group members. Putnam et al. (1989) demonstrated that, when participants were taught social skills, observed, and given individual feedback as to how frequently they engaged in the skills, their relationships became more positive.

1.4.5 Group Processing

Promotive interaction may be enhanced by group members periodically reflecting on how well they are functioning and planning how to improve their work processes. A *process* is an identifiable sequence of events taking place over time, and *process goals* refer to the desired sequence of events instrumental in achieving outcome goals. *Group processing* may be defined as reflecting on a group session to: (a) describe what member actions were helpful and unhelpful and (b) make decisions about what actions to continue or change. The purpose of group processing is to clarify and improve the effectiveness of the members in contributing to the joint efforts to achieve the group's goals.

Yager et al. (1986) examined the impact on achievement of: (a) cooperation in which members discussed how well their group was functioning and how they could improve its effectiveness; (b) cooperation without any group processing; and (c) individualistic efforts. The results indicate that the high-, medium-, and low-achieving participants in the cooperation with group processing condition achieved higher on daily achievement, post-instructional achievement, and retention measures than did the participants in the other two conditions. Participants in the cooperation without group processing condition, furthermore, achieved higher on all three measures than did the participants in the individualistic condition.

Putnam et al. (1989) conducted a study in which there were two conditions: cooperation with social skills training and group processing and cooperation without social skills training and group processing. They found more positive relationships developed between handicapped and nonhandicapped participants in the cooperative skills and group processing condition and that these positive relationships carried over to post-instructional free-time situations.

Johnson et al. (1990) conducted a study comparing cooperation with no processing, cooperation with instructor processing (instructor specified cooperative skills to use, observed, and gave whole class feedback as to how well participants were using the skills), cooperation with instructor and participant processing (the instructor specified cooperative skills to use, observed, gave whole class feedback as to how well participants were using the skills, and had groups discuss how well they interacted as a group), and individualistic efforts. All three cooperative conditions performed higher than did the individualistic condition. The combination of instructor and participant processing resulted in greater problem solving success than did the other cooperative conditions.

Finally, Archer-Kath et al. (1994) found that group processing with individual feedback was more effective than was group processing with whole group feedback in increasing participants': (a) achievement motivation, actual achievement, uniformity of achievement among group members, and influence toward higher achievement within cooperative groups; (b) positive relationships among group members and between participants and the teacher, and; (c) self-esteem and positive attitudes toward the subject area.

1.5 Teacher's Role in Cooperative Learning

Ideally, teachers are trained to take their existing lessons and restructure them to be cooperative. *Cooperative learning* is the instructional use of small groups so that students work together to maximize their own and each other's learning (Johnson et al. 1998a, b, 2002). Any lesson in any subject area for any age student can be done cooperatively. There are three types of cooperative learning—formal, informal, and cooperative base groups.

1.5.1 Formal Cooperative Learning

Formal cooperative learning consists of students working together, for one class period to several weeks, to achieve shared learning goals and complete jointly specific tasks and assignments (Johnson et al. 1998a, b, 2002). In formal cooperative learning groups the teachers' role includes (see Fig. 1.4):

1. *Making preinstructional decisions.* Teachers: (a) formulate both academic and social skills objectives; (b) decide on the size of groups; (c) choose a method for assigning students to groups; (d) decide which roles to assign group members; (e) arrange the room; and (f) arrange the materials students need to complete the assignment. In these preinstructional decisions, the social skills objectives specify the interpersonal and small group skills students are to learn. By assigning students roles, role interdependence is established. The way in which materials are distributed can create resource interdependence. The arrangement of the room can create environmental interdependence and provide the teacher with easy access to observe each group, which increases individual accountability and provides data for group processing.

Grade level: _____ Subject Area: _____ Date: _____
Lesson:

_____

Objectives

Academic:

_____

Social Skills:

_____

Preonstructional Decisions

Group Size: _____ Method of Assiging Students: _____
Roles:

_____

Room Arrangement:

_____

Materials:

_____

  ◊ One Copy Per Group   ◊ One Copy Per Group
  ◊ Jigsaw   ◊ Tournament
  ◊ Other:

_____

Explain Task And Cooperative Goal Structure

1. Task:

_____

2. Criteria For Success:

_____
_____

3. Positive Interdependence:

_____
_____

4. Individual Accountability:

_____

5. Intergroup Cooperation:

_____

6. Expected Behaviours:

_____
_____
_____

Monitoring And Intervening

1. Observation Procedure: _____ Formal _____ Informal
2. Observation By: _____ Teacher _____ Students _____ Vistors

Fig. 1.4 (continued)

3. Intervening For Task Assistance:

_____

_____

4. Intervening For Teamwork Assistance:

_____

_____

5. Other:

_____

_____

Evaluating And Processing

1. Assessment Of Members' Individual Learning:_____

_____

2. Assessment Of Group Productivity:

_____

_____

3. Small Group Processing:

_____

_____

4. Whole Class Processing:

_____

_____

5. Charts And Graphs Used:

_____

_____

6. Positive Feedback To Each Student:

_____

_____

7. Goal Setting For Improvement:

_____

_____

8. Celebration:

_____

_____

9. Other:

_____

_____

Fig. 1.4 Cooperative lesson planning form

2. *Explaining the instructional task and cooperative structure.* Teachers: (a) explain the academic assignment to students; (b) explain the criteria for success; (c) structure positive interdependence; (d) structure individual accountability; (e) explain the behaviors (i.e., social skills) students are expected to use; and (f) emphasize intergroup cooperation (this eliminates the possibility of competition among students and extends positive goal interdependence to the class as a whole). Teachers may also teach the concepts and strategies required to complete the assignment. By explaining the social skills emphasized in the lesson, teachers operationalize: (a) the social skill objectives of the lesson and (b) the interaction patterns (such as oral rehearsal and jointly building conceptual frameworks) teachers wish to create.

3. *Monitoring students' learning and intervening to provide assistance in: (a) completing the task successfully or; (b) using the targeted interpersonal and group skills effectively.* While conducting the lesson, teachers monitor each learning group and intervene when needed to improve taskwork and teamwork. Monitoring the learning groups creates individual accountability; whenever a teacher observes a group, members tend to feel accountable to be constructive members. In addition, teachers collect specific data on promotive interaction, the use of targeted social skills, and the engagement in the desired interaction patterns. This data is used to intervene in groups and to guide group processing.

4. *Assessing students' learning and helping students process how well their groups functioned.* Teachers: (a) bring closure to the lesson; (b) assess and evaluate the quality and quantity of student achievement; (c) ensure students carefully discuss how effectively they worked together (i.e., process the effectiveness of their learning groups); (d) have students make a plan for improvement; and (e) have students celebrate the hard work of group members. The assessment of student achievement highlights individual and group accountability (i.e., how well each student performed) and indicates whether the group achieved its goals (i.e., focusing on positive goal interdependence). The group celebration is a form of reward interdependence. The feedback received during group processing is aimed at improving the use of social skills and is a form of individual accountability. Discussing the processes the group used to function, furthermore, emphasizes the continuous improvement of promotive interaction and the patterns of interaction need to maximize student learning and retention.

1.5.2   Informal Cooperative Learning

Informal cooperative learning consists of having students work together to achieve a joint learning goal in temporary, ad-hoc groups that last from a few minutes to one class period (Johnson et al. 1998b, 2002). During a lecture, demonstration, or film, informal cooperative learning can be used to focus student attention on the material to be learned, set a mood conducive to learning, help set expectations as to what will be covered in a class session, ensure that students cognitively process and rehearse the material being taught, summarize what was learned and pre-cue the next session, and provide closure to an instructional session. The teacher's role for using informal cooperative learning to keep students more actively engaged intellectually entails having focused discussions before and after the lesson (i.e., bookends) and interspersing pair discussions throughout the lesson. Two important aspects of using informal cooperative learning groups are to: (a) make the task and the instructions explicit and precise, and; (b) require the groups to produce a specific product (such as a written answer). The procedure is as follows.

1. *Introductory Focused Discussion*: Teachers assign students to pairs or triads and explain: (a) the task of answering the questions in a 4–5-min time period and (b) the positive goal interdependence of reaching consensus. The discussion task is aimed at promoting advance organizing of what the students know about the topic to be presented and establishing expectations about what the lecture will cover. Individual accountability is ensured by the small size of the group. A basic interaction pattern of eliciting oral rehearsal, higher-level reasoning, and consensus building is required.

2. *Intermittent Focused Discussions*: Teachers divide the lecture into 10–15-min segments. This is about the length of time a motivated adult can concentrate on information being presented. After each segment, students are asked to turn to the person next to them and work cooperatively in answering a question (specific enough so that students can answer it in about three minutes) that requires students to cognitively process the material just presented. The procedure is:

(a) Each student formulates his or her answer.
(b) Students share their answer with their partner.
(c) Students listen carefully to their partner's answer.
(d) The pairs **create** a new answer that is superior to each member's initial formulation by integrating the two answers, building on each other's thoughts, and synthesizing.

The question may require students to:

(a) Summarize the material just presented.
(b) Give a reaction to the theory, concepts, or information presented.
(c) Predict what is going to be presented next; hypothesize.
(d) Solve a problem.
(e) Relate material to past learning and integrate it into conceptual frameworks.
(f) Resolve conceptual conflict created by presentation.

Teachers should ensure that students are seeking to reach an agreement on the answers to the questions (i.e., ensure positive goal interdependence is established), not just share their ideas with each other. Randomly choose two or three students to give 30-s summaries of their discussions. Such *individual accountability* ensures that the pairs take the tasks seriously and check each other to ensure that both are prepared to answer. Periodically, the teacher should structure a discussion of how effectively the pairs are working together (i.e., group processing). Group celebrations add reward interdependence to the pairs.

3. *Closure Focused Discussion*: Teachers give students an ending discussion task lasting 4–5 min. The task requires students to summarize what they have learned from the lecture and integrate it into existing conceptual frameworks. The task may also point students toward what the homework will cover or what will be presented in the next class session. This provides closure to the lecture.

Informal cooperative learning ensures students are actively involved in understanding what is being presented. It also provides time for teachers to move around the class listening to what students are saying. Listening to student discussions can give instructors direction and insight into how well students understand the concepts and material being as well as increase the individual accountability of participating in the discussions.

1.5.3   Cooperative Base Groups

Cooperative base groups are long-term, heterogeneous cooperative learning groups with stable membership (Johnson et al. 1998b, 2002). Members' primary responsibilities are to: (a) ensure all members are making good academic progress (i.e., positive goal interdependence); (b) hold each other accountable for striving to learn (i.e., individual accountability); and (c) provide each other with support, encouragement, and assistance in completing assignments (i.e., promotive interaction). In order to ensure the base groups function effectively, periodically teachers should teach needed social skills and have the groups process how effectively they are functioning. Typically, cooperative base groups are heterogeneous in membership (especially in terms of achievement motivation and task orientation), meet regularly (for example, daily or biweekly), and last for the duration of the class (a semester or year) or preferably for several years. The agenda of the base group can include academic support tasks (such as ensuring all members have completed their homework and understand it or editing each other's essays), personal support tasks (such as getting to know each other and helping each other solve nonacademic problems), routine tasks (such as taking attendance), and assessment tasks (such as checking each other's understanding of the answers to test questions when the test is first taken individually and then retaken in the base group).

The *teacher's role* in using cooperative base groups is to: (a) form heterogeneous groups of four (or three); (b) schedule a time when they will regularly meet (such as beginning and end of each class session or the beginning and end of each week); (c) create specific agendas with concrete tasks that provide a routine for base groups to follow when they meet; (d) ensure the five basic elements of effective cooperative groups are implemented; and (e) have students periodically process the effectiveness of their base groups.

The longer a cooperative group exists, the more caring their relationships will tend to be, the greater the social support they will provide for each other, the more committed they will be to each other's success, and the more influence members will have over each other. Permanent cooperative base groups provide the arena in which caring and committed relationships can be created that provide the social support needed to improve attendance, personalize the educational experience, increase achievement, and improve the quality of school life.

1.5.4   Integrated Use of All Three Types of Cooperative Learning

These three types of cooperative learning may be used together (Johnson & Johnson 1999). A typical class session may begin with a base group meeting, which is followed by a short lecture in which informal cooperative learning is used. The lecture is followed by a formal cooperative learning lesson. Near the end of the class session another short lecture may be delivered with the use of informal cooperative learning. The class ends with a base group meeting.

1.6   Conclusions and Summary

Teachers who wish to use cooperative learning should ideally base their classroom practices on theory validated by research. The closer classroom practices are to validated theory, the more likely they will be effective. When more directly practice is connected to theory, furthermore, the more likely practice will be refined, upgraded, and improved over the years. There are, however, few classroom practices that are directly based on validated theory. The close relationship between theory, research, and practice makes cooperative learning somewhat unique. It also creates a set of issues for teachers using cooperative learning.

The first issue is understanding the nature of social interdependence. *Social interdependence* is created when goals are structured so that the accomplishment of a person's goal is affected by others' actions. The interdependence may be positive (which results in individuals working cooperatively to achieve their mutual goals) or negative (which results in individuals competing to see who will achieve the goal). The absence of interdependence indicates no connection between people's attempts to achieve their goals. In cooperative situations, students' actions substitute for each other, students are inducible, and a positive cathexis is created toward other's actions. In competitive situations, the opposite psychological processes may be found. The fundamental premise of social interdependence theory is that the way in which goals are structured determines how individuals interact, and those interaction patterns create outcomes. Positive goal interdependence tends to result in promotive interaction, negative goal interdependence tends to result in oppositional interaction, and no interdependence tends to result in no interaction.

The second issue is understanding the research validating social interdependence theory. There are hundreds of studies indicating that cooperation, compared to competitive and individualistic efforts, tends to result in greater effort to achieve, more positive relationships, and greater psychological health. The diversity of this research provides considerable generalizabiity to the findings.

The third issue is to understand the five basic elements that make cooperation work. There is nothing magical about putting students in groups. Students can compete with groupmates, students can work individualistically while ignoring groupmates, or students can work cooperatively with groupmates. In order to structure cooperative learning effectively, teachers need to understand how to structure positive interdependence, individual accountability, promotive interaction, appropriate use of social skills, and group processing into learning situations.

The fourth issue is to understand the diversity of cooperative learning. When the five basic elements may be effectively implemented in formal cooperative learning situations (formal cooperative learning may be used to structure most learning situations), informal cooperative learning situations (informal cooperative learning may be used to make didactic lessons cooperative), and cooperative base groups (which are used to personalize a class and the school). Together they provide an integrated system for instructional organization and design (as well as classroom management). When utilizing these three types of cooperative learning, any learning situations in any subject area with any age students and with any curriculum can be structured cooperatively.

References

Archer-Kath, J., Johnson, D. W., & Johnson, R. (1994). Individual versus group feedback in cooperative groups. *Journal of Social Psychology, 134,* 681–694.

Aronson, E., Blaney, N., Stephan, C., Sikes, J., & Snapp, M. (1978). *The jigsaw classroom.* Beverly Hills, CA: Sage.

Blau, P. (1954). Co-operation and competition in a bureaucracy. *American Journal of Sociology, 59,* 530–535.

Brewer, M., & Kramer, R. (1986). Choice behavior in social dilemmas: effects of social identity, group size, and decision framing. *Journal of Personality and Social Psychology, 50,* 543–549.

Crawford, J., & Haaland, G. (1972). Predecisional information seeking and subsequent conformity in the social influence process. *Journal of Personality and Social Psychology, 23,* 112–119.

Crombag, H. (1966). Cooperation and competition in means interdependent triads: A replication. *Journal of Personality and Social Psychology, 4,* 692–695.

De Cremer, D., & Van Kijk, E. (in press). Reactions to group success and failure as a function of group identification: A test of the goal transformation hypothesis in social dilemmas. *Journal of Experimental Social Psychology.*

De Cremer, D., & Van Vjugt, M. (1999). Social identification effects in social dilemmas: A transformation of motives. *European Journal of Social Psychology, 29,* 871–893.

Deutsch, M. (1949a). A theory of cooperation and competition. *Human Relations, 2,* 129–152.

Deutsch, M. (1949b). An experimental study of the effects of cooperation and competition upon group process. *Human Relations, 2,* 199–231.

Deutsch, M. (1958). Trust and suspicion. *Journal of Conflict Resolution, 2,* 265–279.

Deutsch, M. (1960). The effects of motivational orientation upon trust and suspicion. *Human Relations, 13,* 123–139.

Deutsch, M. (1962). Cooperation and trust: Some theoretical notes. In M. Jones (Ed.), *Nebraska symposium on motivation* (pp. 275–319). Lincoln, NE: University of Nebraska Press.

Frank, M. (1984). *A comparison between an individual and group goal structure contingency that differed in the behavioral contingency and performance-outcome components.* Unpublished doctoral thesis, University of Minnesota.

Gabbert, B., Johnson, D., & Johnson, R. (1986). Cooperative learning, group-to-individual transfer, process gain and the acquisition of cognitive reasoning strategies. *Journal of Psychology, 120*(3), 265–278.

Gerard, H., Wilhelmy, R., & Conolley, E. (1965). Conformity and group size. *Journal of Personality and Social Psychology, 8,* 79–82.

Haines, D., & McKeachie, W. (1967). Cooperative versus competitive discussion methods in teaching introductory psychology. *Journal of Educational Psychology, 58*(6), 386–390.

Harkins, S., & Petty, R. (1982). The effects of task difficulty and task uniqueness on social loafing. *Journal of Personality and Social Psychology, 43,* 1214–1229.

Hooper, S., Ward, T., Hannafin, M., & Clark, H. (1989). The effects of aptitude composition on achievement during small group learning. *Journal of Computer-Based Instruction, 16,* 102–109.

Horney, K. (1937). *The neurotic personality of our time.* New York: Norton.

Hwong, N., Caswell, A., Johnson, D. W., & Johnson, R. (1993). Effects of cooperative and individualistic on prospective elementary teachers' music achievements and attitudes. *Journal of Social Psychology, 133*(1), 53–64.

Indik, B. P. (1965). Organization size and member participation: Some empirical tests of alternate explanations. *Human Relations, 15,* 339–350.

Ingham, A., Levinger, G., Graves, J., & Peckham, V. (1974). The Ringelmann effect: Studies of group size and group performance. *Journal of Personality and Social Psychology, 10,* 371–384.

Johnson, D. W. (1970). *The social psychology of education.* New York: Holt, Rinehart & Winston.

Johnson, D. W. (1974). Communication and the inducement of cooperative behavior in conflicts: A critical review. *Speech Monographs, 41,* 64–78.

Johnson, D. W. (2003). Social interdependence: The interrelationships among theory, research, and practice. *American Psychologist, 58*(11), 931–945.

Johnson, D. W. (2006). *Reaching out: Interpersonal effectiveness and self-actualization* (9th edn). Boston: Allyn & Bacon.

Johnson, D. W., & Johnson, F. (2006). *Joining together: Group theory and research* (9th edn). Boston: Allyn & Bacon.

Johnson, D. W. & Johnson, R. (1974). Instructional goal structure: Cooperative, competitive, or individualistic. *Review of Educational Research, 44,* 213–240.

Johnson, D. W., & Johnson, R. (1979). Conflict in the classroom: Controversy and learning. *Review of Educational Research, 49,* 51–70.

Johnson, D. W., & Johnson, R. (1981). Effects of cooperative and individualistic learning experiences on interethnic interaction. *Journal of Educational Psychology, 73*(3), 454–459.

Johnson, R., & Johnson, D. W. (1982). Effects of cooperative, competitive, and individualistic learning experiences on cross-ethnic interaction and friendships. *Journal of Social Psychology, 118,* 47–58.

Johnson, D. W., & Johnson, R. (1984). The effects of intergroup cooperation and intergroup competition on ingroup and outgroup cross-handicap relationships. *The Journal of Social Psychology, 124,* 85–94.

Johnson, D. W., & Johnson, R. (1989). *Cooperation and competition: Theory and research.* Edina, MN: Interaction Book Company.

Johnson, D. W., & Johnson, R. (1992). *Positive interdependence: Activity manual and guide.* Edina, MN: Interaction Book Company.

Johnson, D. W., & Johnson, R. (1994). *Leading the cooperative school* (2nd edn). Edina, MN: Interaction Book Company.

Johnson, D. W., & Johnson, R. (1999). *Learning together and alone: Cooperative, competitive, and individualistic learning* (5th edn). Boston: Allyn & Bacon.

Johnson, D. W., & Johnson, R. (2002). Cooperative learning methods: A meta-analysis. *Journal of Research in Education, 12*(1), 5–14.

Johnson, D. W., & Johnson, R. (2005). New developments in social interdependence theory. *Genetic, Social, and General Psychology Monographs, 131*(4), 285–358.

Johnson, D. W., & Johnson, R. (2007). *Creative controversy: Academic conflict in the classroom* (4th edn). Edina, MN: Interaction Book Company.

Johnson, D. W., Johnson, R., & Holubec, E. (1998a). *Cooperation in the classroom* (6th edn). Edina, MN: Interaction Book Company.

Johnson, D. W., Johnson, R., & Holubec, E. (1998b). *Advanced cooperative learning* (3rd edn). Edina, MN: Interaction Book Company.

Johnson, D. W., Johnson, R., & Holubec, E. (2002). *Circles of learning* (5th edn). Edina, MN: Interaction Book Company.

Johnson, D. W., Johnson, R., Ortiz, A., & Stanne, M. (1991). Impact of positive goal and resource interdependence on achievement, interaction, and attitudes. *Journal of General Psychology, 118*(4), 341–347.

Johnson, D. W., Johnson, R., Roy, P., & Zaidman, B. (1985). Oral interaction in cooperative learning groups: Speaking, listening, and the nature of statements made by high-, medium, and low-achieving students. *Journal of Psychology, 119*, 303–321.

Johnson, D. W., Johnson, R., Stanne, M., & Garibaldi, A. (1990). The impact of leader and member group processing on achievement in cooperative groups. *Journal of Social Psychology, 130*, 507–516.

Johnson, D. W., & Noonan, P. (1972). Effects of acceptance and reciprocation of self-disclosures on the development of trust. *Journal of Counseling Psychology, 19*(5), 411–416.

Johnson, D. W., Skon, L., & Johnson, R. (1980). Effects of cooperative, competitive, and individualistic conditions on children's problem-solving performance. *American Educational Research Journal, 17*(1), 83–94.

Kerr, N. (1983). The dispensability of member effort and group motivation losses: Free-rider effects. *Journal of Personality and Social Psychology, 44*, 78–94.

Kerr, N. (1989). Illusions of efficacy: The effects of group size on perceived efficacy in social dilemmas. *Journal of Experimental Social Psychology, 25*, 297–313.

Kerr, N., & Bruun, S. (1981). Ringelmann revisited: Alternative explanations for the social loafing effect. *Personality and Social Psychology Bulletin, 7*, 224–231.

Kerr, N., & Bruun, S. (1983). The dispensability of member effort and group motivation losses: Free-rider effects. *Journal of Personality and Social Psychology, 44*, 78–94.

Koffka, K. (1935). *Principles of gestalt psychology*. New York: Harcourt, Brace.

Kramer, R., & Brewer, M. (1984). Effects of group identity on resource use in a simulated commons dilemma. *Journal of Personality and Social Psychology, 46*, 1044–1057.

Latane, B., Williams, K., & Harkins, S. (1979). Many hands make light the work: The causes and consequences of social loafing. *Journal of Personality and Social Psychology, 37*, 822–832.

Laughlin, P., & McGlynn, R. (1967). Cooperative versus competitive concept attainment as a function of sex and stimulus display. *Journal of Personality and Social Psychology, 7*(4), 398–402.

Lew, M., Mesch, D., Johnson, D. W., & Johnson, R. (1986a). Positive interdependence, academic and collaborative-skills group contingencies and isolated students. *American Educational Research Journal, 23*, 476–488.

Lew, M., Mesch, D., Johnson, D. W., & Johnson, R. (1986b). Components of cooperative learning: Effects of collaborative skills and academic group contingencies on achievement and mainstreaming. *Contemporary Educational Psychology, 11*, 229–239.

Lewin, K. (1935). *A dynamic theory of personality*. New York: McGraw-Hill.

Lewin, K. (1948). *Resolving social conflicts*. New York: Harper.

Matsui, T., Kakuyama, T., & Onglatco, M. (1987). Effects of goals and feedback on performance in groups. *Journal of Applied Psychology, 72*, 407–415.

Mayer, A. (1903). Uber einzel-und gesamtleistung des scholkindes. *Archiv fur die Gesamte Psychologie, 1*, 276–416.

Mesch, D., Lew, M., Johnson, D. W., & Johnson, R. (1986). Isolated teenagers, cooperative learning and the training of social skills. *Journal of Psychology, 120*, 323–334.

Mesch, D., Johnson, D. W., & Johnson, R. (1988). Impact of positive interdependence and academic group contingencies on achievement. *Journal of Social Psychology, 128,* 345–352.

Messick, D., & Brewer, M. (1983). Solving social dilemmas: A review. *Review of Personality and Social Psychology, 4,* 11–44.

Moede, W. (1927). Die richtlinien der leistungs-psycholgie. *Industrielle Psychotechnik, 4,* 193–207.

Morgan, B., Coates, G., & Rebbin, T. (1970). *The effects of Phlebotomus fever on sustained performance and muscular output.* Tech. Rep. No. ITR-70-14. Louisville, KY: University of Louisville, Performance Research Laboratory-36697.

Montagu, A. (1966). *On being human.* New York: Hawthorn.

Naught, G., & Newman, S. (1966). The effect of anxiety on motor steadiness in competitive and non-competitive conditions. *Psychonomic Science, 6,* 519–520.

Olson, M. (1965). *The logic of collective action.* Cambridge, MA: Harvard University Press.

Ortiz, A., Johnson, D. W., & Johnson, R. (1996). The effect of positive goal and resource interdependence on individual performance. *Journal of Social Psychology, 136*(2), 243–249.

Petty, R., Harkins, S., Williams, K., & Latane, B. (1977). The effects of group size on cognitive effort and evaluation. *Personality and Social Psychology Bulletin, 3,* 575–578.

Pittman, T., Davey, M., Alafat, K., Wetherill, K., & Kramer, N. (1980). Informational versus controlling verbal rewards. *Personality and Social Psychology Bulletin, 6,* 228–233.

Putnam, J., Rynders, J., Johnson, R., & Johnson, D. W. (1989). Collaborative skills instruction for promoting positive interactions between mentally handicapped and nonhandicapped children. *Exceptional Children, 55,* 550–557.

Raven, B., & Eachus, H. (1963). Cooperation and competition in means-interdependent triads. *Journal of Abnormal and Social Psychology, 67,* 307–316.

Rosenbaum, M., Moore, D., Cotton, J., Cook, M., Hieser, R., Shovar, N., & Gray, M. (1980). Group productivity and process: Pure and mixed reward structures and task interdependence. *Journal of Personality and Social Psychology, 39*(4), 626–642.

Rosenberg, L. (1961). Group size, prior experience, and conformity. *Journal of Abnormal and Social Psychology, 63,* 436–437.

Ryan, R. (1982). Control and information in the intrapersonal sphere: An extension of cognitive evaluation theory. *Journal of Personality and Social Psychology, 43,* 450–461.

Skinner, B. (1968). *The technology of teaching.* New York: Appleton-Century-Crofts.

Skon, L., Johnson, D. W., & Johnson, R. (1981). Cooperative peer interaction versus individual competition and individualistic efforts: Effects on the acquisition of cognitive reasoning strategies. *Journal of Educational Psychology, 73,* 83–92.

Sweeney, J. (1973). An experimental investigation of the free-rider problem. *Social Science Research, 2,* 277–292.

Thomas, D. (1957). Effects of facilitative role interdependence on group functioning. *Human Relations, 10,* 347–366.

Triplett, N. (1898). The dynamogenic factors in pacemaking and competition. *American Journal of Psychology, 9,* 507–533.

Turner, E. B. (1889). A three-year study of the physiology of pacing and waiting races. Cited in N. Triplett (1898), The dynamogenic factors in pacemaking and competition. *American Journal of Psychology, 9,* 507–533.

Webb, N., & Cullian, L. (1983). Group interaction and achievement in small groups: Stability over time. *American Education Research Journal, 20*(3), 411–423.

Wertheimer, M. (1923). Untersuchungen zur Lehre von der Gestalt: II. *Psychologische Forschung, 4,* 301–350.

Wicklund, R., & Brehm, J. (1976). *Perspectives on cognitive dissonance.* Hillsdale, NJ: Erlbaum.

Williams, K. (1981). *The effects of group cohesiveness on social loafing.* Paper presented at the annual meeting of the Midwestern Psychological Association, Detroit.

Williams, K., Harkins, S., & Latane, B. (1981). Identifiability as a deterrent to social loafing: Two cheering experiments. *Journal of Personality and Social Psychology, 40,* 303–311.

Yager, S., Johnson, R., Johnson, D. W., & Snider, B. (1986). The impact of group processing on achievement in cooperative learning groups. *Journal of Social Psychology, 126,* 389–397.

Chapter 2
Beyond the Classroom and into the Community: The Role of the Teacher in Expanding the Pedagogy of Cooperation

Rachel Hertz-Lazarowitz

Abstract The chapter presents four systemic cooperative learning (CL) long-term programs conducted in northern Israel, with Arabs and Jewish schools in mixed cities or neighboring communities. In each of those programs the teachers-educators expanded their roles implementing reforms based on cooperation. The first program extended the classic method of Group Investigation (GI) to Innovative Technology (IT) sites of learning. The second program expanded the "face to face" model of "The Six Mirrors of the Classroom" to classrooms using complex investigations in the open spaces and the highway of technology. The third broadened the role of teachers to become facilitators of a CL school-family partnership within the school and across schools. The fourth, formed a principals community of leaders, who based on cooperation transformed their vision, skills and knowledge to generate a vision of critical cooperative pedagogy aimed to empower and bring equality to the schools and the community at large.

2.1 Introduction

This chapter presents the position that teachers roles can be expanded to realize broader visions of bringing Cooperative Learning (CL) into the future. The work was conducted in northern Israel, where Arabs and Jews live in geographical proximity to one another in either mixed cities or neighboring communities. Many teachers and principals were highly motivated to make a critical change in their schools and beyond. They had a vision and a mission to make a difference in their deprived communities and to use CL as a vehicle for empowerment and greater equality (Hertz-Lazarowitz 1999, 2005).

Four paths are suggested for restructuring CL into new challenges. The first is extending the classic method of Group Investigation (GI) to Innovative Technology (IT) sites of learning, where the teachers and their students are the designers of the future GI classrooms and the IT curricula for computer-supported cooperative learning. The second path is expanding the "face to face" model of "The Six Mirrors of the Classroom" to include learning at the open spaces and the highway of technology, using cooperative learning. The third path is broadening the role of teachers to become agents of a school-family partnership within the school and across schools, thereby reducing national/religious segregation and creating a mixed community. The fourth path – and the most challenging one – is principals' commitment to use the vision, skills and knowledge of CL to become agents of critical cooperative pedagogy aimed at decreasing injustice in schools and in society at large. These four paths were systemic-and holistic reforms, based on cooperation, positive interdependence and a community approach. Each of the four paths described in the chapter demonstrate how CL can inspire and revolutionize educators' roles.

From the basic Group Investigation (GI) practiced by individual teachers in CL classrooms, teachers in their peer learning communities (TPLC) moved to design the method (GI) based on the "six mirrors of the classroom model" to the classrooms of the future using complex technology as additional source for investigation. Then the teachers and the principals moved beyond the classroom to School-Family Partnerships to include families of the children in all the schools in the community in large. Finally the same systemic holistic approach based on cooperation, created a community of principals leadership that transformed the educational vision of the system.

During 1993–2004, the implementation of Cooperative Learning was intensively applied and researched in Arab and Jewish schools in Acre, a mixed Arab-Jewish city, as well as in other cities in northern Israel. The methods integrated elements of Group Investigation into Slavin's method of Success for All (SFA) and into the Israeli program for literacy development (ALASH) (Hertz-Lazarowitz 2001; Hertz-Lazarowitz & Schaedel 2003). During these years, the working models expanded the scope of CL beyond the classroom and the school, empowering teachers and principals to transform their knowledge and vision of cooperation to their own communities. Innovative methods of GI and complex classroom contexts were introduced in many Arab and Jewish schools on all grade levels and in various subjects.

2.2 The Technological Innovative (TI) Group Investigation Model

Group Investigation (GI) was a milestone for CL in Israel and was considered a revolution because it went against the traditional teaching methods that were rooted in the national ideology of creating a new nation of Israeli-Jews in the homeland (Hertz-Lazarowitz & Zelniker 1995). The former methods were not sensitive to the diverse ethnic groups within the Israeli-Jewish student population and were unjust to the Arab citizens of Israel (Al-Haj 1998; Azaiza et al, in press).

Values of cooperative investigation are deeply rooted in the cultures of both Jews and Arabs. For the Jews, the old Talmudic saying of "Chavruta or Mituta" translated to "learning with a partner or death." The Arab culture is also based on collectivism, closeness, and cooperation (Dwairy 2004). GI is ideologically different from the CL methods developed in the USA (Lazarowitz & Hertz-Lazarowitz 1998; Sharan & Sharan 1992), which were based on behaviorist approaches, packaged curricula, external rewards, and competition between groups (Johnson et al. 2000; Kagan 2001; Slavin et al. 2003).

2.2.1 Teachers as Peer Learners

Group Investigation was a major source of influence on working with Teachers as Peer Learners with Computers (TPLC) in their professional development. In GI teachers are perceived as facilitators of intellectual and social development of the students (Almog & Hertz-Lazarowitz 1999; Gillies & Ashman 2003; Gillies & Boyle 2005). The goal of TPLC was to create a curriculum for GI in the new complex learning environment. The Group Investigation process was restructured into six stages and revitalized as a main model in the cooperative learning movement in many cultures (Hertz-Lazarowitz & Zelniker 1995; Joyce & Weil 1986). Four major features characterize GI: investigation, interaction, interpretation, and intrinsic motivation. The unique character of GI lies in the integration of these four basic features within the meaningful context of an issue worthy of investigation (Sharan & Sharan 1992).

Investigation refers to the general orientation toward learning adopted by the teacher and student. When a group of learners is carrying out a group investigation project, it becomes an inquiry community with a common purpose, and each participant serves as an investigator who coordinates his/her inquiry with other members of the group. Thus, in Thelen's (1960) words, the class is both an inquiry community and a community of inquirers.

Interaction is essential to the successful use of group investigation. Students and teachers need to learn and practice effective interaction as they work in groups. Peer learning in GI is the vehicle by which students and teachers encourage one another, elaborate on each others ideas, help each other to focus on the task, and confront one anothers ideas with opposing points of view. Intellectual and social interactions are the means by which learners rework their personal knowledge in light of the new knowledge gathered by the group in the course of the investigation.

Interpretation of the combined findings is a process of negotiation between personal knowledge and new knowledge, and between ideas and information contributed by other members of the group. Facilitating the process of interpretation through group interaction is consistent with Dewey's view (1927) of education, as well as with the constructionist approach to cognition (Vygotsky 1978). Group Investigation provides learners with the opportunity to interact with others who have investigated different aspects of the same general topic and who have contributed different perspectives on that topic. Within this context, interpretation is a social, cognitive, and intellectual process par excellence.

Intrinsic motivation in GI refers to the way that GI motivates learners to take an active role in determining what and how they will learn. It motivates students and teachers to choose investigation issues that are connected to their own needs, experiences, feelings, and values that are relevant to the general community. The decision of the topic for GI is a social act that can empower thinking and critical perspectives among the GI participants. A meaningful investigation is an expression of a choice.

2.2.2   The GI Model

The classical GI method, as proposed in Israel in the late seventies, was implemented at all levels of schooling in Israel. Research on GI indicated positive outcomes in general in academic, cognitive, social, and emotional aspects as compared to other methods (Hertz-Lazarowitz 1992; Hertz-Lazarowitz & Schaedel 2003; Lazarowitz, 2007; Sharan & Hertz-Lazarowitz 1981; Sharan et al. 1984).

In the new learning environment, investigation can occur over a wide range of topics by using advanced technology, promoting peer interaction, constructing interpretation, and bringing social and moral perspectives to the learning environment. However, the process of GI needs to be updated for use in the future, with its complexity of technological developments and multi-faceted environments and communities. Still, we shall argue that its six-stage model is generic enough to guide the process of social investigation in the TPLC and in the classrooms.

2.2.2.1   The Six Stages of the GI Model

Stage 1: Class determines sub-topics and organizes into research groups.
Stage 2: Groups plan their investigation.
Stage 3: Groups carry out their investigation.
Stage 4: Groups plan their presentation/feedback.
Stage 5: Groups make their presentation.
Stage 6: Teacher and students evaluate their project.

2.2.3   Curriculum of the TPLC

The intent of the TPLC curriculum was to help teachers prepare for the classroom of the future. In the project (Almog & Hertz-Lazarowitz 1999; Salomon 2002), the investigation topic chosen was *Planning the City of the Future*. The investigation of this topic had two phases: studying an existing city – in our case, Haifa – wherein most of the participants lived, and then, based on this phase of the investigation, planning the city of the future.

Teachers in the TPLC program shared motivation to implement this educational innovation (Abrami et al. 2004). The teachers participated in 11 sessions in which they researched and learned new, complex interdisciplinary topics using advanced technology (word processor, multi-media software, and data banks) and worked in cooperative and collaborative investigative working teams. A typical session usually lasted 3–4 h and can be described according to the following four areas: cognitive, social, technological, and curricular. (1) the cognitive area, which included generating questions, clarifying concepts, and working on research; (2) the social area, which included helping by mutual explanation, talking and reflecting with peers about mistakes, and taking roles to facilitate group work; (3) the technological area, which included defining key terms for searching databases, revising a written text with a word processor, and preparing a multimedia product; and (4) the curricular area, which included deciding on resources, learning diverse content related to urban life, and planning an interdisciplinary unit.

The goal of the TLPC was to give the teachers the knowledge in the mode that will afford their experiential learning as teachers and as students of GI.

2.2.4   Steps of GI in Teachers Peer Learning Professional Development Curriculum

The 11 steps presented in the paragraph are corresponding to the six stages of the GI method.

Step 1 and step 2 are introductory practices related to the organization of the classroom, the practice of the social-academic skill needed to start CL, and introduction to the use of advanced technology.

1. Cooperative learning: Ways of dividing the class into learning groups; obtaining skills in cooperation and in prosocial behavior such as: information exchange, active thinking by exchanging ideas, effective communication, tolerance, openness, sensitivity, and the ability to admit mistakes.
2. The Use of advanced technology: Learning to use the computer, work with multi-media software and data banks (local and abroad).
3. Formulating the topic for investigation and dividing it into sub-topics: Brainstorming; discussing ways of dividing complex subjects into sub-topics; and defining methods of organizing topics and sub-topics hierarchically.

4. Raising questions for investigation and problem solving: Arranging the questions hierarchically and, according to related topics, exchanging questions with peers and discussing ways of obtaining answers.

Step 3 and step 4 begins the GI method – It corresponds to the first stage of GI "Class determined sub units and organize into research group."

5. Creating and planning a work program: Discussing decisions related to scheduling; dividing tasks; and assigning authority, responsibility, and roles to team members.
6. Gathering information with advanced computer-network technology: Conducting academic investigation using various resources and computerized data banks; making judgments about the information; and expanding and reducing the information.
7. Dealing with nontextual information: Working with maps, tables, graphs, and photographs.
8. Analysis and comprehension of texts: Working on academic and scientific literacy; discussing a variety of text structures; strategic reading aimed at formulating questions; abstracting; distinguishing main issues; and identifying key terms as a guide for further research.

Steps 5, 6,7, and step 8, correspond to the third stage of GI: "Group carry out their investigation". This stage is the heart of the GI method and is done in the topic that the interest groups chose. Technology was one of the tools the students used.

9. The writing process: Approaching writing as a process, including drafting, reviewing, editing, peer reviewing, and publishing. The final product should be a multimedia and written professional product.

Steps 9 correspond to the fourth stage of GI: "Groups plan their presentation/ feedback"

10. Preparing and presenting an oral report: Working on the structure of the report for the TPLC and examining in what ways it differs from a traditional written presentation; skill-building for a multimedia presentation, emphasizing the rhetoric of presentations and the use of audio-visual devices.

Step 10 correspond the stage 5 of the GI; "Groups make their presentation"

11. Evaluation: Developing criteria for creating a variety of ways to evaluate each teams multimedia products and sub-products. The evaluations take place within groups, between groups, and with experts in the community.

Step 11 corresponds to the sixth stage of the GI method: Teacher and student evaluate their project. The project is a group cooperative outcome.

The TLPC workshop was a year-long process, while the teachers served in two roles – the first as a community of peers and the second as implementers of the TI Group Investigation in their classrooms at the junior high school level in northern Israel. This inquiry project followed former models of teachers as a community of peers that were developed in elementary schools (Hertz-Lazarowitz & Calderon 1994; Sharan et al. 1984; Slavin & Calderon 2001). Those models showed positive outcomes for teachers and students.

2.3 The Six Mirrors of the Classroom: Into the Future Classroom

The work with teachers and students in the transition from the traditional classroom to the GI classroom in Israel demanded contact and ongoing observation and conceptualization of the dynamic between teachers and students in the classroom. During this process, a long-term plan of observational-process studies was conducted to describe the six-mirror model of the classroom (Hertz-Lazarowitz 1992). The model consists of six "mirrors," a term chosen to portray the view that the dimensions which characterize the classroom are interrelated and reflected in one another: Structure and activities in one dimension have implications for what is possible in another dimension.

In the model, harmony among the mirrors and the levels within each mirror positively affect the social and cognitive development of the students. For example, if the teacher maintains central control of the classroom (mirror three, level one), and asks her students to work cooperatively (mirror six, level three) on a given learning task, this creates a disharmony between the mirrors and will be reflected in students' behavior, as the students will be unable to engage in multilateral investigation. However, if the learning task is designed to bring together the parts of a horizontal work division and then to find a creative solution for the problem – such as in the planning of a future city – while the teacher aims her instructional behavior at supporting and helping different groups, then there is harmony between the mirrors and the learners will be engaged and observed in performing a high level of academic and social behavior (mirrors five and six)

The model has served as a conceptual framework enabling teachers to analyze the mirrors and to be trained to gradually design their classrooms to become a CL and a GI learning environment. The development of innovative technology has made attainable what was once merely a dream – the use of the computer as a personal tool, much like a notebook and pen (Hertz-Lazarowitz & Bar Natan 2002). Likewise, every new technological development can be expected to interact with and change some basic features in the learning environment. *Technological development, with scaffolding cognitive aspects of students thinking*, has the potential to eventually revolutionize the classroom (Lockhorst 2004; O'Donnell & King 1999; Resta et. al. 1999). However, this revolution for future learning/teaching environment has to take place with an integrative understanding of the interdependence of the different mirrors, and specially to work on the advancement of students' academic-social skill in CL. The design of the learning task will be mostly affected by technology (Ronen et al. 2006). However, the parallels of discourse between the mirrors of teachers' instruction and students' behavior, will continue to be a significant factor in the future classroom (Webb et al. 2006).

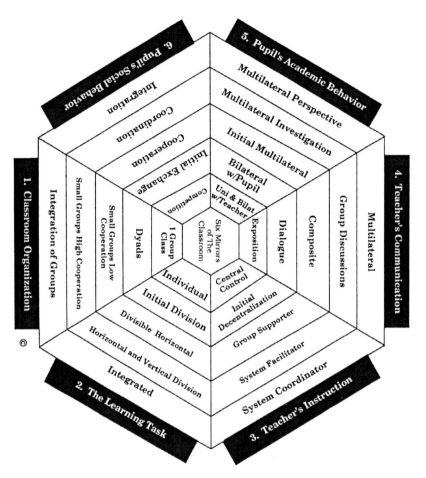

Fig. 2.1 Six mirrors of the classroom (Hertz-Lazarowitz 1992)

2.3.1   Mirror One: The Physical Organization of the Learning and Teaching Space

The future classroom, with advanced technologies and collaborative teams, should be organized in a flexible manner in order to meet both the traditional and innovative organization of learning teams. The physical setting of the classroom will have to accommodate human engineering aspects, peer learning, and computer demands. The classroom will have to become a flexible place for teachers and students to work. In the future, teachers may also give instructions via their computer network, and communication will flow from the teacher's computer to the students' personal computers and vice versa. The classroom will become a decentralized organization, with many smaller units (groups or teams) operating simultaneously. This organization of "group of groups" fits group learning and the high-technology environment.

The possibility of turning a classroom into a community of peers and computers will allow a dynamic presentation of information and products involved in learning projects. The change in instruction and learning will have to be followed by changes in the design and architecture of other rooms and spaces in the school, such as teachers' rooms, laboratories, and libraries.

2.3.2   Mirror Two: Learning Tasks – Using Peers and Computers as Thinking and Investigation Resources

Teachers, alongside their students, and sometimes following them, are learning to use the computer as a tool to develop skills in thinking and reflection. The computer can help to organize and carry out efforts of high-level learning and teaching and can engage students and teachers in challenging tasks. The computer's power lies in the access to rich and complex bodies of information that can be used to construct meaningful knowledge by investigation. Peers working together with computers interweave interpersonal and task-related learning, which facilitates the exchange of information through communication with other learning teams and with experts beyond the school walls.

The claim that "learning tasks vary in levels of complexity determined by the pattern of division of the tasks and integration of the learning products" (Hertz-Lazarowitz 1992; p. 76) is still relevant. The creation and design of the learning task was and still is the most significant role of the teacher in the "face to face" cooperative learning process (Gillies & Ashman 2003), and will be even more so in the future learning spaces with computer technology. The primary role and responsibility of teachers remains that of facilitating and supervising the quality of students' learning, as reflected in the processes and products derived from the tasks assigned to them.

2.3.3   Mirrors Three and Four: Teachers as Initiators, Producers, and Communicators of Learning

The role of the teacher is presently undergoing major changes. Whereas teachers' roles were traditionally based on historical definitions, such as "the sage or the stage," they are gradually becoming partners in a community of teachers and are increasingly immersed with students as partners in learning – the "guide on the side". The role of teachers as active initiators and actors in the "show of learning and teaching" will be influenced by the metaphor of theater production and interpretation (Schonmann 2006). Teachers will become producers of new classroom curricula and programs, in which new technology and sophisticated teaching materials play an ongoing part. Multidisciplinary teaching, in addition to mono-disciplinary teaching, will become a central part of learning in schools, which in turn will require the establishment and cooperation of multidisciplinary teaching teams.

2.3.4   Mirrors Five and Six: Academic and Social Communication and Behaviors

Open electronic communication with the outside world will expose teachers and students to peers from other schools and cultures. Through computer-mediated communication on the information highway, every classroom can become a real-time, on-line information center. Schools will familiarize their students and teachers with the many services of social institutions, such as research centers, laboratories, banks, newspapers, stock market information, and various resource centers. The small team within the classroom will become the primary social unit of learning. Students will be able to interact with on-line information and to share and discuss ideas and thoughts with a broad community. Examples are: in economics classes, to analyze the latest foreign currency data; in citizenship classes, to review last night's public opinion surveys; in sports, to follow the results of the latest games in various states. In these interactive knowledge-seeking contexts, students will master the most significant academic and social skills needed for citizens in the next century: working with people and on-line information in order to cooperate and collaborate with other people for actual learning, analyzing, and decision making.

The teacher in this classroom will need to be a skilled computer user and well versed in complex and varied information networks. This teacher will also need to be able to guide students to use technology in an enlightened way. Transforming information into knowledge in a context of moral and ethical dilemmas previously unknown to the teacher can be eased by working in teams and communities of teachers and by establishing such communities in the classroom. Writing is the powerful force for students and teachers working as communities through the use of telecommunication and intensive peer interaction (Morton 1996).

Many of the CL and IT innovations might fail because teachers make sporadic and partial changes. The model gives teachers a deep understanding of the whole learning environment and enables them to apply the principles of designing the mirrors so that they can create a powerful learning context. We found that this holistic perception transforms teachers' actions and positively affects students' development. Teachers in various educational settings have reported that the model created a multidimensional vision of their work and made them think and work simultaneously on the six-mirror dimensions.

Since the summary of research (Hertz-Lazarowitz 1992), the two models; the GI model and the six mirrors of the classroom model were combined in our field work. It has been used in Computer Mediated Instruction in junior high school social studies curricula (Almog & Hertz-Lazarowitz 1999; Salomon 2002); in cooperative methods of writing and literacy development (Hertz-Lazarowitz 2001; Hertz-Lazarowitz & Bar-Natan 2002; Hertz-Lazarowitz & Schadeal 2003). CL based on GI was implemented in science education at the secondary level of schooling (Lazarowitz & Hertz-Lazarowitz 1998). For example: Science-Technology-Environment and Peace Society (STEPS) was studied by Khalil & Lazarowitz, (2002) with ninth grade Arab and Jewish students in neighboring communities in the Galilee. Salit Ron used the Jigsaw-GI combined method with 11th and 12th grade students to study the complex subject of evolution (Ron & Lazarowitz 1995). The field work and research using GI in biology at the secondary level are summarized by Lazarowitz 2007.

Recently a new computerized system Collaborative e Learning Structures (CeLS) was developed in Israel, (Ronen et al. 2006). CeLS is a web-based system designed to create and reuse collaborative instruction by creating and conducting structured asynchronous collaborative activities and incorporate them in the existing instructional setting for all subjects and levels.

CeLS is currently under experimental implementation with communities of teachers, that search for existing activities, or create new collaborative structures using basic building blocks to suit their specific needs and instructional goals.

2.4   Into the Community: Teachers' Role in School-Family Partnership

Teachers in Israel extend their roles into the community. In 1998–2000, a two-year School-Family Partnership (SFP) program was implemented in Acre, a mixed Jewish-Arab city in Israel, to promote parents' role as the facilitators of their children's literacy development and to advance coexistence between Arab and Jewish parents. The SFP program was part of a five-year (1995–2000) holistic project designed to bring about a systemic change in Acre (Hertz-Lazarowitz 1999; Zelniker & Hertz-Lazarowitz 2005).

Two studies were conducted within the SFP program. In the first (1999), 174 Arab parents and 111 Jewish parents of first-grade children responded to a 31-item Parents' Literacy Questionnaire. In addition, interviews were conducted with mothers, teachers, and children. The questionnaire (Hertz-Lazarowitz & Horovitz 2002), yielded seven factors related to parents' perceptions and attitudes: (a) encouraging reading; (b) school assistance; (c) enriching the home literacy environment; (d) keeping the School-Family Partnership; (e) teachers' providing of support for their child; (f) parent-child interaction; and (g) knowing the CL method used in school for reading and writing.

In the second study (2000), 120 Arab parents and 30 Jewish parents responded to an Inter-group Coexistence Questionnaire. The 34 items related to five domains: parents' exposure to media in Hebrew and Arabic; parents' acceptance of Arab definitions of identity; readiness for relations; contact; and equality demands.

2.4.1   SFP Workshop Activities

Epstein's model of School-Family Partnership (Epstein & Sanders 2006) served as the basis for the program. A novel element of coexistence was introduced by the teachers and the principals in Acre by bringing together Jewish and Arab parents and teachers across schools for a year of structured workshops on themes of literacy development and inter-group contact. The coexistence component was suggested by the principals and teachers of several schools, as it was necessary and critical for advancing inter-group relations and equality in Acre's educational system. In order to achieve this purpose, the work was planned and implemented jointly by Arab and Jewish participants in cross-school and cross-national workshops focusing on literacy development and coexistence issues. Workshops conducted during the two-year period were documented as written protocols, as well as less formal reports including written and oral feedback provided by participating parents and teachers.

Literacy-Related Activities: Literacy-related activities took place within the SFP program as well as in the classroom. There were two main settings for training parents of first graders: one consisted of bi-weekly meetings of parents and teachers in each school, which served to strengthen the contact between the classroom teachers and the parents as well as to inform parents about the SFA program and its various components. The second setting consisted of monthly workshops in which parents and teachers across schools practiced and discussed literacy-related activities in the two cultures.

Within the literacy-related workshops, parents were encouraged to advance literacy at home by assembling a small library with books recommended by the teachers and by reading stories to the children on a daily basis. In addition, parents were encouraged to get involved with and help their children with their homework and to initiate discussion of various topics, such as cultural events and holidays and stories about the city. Parents were also encouraged to learn about the SFA program by visiting the classroom and joining a group of volunteer teacher's helpers in the class. Parents and teachers exchanged written communication by means of information and feedback sheets.

Once a month, there was an open day when teachers presented parents with activities related to the curriculum, such as parent-child cooperative writing of a family story. Other activities practiced and/or discussed on the open days and at the workshops included reading and writing with the children in their first language, discussing literature from each culture, meeting authors of Jewish and Arab literary works, listening to storytellers from each culture, telling about their group's history in Acre, and bringing more technology to the classroom.

Coexistence-related activities: Coexistence-related activities in the parents' workshop included the use of expressive means to increase personal closeness and mutual acceptance, such as singing, dancing, telling personal stories about their own and their children's education, sharing memories, sharing past and present experiences of coexistence in Acre, and building shared visions for the future of inter-group relations and education in Acre. In the workshops, parents discussed municipal resource allocation and policies of equality and discrimination. Parents formulated the construction of joint educational task forces and education-related plans for Acre, such as getting more instructional help for Jewish and Arab at-risk children and adding a wing to the Arab school building. Parents were interested in advancing positive inter-group relations and were encouraged to engage in joint civic activism to benefit both Arab and Jewish children in Acre.

In addition to the workshops, there were numerous open days when parents came to school, participated in classes with their children, and took part in activities shared with their children and the teachers. According to the teachers, the parents' participation and involvement was greater than in the period preceding the SFP program. As stated by one of the teachers, Miri Yunger, "Since the implementation of the School-Family Partnership program, the parents have become more involved. Many parents have become aware of the importance of literacy at home and the encouragement of literacy development at home."

Overall, the findings indicated that the Arab parents perceived themselves as learning to become more effective facilitators of literacy development for their children than the Jewish parents, as well as more effective facilitators of coexistence than the Jewish parents. The teachers in Acre expanded their role and added the mission of working with parents in their school and across segregated schools throughout the country. The School-Family Partnership positively affected the home literacy of the parents and created a bond between parents-teachers and the children, and a peaceful community of Arab and Jewish parents (Hertz-Lazarowitz 2004; Zelniker & Hertz-Lazarowitz 2005).

2.5 Teachers and Principals Transform CL to a Critical Pedagogy for Civil Action

In the work in Acre (1995–2000), a city-wide plan was developed in which different Investigative Task Forums (ITFs) were created to increase the participation of all members of the community. Each ITF was based on the GI structures: The group in the ITF had to engage a community-related problem, brain storm, investigate, discuss, suggest solution and present plans for change by action. The ITF represented the highly diverse groups within this mixed city – Arabs and Jews, religious and secular, public and private schools (Hertz-Lazarowitz 1999).

Among the ITFs created were a forum of principals and a forum of teachers-leaders, which were the most active of all the bodies that were established in the city. Those two forums, mainly the principals' forum, were analyzed (Eden & Hertz-Lazarowitz 2002) for their potential of becoming a critical force for change in the city. The holistic project and the CL program (SFA and ALASH) were implemented in Acre for one purpose, namely, professional growth that would advance the children and the city (Gordon 1996). The teachers and mainly the principals perceived the ITF as an opportunity to become organized and to establish several forums to advance their own purposes of achieving educational-political power in order to generate social change in the city. In so doing, they were transformed from professional leaders with rational-technical skills to avant-garde intellectual agents for change in the community.

One of their main goals was to change the nature of their dependence on the municipality against which they acted. The internal factors that helped them to attain their goals were the ability of the teachers and principals to organize due to their vision, skill, and level of education. In the process of their struggle, the members became aware of the political nature of their work. As a result, they redefined their role and degree of commitment from one of "narrow egoism," serving their own schools and causing them to compete with each other, to a "wide [holistic] outlook" of commitment to the entire educational system. By cooperating in this way, they brought the whole system under their aegis and thus gathered strength. For the first time, they were able to act according to their belief that "if there is no progress in education, there is no progress and prosperity in the city."

The principals and the teachers gathered to create a professional body with the aim of improving their function. Dialectically, they evolved from a body aiming to improve its professional-objective performance to one of intellectual change agents who understand that their work is not only pedagogical, but rather dependent on a wider social context requiring their acting as a local political leadership group aimed at improving the entire community (Giroux 1988). They showed that from a system in deep crisis, which was blamed for the poor academic achievements of students, the principals and teachers could come forward, assume leadership, and transform not only the educational system but the entire community, thus changing patterns of relations between bodies within the educational system and with other societal institutions.

The principals saw their greatest achievements in the following areas: *collecting debts* which had accumulated over eight years and had not been paid by the municipality; *openly obtaining information* about their financial situation from the municipality for the first time, allowing them to plan maintenance and renovation work within the framework of the budget; *supporting individual schools with their unique problems*, such as in the case of an affirmative-action strike in an Arab high school; *mediating between disputing principals* in order to positively impact the culture of work relations; *allocating resources for the schools* to provide for greater equality, especially for the Arab schools and the ultra-Orthodox Jewish schools (partially State-run schools) that had been discriminated against for many years; and *supporting city-wide processes of evaluation* so that information about each school's academic outcomes will be open to the community (Eden & Hertz-Lazarowitz 2002; Hertz-Lazarowitz 2004).

2.6   Future Prospects

In its essence, CL is a critical pedagogy because it raises basic questions regarding our nature as social beings. CL is based on perceiving the human being as a positive social being that is driven by cooperation and pro-social and humanistic motives (Deutsch 1973). According to this pedagogy, every child and every teacher has a voice and a contribution to make and can fulfill their potential within pro-social and caring schools (Aronson 2000; Kohn 2000).

The Cooperative Learning reform in Israel was the first critical pedagogy to be implemented in the State schools and was successful in changing two major injustices within the Israeli educational system. First, CL advanced social and academic integration and greater equality in the educational experience and outcomes for the different Jewish ethnic groups. Second, CL decreased the full segregation between the Arab sector and the Jewish sector in many communities due to the collaborative efforts of Arab and Jewish educators (Azaiza et al, in press; Hertz-Lazarowitz & Schaedel 2003).

GI work began with a commitment to apply the method in the classroom through complex models, and it was transformed to a vision of creating a critical pedagogy of cooperation in schools, cities, and regions that will make a difference. The teachers and the principals contributed to the growing awareness of multiculturalism due to the fact that CL was the first pedagogy to be implemented and researched in the Arab schools alongside the Jewish schools in northern Israel. Turning CL into a vision of a critical pedagogy may be the result of the unique structure and characteristics of Israel. The country is small, young, and has a highly diverse population, with multiple religions and multiple cultures living in an intractable state of conflict and war, but still looking for coexistence (Al-Haj 1988; Hertz-Lazarowitz et al, 2004).

The expansion of the roles of teachers in Israel is derived from genuine professional and personal contact between communities of Arab and Jewish educators, many of them women who were influenced to become a political-educational force that can make a difference in their various communities (Oplatka & Hertz Lazarowitz 2006). They perceive cooperation from a broader perspective as a lever and a vision of greater commitment, recognition, sensitivity, and concern for minorities and different cultural and religious groups in Israel (Azaiza et al, in press).

Five years of continuous work and research validated the positive impact of the work that the teachers invested in students' academic outcomes. A high quality of implementation of the cooperative learning methods resulted in higher academic achievements among the students (Hertz-Lazarowitz 2001, 2004; Zelniker & Hertz-Lazarowitz 2005, 2006). Our follow-up studies indicated that in about half of the CL schools, the teachers and principals continue to work with parents, with teachers across schools, and with the community at large, as it has become part of their professional roles. The principal forum is still active as change agents.

The principals and teachers in northern Israel have shown that educators can free themselves from technical-objective thinking and can view education as a political matter related to the power structure of society. But their liberation is not complete. It will only be so when the relationship moves beyond functional cooperation and is transformed so that all people are emancipated from boundaries that cause hostility and are truly treated as part of the community. Power is a requisite for social change, but cooperation and emancipation means a different view of human relations, which many principals and teachers have yet to attain.

Acknowledgments The author wishes to thank the many children, teachers, principals, parents, trainers, administrators, and University students that worked to transform the Arab and Jewish schools in the northern region of Israel to become places of greater cooperation, justice and equality. Special thanks are due to Dr. Bruria Schaedel for her leadership of the field work in many schools and to Mohammed Ali-Said, a writer, a teacher and a trainer, for his contribution to applying CL in the Arab schools. Appreciation is also extended to my coauthors in previous

publications, Tamar Almog, Margarita Calderon, Devorah Eden, Reuven Lazarowitz, Bruria Schaedel, and Tamar Zelniker, for their contribution to this chapter.
I thank Bat Sheva Vitner- Simon for her help in finalizing this paper.

References

Abrami, P. C., Poulsen, C. & Chambers, B. (2004). Teacher motivation to implement an educational innovation: Factors differentiating users and non-users of cooperative learning. *Educational Psychology*, 24 (2), 201–216.

Al-Haj, M. (1998). *Education, Empowerment and Control: The Case of the Arabs in Israel.* Albany: SUNY Press.

Almog, T. & Hertz-Lazarowitz, R. (1999). Teachers as peer learners: Investigation in an advanced technological learning environment. In A. M. O'Donnell & A. King (Eds.), *Cognitive Perspectives on Peer Learning* (pp. 285–313). Mahwah, NJ: Lawrence Erlbaum.

Aronson, E.(2000). *Nobody Left to Hate.* New York: W.H. Freeman and company.

Azaiza, F., Mor-Sommerfeld, A., Zelniker, T. & Hertz-Lazarowitz, R. (in press). A critical multicultural perspective: The segregated educational saga of the State of Israel 1948–2006. *The Journal for Critical Education Policy Studies (JCEPS).*

Deutsch, M. (1973). *The Resolution of Conflict.* New Haven: Yale University Press.

Dewey, J. (1927). *The School and Society.* Chicago, IL: The University of Chicago Press.

Dwairy, M. (2004). Culturally sensitive education: Adapting self-oriented assertiveness training to collective minorities. *Journal of Social Issues*, 60 (2), 423–436.

Eden, D. & Hertz-Lazarowitz, R. (2002). The political power of school principals in Israel: A case study. *Journal of Educational Administration.* 40 (3), 211–230.

Epstein, J. L. & Sanders, M.G. (2006). Prospects for change: Preparing educators for school, family, and community partnerships. *Peabody Journal of Education*, 81 (2), 81–120.

Gillies, R. M. & Ashman, A. F. (Eds.). (2003). *Co-Operative Learning: The Social and Intellectual Outcomes of Learning in Groups.* London: RoutledgeFalmer.

Gillies, R. M. & Boyle, M. (2005). Teachers' scaffolding behaviours during cooperative learning. *Asia-Pacific Journal of Teacher Education, 33* (3), 243–259.

Giroux, H. (1988). *Teachers as Intellectuals.* New York: Bergin & Garvey.

Gordon, D. (1996). *Restructuring and holism as principles of systemic change: The case of the 36-community project in Israel*, Ministry of Education, Culture and Sports, Jerusalem (Hebrew).

Hertz-Lazarowitz, R. (1992). Understanding students' interactive behavior: Looking at six mirrors of the classroom. In R. Hertz-Lazarowitz & N. Miller (Eds.), *Interaction in Cooperative Groups* (pp. 71–102). New York: Cambridge University Press.

Hertz-Lazarowitz, R. (1999). Cooperative learning and group investigation in Israel's Jewish-Arab schools: A community approach. *Theory into Practice 38* (2), 105–113.

Hertz-Lazarowitz, R. (2001). Success for all (SFA) in Israel: A community research and evaluation model. In R. E. Slavin & N. A. Madden (Eds.), *Success for All: Research and Reform in Elementary Education* (pp.149–177). Mahwah, NJ: Lawrence Erlbaum.

Hertz-Lazarowitz, R. (2004). Existence and Co-existence in Acre: The Power of Educational Activism. *Journal of Social Issues*, 60 (2), 357–373. http://construct.haifa.ac.il/~rachelhl/index.htm.

Hertz-Lazarowitz, R. (2005).Cooperative Learning in Israel. IASCE Newsletters. http://www.iasce.net.

Hertz-Lazarowitz, R. & Bar Natan, I. (2002). Writing development of Arab and Jewish students using cooperative learning (CL) and computer mediating communication (CMC). *Computers and Education*, 39, 19–36.

Hertz-Lazarowitz, R. & Calderon, M. (1994). Implementing cooperative learning in the elementary schools: The facilitative voice for collaborative power. In: Sharan, S. (Ed.). *Handbook of Cooperative Learning Methods* (pp. 300–318). New York: Greenwood.

Hertz-Lazarowitz, R. & Horovitz, H. (2002). *The impact of School-Family Partnership (SFP) on parents' attitudes and children reading and writing in first grade.* Paper presented at the 11th International Roundtable on School, Family and Community Partnerships (in cooperation with AERA). New Orleans, LA.

Hertz-Lazarowitz,R. & Schaedel, B. (2003). *Literacy Development and Cooperative Learning: Research and Development in Arab and Jewish Schools.* Haifa: Ach Publishers (Hebrew).

Hertz-Lazarowitz, R. & Zelniker, T. (1995). Cooperative learning in the Israeli context: Historical, educational and cultural perspectives. *International Journal of Educational Research, 23,* 267–285.

Hertz-Lazarowitz, R., Zelniker. T., White-Stephan, C. & Stephan, W. G. (2004.). (Eds.). Arab-Jewish coexistence programs. *Journal of Social Issues, 60* (2), 237–452.

Johnson, R. T., Johnson D. W. & Stanne, M. B. (2000). Cooperative Learning Methods: A Meta-Analysis. University of Minnesota. http://www.co-operation.org/pages/cl-methods.html

Joyce, B. & Weil, M. (1986). *Models of teaching.* Englewood Cliffs, N.J: Prentice Hall.

Kagan, S. (2001). Teaching for Character and Community, *Educational Leadership, 59* (2), 50–55.

Khalil, M. & Lazarowitz, R. (2002). *Developing a learning unit on the science-technology-environment-peace-society mode. Students' cognitive achievements and attitudes toward peace.* The Annual Meeting of The National Association of Research in Science Teaching, (NARST). New Orleans, 7–10 April.

Kohn, A. (2000). The schools our children deserve: Moving beyond Traditional Classrooms and "Tougher Standards", Boston: Houghton Mifflin. http://books.google.com/books?id = NXead57GHSwC&dq = Kohn + a.&psp = 9

Lazarowitz, R. & Hertz-Lazarowitz, R. (1998). Cooperative learning in science curriculum. In B.J. Fraser & K.G. Tobin (Eds.), *International handbook of science education* (pp. 449–471). Dordrecht, Netherlands: Kluwer Academic Publishers.

Lazarowitz, R.G. (2007). High School Biology Curricula Development: Implementation, Teaching and Evaluation. From the 20th to 21st Century. In: Sandra K. Abell & Norman G. Lederman (Eds.), *Handbook of Research on Science Education* (pp. 561–598). Mahwah, NJ: Lawrence Erlbaum.

Lockhorst, D. (2004). Design Principles for a CSCL Environment in Teacher Training. Proefschrift Universiteit Utrecht, Nederlands. http://elearning.surf.nl/docs/e-learning/proefschrift_lockhorst.pdf.

Morton, C. (1996). The modern land of Laputa. *Phi Delta Kappan, 77*(6), 416–419.

O'Donnell, A.M. & King, A. (Eds.). (1999). *Cognitive Perspectives on Peer Learning.* Mahwah, NJ: Lawrence Erlbaum.

Oplatka, I. & Hertz-Lazarowitz, R. (Eds.). (2006). *Women principals in a multicultural society: New insights into feminist educational leadership.* Rotterdam, The Netherlands: Sense Publishers.

Resta, P., Christal, M., Ferneding, K. & Kennedy Puthoff, A. (1999). CSCL as a Catalyst for Changing Teacher Practice. Computer Support for Collaborative Learning.http://sll.stanford.edu/projects/CSCL99/papers/wednesday/Paul_Resta_488.pdf#search = %22role%20of%20 teacher%20in%20cscl%22.

Ron, S. & Lazarowitz, R. (1995).*Learning Environment and Academic Achievement of High School Students Who Learned Evolution in a Cooperative Mode.* Paper presented at the annual meeting of the National Association for Research in Science Teaching (NARST), San Francisco, CA., April 22–25.

Ronen, M., Kohen-Vacs, D. & Raz-Fogel, N. (2006). *Adopt & Adapt: Structuring, Sharing and Reusing Asynchronous Collaborative Pedagogy.* International Conference of the Learning Sciences, ICLS 2006 Indiana University, Bloomington.

Salomon, G. (2002). Technology and pedagogy: Why don't we see the promised revolution? *Educational Technology, 42* (2), 71–75.

Schonmann, S. (2006). Theatrical representations of teaching as performance. In J. Brophy & S. Pinnegar (Eds). *Learning from Research on Teaching: Perspective, Methodology, and Representation: Advances in Research Theory, Volume* 11, (pp. 287–316), Oxford: Elsevier.

Sharan, S. & Hertz-Lazarowitz, R. (1981). *Changing schools: The Small Group Teaching (SGT) Project in Israel.* Tel Aviv: Ramot Publishing, Tel Aviv University, Second Edition: 1984. (Hebrew).

Sharan, S., Kussel, P., Hertz-Lazarowitz, R., Raviv, S., Bejerano, Y. & Sharan, Y. (1984). *Cooperative Learning in the Classroom: Research in Desegregated Schools.* Hillsdale, NJ: Lawrence Erlbaum.

Sharan, S. & Sharan Y.(1992). *Expanding Cooperative Learning through Group-Investigation.* New York: Teacher College, Columbia University.

Slavin, R.E. & Calderon, M. (2001).(Eds.). *Effective programs for Latino students.*

Mahwah, New Jersey: Lawrence Erlbaum.

Slavin, R.E., Hurley, E. & Chamberlain, A. (2003). Cooperative learning and achievement: Theory and research. In W. Reynolds & G. Miller (Eds.), *Handbook of Psychology.* Vol 7 (pp. 177–198). New York: Wiley & Sons.

Thelen, H. (1960). *Education and the human quest.* New York: Harper and Row.

Vygotsky, L. S. (1978). *Mind in Society: The Development of Higher Psychological Processes.* In M. Cole, V. John-Steiner, S. Scribner, & E. Souberman (Eds.). Cambridge, MA: Harvard University Press.

Webb, N., Nemer, K. M. & Ing, M. (2006). Small-Group Reflections: Parallels Between Teacher Discourse and Student Behavior in Peer-Directed Groups, *Journal of the Learning Sciences, 2006,* 15, 63–119.

Zelniker, T. & Hertz-Lazarowitz, R. (2005). School-family partnership for coexistence in the city of acre; promoting Arab and Jewish parents' role as facilitators of children's literacy development and as agents of coexistence. *Language, Culture and Curriculum, 18* (1), 114–138.

Zelniker, T. & Hertz-Lazarowitz, R. (2006). *Long Term effects of Community Empowerment and Leadership Building in An Arab-Jewish City in Israel.* Paper presented in the International Society for the Study of Organization Behavior and Work Values (ISSOW), Tallinn, Estonia, June 25–29.

Chapter 3
Pupil Grouping for Learning: Developing a Social Pedagogy of the Classroom

Ed Baines, Peter Blatchford, and Peter Kutnick

Abstract Studies of grouping practices in everyday classrooms in England show that the potential of group work as a pedagogic approach, that can enhance learning and active engagement among pupils, is not being realised. Three main principles for the effective use of group work in schools are highlighted. These are that teacher practices should focus on enhancing pupils' relational skills, carefully structuring the classroom and group context and on providing structure and support to group interactions. These principles and their associated practices form the core of a recent UK group work program for teachers. Results from a year long evaluation of this program show that pupils made greater progress in general and specific measures of attainment and were more likely to show behaviours indicative of effective group interactions than pupils in a comparison group. Findings emphasise the need for educators to implement a social pedagogic approach, rather than individualised approaches, to teaching and learning in classrooms.

In this chapter we broaden consideration of the role and purposes of putting children in groups for learning. Our central premise is that children are always found seated or working in some form of grouping in their classrooms, but many of these groupings actually inhibit learning and the motivation to learn. This chapter will consider the use of pupil groups within the natural classroom context to help to understand why they may not be effective in promoting learning, and how they may be changed to support learning.

Our view of effective group work in classrooms moves away from examining group work in terms of a short-term (often experimental) approach in which group working skills are de-contextualised from the general classroom context. The chapter will focus largely on research related to elementary/primary schools and will provide a review of current grouping practices in classrooms, particularly in England. The chapter has four main sections: first, there is a review of research on group work in schools drawing on what we know from naturalistic studies of classrooms; second, we consider how this review has informed the key principles of a recent UK group work program; third, the results of a large scale quasi-experimental evaluation of this program will be presented; and fourth, we conclude points with implications for everyday practice and policy in schools.

3.1   The Grouping of Pupils in Classrooms

Since children have been formally educated in schools and classrooms, they have been placed in various forms of groupings including individuals, dyads, groups and whole class groups (see Baines et al. 2003). Over the last century, many studies have been undertaken to assess whether learning within these groupings is more effective in particular forms (see, e.g., Pepitone 1980; the Plowden Report 1967; Slavin 1995). While it has been commonly thought that learning and social benefits accrue from effective group work, there has not been common agreement over what group work is, and how it can be made effective. Many of the literature reviews over the last 20 years lead to a range of conclusions (see e.g., Kutnick et al. 2005; Lou et al. 1996; O'Donnell & King 1999; Slavin et al. 2003; Webb & Palincsar 1996). These conclusions include the following points: that children work more effectively in smaller than larger groups; the co-operative and collaborative approaches to group work are, generally more effective than individualistic and competitive approaches; there are modest academic gains; and pro-social and pro-school attitudes improve significantly in co-operative/collaborative groups.

The main theories underlying group working in classrooms are psychological (derived from behavioural, developmental, social, and humanistic psychology) and sociological (concerned with social justice and inclusion). Psychological theory focuses on individual and social processes while sociological theory places emphasis on the social context of cooperation and group work. Psychological theories concerning group work have been dominated by behavioural, cognitive, and relational theories (see discussions by Damon & Phelps 1989; Littleton et al. 2005) and have been associated with two distinct outcomes, learning/school achievement and social/pro-school attitudes. Only lately have reviewers differentiated these outcomes (see especially Gillies & Ashman 2003; and for a fuller description of the relationship between these theories and outcomes, Kutnick et al. 2005). Sociological studies tend to describe group activities (e.g., Cohen 1994) and evaluate tasks and group structures associated with classroom groups that work more or less effectively.

Studies concerning group work in classrooms can be divided into two broad categories, representing naturalistic descriptions and experimental change (some are based upon preliminary naturalistic study) of classroom activity (Kutnick et al. 2002). This division provides a useful starting point for this chapter. Whereas many chapters in this volume provide reviews of experimental approaches for the use of cooperative learning in classrooms, we refer only briefly to experimental studies and, instead, concentrate on naturalistic studies, notably those undertaken in England, as these studies provide the basis for the development (with teachers) of a program to enhance the cognitive and social effects of group work in classrooms.

Experimental studies tend to arise from, or can be associated with, theoretical orientations that are predominantly psychological. Theories underlying cooperative learning (Johnson & Johnson 2003; Slavin 1995) have described their roots in social psychological theories of Deutsch (1949) and Lippitt and White (1943) that stress the advantages of interdependence within (heterogeneous) groups and Allport's (1954) operationalisation of contact theory. When the social psychological focus on interdependence is applied to classroom studies, especially in comparisons of co-operative learning to traditional learning, findings show consistent enhanced relational and pro-school attitude development among pupils, and moderate learning gains. Experimentally-based, collaborative approaches in classrooms acknowledge the importance of interpersonal relations for the sharing and co-construction of knowledge. They often focus on the role of classroom talk and these can be reviewed through the extensive range of studies by Webb and her colleagues and by Mercer and colleagues (e.g., Mercer 2000; Webb & Mastergeorge 2003). These studies have explored interpersonal language that supports group work in class-rooms and have developed effective programs to enhance child talk/knowledge within particular curricular areas. While these studies are insightful in identifying where groups are ineffective and for recommending particular interpersonal and communicative methods to enhance group work, few consider the whole classroom context within which group work takes place.

Naturalistic studies generally take into account the whole classroom context, often including a number of sociological concerns such as social inclusion and participation of all children within the classroom. For convenience here, we divide naturalistic studies into two phases: studies between 1980 and 2000 that have identified a range of problems associated with classroom group work, and recent studies that see classrooms as a social pedagogic context within which pupil groups may promote or inhibit classroom learning and motivation.

From the first phase of naturalistic studies, three dominant themes arise. First, while children experience classroom activity in groups, these groups may vary in size and phase of lesson. Second, children often do not work productively in groups. Finally, teachers are not confident in their use and support of group work.

Descriptions of elementary/primary classrooms (see Galton et al. 1980, 1999) show that the term, pupil group, can relate to a range of sizes and purposes.

Children may be found in large groups (such as the whole class), in small groups (usually about four to six children, seated around a classroom table), and in pairs or triads (sometimes sharing a table with other pairs). Additionally, pupils may be found working as individuals, often sharing table space with others. These different group sizes are often associated with phases of a lesson – with large groups/whole class coming together at the beginning and end of a lesson and with smaller groups being used in the middle of a lesson.

Pedagogically, group size may relate to the variety of learning tasks that characterise a lesson; broad categories of learning task include new/cognitive knowledge, extension of existing knowledge and practice/revision of knowledge (from Norman 1978; and used in Bennett et al. 1984; Edwards 1994). These studies can be integrated to show a relationship between group size and learning task described more fully in Kutnick (1994). For practice tasks, children work better as individuals than in any larger group that may distract the child (Jackson & Kutnick 1996). For cognitive tasks, pairs of pupils or pupil-tutor dyads are more effective in promoting understanding than individuals or larger groups (see Kutnick & Thomas 1990; Littleton et al. 2004; Perret-Clermont 1980). For extension of understanding, small groups are recommended, especially in cooperative learning studies (see Johnson & Johnson 1994; Slavin 1995). Finally, the whole class is best used for presentation of new tasks that allow for teacher-child (dyadic) follow-ups.

While all task types are found in elementary/primary schools (Baines et al. 2003; Bennett et al. 1984) children's seating is most likely to be in small groups around small tables. Hence, studies such as Galton et al. (1980) and Galton et al. (1999) have identified a number of disparities. For example, children are most often found seated in small groups for up to 80% of their classroom time while being assigned individual tasks. The quality of talk within small groups is also likely to be at a low cognitive level. Other disparities can also be detected in this first phase of naturalistic studies such as the assignment to, and use of, small groups based on distribution of furniture in the classroom (Dreeben 1984); differentiation of pupils by ability-based seating (Ireson & Hallam 2001); teacher difficulties in the selection and design of tasks that legitimise group interaction (Bennett & Dunne 1992; Harwood 1995); and the resistence by teachers to move tables to accommodate individual, paired, small or large group seating for specific learning tasks (Hastings & Chantry 2002).

Many children, as well as their teachers, do not like working in groups (Cowie & Rudduck 1988). Galton (1990), for example, found that children often feel insecure and threatened when told to work in groups and pupils responded to this threat by withdrawal from participation or looking to the teacher to give legitimacy to their responses within groups. Teachers have expressed particular concern about loss of classroom control, increased disruption and off-task behaviour (Cohen & Intilli 1981; see Cohen 1994), children having difficulty learning from one another (Lewis & Cowie 1993), the time consuming nature of group work, the assessment of children when working in interactive groups (Plummer & Dudley 1993), and the limitation of positive outcomes to the more academically able students. Teachers have also expressed the view that pupils, particularly boys, will misbehave during group work and that discussion within group work may cause conflict between pupils (Cowie 1994).

Findings from this first phase of naturalistic studies often make depressing reading for those who are aware of the success of experimentally oriented studies. In spite of this, research on the first phase has identified where problems exist in the implementation of effective group work in classrooms. The overall problem is the lack of coordination between the size of pupil groupings, their composition, pedagogic purpose of learning task and interactions among group members. In short, there is little awareness of social pedagogical relationships in the classroom. It is little surprise, therefore, that pupils and their teachers do not express confidence or liking of group work, and both feel threatened by group work.

In the second phase of naturalistic studies, a clearer understanding of the bases for success and failure of group work in the classroom is established. The social pedagogic approach drawn upon by the authors focuses on relationships between pupil groups (their size and composition), learning tasks, supportive interactions with peers and teachers, and whether pupils have received training for effective group working (see Blatchford et al. 2003). Evidence referred to in this phase arises mainly from mapping classrooms while pupils engage in learning tasks and from interviews with teachers. For a more extensive discussion of mapping as a systematic, multi-dimensional description of grouping practices and more on data reported below see Baines et al. (2003), Blatchford et al. (1999), and Kutnick et al. (2002).

Studies on mapping in elementary/primary schools generally show that the majority of pupils are seated in small groups (50% of mapping exercises), with whole class groupings accounted for a further 20%. In only 2% of observations were individuals seated alone. Larger groups, as might be expected by their size, were mixes of boys and girls and mixed-ability. Smaller groups tend to be single-sex, single-ability, and friendship based. The predominant learning task type used in classrooms was practice tasks and the least likely task was new knowledge/cognition. While virtually all children were found seated in pairs or larger groupings, over 60% of the assigned tasks required children to work individually. Teachers and other adults in the classroom were only able to work with approximately one-third of the pupil groups in their classrooms at one time.

While most of the observations found children seated in pairs or larger groups, only a quarter of the nearly 200 teachers participating in the study stated that they prepared their classes for group working. The majority of these teachers cited 'circletime' as their only form of group work preparation. Other social pedagogic concerns about group work included the following:

1. The small groups that dominated classroom experience were likely to be composed of same-sex and same-ability pupils, providing contexts of social exclusion rather than inclusion in the classroom. This was especially true of low-attaining boys who were mainly assigned individual tasks where they were not asked to interact or discuss the task with others, and high-attaining girls.
2. In findings similar to the first phase of naturalistic research results, but more extensively explored, there was no clear relationship between the size of groups and the learning tasks/interaction assigned. Most pupil groups were assigned practice tasks that required children to work alone.

3. Adults in the classrooms tended to work with the whole class, large groups, or with individuals, leaving most of the small groups to work autonomously from teacher or adult support.
4. Adults were present in virtually all of the observations within which new knowledge/cognition was presented restricting opportunities for pupils to co-construct and develop their own new knowledge further.

As a result of this systematic description of the range and use of pupil groupings in authentic elementary/primary school classrooms, three main concerns are identified that underpin the SPRinG (Social Pedagogic Research into Group-work) project. These concerns form the basis for the remainder of the chapter and are listed below.

1. *Relationships are fundamental for effective group working.* As identified in the description of the first phase of naturalistic studies, pupils often feel threatened and do not understand how to work in a group with their peers. We found that teachers had not overcome this lack of group work skills in their classrooms. Conversely, we also found that most teachers and pupils appreciated that supportive relationships are essential for the promotion of learning, that is, relationships that build upon trust between peers and children with teachers, and the ability to communicate effectively and jointly resolve problems with partners (Hall 1994; Kutnick et al. 2005).
2. *Effective group work involves an effective classroom context.* If group work is to be effective, pupils must be able to work in a socially inclusive manner with all other members of their class and not be dominated by same-gender and friend-ship preference groups as noted in Kutnick & Kington (2005), and Kutnick et al. (2005). For pupils to draw upon supportive relationships and be less dependent on their teachers in their learning, the physical layout (e.g., seating and furniture), and the curriculum and interactional contexts of the classroom (e.g., group composition and size) must be co-ordinated to support group work.
3. *Adults need to structure and support group work experiences.* Teachers are essential for the organisation of the learning experience of their pupils, but as described above they rarely draw upon social pedagogic principles that would relate pupil group size and composition to learning task and interaction and which would promote group working among the children.

3.2 Social Pedagogic Research into Group Work

The main impetus for the Social Pedagogic Research into Group Work project (SPRinG) was to address the three concerns listed immediately above. To do this successfully suggested a new approach to conceptualising classroom group work, an approach that would ground itself in the reality of everyday school life and the concerns of teachers and pupils, and integrate group work into the fabric of the school day. This is not so much an alternative pedagogy but a realisation and application of social pedagogy. We were interested in an inclusive view of classroom groups that sought to integrate findings from previous research into a more general application. The project reported here took place from 2001 to 2005.

In collaboration with teachers over the course of the second year of the project we developed approaches and materials at three sites – KS1 (5–7 years) at the University of Brighton, KS2 (7–11 years) at the Institute of Education, University of London, and KS3 (11–14 years) at the University of Cambridge. This paper is concerned with KS1 and KS2, which covers the primary school stage in England.

The SPRinG approach was based on three key principles in line with the three concerns above.

3.2.1 A Relational Approach

A key feature of the SPRinG program is that *group work skills have to be developed* (Cohen 1994; Webb & Farivar 1994). It is well known (see Gillies 2003) that pupils need to have the skills to communicate effectively through listening, explaining, and sharing ideas. But effective group work also depends on pupils learning to trust and respect each other (Galton 1990) and having skills to plan and organise their group work, make considered group decisions, reach a compromise and avoid petty disputes. The approach is based on a naturalistic study of close social relationships (Kutnick & Manson 1998) and has been devised to overcome problems associated with social skills training programs. Ogilvy (1994) suggested that pupils' group work skills are unlikely to be long lasting if they are approached in isolation and specific just to group work. Such a relational approach to group working skills will benefit from integration into more general rules and ways of behaving in the class. Indeed, integration can create classroom norms for social inclusion. One message that has emerged strongly from our work is the importance of not allowing personality types or group conflict to dictate the success, or failure, of groups. If not addressed directly then difficulties between pupils may lie below the surface and inhibit classroom learning.

3.2.2 Preparation of the Classroom Context for Group Work

The SPRinG approach also rests on the view that group work has to be considered strategically in the wider context of the whole classroom. This includes three main dimensions: (a) classroom level factors such as classroom layout, furniture, and seating arrangements and class size; (b) characteristics of groups such as their size and number, their composition and their stability; and (c) group work tasks and the way these are integrated into, and used to support learning within, a lesson and the curriculum. The aim is to integrate group-work into all class and curricular activities. A fundamental proposition is that effective group work can be facilitated by structuring the group work context in a number of key ways. For instance, by organising classroom seating arrangements and increasing the proximity of pupils to reduce noise and encourage group interaction, by ensuring group size (usually 2–4 pupils) is appropriate to the experience of pupils and the task at hand, and where possible maintaining stable groups as they can reduce insecurities and conflict.

One common assumption, which can hinder the development of group work, is the view that curriculum demands leave no time for group work. It is important that we do not examine small group learning independently of the curriculum and the culture of the classroom (Slavin et al. 2003; Webb & Palincsar 1996). While much research on group work has tended to be rather curriculum specific, or extra-curricular, our aim was to encourage the development of group work skills that are both generic and also applicable to specific curriculum areas. Previous research would suggest that if effective learning is to take place the relationship between the task and the quality of group interaction is important (Bossert et al. 1985). It is important that learning tasks are set up in a way that is conducive to working together and not independent work.

3.2.3   Involvement of Teachers in the Support of Group Work

A major part of the program was devoted to the development of classroom and interactive strategies to assist teachers to promote and support high quality group processes. We suggest several ways of conceiving how teachers can make group work productive. One way is by lowering the risk for pupils (Doyle 1986) while ensuring the challenge remains high through scaffolding of the task, and arranging the group context and interactions. When it comes to supporting group work, scaffolding has not been fully researched but will involve adapting and structuring the group work context and the task (see Palincsar & Herrenkohl 1999; Tolmie et al. 2005). The teacher will need to structure lessons carefully to facilitate learning in groups and encourage reflection on group processes. It is important for the teacher to replace some direct teaching with time for monitoring pupil behaviour and interaction in groups.

3.3   Implementation and Evaluation of the SPRinG Program

The SPRinG program was based on the three key principles described above and involved a set of lesson plans to help teachers develop pupils' social, communication, advanced group work skills, and integrate group work into the curriculum. The development phase was followed by an evaluation phase that extended over a further school year, a far longer time frame than many studies. Involvement required attendance at regular half-day meetings over the course of the year and a willingness and commitment to implement the SPRinG program. Meetings involved presenting the SPRinG ideas and practices, discussions of these ideas and sharing of further practices and other aspects related to the evaluation of the program. Teachers were given a handbook that was designed in the previous year on the basis of a collaboration between the research team and a different group of teachers. The Handbook was based on research evidence as far as possible but also teachers' experiences during the development phase. Teachers were also visited through the year; during these visits observations could be made and teachers could discuss their group working practices.

3.4   Results from the Evaluation of SPRinG

In this section we give a brief overview of results from the extensive evaluation of SPRinG. More complete results can be found in Baines et al. (in press), Blatchford et al. (2006), Blatchford et al. (2005), and Kutnick et al. (in press). The main research questions asked whether the group-work program led to increases in learning/attainment, behavioural and dialogue patterns supportive of learning, and favourable motivational patterns and attitudes to learning. The exact designs, as well as samples and measures, varied between the two sites, but at each there was an experimental group involved in the SPRinG program, extending over one year, and a control group of teachers and classes equally committed but who pursued their normal classroom activities and did not work on the principles and activities in the SPRinG program. No attempt was made to alter the style of teaching in the control group. Some teachers may have used group work as part of their normal approach to teaching but they predominantly used whole class teaching and individual work. To address the research questions, pupils in experimental and control classes were assessed on three outcome measures: attainment/learning, classroom behaviour and motivation/attitudes. At KS1 (4–7 years) there were 19 classes and 474 pupils in the experimental group and 18 classes and 506 pupils in the control group. At KS2 (7–11 years) there were 32 classes and 849 pupils in the experimental group and 40 classes and 1,027 pupils in the control group. In SPRinG classes, teachers were asked to do a minimum of three group work activities per week. These were initially separate from the curriculum but gradually integrated into normal curricular teaching.

3.5   Attainment Differences

3.5.1   Macro Attainment at the Beginning and End of the School Year

Attainment test scores were collected for KS1 using measures developed by the Performance Indicators in Primary Schools project of the Curriculum Evaluation and Management Centre at the University of Durham. They were conducted at the beginning and the end of the school year and covered curriculum-related areas of reading/literacy and mathematics.

Macro attainment measures in science were collected at the beginning and end of the school year at KS2. Science tests did not exist for Years 3–5 and so three specially designed tests were constructed. These were based on items drawn from government devised national tests. All items related to the themes of physical processes and materials and their properties. The tests were designed to cover all types of knowledge and required interpretation of diagrams, tables and graphs.

Statistical analysis for both KS1 and KS2 was undertaken using multilevel modelling that standardised attainment outcome scores by year in school and modelled effects of experimental versus control main effects, controlling for pre-test scores. A number of other variables were also factored into the model (e.g., pupil gender, initial attainment level, and year group) to examine main independent effects on outcomes and possible interactions with condition (experimental vs. control), for example, to see if the effect of SPRinG varied by gender or initial attainment level.

Results showed significant differences in favour of the SPRinG classes (see Table 3.1). As regression coefficients are standardised they can be interpreted as effect sizes in standard deviation units. It can be seen that at KS1 in reading/literacy children in the experimental condition improved more than those in the control group (effect size = 0.23). In mathematics, children in the experimental classes improved more than control children, with a large effect size (0.71), though this related only to the Year 2 children. No significant interactions were found between SPRinG versus

Table 3.1 The effect of SPRinG vs. Control and other explanatory variables on attainment results at KS1 and KS2

Outcome variable	Coefficient (SE)	p-value
Key stage 1		
Reading/literacy		
Group (SPRinG vs. control)	0.23 (0.10)	<0.05
Sex (males vs. females)	−0.10 (0.05)	<0.05
Mathematics		
Year 1 group (SPRinG vs. control)	0.0 (0.13)	0.99
Year 2 group (SPRinG vs. control)	0.71 (0.13)	<0.001
Key stage 2		
Macro science test		
Group (SPRinG vs. control)	0.208 (0.083)	0.01
Evaporation items on science macro test		
Group (SPRinG vs. control)	0.429 (0.081)	<0.001
% pupils eligible for FSM	−0.111 (0.022)	<0.001
Forces items on science macro test		
Group (SPRinG vs. control)	0.294 (0.077)	<0.001
% pupils eligible for FSM	−0.074 (0.021)	<0.001
Evaporation micro test		
Group (SPRinG vs. control)	0.576 (0.220)	0.009
% pupils with EAL	−0.076 (0.025)	0.002
Macro science test with evaporation and forces items omitted		
Group (SPRinG vs. control)	0.089 (0.17)	0.37

Only one control school was able to take on the forces unit, and so results were not analysed control and other factors (e.g., sex and initial attainment of children) indicating that SPRinG benefited all pupils in these classes. Table 3.1 also shows that at KS2 SPRinG pupils showed modest progress over the school year than the control group on the overall macro science test, and the two macro sub-tests covering the areas of evaporation/condensation and forces (effect sizes of 0.21, 0.43 and 0.29 respectively). No interaction effects were found, again indicating that all groups of children in the SPRinG classes benefited (see Baines et al., in press).

3.5.2 Micro Science Attainment: Evaporation and Forces

For the purposes of the evaluation at KS2, activities and teachers' notes and micro tests were also specially constructed for the science topics of evaporation/condensation and forces. The two sets of group work activities extended over at least two and a half hour long lessons and were completed in the Spring and Summer terms respectively. These micro assessments more closely connected learning and attainment to particular instances of the use of group work for learning a particular topic. If we found effects of SPRinG on attainment at both micro and macro levels there would be a strong case for concluding that these effects were due to the group work intervention. Micro tests were based on Government curriculum guidance and consistent with expected coverage of these topics, but gave a central place to group work activities. The activities covered higher order problem solving skills (e.g., that involved thinking about and discussing particular scientific concepts, planning controlled science experiments). For both SPRinG and control samples, pretests were built into the start of the lessons and we asked for posttests to be conducted two weeks after the activities were completed. Teachers in control classes covered similar science topics to those in the SPRinG group, including evaporation and forces (because they follow Government schemes of work), but the main difference was that the same topics were taught in a different way to that used in SPRinG classrooms, and the control pupils had not experienced group work skills training. Group work may have been used but probably not as extensively as in the SPRinG sample.

Results for evaporation micro tests are again shown in Table 3.1. Pupils in the SPRinG group had scores that were over 0.58 standard deviations greater than pupils in the control group (see Baines et al., in press).

3.6 Observation Measures

3.6.1 On the Spot Observations

Systematic on-the-spot (OTS) observations of pupil behaviour and interactions were undertaken in each experimental and control class at the beginning and end of the school year. The OTS method recorded behaviour during normal classroom activities, so tested whether involvement in group-work transferred to usual classroom activities. Researchers focussed on six target children (balanced for sex and ability) selected randomly from each class. The schedule was similar to that used in Blatchford et al. (2005) and involved a 10-s time sampling technique with categories describing time spent in different work settings, school subject, and a description of how children behaved when in three social modes: with their teachers, with other children, and when not interacting. Each of these three modes contained mutually exclusive categories that covered engagement in work, procedural, social and off-task activity.

Multi-level logistic regression analyses at KS1 and KS2 showed clear differences between the SPRinG and control pupils on the key observation measures and their behaviour changed in predicted ways over the school year (for further details see Blatchford et al. 2006; Kutnick et al., in press):

1. SPRinG classes dramatically increased the amount of group work and this was at the expense of individual work. Control classes maintained individual and whole class settings.
2. In SPRinG classes pupils engaged in more task-related interactions with each other. Conversely, control pupils spent more time in off-task interactions.
3. SPRinG pupils' interactions were far more likely to be high (cognitive) level and this increased over the year.
4. SPRinG pupils engaged in more sustained interactions (and increasingly over the year) and made more substantial contributions, while control children's interactions were more commonly coded as intermittent.
5. SPRinG teachers were more likely to monitor interactions and less likely to directly teach pupils. The SPRinG program affected the behaviour of all ability levels and year groups equally.

3.6.2   Video Observation Analysis

At KS1, analysis of videotapes of micro testing focused on pairs of children designing concept maps (23 pairs: 11 experimental, 12 control) and were analysed with Fogel's (1993) relational coding system for interpersonal activity that noted time on/off-task, whether speech was reciprocated (co-regulated) or controlled by one individual, and whether partners did/did not work with each other (disengaged). Paired work was undertaken as a classroom activity and one randomly selected pair of children in each class was recorded on this activity during the spring and on a similar activity in the summer term. Over these two terms SPRinG pupils engaged in significantly more on-task conversation and more co-regulated speech than control pupils who showed more disengaged behaviour than SPRinG pupils.

At KS2, detailed analysis of pupil talk and involvement in group-work was conducted on videotapes of researcher-designed group-work activities. These were filmed in the summer term and involved groups of usually four pupils working on the group-work activity within their usual classroom context. The video analysis tested whether SPRinG and control pupils differed in predicted ways when involved in the same selected group-work task. It allowed a more fine-grained description of classroom talk and group-working. The tasks were specially designed non-curricular tasks. One concerned 'Who should get the pay rise?' and the other 'Who should be the class representative.' The activity involved a short piece of background, a description of several people who were possible contenders, and the task was to discuss and agree on who should be chosen and why. The activity took about 20 min. A total of 31 SPRinG and 29 control groups were filmed. Observation categories related to groups and covered: (a) the degree to which all participated within the group and are engaged on-task, (b) socio-emotional (group maintenance vs. blocking), (c) sustained topic focus versus changeable topic focus, and (d) pupil-pupil interaction/ dialogue in terms of collaborative discussion (inferential talk vs. text based talk), meta-group talk, sharing information, disputational talk, procedural, reading out task, off-task. The videotaped interaction was coded every 20 s. Results showed significant effects in favour of SPRinG groups. In SPRinG groups there was more involvement of all group members, more instances of a sustained topic focus, more higher order inferential talk, while in control classes there was more off-task talk, more group blocking, more changeability in topic focus, and more procedural talk than in the control condition (see Blatchford et al. 2006).

3.6.3 Attitudes and Motivation

Measures were derived from pupil self-completed questionnaires. The questionnaires formed scales including: Attitudes to Group working (liking group work, effective group working, cooperative learning); Personality (confident/assertive v. timid/passive); and Peer relations (truculent, activator). Results were less clear cut than those on attainment and behaviour although at KS1, pupils showed developing preferences for paired and small group work over individual work, and at KS2 involvement in SPRinG arrested deteriorating attitudes to science and to working well as a group that were evident in the control group. There was also a significant gain in mastery motivation for the SPRinG sample only.

3.7 Conclusion

In this paper we started by arguing that although research shows that group work can be a productive part of classroom activity, naturalistic observational studies of classrooms show little group work taking place and few opportunities for the development of relational/group working skills. Group work is, therefore, not legitimised in classrooms and pupils are left dependent on the teacher for cognitive information, and procedural and behavioural support. In parallel work (Blatchford et al. 2004) we have found that teachers in English schools have a strong belief in the value of addressing the individual needs of pupils. This lack of group working and the individual focus combine with perceived pressures arising from the curriculum and the classroom context (especially when they have large numbers of children in their class) and result in traditional, didactic views of pedagogy. Teachers feel forced to lead activities and engage in more whole class teaching sessions than they might like. In consequence pupils can become passive in their learning, spending much time listening to the teacher. Although some teachers are aware that all is not well, it is difficult for them to develop alternative pedagogic approaches, like group work, especially when this could mean introducing practices in opposition to the rest of the school. Moreover, in the UK at least, group work does not figure significantly in current educational policy and advice or, at most, has a very minor role. When group work is mentioned, it is in effect a teacher or adult led context, little different pedagogically from whole class teaching, or individual work when seated in groups.

Results from the large scale evaluation of the SPRinG program show that group work does not, as some teachers feared, get in the way of progress in mainstream curriculum areas or exacerbate conflict between pupils. Indeed, group work has a significant effect in terms of pupils' measured progress. The effect sizes associated with the difference between the SPRinG and control groups are equivalent to an average pupil moving up into the top third of the class. The SPRinG programme also has positive effects on interactive and behavioral processes. It was instrumental in affecting three key aspects of group-work: more active, sustained engagement in group activities; more connectedness within the group; and more higher order, inferential forms of reasoning.

We suggest, therefore, that teachers and schools could help themselves by making more use of group work as a way of facilitating pupil involvement – it offers learning possibilities for pupils not provided by either teacher led situations or individual work, and is more in keeping with current learning and developmental theories based on social construction (Blatchford et al. 2003). Readers of this chapter need to remember that the development of an effective social pedagogy of group working cannot be undertaken as a quick fix to current problems in the classroom. With regard to our three principles: effective group working is based on effective and supportive relationships between children, and between teachers with pupils and will take time to develop. The classroom context must be changed to support group working by co-ordinating furniture arrangements, group sizes and composition, and learning tasks. Finally, teachers need to legitimise, support and integrate group working practices into their classrooms and curriculum.

It seems to us that we need to rethink both informal and formal pedagogical theories to allow group work a much more central role in educational policy and school practice. This is not just the responsibility of teachers and will need to involve school leaders and policy makers. The SPRinG study has provided a number of useful insights into the ways in which teachers can integrate effective group working into classrooms. Teachers must move away from sole reliance on an individualised pedagogy, and they should consider the role of social pedagogy within their classes that can lead to an understanding that it is the social context within their classroom that can promote or inhibit learning. To successfully implement this social pedagogic approach, teachers need to plan for, and integrate, a relational approach to support pupils' group working. They need to create teaching and learning strategies that make use of various group sizes and structures and ensure that they legitimise the use of groups in their classrooms.

Acknowledgements This research was funded by the Economic and Social Research Council (ESRC) of the UK under its Teaching and Learning Research Programme. Thanks are due to the ESRC for their support, and to the teachers, head-teachers and pupils from the participating schools for their assistance and commitment to the project.

References

Allport, G. (1954). *The Nature of Prejudice*. Cambridge, MA: Addison Welsley.

Baines, E., Blatchford, P., & Chowne, A. (in press). Improving the effectiveness of collaborative group work in primary schools: effects on Science attainment. *British Education Research Journal*.

Baines, E., Blatchford, P., & Kutnick, P. (2003). Changes in grouping practice over primary and secondary school. *International Journal of Educational Research*, 39, 9–34.

Bennett, N., & Dunne, E. (1992). *Managing Classroom Groups*. Hemel Hempstead: Simon & Schuster Education.

Bennett, N., Desforge, C., Cockburn, A., & Wilkinson, B. (1984). *The quality of pupil learning experiences*. London: LEA.

Blatchford, P., Baines, E., Rubie-Davies, C., Bassett, P., & Chowne, A. (2006). The effect of a new approach to group-work on pupil-pupil and teacher-pupil interactions. *Journal of Educational Psychology*, 98, 750–765.

Blatchford, P., Bassett, P., & Brown, P. (2005). Teachers' and pupils' behaviour in large and small classes: a systematic observation study of pupils aged 10/11 years. *Journal of Educational Psychology*, 97, 454–467.

Blatchford, P., Galton, M., Kutnick, P., & Baines, E. (2005). *Improving the Effectiveness of Pupils Groups in Classrooms*. ESRC/TLRP final report.

Blatchford, P., Kutnick, P., & Baines, E. (1999). *The Nature and Use of Classroom Groups in Primary Schools*. Final report to ESRC, held at British Library.

Blatchford, P., Kutnick, P., Baines, E., & Galton, M. (2003). Toward a social pedagogy of classroom group work. *International Journal of Educational Research*, 39, 153–72.

Blatchford, P., Russell, A., Bassett, P., Brown, P., & Martin, C. (2004). *The Effects and Role of Teaching Assistants in English Primary Schools (Years 4 to 6) 2000–2003*. Results from the Class Size and Pupil-Adult Ratios (CSPAR) Project. Final Report. (Research Report 605 ISBN 1 84478 373 1) DfES (http://www.dfes.gov.uk/research/data/uploadfiles/RR605.pdf).

Bossert, S., Barnett, B., & Filby, N. (1985). Grouping and instructional organisation. In P. Peterson, L. Wilkinson & M. Hallinan (Eds.), *The Social Context of Instruction* (pp. 39–51). Orlando, FL: Academic Press.

Cohen, E. (1994). Restructuring the classroom: conditions for productive small groups. *Review of Educational Research*, 64, 1–35.

Cohen, E.G., & Intilli, J.K. (1981). *Interdependence and Management in Bilingual Classrooms*. Final Report No. NIE-G-80-0217. Stanford University, School of Education.

Cowie, H. (1994). Co-operative group work: a perspective from the U.K. *International Journal of Educational Research* (special issue on co-operative learning in social contexts).

Cowie, H., & Rudduck, J. (1988). Learning together – Working together. In Vol. 1: *Cooperative Group Work* – An Overview and Vol. 2: *School and Classroom Studies*. London: BP Educational Service.

Damon, W., & Phelps, E. (1989). Critical distinctions among three approaches to peer education. *International Journal of Educational Research*, 13, 9–19.

Deutsch, M. (1949). A theory of cooperation and competition. *Human Relations*, 2, 129–52.

Doyle, W. (1986). Classroom organization and management. In M.C. Wittrock (Ed.) *Handbook of Research on Teaching*, 3rd edn (pp. 392–431). New York: Macmillan.

Dreeben, R. (1984). First-grade reading groups: their formation and change. In P. Peterson, L. Wilkinson & M. Hallinan (Eds.) *The Social Context of Instruction* (pp. 69–84). Orlando, FL: Academic Press.

Edwards, A. (1994). The curricular applications of classroom groups. In P. Kutnick & C. Rogers (Eds.), *Groups in Schools* (pp. 177–194). London: Cassell.

Fogel, A. (1993). Developing through relationships; Origins of Communication, Self, and Culture. Harlow: Prentice-Hall.

Galton, M. (1990). Grouping and groupwork. In C. Rogers & P. Kutnick (Eds.) *The Social Psychology of the Primary School* (pp. 11–30). London: Routledge.

Galton, M.J., Hargreaves, L., Comber, C., Wall, D., & Pell, A. (1999). *Inside the Primary Classroom: 20 Years On*. London: Routledge.

Galton, M.J., Simon, B., & Croll, P. (1980). *Inside the Primary Classroom*. London: Routledge & Kegan Paul.

Gillies, R. (2003). Structuring cooperative group work in classrooms. *International Journal of Educational Research*, 39, 35–49.

Gillies, R., & Ashman, A. (2003). A historical review of the use of groups to promote socialization and learning. In R. Gillies & A. Ashman (Eds.), *Co-Operative Learning* (pp. 1–18). London: Routledge Falmer.

Hall, E. (1994). The social relational approach. In P. Kutnick & C. Rogers (Eds.), *Groups in Schools* (pp. 129–142). London: Cassell.

Harwood, D. (1995). The pedagogy of the world studies 8–13 project: the influence of the presence/ absence of the teacher upon primary children's collaborative group work. *British Educational Research Journal*, 21, 587–611.

Hastings, N., & Chantry, K. (2002). *Reorganising Primary Classroom Learning*. Buckingham: Open University Press.

Ireson, J., & Hallam, S. (2001). *Ability Grouping in Education*. London: Sage.

Jackson, A., & Kutnick, P. (1996). Group work and computers: the effects of type of task on children's performance. *Journal of Computer Assisted Learning*, 12, 162–71.

Johnson, D. W., & Johnson, R.T. (1994). Collaborative learning and argumentation. In P. Kutnick & C. Rogers (Eds.), *Groups in Schools*. London: Cassell.

Johnson, D. W., & Johnson, F. (2003). *Joining Together: Group Theory and Research*. Boston, MA: Allyn & Bacon.

Kutnick, P. (1994). Use and effectiveness of groups in classrooms. In P. Kutnick & C. Rogers (Eds.), *Groups in Schools* (pp. 13–33). London: Cassell.

Kutnick, P., Blatchford, P., & Baines, E. (2002). Pupil groupings in primary school classrooms: sites for learning and social pedagogy. *British Educational Research Journal*, 28 (2), 189–208.

Kutnick, P., Blatchford, P., & Baines, E. (2005). Grouping of Pupils in Secondary School Classrooms: possible links between pedagogy and learning. *Social Psychology of Education*, 8, 1–26.

Kutnick, P., & Kington, A. (2005). Children's friendships and learning in school; cognitive enhancement through social interaction? *British Journal of Educational Psychology*, 75, 1–19.

Kutnick, P., & Manson, I. (1998). Social life in the classroom: towards a relational concept of social skills for use in the classroom. In A. Campbell & S. Muncer (Eds.), *The Social Child* (pp. 165–188). Hove: The Psychology Press.

Kutnick, P., Ota, C., & Berdondini (in press). Improving the effects of groupworking in classrooms with young school-aged children; facilitating attainment, interaction and classroom activity. *Learning and Instruction*.

Kutnick, P., Sebba, J., Blatchford, P., Galton, M., & Thorp, J., with Ota, C., Berdonini, L., & MacIntyre, H. (2005). *An Extended Review of Pupil Grouping in Schools*. London: DfES.

Kutnick, P., & Thomas, M. (1990). Dyadic pairings for the enhancement of cognitive development in the school curriculum; some preliminary results on science tasks. *British Educational Research Journal*, 16, 399–406.

Lewis, J. & Cowie, H. (1993). Cooperative group work: Promises and limitations a study of teachers' values. *Education Section Review*, 17, 77–84.

Lippitt, R. & White, R.R. (1943). The social climate of children's groups. In R.G. Barker, J.S. Kounin & H.F. Wright (Eds.), *Child Behaviour and Development*. New York: McGraw-Hill.

Littleton, K., Meill, D., & Faulkner, D. (2004). *Learning to Collaborate/Collaborating to Learn*. New York: Nova Scene.

Littleton, K., Mercer, N., Dawes, L., Wegerif, R., Rowe, D., & Sams, C. (2005). Talking and thinking together at Key Stage 1. *Early Years*, 25, 167–182.

Lou, Y., Abrami, P.C., Spence, J.C., Poulsen, C., Chambers, B., & d'Apollonia, S. (1996). Within-class grouping: a meta-analysis. *Review of Educational Research*, 66, 423–458.

Mercer, N. (2000). *Words and Minds: How We Use Language to Think Together*. London: Routledge.

Norman, D. A. (1978). Notes towards a complex theory of learning. In A. M. Lesgold (Ed.), *Cognitive Psychology and Instruction*. (pp. 39–48). New York: Plenum.

O'Donnell, A. M., & King, A. (Eds.) (1999). *Cognitive Perspectives on Peer Learning*. Mahwah, NJ: Lawrence Erlbaum Associates.

Ogilvy, C.M. (1994). Social skills training with children and adolescents: A review of the evidence on effectiveness. *Educational Psychology*, 14, 73–83.

Palincsar, A., & Herrenkohl, L. (1999). Designing collaborative contexts: lessons from three research programs. In A. M. O'Donnell & A. King (Eds.), *Cognitive Perspectives on Peer Learning* (pp. 151–177). Mahwah, NJ: Lawrence Erlbaum Associates.

Pepitone, E. (1980). *Children in Co-Operation and Competition*. Lexington, MA: Lexington Books.

Perret-Clermont, A.-N. (1980). *Social Interaction and Cognitive Development in Children*. London: Academic Press.

Plowden Report (1967). *Children and Their Primary School*. London: HMSO.

Plummer, G., & Dudley P. (1993). *Assessing Children Learning Collaboratively*. Chelmsford: Essex Development Advisory Service.

Slavin, R. (1995). *Cooperative Learning* (2nd edn). Boston: Allyn & Bacon.

Slavin, R., Hurley, E. A., & Chamberlain, A. (2003). Cooperative learning and achievement: theory and research. In W.M. Reynolds & G.E. Miller (Eds.), *Handbook of Psychology: Educational Psychology* (Vol.7, pp.177–198) New York: Wiley.

Tolmie, A., Thomson, J., Foot, H., Whelan, K., Morrison, S., & McLaren, B. (2005). The effects of adult guidance and peer discussion on the development of children's representations: Evidence from the training of pedestrian skills. *British Journal of Psychology*, 96, 181–204.

Webb, N., & Farivar, S. (1994). Promoting helping behavior in cooperative small groups in middle school mathematics. *American Educational Research Journal*, 31, 369–395.

Webb, N. & Mastergeorge, A. (2003). Promoting effective helping behaviour in peer directed groups. *International Journal of Educational Research*, 39, 73–97.

Webb, N. M., & Palincsar, A. S. (1996). Group processes in the classroom. In D. C. Berliner & R. C. Calfee (Eds.), *Handbook of educational psychology* (pp. 841–873). New York: Macmillan.

Chapter 4
Structuring Peer Interaction to Promote Higher-Order Thinking and Complex Learning in Cooperating Groups

Alison King

Abstract A major challenge for teachers who implement cooperative learning tasks that have cognitively advanced goals is how to promote the kind of group interaction required to achieve those goals. Such complex learning requires learners to go beyond mere review of information or retrieval of previously-acquired knowledge to engage in thinking analytically about that knowledge, relating it to what they already know, and using that knowledge to construct new knowledge, solve new problems, and address new issues. This chapter presents Guided Reciprocal Peer Questioning, a strategy that structures the interaction within a cooperating group to stimulate the cognitive and metacognitive processing appropriate to complex learning tasks. Guided Reciprocal Peer Questioning has been found to be effective in promoting complex learning in a number of classroom contexts for groups of learners ranging from fourth graders to graduate students in a variety of subject areas. The teacher's role in implementing this strategy is described along with the theoretical and research bases for the strategy's effectiveness.

Many classroom cooperative learning tasks involve learners working together to complete a particular assignment or solve a specific, clear-cut problem; while other tasks entail learners reviewing and retelling material already read or covered in class with the twin goals of achieving a basic understanding of concepts and procedures, and then committing that material to memory. In contrast, still other cooperative learning tasks have more cognitively advanced goals that call for learners to achieve a deeper comprehension of material, construct new knowledge, solve problems that have more than one possible answer, create something original, or make sophisticated decisions. These learning tasks require different interactions among learners. The former tasks, being primarily based on memorization and reproduction of information, call for interaction focused largely on exchanging factual material, while the latter tasks require interaction that induces higher-order thinking and results in complex learning.

Guided Reciprocal Peer Questioning is a cooperative learning strategy that has been developed for structuring the kinds of group interaction that promote higher-order thinking and complex learning (e.g., King 1989, 1990, 1994, 2006; King et al. 1998). The effectiveness of the strategy has been demonstrated in a number of controlled research studies conducted in classroom settings.

The remainder of this chapter consists of several sections, the first of which presents a brief analysis of how interaction and activity in groups affects learning with emphasis on five cognitive activities that promote complex learning. The next section describes the Guided Reciprocal Peer Questioning strategy and delineates the teacher's role in implementing the strategy. The following section explains why and how the strategy is effective, including the cognitive and metacognitive processes induced in learners while using the strategy, and incorporates findings from a set of research studies. The concluding section briefly discusses how this cooperative group strategy can promote self-regulated learning by individual learners when working on their own.

4.1   Group Interaction and Learning

Learning is generally defined as cognitive change, that is, some addition to a learner's knowledge structures or reorganization and reconstruction of that learner's existing knowledge. This change occurs as connections are made between new material and prior knowledge and then integrated into the learner's existing knowledge base. The more complex the learning, the more complex those cognitive changes are. According to socio-cognitive learning theory (e.g., Mugny & Doise 1978, Vygotsky 1978), cognitive change is strongly influenced by interaction and activity with others.

Several lines of research have demonstrated that different interactions promote different kinds of learning (e.g., Chan et al. 1992; King 1994; Webb & Palincsar 1996) and are, therefore, conducive to different cooperative learning tasks. For example, factual questioning and responding are highly effective for knowledge retelling tasks that call for interaction that consists merely of requesting and providing information because fact questions tend to elicit facts. However, such fact-based interaction is ineffective for complex learning tasks, which involve analyzing and integrating ideas, constructing new knowledge, and solving novel problems, because fact questions seldom elicit responses that are sufficiently thoughtful (Cohen 1994; King 1994).

It is rare for collaborating learners to engage spontaneously in effective interaction or match their type of interaction to the task at hand without some form of explicit prompting or other guidance by their teachers (Bell 2004; Britton et al. 1990; Cohen 1994; King 1994; King & Rosenshine 1993; Kuhn 1991). In fact, research has shown that, even when given instructions to work collaboratively on a task, learners generally tend to interact with each other at a concrete level in a specific step-by-step manner rather than at an abstract, planful level unless the teacher intercedes with explicit guidance in how to interact (Vedder 1985; Webb et al. 1986). Learners also do not consistently activate and use their relevant prior knowledge without specific prompting (see Pressley et al. 1987). For this reason, classroom teachers and researchers have developed various ways to structure and regulate the interaction within collaborating groups so that learners are required to interact in ways that induce the cognitive processes appropriate to the learning task. Depending on the task at hand, those structures require learners to assume designated roles, follow a prescribed sequence of activities, or sometimes even engage in a particular pattern of dialogue (e.g., Dansereau 1988; King 1997; Palincsar & Brown 1984).

For simple review and work-completion cooperative tasks, teachers often structure group interaction by assigning teacher-learner roles such as teller and listener or summarizer and checker, setting out certain steps to be followed, or distributing work roles such as recorder, clarifier, group facilitator, or consensus checker. However, for complex learning tasks learners need to engage more deeply with new material, that is, they need to think about the knowledge they have already acquired and actively make connections between that new material and their relevant prior knowledge. This calls for interaction that induces in learners sophisticated cognitive processes such as inferencing, speculating, comparing and contrasting, justifying, explaining, questioning, hypothesizing, evaluating, integrating ideas, logical reasoning, and evidence-based argumentation. According to Graesser's constructionist theory of comprehension (Graesser et al. 1994), this kind of cognitive processing is essential to constructing understanding and according to Kintsch's (1988) construction-integration theory, such cognitive processing promotes building coherent highly-integrated mental representations.

4.2 Effective Cognitive Activities for Complex Learning in Groups

Effective group cognitive activities induce cognitive processes in group members, which then results in complex learning. An important distinction is being made here between cognitive *activities* and cognitive *processes*. Cognitive activities are observable by others (and generally involve verbalizations) while cognitive processes take place within the individual. When a learner is engaged in cognitive activity, that cognitive *activity* induces cognitive *processing* in the learner.

Several group activities that have been found to induce higher-order cognitive processes include: explaining concepts and processes (e.g., Chi et al. 1994); asking thought-provoking questions (e.g., King 1994); elaborating on content (e.g., Webb 1989); argumentation (e.g., Kuhn 1991); and modeling of cognition (e.g., Dansereau 1988; King 1994, 2006). All of these activities can be orchestrated by structuring the interaction within a cooperating group. Guided Reciprocal Peer Questioning structures group interaction so that these activities are engaged in as needed.

In interaction and activity individual learners continually use each other's ideas, reasoning, explanations, and argumentation to modify their own thinking and restructure their own knowledge. Moreover, during interaction that involves activity such as explaining concepts, asking questions, elaborating on ideas, and argumentation, learning is enhanced even more for the individual learner who is generating the explanation, creating the question, formulating the elaboration, and constructing the argument. This occurs because such extensive cognitive processing involved causes that individual to reconceptualize the material and alter that individual's own knowledge structures. Each of the five cognitive activities listed above induces specific cognitive processes in the learner.

Explaining. Explaining something to someone else is a cognitive activity – a high-level one because it requires going beyond simply describing something or summarizing a previously memorized explanation: an explanation focuses on why and how. High-level explaining to others induces a number of cognitive processes in the explainers:

- accessing their existing knowledge about the topic;
- clarifying their understanding of the phenomenon;
- thinking about and presenting the material in new ways (such as relating it to the other's prior knowledge or experience, translating it into terms familiar to the other);
- generating new examples;
- evaluating their existing knowledge for accuracy and gaps;
- thinking analytically about the material to make connections between the phenomenon being explained and the other's prior knowledge; and
- integrating and reorganizing knowledge (Bargh & Schul 1980; Brown & Campione 1986).

Again, one of the reasons that explaining is such a powerful learning activity is that the explainer is the one engaged in doing all of that cognitive processing involved in explaining (see also Webb, this volume). Of course, receiving explanations helps others in the group to fill in gaps in understanding, clarify and reorganize existing knowledge, and in general reconceptualize material explained.

Asking thought-provoking questions. Although factual questions and comprehension questions play an important role in learning as their responses can demonstrate whether certain information has been acquired and the extent of understanding achieved, neither of these types of question require much cognitive effort either to formulate or to answer. Both merely call for the restatement of knowledge already acquired, either verbatim retelling of it or a reconstructed version paraphrased to show understanding. In contrast, thought-provoking questions are more likely to induce high-level cognitive processing in both the questioner and responder. Thought-provoking questions go beyond asking for reproduction of the presented material or reconstruction of it. That is, the answer to the question must not have been given in the materials provided. Rather, those materials provide the information needed to think about the stated issue, idea, process. Responding to a thought-provoking question calls for higher-level cognitive processing. To answer such questions one must make inferences, generate relationships among ideas, draw conclusions, develop elaborated rationales or justifications, formulate hypotheses and seek evidence to support or reject them, analyze ideas for their significance, determine their implications, or evaluate strengths and weaknesses and possible outcomes.

Simply posing a thought-provoking question is an activity that triggers higher-level cognitive processes in individuals (see King 1989, self-questioning). In generating such questions the questioner must identify the main ideas and think about how those ideas relate to each other and to their own prior knowledge and experience. Generating questions (even without answers) requires cognitive processing that can help the questioner to build an extensive cognitive representation of the material.

Such questioning can be a valuable learning activity in a collaborative learning context and results of several research programs have confirmed that asking and answering thought-provoking questions promotes complex learning (e.g., Graesser 1992; King 1989, 1994, 2006; Lepper et al. 1990).

Elaborating. Elaborating on an issue, topic, or idea is another activity that induces cognitive processing such as adding details, giving examples, generating images, and in general relating the new material to what is already known. When elaborations are made by a learner, those elaborations are incorporated into learners' existing knowledge; and, as a consequence, their mental representations are reorganized and increased in complexity, thus improving understanding and recall (e.g., Dansereau 1988). A number of researchers have demonstrated the effectiveness of elaboration as a method for learning new material (e.g., O'Donnell & Dansereau 1992; Pressley et al. 1987; Webb 1989). Both the elaborator and others in the group learn through elaboration, but again, the one doing the elaborating tends to learn most.

Argumentation. During reasoned argument adequate and convincing evidence or reasoning is given to support claims, statements and other assertions (Kuhn et al. 1997). Although a primary purpose of argument is to convince others of a belief or claim, argumentation also functions to clarify thinking, explore an issue, and arrive at a deeper understanding of that issue (Wright 1995). During collaboration when a learner makes an assertion, such as arriving at a conclusion, a statement of cause and effect, an hypothesis to account for some phenomenon, an explanation, a theory of how things are, that assertion induces evidence-based thinking in others, that is, that assertion elicits evidence or reasoning that supports it (Kuhn et al. 1997). Any collaborative activity provides a setting for learners to develop and practice argumentation skills because interaction within a group often reveals inconsistencies between learners' notions of a topic. Individual learners discover that their own understanding of an aspect of the content, their opinions about an issue, their perceptions, assumptions, values or even their basic factual information about the material may not be shared by others in the group and may even differ to a great extent from others. When such cognitive discrepancies arise learners have opportunities to generate, compare and evaluate multiple conclusions, theories, counter theories, counter arguments, and rebuttals along with any supporting evidence provided. In fact, during this verbal interaction, learners are not just exchanging theories and rebuttals; they are negotiating meaning and arriving at re-conceptualized and deeper understanding about the topic or issue being argued. Engaging in such cognitive processing induced by constructive argumentation can promote complex learning (Kuhn et al. 1997). Furthermore, jointly constructed meanings can be internalized by individuals as their own revised mental representations of the topic or issue.

However, even adults rarely engage in reasoned argumentation without specific guidance and scaffolding. For example, most adults have been found to make assertions that they are unable to support with evidence or logical reasoning even when prompted (Kuhn 1991). Interaction during collaborative learning can be structured to guide and support learners' reasoned argumentation during complex learning tasks (Kuhn 1991)

Modeling of cognition. Modeling of cognition is a general phenomenon of learning through interaction. Although not usually an intentional activity, modeling of cognitive processes is a very powerful way of learning during interaction. In contrast to *behavioral* modeling (observational learning) that occurs when we observe other's actions and then imitate them, cognitive modeling is modeling of various cognitive processes. Unlike actions, cognitive processes are internal to the individual and are only made observable to others through thinking aloud.

Making thinking explicit by thinking aloud in a collaborative group context provides opportunities for group members to learn new ways of thinking, refine their existing strategies, and develop other cognitive processes through modeling. Individuals may notice ways in which others use language, strategies, skills, and patterns of argument and imitate them. When individual learners observe and imitate their peers' use of cognitive processes, they modify and refine their own processing by modeling their own reasoning, argumentation style, questioning and problem-solving strategies on those of other group members. Of course, before any of this cognition can be modeled during interaction, it first must occur, either spontaneously or through some form of prompting.

Metacognition in cooperating groups. Metacognitive processes can play a major role during collaborative learning. Monitoring and regulating learning during collaboration induce corresponding metacognitive processes in individual learners, and cooperating learners can mutually regulate their joint learning. Metacognitive processing can also be modeled during interactions.

4.3   Guided Reciprocal Peer Questioning

Guided Reciprocal Peer Questioning is a strategy for structuring interaction in groups. It has been found to promote learning that is based on, but goes beyond, material read or presented in class (e.g., King 1989, 1994; King & Rosenshine

1993). Learners from elementary grades to university have used Guided Reciprocal Peer Questioning successfully in a variety of subject areas. The Guided Reciprocal Peer Questioning strategy is designed to engage learners in activities that induce complex cognitive processing. The strategy functions by guiding learners' discussions of the material so that thinking and learning moves to progressively more complex levels.

4.3.1 The Strategy

In Guided Reciprocal Peer Questioning learner questioning and responding is guided so as to activate prior knowledge of the topic to be discussed first, then consolidate understanding, and consequently elicit inferencing, explanation, integration of ideas, and connections among ideas and information within the presented material and between that material and relevant prior knowledge. Simply put, group members learn how to:

- ask questions that elicit explanations and inferences;
- answer questions with relevant thoughtful responses (e.g., explanations & inferences);
- build on each other's responses; and
- assess and monitor each other's understanding.

During cooperative learning sessions they use these skills by asking and answering questions in a reciprocal manner. The strategy is most often used as a way of processing, integrating, and extending material presented by the teacher or covered in assigned readings. (ASK to THINK-TEL WHY®©,[1] King (in press) is a more complex version of Guided Reciprocal Peer Questioning used for peer tutoring.)

After a teacher presentation on a topic and/or after reading material on the topic, learners create questions related to the material covered. The teacher provides a set of general question starters that the learners use as a model to guide them in writing their own questions, which are specific to the material presented or read. Two kinds of question starters are provided: comprehension ones (e.g., "What does _____ mean?" and "Summarize _____ in your own words.") and thought-provoking ones (such as "How is _____ similar to _____?" and "Explain why _____"). Figure 4.1 shows a list of sample guiding question starters. These general questions are content free so they can be used with any subject matter. To create their own

---

[1] Materials for training and/or use of "ASK to THINK –TEL WHY©® are copyrighted and are available only with the author's written permission. "ASK to THINK –TEL WHY©® is a registered trademark and the learning procedure itself is copyrighted by Alison King, 1994a, 1997, 1998 and 1999. Neither the names ASK to THINK –TEL WHY©® or ASK to THINK nor the particular learning procedure known by that name and described herein may be used for any commercial, teaching, or training purpose or any other purpose whatsoever without prior written permission from Alison King.

Comprehension Review Questions
What does ... mean?
What caused ...?
Describe ... in your own words.
Summarize ... in your own words
Thought-Provoking Questions
Explain why . . . .
(Explain how . . . .)
How would you use . . . to . . . ?
What is the significance of ...?
What is the difference between . . . and . . . ?
How are . . . and . . . similar?
What is a new example of . . . ?
What do you think would happen if . . . ?
What conclusions can you draw about . . .?
Compare . . . and . . . with regard to . . ..
What do you think causes . . .? Why?
How might . . . affect . . . ?
What are the strengths and weaknesses of...?
Which ... do you think is best and why?
How is ...related to... that we studied earlier?
Do you agree or disagree with this statement: ...?
What evidence is there to support your answer?

Fig. 4.1 Sample comprehension and thought-provoking question starters for use in Guided Reciprocal Peer Questioning

content-specific questions, learners select several of these content-free question starters and then complete the starters by filling in the blanks with relevant content from the presentation or readings (e.g., "How is the human process of digestion similar to the process of photosynthesis that we studied last month?" and "Explain why the storm is relevant to the theme of this story?") Then they engage in peer questioning, taking turns to pose questions to their group and answering each other's questions in a reciprocal manner. In this way student discussion and processing of the new material is heavily influenced by the nature of the questions they themselves generate.

To guide their responding, learners are taught a procedure ("TEL WHY", King 1994) for explaining, elaborating, and inferencing so that their answers to the thought-provoking questions are more likely to be correspondingly thoughtful. Figure 4.2 shows the acronym for the TEL WHY procedure along with reminders for learners regarding what each letter refers to and how this component of the strategy is used. TEL WHY is intended to emphasize the self-explanation aspect of the strategy and prompt learners to tell how and why, using their own words to do so, and connecting the idea being explained to something already known. The acronym is also expected to keep learners' attention focused on these characteristics of effective explanations, elaboration, and inferences.

The TEL WHY Procedure in Guided Reciprocal Peer Questioning		
T		Tell---what you know to your group
E		Explain -- the why and the how about something -don't just tell what it is or describe it or summarize it
L		Link -- connect what you are telling about to something your partner already knows about so they'll be sure to understand. Connect two things or ideas or link together a procedure and an idea
W	tell	Why
H	tell	How
Y	use	Your own words

Fig. 4.2 TEL WHY Explanation Guide adapted from King (1994)

Learners also learn to sequence their questioning and responding from comprehension to thinking. This questioning sequence is intended to move discussion from
review and consolidation of already-learned material to higher-level thinking about
that material and this results in complex learning.

4.3.2 Teaching Guided Reciprocal Peer Questioning

This strategy has been implemented successfully by classroom teachers with
collaborative learning groups at university level, high school, middle school, and as
young as fourth grade. However, for successful use of the strategy teachers must
provide extensive training, modeling, guidance, and application practice in skills of
question asking, question sequencing, explaining, and inferencing. A useful way to
begin teaching this strategy is to inform students that making up their own questions and answering their own and each other's questions will help them to learn.

Teaching questioning. First, the two kinds of questions should be introduced and
differentiated. For younger children it is generally useful to label the comprehension
questions "memory questions" or "review questions" and to refer to the thought-
provoking questions as "thinking questions" as these terms capture their essential
difference. Memory/review questions require learners only to remember and repeat
material memorized from the lesson or readings, while thinking questions require
learners to not only to remember information presented but also think about that
information in some way, such as linking two ideas from the presentation together
or connecting the lesson material to prior knowledge. In essence, a memory question
is one where the answer is clearly stated in the material read or presented.
A thought-provoking question is one whose answer is not explicitly stated in the
provided material but must be inferred (by "reading between the lines") or generated
by the learner in some other way.

The teacher needs to make clear the difference between writing memory/review
questions and writing thinking. The teacher can use the question starters in Fig. 4.1

for examples and as a guide for practice in generating the two kinds of questions. Memory/review questions check how well the material is understood, ask for definitions and summaries in the learner's own words, or ask for retelling about something learned – but in the learner's own words, not the teacher's words, for example, "What does circulatory system mean?" and "Describe in your own words how the circulatory system works." Teachers need to provide time for learners to practice making up a few of their own memory questions using the starters in Fig. 4.1. Questions can be based on the content of a previous lesson or reading assignment. The teacher may need to demonstrate how to do so using the question starters as a guide.

Generating thinking questions can be presented as linking two ideas from the lesson together (e.g., "What is the difference between arteries and veins?" and "Explain how what happens in the heart affects what happens in the arteries."). Thought-provoking questions require going beyond the material presented to think *about* that material; that is (again), the "answer" to the question must not have been given in the lesson or reading materials provided. Instead, those materials provide the information needed to think about the stated concept, issue, entity, experience, procedure, or process to generate relationships among ideas, make inferences, draw conclusions, develop elaborated rationales or justifications, generate hypotheses and seek evidence to support or reject them, analyze them for their significance, determine their implications, evaluate strengths and weaknesses and possible outcomes. Thought-provoking questions induce thinking and can stimulate a sustained discussion; therefore, teachers must emphasize that no thought provoking question can be answered by either "Yes" or "No" or by something already stated in the materials read.

Teachers can distribute copies of the question starters shown in Fig. 4.1 (or a subset of those) on index cards to be distributed so that each student has one, or display them to the class on a chart or overhead projector. Using material from a recent lesson, the teacher should model for students how to generate thinking questions using the question starters as a guide. Examples and modeling should be provided for each generic question starter. Then students can write their own questions using the question starters, again, based on content already covered in class. Teachers must provide sufficient coaching, practice and feedback and this takes time, but the dividends are well-developed questioning skills. An example of teacher cognitive modeling of generating thinking questions follows. After a presentation on migration, teacher says:

> "Let's see, I guess I'll start by listing some of the things covered in the lesson. Of course one thing was migration – and that whales and birds and some butterflies migrate; and so do some people. A question might be "What animals migrate?", but that's too easy. And it's just a memory question. We covered that in class. I want to make up thoughtful questions – like "Explain why Monarch butterflies migrate." That's a good one because I want to be sure that I really understand that (more fully than it was explained in the lesson) first – before I go any further. Now I'll look at the question starters again for ideas about another question. What I still wonder about, and we didn't already cover this, is what happens to the land and the animals in the areas where the birds migrate to –they must have some effect on it in terms of the ecology –for example, some effect on the insects and other food that they eat. And also when they leave an area it must change the ecology of that area too. So my next question will be "How does migration affect the ecology of the area left and the area migrated to?"

Although some teachers may feel uncomfortable thinking aloud, it can be a very powerful way to reveal the internal process of making up thought-provoking questions.

It is effective to emphasize that some thinking questions link ideas from the presentation with ideas outside of the presentation; that is, things already known about (prior knowledge or experience). Examples of these kinds of thinking questions are "Explain how the circulatory system is similar to a tree." "What do you think would happen if our hearts were smaller?" "How is the circulatory system related to the other systems of the body we've already studied?" Again, teachers must provide modeling, coaching, and practice in how to generate those kinds of questions.

Teaching the TEL WHY procedure. Although the TEL WHY procedure depicted in Fig. 4.2 is self-explanatory, it can be effective to use an example to show learners the difference between a response that is merely a description and one that shows elaboration, explanation, and inference. Below is an example that shows the difference between a description of the circulatory system and an elaborated explanation showing the why and how of the circulatory system. This example was used in a study with fourth-graders using Guided Reciprocal Peer Questioning.

Comparing a description of the circulatory system and an elaborated explanation showing the why and how of the circulatory system.

Description of the circulatory system

The circulatory system is made up of the heart, veins, arteries and blood. Some of the arteries and veins are small and some are large. The heart pumps blood through the arteries and veins

The Why and How of the Circulatory System

We need a circulatory system in our bodies to move the blood around to all parts of the body because the blood carries oxygen, which is food for the cells of the body. All parts of the body need the oxygen in order to grow and function. The circulatory system is just a way of getting that oxygen moved around. The tubes the blood moves in are the arteries and veins. The arteries and veins are all connected, like highways and roads, so they can transport blood to any place in the body. Near the heart the arteries and veins are large because they have a lot of blood to carry, and as they get closer to one part of the body or to a cell they become much smaller (like freeways, highways, streets, roads, and dirt paths) because they have less blood to carry. They can also be seen as being like branches of a tree that get smaller as they get closer to the leaves because they don't have so much to carry to only one leaf. The heart is a pump and it pushes the blood so that it keeps moving around in the network of arteries and veins. The heart pumps by squeezing in and then releasing over and over and over (like making a fist and relaxing it).

It is helpful to point out to learners that good explanations make use of explaining links, connections that are captured by such words such as "because," "therefore," "consequently," and "in order to" that tie phrases together and make it clear that a relationship exists and what the nature of the relationship is (e.g., causal, comparative).

Teaching question sequencing. Teachers can generally best teach question sequencing while learners are actually using the strategy. Essentially, questions are sequenced from review questions to thinking questions so that students establish a shared understanding of known material before asking each other to think about that material. Below is an example of a short sequence of questions taken from a transcript from a high school tutoring project.

Review Question	How does increase in carbon dioxide affect the earth's atmosphere?
Review Question	What does "greenhouse effect" mean?
Thinking Question	How are the terms "greenhouse effect" and "global warming" similar and different?
Thinking Question	What do you think would happen to the people in our community if the temperature of the atmosphere increased a great deal?

If group members cannot answer a question or if an answer is incorrect, they need to be taught to ask a related review question and then build up to ask the incorrectly-answered question once more. If an answer is not complete, the others in a group can ask probing questions.

Learners will need practice using their questioning and responding skills in a group setting by discussing presented materials using the list of question starters and TEL WHY as guides and prompts. Additional teacher modeling and scaffolding may be needed.

Putting it all together. After training and practice in the questioning, responding and question sequencing, learners are ready to implement the Guided Reciprocal Peer Questioning strategy. Following a teacher's presentation or reading assignment, students choose several appropriate questions to use as a guide to create their own specific questions on the material presented. In this question-generation step of the strategy, learners work independently. Memory/review questions are not difficult to pose and can be created "on the fly" but thought-provoking questions take time to generate, so learners need time to individually write out two or three thoughtful questions on material from the presentation. Then they work cooperatively in pairs or small groups to take turns asking and answering each other's questions in a reciprocal manner. Thus, group discussion and processing of the new material is guided by the questions they themselves generate. If learners follow the form of the general thought-provoking questions, their specific questions will be thought-provoking; therefore, their discussion is almost guaranteed to be thoughtful.

It is important that students not use the Guided Reciprocal Peer Questioning strategy in a rote learning manner but in a meaningful way. For example, learners need to be reminded not just to ask and answer their questions in a rigid turn-taking manner, but by engaging in a full discussion. In this way, group members contribute multiple responses to one question, each response building on the previous ones, before going on to another question. In some cases within one 10-min discussion session only one question gets discussed because the discussion that ensues from that question is so extensive. An effective way to get learners to extend discussion of a particular point is to teach them to ask probing or follow-up questions such as: "Can you expand on that?" "I don't understand. What do you mean by that?" "Can you give an example of what you mean?" "Tell me more about that." Another rote use of the strategy occurs when learners simply use the first two question starters on the list to generate questions rather than thoughtfully choosing question starters that are most suited to their learning needs.

4.4   Effectiveness of Guided Reciprocal Peer Questioning

There are a number of distinct components and aspects of the Guided Reciprocal Peer Questioning strategy: thought-provoking questioning, TEL WHY, peer modeling of cognition, the metacognitive emphasis, structured sequence of questioning, and learner choice. Results of controlled componential analysis studies on the contributions of these various components and aspects of the strategy have revealed that all aspects play a vital role but it is the combination that makes the strategy most effective. However, the component that could be singled out as making the greatest contribution is the question starters, and it is likely that the strategy's effectiveness can be attributed primarily to the format of those guiding questions.

4.4.1   Role of the Question Starters

The Guided Reciprocal Peer Questioning strategy uses thought-provoking question starters to induce cognitive processes in learners. Furthermore, different kinds of thought-provoking question starters are used to induce a variety of cognitive processes. Specifically, the format of those question starters guide and support learners to generate specific kinds of questions that prompt them to think about and discuss the material in specific ways such as comparing and contrasting, inferring cause and effect, noting strengths and weaknesses, evaluating ideas, explaining, and justifying. Figure 4.3 shows a variety of question starters and the cognitive processes they are designed to induce.

The resulting variety of specific questions is expected to prompt different ways of thinking about the material by inducing a variety of cognitive processes in the learner. As a result, during discussion learners are expected to make those same kinds of connections among ideas. Presumably, the mental representations they construct reflect those same explicit links between and among the ideas in that material and between the material and learners' prior knowledge. Thus, asking and answering thinking questions is expected to not only increase the number of connections learners make in their knowledge structures, but also create a variety of connections (e.g., comparative connections, evaluative connections, explanatory connections). Such additional and varied links result in elaborately connected and richly integrated complex mental representations that are both stable over time and contain numerous and varied cues for retrieval and provide a solid base for additional complex learning (see Kintsch 1988, Construction-Integration model of comprehension).

Guided Reciprocal Peer Questioning has been used by fourth and fifth graders to help them learn material presented in science lessons (King 1994; King & Rosenshine 1993), by ninth graders to learn from teacher presentations in history classes (King 1991), and by university students to learn from lectures in psychology, anthropology, political science, and education (e.g., King 1989, 1990, 1992, 1993). Guided Reciprocal Peer Questioning has been compared to other learning approaches at various grade levels. For example, results of research involving

Different types of questions are used to induce a variety of cognitive processes	
Thought-provoking Question Starters	Cognitive Processes
induced	
What are the implications of _____ for _____?	inferencing
What do you think causes ____?	inferencing
How are _____ and _____ similar?	comparing, contrasting, inferencing
What is the difference between ___and ___in terms of ___?	contrasting, applying criteria
Why (How) is _____ significant to _____ ?	inferencing, analysis
What evidence is there to support the contention that ____?	evaluation, evidence-based reasoning
How could _____ be useful in addressing the issue of ____?	analysis, generating applications
Which _____ is the best: _____ or _____? And why?	evaluation with rationale
Why is _____ relevant to the issue (problem) of _____?	inferencing, evaluation
What is a new example of ____?	generating examples
How might the discrepancy between __ and __be explained?	comparing, contrasting, inferencing
What might be a counter-argument for _____?	reasoning logically
What is another way to look at _____?	assuming different perspectives
What disadvantage might there be to using ____ with ____?	speculating, inferencing
Is it possible that _____? Why or why not?	evaluation with rationale
What do you think would happen if _____? Explain.	inferencing, predicting, hypothesizing
What is _____ analogous to?	analogical/metaphorical analysis
Why is _____ happening?	inferencing, analysis
What are possible solutions to the problem of _____?	synthesis of ideas
Do you agree or disagree with this statement:____?	analysis, evaluation
Support your answer.	justifying

Fig. 4.3 Questions to induce cognitive processes

university students using Guided Reciprocal Peer Questioning to study lectures showed better understanding of content than did learners who studied the material independently (King 1989) or engaged in small-group unstructured discussion of the material (King 1989), generated summaries of the material (King 1992), studied in small groups using student-generated questioning and answering without the guidance of the question starters (King 1990), or used guided questioning and answering with provided (but similar) thought-provoking questions (King 1993). Furthermore, analyses of the verbal interaction, tape-recorded during learners' questioning and answering sessions, showed that the questions used by students in the Guided Reciprocal Peer Questioning conditions elicited inferences, explanations, and other high-level thinking from others in their groups (King 1990, 1992, 1994; King & Rosenshine 1993).

The value of question sequencing, the TEL WHY component, and peer modeling of cognitive processes have been shown throughout this chapter, and their contribution to the strategy's effectiveness will be only briefly mentioned in this section. Sequencing question-asking by asking review questions before thinking questions helps learners to gain access to prior knowledge and establish a shared knowledge base. It makes it more likely that the thinking questions will lead to more complex learning because that learning will have been built on a more solid base. The TEL WHY procedure centers on developing elaborated useful explanations and inferences. TEL WHY guides and supports learners in generating cognitively sophisticated responses to thinking questions. This is a key to reorganizing existing knowledge structures and building new knowledge. According to theories of generative learning (Wittrock 1990), learners own elaborations are personally significant to them and, therefore, are more memorable. It should be noted that peer modeling of cognitive processes goes on throughout any cooperative learning experience. Learners are observing each other's externalized cognitive processing (through thinking aloud) whether it is effective cognition or not. Simple verbatim repetition of material is as much a candidate for imitation as complex strategizing, hypothesizing, and justifying. When skilled peers demonstrate accurate use of questioning, explaining, and elaborating during Guided Reciprocal Peer Questioning, they become ideal models for others to observe and imitate.

4.4.2 The Role of Metacognition

Metacognition includes monitoring, regulating, and evaluating one's own thinking and learning (see Hacker 1998). Like cognitive processes, metacognitive processes take place within the individual. The Guided Peer Questioning strategy has a metacognitive component built into it. When learners deliberately select particular question starters to guide them in generating questions, they are using the strategy in a metacognitive way. They are intentionally guiding their own cognitive processing based on their perceived learning needs. In addition to guiding cognitive processes in this way, the Guided Reciprocal Peer Questioning strategy functions in a second metacognitive component. The strategy can be used for monitoring comprehension. Asking and answering review and thinking questions functions as a self-testing experience, giving students the chance to monitor and evaluate their understanding of the material covered. If a learner is unable to answer a review question correctly, this indicates a gap in understanding or even a misunderstanding and the learner can proceed to regulate learning by asking for additional information, clarification, explanation and such. Such awareness of what one knows and what one does not know must precede regulation of learning. Furthermore, by assessing each other's memory for material and their understanding of it, questioners are also monitoring their own comprehension and can attempt to regulate their own learning by repairing gaps in their own knowledge base. When learners are unable to pose thought-provoking questions, they probably do not understand the ideas presented Once learners have made themselves aware of their learning deficits, they can look forremedies, such as filling in their gaps in information, and correcting misunderstandings. In this way monitoring learning improves the accuracy of the students' mental representations of the presented material.

Like cognition, metacognition can be modeled. Externalizing thinking by thinking aloud during cooperative learning exemplifies metacognition in action. When learners observe their peers monitoring their own thinking and problem solving in this manner it is likely that they will imitate these models of metacognition.

4.4.3   The Role of Learner Control

The degree of learner autonomy that Guided Reciprocal Peer Questioning affords has been found to play an important role in the strategy's effectiveness (King 1993). Individuals using Guided Reciprocal Peer Questioning have a great deal of control over both the questions that are asked and the answers that are generated. Although they are guided by the general question starters, learners are free to choose which of those question starters to use and free to create whatever specific questions they wish to on whatever aspect of the content they choose.

Both motivational and cognitive rationales have been advanced to account for the value of learner control in learning contexts. From a motivational perspective, putting learners in control of their own learning may improve their subsequent achievement, in part because it enhances their intrinsic motivation and sense of autonomy (e.g., Reigeluth & Stein 1983). From a cognitive perspective, it has also been argued that learners who control their own learning are likely to select, encode, and store information based on their own knowledge structures, rather than externally-imposed conceptual organizers, and this makes the information more personally relevant and therefore more memorable. In this context, learners (rather than their teachers) are making the decisions about what they already understand, what they do not yet understand, and what they need to study further. Because the individual learner is the one who is experiencing the gaps in knowledge, it could be argued that it is the learner who is the one best suited to decide how to fill in those gaps. Teacher-provided questions may or may not match that particular individual's learning needs; whereas a learner's self-generated questions presumably are highly relevant to that student's own learning. Similarly, when learners generate their own explanations and other elaborations during learning (rather than having them provided by the teacher, another learner, or the text book), those self-generated responses are consistent with the individual's knowledge base and personal experience. Therefore they are more likely to be remembered by that particular learner.

In a study to determine the role of learner control in the Guided Reciprocal Peer Questioning strategy, university students in small groups used the strategy to guide discussions of material presented in lectures (King 1993). Students in a learner-control condition used thought-provoking general question starters to guide them in generating discussion questions specific to the lecture, whereas those in an experimenter-control condition were provided with similar lecture-specific questions generated by students in the same course during the previous semester using identical question starters. On tests of lecture comprehension students who generated their own questions outperformed students provided with others' questions.

4.5 Guided Reciprocal Peer Questioning and Self-Regulated Learning

Guided Reciprocal Peer Questioning appears on the surface to be antithetical to self-regulated learning. However, according to Vygotskian thinking, any verbal prompts provided externally can be internalized as inner speech by a learner. Those prompts can then be used by the learner at a later time to self-prompt actions and cognitions in similar situations (Rogoff 1990; Vygotsky 1978).

According to Vygotsky (1978), an adult (or more capable peer) can teach skills and strategies for thinking during interaction with a child by providing prompting and assistance. This process is referred to as guiding cognitive performance or intellectual scaffolding. Over time, as the child uses thinking, problem-solving and decision-making strategies through prompting and assistance, the child will gradually require less and less prompting and assistance, and eventually be able to do the thinking independently without any guidance from another person. As the child gains ability to perform the task, (or solve the problem or analyze the information) that child is internalizing the thinking involved. In an adult-child interaction the dialogue becomes an inner monologue for the child. The child internalizes the guiding words and questions of the adult so that the child eventually uses these same words and questions to generate independent thinking during the task. The child is then thought to be self-regulated in the use of that (now internalized) thinking process and can perform the task or solve the problem or analyze the information independently of the adult. In Vygotsky's terms, the thinking process has moved from being other-regulated (by the parent, caregiver, or teacher) to being self-regulated (by the child).

In Guided Reciprocal Peer Questioning, aspects of the actual dialogue used during the interaction between learners (the actual questions asked and answers generated as well as ways of strategizing and reasoning) can become internalized by learners. For example, internalizing the actual dialogue as inner speech allows learners to engage in self-talk (e.g., posing the questions to themselves, generating self-explanations) to prompt cognitive and metacognitive processing in similar situations later.

References

Bargh, J. A., & Shul, Y. (1980). On the cognitive benefits of teaching. *Journal of Educational Psychology, 72,* 593–604.

Bell, P. (2004). Promoting students' argument construction and collaborative debate in the classroom. In M. C. Linn, E. A. Davis, and P. Bell (Eds.), *Internet environments for science education* (pp. 114–144). Mahwah, NJ: Erlbaum.

Biancarosa, G., & Snow, C. E. (2004). Reading next – *A vision for action and research in middle and high school literacy: A report from the Carnegie Corporation of New York.* Washington, DC: Alliance for Excellent Education.

Britton, B. K., Van Dusen, L., Glynn, S. M., & Hemphill, D. (1990). The impact of inferences on instructional text. In A.C. Graesser & G.H. Bower (Eds.), *Inferences and text comprehension* (pp. 53–87). San Diego: Academic Press.

Brown, A. L., & Campione, J. C. (1986). Psychological theory and the study of learning disabilities. *American Psychologist, 41,* 1059–1068.

Chan, C. K. K., Burtis, P. J., Scardamalia, M., & Bereiter, C. (1992). Constructive activity in learning from text. *American Educational Research Journal, 29,* 97–118.

Chi, M. T. H., deLeeuw, N., Chiu, M. H., & LaVancher C. (1994). Eliciting self explanations improves understanding. *Cognitive Science, 18,* 439–477.

Cohen, E. G. (1994). Restructuring the classroom:Conditions for productive small groups. *Review of Educational Research, 64,* 1–35.

Dansereau, D. F. (1988). Cooperative learning strategies. In C. E. Weinstein, E.T. Goetz, and P. A. Alexander (Eds.), *Learning and study strategies: Issues in assessment, instruction, and evaluation* (pp. 103–120). New York: Academic Press.

Graesser, A. C. (1992). *Questioning mechanisms during complex learning.* Technical report, Cognitive Science Program, Office of Naval Research, Arlington.

Graesser, A., Singer, M., & Trabasso, T. (1994). Constructing inferences during narrative text comprehension. *Psychological Review, 35,* 371–395.

Hacker, D. (1998). Definitions and empirical foundations. In D. Hacker, J. Dunlosky, & A. Graesser (Eds.), *Metacognition in educational theory and practice* (pp 1–23). Mahwah, NJ: Erlbaum.

King, A. (1989). Effects of self-questioning training on college students' comprehension of lectures. *Contemporary Educational Psychology, 14,* 1–16.

King, A. (1990). Enhancing peer interaction and learning in the classroom through reciprocal questioning. *American Educational Research Journal, 27,* 664–687.

King, A. (1992). Comparison of self-questioning, summarizing, and notetaking-review as strategies for learning from lectures. *American Educational Research Journal, 29,* 303–323.

King, A. (1993). Autonomy and question asking: The role of personal control in guided student-generated questioning, invited article for Special Issue of *Learning and Individual Differences: Question Asking and Strategic Listening Processes: Individual Differences and Their Consequences, 6,* 162–185.

King, A. (1994). Guiding knowledge construction in the classroom: Effects of teaching children how to question and how to explain. *American Educational Research Journal, 30,* 338–368.

King, A. (2007). Scripting collaborative learning processes: A cognitive perspective. In F. Fischer, H. Mandl, J. Haake, & I. Kollar (Eds.), *Scripting computer-supported collaborative learning: Cognitive, computational, and educational Perspectives* (pp. 13–37). New York: Springer.

King, A. (in press). Beyond literal comprehension: A strategy to promote deep understanding of text. In D. S. McNamara (Ed.), *Reading Comprehension Strategies: Theories, Interventions, and Technologies,* Mahwah, NJ: Erlbaum.

King, A., & Rosenshine, B. (1993). Effects of Guided Cooperative Questioning on children's knowledge construction. *Journal of Experimental Education, 61,* 127–148.

King, A., Staffieri, A., & Adelgais, A. (1998). Mutual peer tutoring: Effects of structuring tutorial interaction to scaffold peer learning. *Journal of Educational Psychology, 90,* 134–152.

Kintsch, W. (1988). The role of knowledge in discourse comprehension: A constructive-integration model. *Psychological Review, 95,* 163–182.

Kuhn, D. (1991). *The skills of argument*. New York: Cambridge University Press.
Kuhn, D., Shaw, V., & Felton, M. (1997). Effects of dyadic interaction on argumentative reasoning. *Cognition and Instruction, 15*, 287–315.
Lepper, M. R., Aspinwall, L. G., Mumme, D. L., & Chabey, R. W. (1990). Self-Perception and social perception processes in tutoring: Subtle social control strategies of expert tutors. *Self-inference processes: The Ontario Symposium* (217–237). Hillsdale, NJ: Erlbaum.
Mugny, G., & Doise, W. (1978). Socio-cognitive conflict and the structure of individual and collective performances. *European Journal of Social Psychology, 8,* 181–192.
O'Donnell, A. & Dansereau, D. (1992). Scripted cooperation in student dyads: A method for analyzing and enhancing academic learning and performance. In Hertz-Lazarowitz, R. & Miller, N. (Eds.), *Interaction in cooperative groups: The theoretical anatomy of group learning* (pp. 120–141). New York: Cambridge University Press.
Palincsar, A. S., & Brown, A. L. (1984). Reciprocal teaching of comprehension-fostering and monitoring activities. *Cognition and Instruction, 1*, 117–175.
Pressley, M., McDaniel, M. A., Turnure, J. E., Wood, E., & Ahmad, M. (1987). Generation and precision of elaboration: Effects on intentional and incidental learning. *Journal of Experimental Psychology: Learning, Memory, and Cognition, 13*, 291–300.
Reigeluth, C. M. & Stein, F. S. (1983). The elaboration theory of instruction. In C. M. Reigeluth (Ed.), *Instructional DesignTheories and Models: An Overview of Their Current Status* (pp. 335–381). Hillsdale, NJ: Lawrence Erlbaum.
Rogoff, B. (1990) *Apprenticeship in thinking: Cognitive development in social context*. New York: Oxford University Press.
Vedder, P. (1985). *Cooperative learning: A study on processes and effects of cooperation between primary school children*. Gronigen, The Netherlands: University of Gronigen.
Vygotsky, L. S. (1978). *Mind in society: The development of higher psychological processes*. Cambridge, MA: Harvard University Press.
Webb, N. M. (1989). Peer interaction and learning in small groups. *International Journal of Educational Research, 13*, 21–39.
Webb, N., Ender, P., & Lewis, S. (1986). Problem solving strategies and group processes in small group learning computer programming. *American Educational Research Journal, 23*, 243–251.
Webb, N. M., & Palincsar, A. S. (1996). Group processes in the classroom. In D. C. Berliner & R. C. Cafree (Eds.) *Handbook of Educational Psychology* (pp. 841–873). New York: Simon & Shuster Macmillan.
Wittrock, M. C. (1990). Generative processes of comprehension. *Educational Psychologist, 24,* 345–376.
Wright, L. (1995). Argument and deliberation: A plea for understanding. *Journal of Philosophy, 92*, 565–585.

Chapter 5
Cooperative Learning and Literacy Instruction in Middle Level Education

Robert J. Stevens

Abstract The goal of the middle school structure is to create a learning environment that matches the developmental abilities and needs of adolescents. This research attempts to operationalize that goal by integrating reading and English classes in large urban middle schools. In the Student Team Reading and Writing (STRW) program instruction was reconfigured to actively engage students in learning. The program used cooperative learning processes to take advantage of the cognitive, social, and motivational benefits of students working together on academic content. Teachers provided explicit instruction and guided students' interactions during cooperative learning. After a year-long implementation, the research found students in STRW performing significantly higher on reading comprehension, reading vocabulary, and language expression achievement. The author discusses the implications of this research for providing integrated and engaging instruction in middle school.

5.1 Cooperative Learning and Literacy Instruction in Middle Level Education

Discussions about how to best instruct young adolescents (ages 11–14 years) have attempted to focus around matching instruction to the unique characteristics of students in that age range. By early adolescence, students typically have developed a broad knowledge in most academic subjects and have a well-developed foundation in reading and writing skills. Cognitively, young adolescents are developing problem-solving and critical thinking skills that are central to success in secondary and post-secondary education. Yet recent reports suggest that more needs to be done to develop students' literacy skills in middle school and apply them in content areas so the students will be prepared adequately for high school and beyond (Biancarosa & Snow 2004). Other research suggests that the structural and instructional charac-teristics of middle schools are unresponsive to the development and needs of students, resulting in declining student achievement, attendance, and motivation during early adolescence (Eccles & Midgley 1989; Oldfather 1995).

Cognitive mismatch. Descriptive research on middle level education in the United States has documented that students spend much of their time in didactic instruction, with a focus on factual learning (DiCintio & Stevens 1997; Feldlaufer et al. 1988). During the middle school years students develop their ability to learn abstract concepts and are consolidating their ability to consider options and weigh alternative explanations. At this age they are engaging in metacognitive activities like planning, monitoring, controlling, and evaluating their cognitive processes (Steinberg 1993). The more factual, didactic instruction seems to be mismatched to the growing cognitive skills and independent thinking that adolescents are developing.

Social mismatch. Adolescents are also going through significant social development marked by increased desire for control and decision-making. Young adolescent development is characterized by a striving for independence, greater peer orientation, and self-consciousness than in earlier years. Yet middle level education often emphasizes instruction where students are to focus on following directions and less autonomy than what students may have had in the upper elementary grades (Midgley & Feldlaufer 1987). There is also an increase in normative evaluation in middle school, emphasizing social comparison and competition for grades (Gullickson 1985). These social characteristics of middle school instruction run counter to the students' needs and developing abilities.

Typical middle level literacy instruction. Literacy instruction in middle schools typically is departmentalized with students receiving literacy instruction in reading and in English classes. For the most part, these two classes are taught separately with little connection between reading instruction in reading class and the reading of literature, and writing instruction in English class (Biancarosa & Snow 2004; Irvin 1990). There is even less integration of reading instruction than in other content-area classes despite a recognition of the importance of reading to learn in the content areas and the need to focus on teaching students skills to read content-area texts (Anderson et al. 1985; Biancarosa & Snow 2004; Irvin 1990). Studies of instructional practices in developmental reading and remedial reading classes in middle school have found little use of strategy instruction, no integration of reading and writing instruction, and little application of reading strategies to expository (factual) text (Irvin & Connors 1989). These findings from a national survey run counter to the suggestions from research that focus on direct instruction in compre-hension strategies, embedding comprehension instruction in content areas, and integrating reading and writing instruction (Biancarosa & Snow 2004).

Conceptualizing change in middle school literacy instruction. The middle school literature offers a plethora of ideas for changing the nature of middle school literacy instruction to match the skills and abilities of students in early adolescence. For example, comments such as "instruction should be developmentally appropriate" or "teachers should use a variety of instructional tasks" do little to clarify the issue or provide substantive guidance to teachers.

Maehr & Anderman (1993) offered a conceptually based approach to considering the redesign of instruction to make it more developmentally appropriate for early adolescents. Their approach considers cognitive, social, and motivational characteristics of the learner in developing the TARRGET model that looks at tasks, autonomy, resources, recognition, grouping, evaluation, and time variables in redesigning instruction (see Fig. 5.1). TARRGET focuses on alterable variables in an attempt to help educators implement the concepts of developmentally-appropriate instruction in middle school.

5.1.1 Changing Middle School Literacy Instruction

The TARRGET model offers a way to consider restructuring middle school literacy instruction in a way that could address the cognitive and social mismatching frequently observed in middle school instruction and provide a positive motivational approach to schooling at a time when students tend to be less motivated than in previous grades. The resulting restructuring would integrate literacy instruction across at least parts of the curricula, provide more meaningful reading materials and instructional tasks, focus reading instruction on comprehension strategies, and focus language arts instruction on writing skills. These became the goals of the research on restructuring middle school literacy instruction.

Integration of reading and English classes. It is well recognized that there is a great deal of overlap between what is taught in reading and English, and we currently

Tasks	The tasks should be challenging, interesting, and meaningful.
Autonomy	Students should develop more autonomy and control of their learning.
Recognition	Students need recognition of their academic successes and improvement.
Resources	Schools should invest resources in improving schools and instruction.
Grouping	Various kinds of instructional grouping and student learning groups should be used to promote learning
Evaluation	Student evaluation should be based on mastery of the content, improvement, and effort.
Time	Larger blocks of time should be allocated to each class to permit more extended and meaningful learning activities.

Fig. 5.1 The TARRGET model for redesigning instruction
Maehr, M. L., & Anderman, E. M. (1993). Reinventing the middle school for early adolescents: Emphasizing tasks goals. *Elementary School Journal, 93*, 593–601

conceptualize the two as teaching parts of what are a continuum of literacy skills including learning to read, developing comprehension, reading to learn information, and writing to convey information. To take advantage of the inherent connections between reading and English instruction and to facilitate students' ability to transfer what they learn, it is important to have one teacher teach both areas preferably in one class. In this way a teacher could teach learning to read, reading to learn, and writing to express what one learns in an integrated fashion. By integrating the two subjects, it is conceivable to have a double period of time for literacy instruction (for example, instead of a 45-minute period for reading and for English, it could be restructured as a 90-minute block of time for Literacy). A longer class would prove valuable in literacy instruction as it would offer teachers more flexibility to change their instructional activities and, most importantly, allow students to engage in extended writing activities without interruption.

Literature as a basis for reading instruction. An important way to develop adolescent students' motivation for reading is to give them interesting, high-quality reading material (Paris et al. 1991; Wigfield 2004). By integrating reading and English classes this is solved by using good literature, like that normally read in English class, as the basis for vocabulary and reading comprehension instruction. Through the use of literature, students can learn about different genres of writing and can become familiar with famous, well-published authors that they could choose to read more extensively on their own. At the same time, literature can provide very valuable writing models that teachers can use in writing instruction. Students can read and observe the effect of things like the rich descriptions, plot development, and figurative language of good authors in the literature reading, which the teacher could then refer to when they are teaching those elements in the writing portion of their literacy instruction. As such, the writing of famous authors may become both the model and the motivation for students in the writing process.

Meaningful instructional tasks. The use of follow-up activities after traditional reading instruction can be a problem as they often bear little or no relationship to what the students have read. As a result, students might not see these instructional tasks as useful or important (Beck et al. 1979; Ivey & Broaddus 2001; Osborn 1984). This is unfortunate because well-designed follow-up activities can further students' understanding of what they have read and help them develop comprehension skills that are useful in all of their reading.

Explicit instruction on text comprehension strategies. A rich body of research has developed over the past 25 years on comprehension strategies that are effective in significantly improving students' reading performance (National Reading Panel 2000). Most of that research emphasizes the importance of explicit instruction on comprehension strategies and applying those strategies to content-area reading (Biancarosa & Snow 2004). Yet, it is surprising how little explicit instruction on comprehension strategies middle school students receive (Irvin 1990; Pressley 2000). Comprehension strategies help students comprehend what they are reading and have the potential to be generalized to reading across content areas with appropriate instruction. During upper elementary and middle school, students are transitioning from learning to read to reading to learn (Anderson & Armbruster

1984). Much of what students learn in school from upper elementary school is presented in text, so it is important for literacy instruction to teach students strategies for identifying, organizing, and learning information that is presented in text (Paris et al. 1991; Pressley 2000). These comprehension skills should not only be taught, but also applied in content area reading to facilitate students' ability to generalize them to new content and different tasks.

Writing as the focus for language arts instruction. Writing has become much more of a focus in language arts instruction over the past 20 years. Instruction has moved away from a focus on mechanics and grammar skills to developing students' ability to express their ideas in writing (Bridge & Hiebert 1985; Strickland et al. 2001). With this focus on writing and the use of writing process models of instruction, language arts instruction becomes more useful and practical. Embedding mechanics and usage skill instruction in the context of writing provides a direct application and meaningful purpose for skill instruction (Flowers & Hayes 1980; Graham et al. 2005; Graves 1978). Thus, the skills are not an abstraction but become significant because students are more likely to see the usefulness of the instruction for improving their expression of ideas. Students are also motivated by the act of expressing their own ideas as well as sharing their writing with their peers (Flowers & Hayes 1980; Graves 1978).

Using cooperative learning to promote learning and more positive peer relations. The TARRGET model suggests that middle school classrooms should be restructured to promote both learning and positive peer relations. This is particularly important for early adolescents because peer relations take center stage during this period and research suggests that a student's relations with his or her peers play an important role in the student's attachment to school (Parker & Asher 1987). Students who do not develop positive peer relations at this time are much more likely to drop out of school. Yet, students often perceive little support for peer relations in the middle school and often more negative peer relations leading to less attachment to school during these years (Seidman et al. 1994).

Cooperative learning is an alternative classroom structure that has been shown to facilitate academic learning, positive peer relations, and positive attitudes toward school (Johnson & Johnson 1989; Slavin 1990). Typically cooperative learning uses group goals, where for one member of the group to succeed all of the members of the group must succeed. As a result, positive interdependence develops within the group – the peers support and motivate one another, leading to more positive peer relations and more social acceptance of one another. At the same time, the individual accountability promotes each individual's learning, resulting in greater achievement. In essence, cooperative learning uses peers as both an instructional and motivational resource, taking advantage of students' increasing sense of independence and stronger peer orientation during adolescence.

Using cooperative learning to influence student motivation. Cooperative learning also results in important changes in the evaluation processes in the classroom that mesh nicely with the developmental trends of early adolescence. A large portion of the recognition in cooperative learning classrooms depends on the whole groups' success on the task, rather than one student outperforming others. This causes students in cooperative learning to develop mastery goals rather than performance goals (Guthrie & Davis 2003; Nichols 1994). When students have mastery goals, they are more oriented on mastering the content and learning from the instructional tasks, which results in more intrinsic motivation. Conversely, students who have performance goals are less concerned about learning or mastery and more concerned about looking good when compared with others. There are important advantages when students adopt mastery goals. Typically, students with mastery goals develop a deep understanding of what is taught (Meece et al. 1988; Nolen 1988) and are likely to focus on effort as a means of attaining success (Pintrich & Schunk 1996). Students with this type of motivation tend to persevere with learning tasks and develop positive attitudes and attachment to school (Maehr & Anderman 1993).

5.2   Student Team Reading and Writing Program

The Student Team Reading and Writing (STRW) Program was an attempt to use the TARRGET model, as operationalized through the above goals, to design a middle school literacy program that was responsive to the cognitive, social, and motivational needs of early adolescents. The reading part of the program consisted of three principal elements: Literature-related activities, direct instruction in reading comprehension strategies, and selection-related writing. Students work in heterogeneous learning teams to complete all of the instructional tasks. The activities followed a regular cycle that involved teacher presentation, team practice, independent practice, peer preassessment, and individual accountability. The approach is described in some detail below.

5.2.1   Cooperative Learning Teams

Cooperative learning teams were used as a vehicle to get students to engage in academic interactions that would further their understanding of what had been taught (National Reading Panel 2000) and to take advantage of the strong peer orientation of early adolescents. This created a change in the instructional activity in the classroom by giving students more responsibility for their work. It also provided a social and engaging academic environment, rather than the common didactic instruction in middle schools (Epstein & Mac Iver 1992).

Students were assigned to teams of heterogeneous ability. Within the teams students were assigned a partner with whom they worked when they completed their activities. Students' scores on the individual accountability activities (e.g., quizzes) contributed to form a team score. Teams were recognized for their success in attaining prespecified levels of performance on the accountability measures based upon the average score of the team members. Cooperative learning researchers have found that this sort of recognition based on the individual performance of all of the team members develops interdependence on the part of team members and typically is related to positive effects on students' academic performance (Slavin 1983; 1990).

Teacher-led instruction. The teacher has an important role in any effective classroom instruction (Rosenshine & Stevens 1986). In STRW the teacher was the instructional leader in the classroom. All instruction was initiated by a teacher presentation followed by the teacher guiding students' initial practice and providing corrective feedback. During cooperative learning activities, the teacher circulated among the students listening and providing further feedback as needed. This gave the teacher an opportunity to provide students in need with remedial instruction to increase their potential for mastering the content. Similarly, it provided the teacher with an opportunity to assess informally the progress of the students and the adequacy of the initial instruction. Most teachers also found this to be a good opportunity to provide encouragement and praise to motivate students regarding their academic work.

5.2.2   Reading Instruction

Literature-related activities. The students used an American literature anthology as the source for the reading selections. The anthology provided high quality literature written by well-known authors like O. Henry, Langston Hughes, Pearl Buck, and Isaac Asimov. Teachers set the purpose for reading, introduced new vocabulary, reviewed old vocabulary words, and discussed the selection after students have read it. After the students read the literature selection they completed a series of follow-up activities that were specifically related to what they had read. The activities included partner reading, text comprehension, word mastery, main idea summarization, story-related writing, and comprehension strategy activities.

Partner reading. Students read the selection silently then read it orally with their partner. During oral reading the students took turns reading, alternating after each paragraph. The listener followed along and corrected any errors the reader made. This type of repeated reading gave the students a great deal of practice reading orally and has been found to contribute significantly to students reading fluency on the target passage and transfers to increased reading fluency on future reading tasks (National Reading Panel 2000; Stevens & Pipich 2002). Increasing reading fluency is an important skill as it not only helps in word recognition, but also seems to help improve reading comprehension (Faulkner & Levy 1999; Thurlow & van den Broek 1997).

Comprehension of the selection. The students were given written activities that focused on comprehension of the structure and content of the literature selection. The goal of these activities was to enable the students to move beyond factual understanding to deeper comprehension of the passages. Halfway through the selection they stopped reading to do half of their comprehension activities. The partners discussed and wrote answers to questions asking them to describe the characters, setting, and problem in the story and predict how the problem in the story might be resolved. They might also discuss questions related to the author's purpose or style, and the interpretation of figurative language or literary techniques used. After completing the first half of the story and comprehension activities, the students read the second half of the story and completed the comprehension activities related to it.

Research in reading comprehension has found that understanding story structures is important for students' comprehension (Fitzgerald & Spiegel 1983; National Reading Panel 2000) and that discussing predictions and summaries of stories can increase students' comprehension (Palincsar & Brown 1984). The comprehension activities related to the literature selections used both in an attempt to give students practice and feedback on generalizable skills in comprehension.

Teachers engaged students in daily discussions about the selection they were reading. In part the discussion would check their comprehension of the story. In part, the teacher would ask questions about the story to extend students' comprehension and understanding of the selection. For example, the teacher would discuss the use of figurative language and what it meant in the context of the selection or discuss the author's purpose of describing events or characters and how that related to the plot of the story.

Word mastery activities. Much research has shown that development of vocabulary skills in students is an important part of improving their reading skills. Vocabulary instruction prior to reading can improve comprehension of current reading material (Brett et al. 1996; Tomeson & Aarnoutse 1998), increase reading achievement (Brett et al. 1996; Eldredge 1990), and improve students' abilities to see causal connections in what they have read (Medo & Ryder 1993). As students move into middle school there is more emphasis on reading to learn (Stevens et al. 1991). Since vocabulary knowledge is a fundamental building block of those comprehension and learning processes, vocabulary instruction must be a fundamental part of literacy instruction.

The teacher in the STRW projects taught new or difficult words that were related to the selection prior to the students reading the selection. The students learned the meaning of the new words through practice focused on writing meaningful sentences with the vocabulary. A meaningful sentence was one that told what the word meant in the context of the sentence, (i.e., "The gigantic pumpkin was so large it had to be lifted by a crane" and not "That pumpkin is gigantic").

Summarizing the main points of the selection. In previous research, summarizing what has been read in one's own words has been found to be a very effective way to enhance the reader's comprehension and retention of what has been read (Doctorow et al. 1978; Paris et al. 1991; Weinstein 1982) and has been found to be an effective way to remediate poor readers' comprehension problems (Jenkins et al. 1987). After reading and discussing the selection, students in the STRW program summarized the main points of the story to their partner. The partner then checked the summary in terms of the adequacy of its completeness and detail.

Selection-related writing. Part of the purpose of the writing activity was to further students' comprehension and understanding of the selection by writing an extended response to the story or a part of the story (Wittrock 1986). The activity also helped to increase the connection between reading literature and writing by having students transfer the skills and strategies that they learned in writing to constructing good responses for the reading activities.

For each selection the students were given an open-ended writing assignment where they were asked to write in response to a topic related to the selection. For example, the students might have been asked to use their predictions and write a new end to the selection, or compare and contrast characters from the selection or from two different literature selections. Students used a simplified writing process in writing their response to the prompt, in which they discussed their ideas with their partner, drafted a version of the response, revised their writing based upon their partner's feedback, edited their writing, and created a final copy.

Reading comprehension strategy instruction. The STRW teacher gave the students direct instruction on reading comprehension strategies and study strategies on a regular basis. The comprehension strategy instruction applied of a large body of research that has shown that students' reading comprehension can be significantly improved through instruction and practice in specific reading comprehension strategies (e.g., Palincsar & Brown 1984; Pressley 2000; Stevens 1988). Previous research has shown the efficacy of instruction on strategies for identifying main ideas, drawing conclusions, and interpreting figurative language (National Reading Panel 2000). Students were taught when and how to use the strategy and they were taught comprehension monitoring strategies so they could check their appropriate use of the strategies.

The teacher also taught the students study strategies to help them locate, organize, and retain important information that was presented in text. Teaching students strategies for reading and remembering information from text can greatly increase their ability to learn the content because students become actively engaged in understanding and organizing the information they are reading (Anderson & Armbruster 1984; Pressley 2000).

5.2.3 Writing Instruction

The writing part of the program used a writing process approach that focused language arts instruction on improving students' writing. In this way the teacher taught grammar, expression, and mechanics in a more meaningful way to the student because the skills can be understood in the context of the concrete activity of writing (Bridge & Hiebert 1985; Strickland et al. 2001). Also, because learning these skills was contextualized, it was more likely that the skills would be retained. The teacher encouraged the students to use the new skills actively in their writing, further increasing their processing of the information and improving their understanding of the skills.

Writing concept lessons. Once students learned to use all of the steps in the writing process, the teacher provided instruction and models on styles and techniques of writing. The lessons included topics such as improving descriptions, organizing ideas, and getting your audience's attention. There were also lessons on specific styles of writing like explanatory writing, persuasive writing, and writing personal and business letters. The STRW program provided a set of writing concept lessons, but teachers were also encouraged to develop their own lessons based upon students' needs and interests. Often teachers used books by authors that the class was already reading in the literature anthology as models for specific types of writing. An advantage of this instructional strategy was further strengthening of connections between reading and writing.

Integrated language arts lessons. Teachers periodically taught lessons on language mechanics and language usage lessons from a set of materials provided by the STRW program. Teachers were told to select language arts lessons that were appropriate for the students' needs as identified in the teacher's evaluations of the students' writing. The goal of the lessons was to give students skills that would help improve their writing. Each lesson included specific writing-related activities to increase the likelihood that students would transfer what they learned to their own writing. Students were also taught how to edit for the types of errors that were relevant to the newly acquired skill. In subsequent writing process activities the new language mechanics skills were added to the editing checklist so students would apply what they learned in writing and in editing their own work and the writing of their classmates.

5.2.4   The Impact of Student Team Reading and Writing on Urban Middle School Students

The STRW model has been evaluated as a means of restructuring urban middle school literacy instruction in a study involving five middle schools in an urban school district in the eastern United States (Stevens 2003). The schools were configured to include 6th through 8th grades (ages 11 through 14 years). The schools were large, typically drawing students from many elementary schools, and had student enrollments that averaged around 260 students per grade level. The students were predominantly from minority groups and were drawn from the urban core of the city (see demographics in Table 5.1 below). The majority of the students were from lower socio-economic families, as can be see by the percent of the students identified as disadvantaged by guidelines for free or reduced lunch programs. Because of previous low student achievement, relatively high absentee rates, and their large disadvantaged population, all of these schools were considered "at-risk schools" and were eligible for specially funded educational programs. For the evaluation the two schools using STRW were matched based on district-administered achievement test scores to three comparison schools of with similar student populations.

The faculty in each of the schools was diverse in years of teaching experience and averaged 12.7 years of experience, which suggests that these were largely veteran teachers with a few newer teacher sprinkled across the schools (each school had at least one teacher with less than five years of experience). The English and reading teachers had from 2 to 23 years of classroom experience.

Table 5.1 Student demographics

	N	Minority (%)	Disadvantaged (%)
Experimental schools (combined)	1798	80.2	69.1
School 1	893	98.0	73.1
School 2	905	62.6	62.5
Comparison schools (combined)	2118	82.1	70.8
School 3	592	58.4	61.9
School 4	413	76.3	71.4
School 5	1113	97.1	75.4

Training in Student Team Reading and Writing. Teachers in the two schools using STRW were trained during the summer prior to beginning implementation in September. The training was conducted on 5 half-days (3 h) during one week. During the training the author described the instructional processes and the theoretical rationale for them. The author also described the research supporting the processes and how they relate to effective instruction. There was an emphasis on the goals of improving students reading fluency, reading comprehension, and ability to express themselves in writing. The teachers were given a detailed explanation of what to do in the classroom, as well as a detailed teacher's manual for the program. The author also modeled the instructional processes in a simulated lesson where the author (trainer) acted as the teacher and the teachers (trainees) acted as students would in a STRW classroom. The simulation provided both a model for the teacher so they could watch what they were expected to do, but also gave them an understanding of what was expected of their students in the program. On the last day of training the teachers were given the books (literature anthologies) and all of the materials they needed to implement STRW. At that time, the author guided the teachers through the materials, so they would know what each piece was and its role in the program.

Implementation of STRW. Teachers began their implementation of STRW during the first day of school. The district restructured the daily schedule so the teachers had a double period of 90 minutes (combining the time typically allotted to reading and English classes) as opposed to the typical 45, during which they taught reading, language arts, and English using the STRW program. During the first months of the school year, the project staff observed the teachers at least three times a week and acted as coaches to help them improve the quality of their implementation. The author also met with the teachers after school to answer their questions about the program and discuss ways to accommodate the needs of their classes and students in them. These discussions often helped the teachers improve their implementation of STRW. As teachers became more proficient in STRW, the classroom observations became less frequent.

In January and February (the second semester) the project staff observed the participating classes to assess teachers' level of implementation of STRW to determine the treatment fidelity. The project staff had an implementation measure listing desired behaviors that was used to assess the level of implementation in the class that included assessments of both student and teacher behaviors. Each teacher was observed on three randomly selected days for 30 minutes and each observation was unannounced. The project staff had observed the classes regularly during the first semester, so their appearance in the classroom was not unusual and the observations were unobtrusive. Since the STRW instructional activities change from day to day in a five-day cycle, only those behaviors expected for that part of the instructional sequence were rated on each particular observation. The project staff attempted to rate each teacher on different days in order to get a broad sample of their behavior on which to assess their quality of implementation.

Quality of implementation scores were computed for each teacher based upon the percent of expected behaviors that were observed, averaged across the three observations. All of the teachers averaged 83% implementation or higher, with an average level of implementation across all teachers of 91%. This was considered a very high level implementation, and we observed no systematic differences in STRW implementation related to variables like the teacher's years of experience.

5.2.5   Traditional Reading and English Instruction in Comparison Classes

Students in traditional reading and English classes in matched middle schools were used as the comparison group in the evaluation. The traditional structure had departmentalized instruction, with reading and English as two separate classes taught by different teachers. None of the teachers in the comparison group used cooperative learning processes.

Reading. Reading instruction used a basal reading series that students typically read silently followed by completing assignments from the workbook or worksheets provided by the series. These activities may or may not have been related to the theme of the story. There were comprehension skill lessons imbedded in the workbooks, but there was little systematic instruction and intensive practice on any of those skills. Comprehension skills were also taught in isolation, and not integrated with what students read in the reading book.

English. English instruction had three components: literature, grammar, and writing. Teachers would block out a period of time each quarter to read a piece of literature, during which time all instruction in class would be about literature. In the literature component, students read extended pieces of literature from an anthology. Often students read sections of the literature silently and then discussed them in a whole class discussion. Teachers often followed the discussion with questions about the piece that were intended to extend students' comprehension of what they had read. The rest of the instruction during each quarter was focused on grammar and writing. Typically grammar instruction occurred for three or four days a week, and used lessons from a grammar textbook. The approach to grammar instruction was fairly traditional, focusing on identification of parts of speech, and learning to use them correctly in writing sentences and paragraphs. Writing activities typically occurred once a week at most. Students usually were given a topic and asked to write a draft about it. Students were given feedback either from the teacher, who collected and read the drafts, or from other students after having the draft read to them. Some teachers provided students with opportunities to revise their drafts, but this was not consistently used in all classes.

5.2.6   Evaluation Results

This evaluation used a multiple choice format standardized achievement test to evaluate the effects of the STRW program as compared to more traditional middle school reading and English instruction. The school district administered the California Achievement Test (CTB/McGraw-Hill 1986), a nationally-normed test commonly used in schools that measured student's performance on reading vocabulary, reading comprehension, language expression, and language mechanics (as well as math, social studies, and science). Based upon data from the previous year (used as a pretest) the students in the STRW schools had similar performance to those in the comparison schools, suggesting that the schools were comparable on initial achievement.

When evaluating this program near the end of the school year, we administered a different form of the California Achievement Test in May. The evaluation revealed that students across the three grade levels benefited from the STRW program and that there were no differential effects based upon grade level (Stevens 2003). Students in the STRW program have significantly higher achievement on measures of reading vocabulary, reading comprehension, and language expression than those who did not participate. There were no differences on measures of language mechanics. In the three areas of significant effects, students in STRW outperformed students in traditional instruction by fairly substantial amounts, scoring a third of a standard deviation higher in reading vocabulary (effect size = +0.33), a quarter standard deviation higher in reading comprehension (effect size = +0.25), and more than a third standard deviation in language expression (effect size = +0.38) (Stevens 2003).

5.3   Discussion

This project used the theory-based TARRGET model to develop an instructional program for middle level students that was developmentally appropriate, instructionally engaging, and motivationally stimulating. At its core, the Student Team Reading and Writing program uses research-based instructional practices, teacher-directed instruction, good literature as a basis for instruction, cooperative learning processes, and integrated reading and English instruction. The combination of these components resulted in a program that when implemented for the entire school year yielded significantly higher student achievement in vocabulary, comprehension, and language expression than achieved before. These findings are important given recent research and reviews suggesting that in the United States there is a critical need to extend our research in effective literacy instruction into the middle grades, and integrate literacy instruction into content areas to make it more relevant and valuable for the students as they are pushed to apply their reading and writing skills (Biancarosa & Snow 2004).

The STRW program reconceptualized the tasks, autonomy, recognition, resources, grouping, evaluation, and time in a typical middle school. The tasks were developed to engage the students in relevant activities by using good literature as a basis for reading instruction. Follow-up activities in reading were related to and expanded on the literature students had just read, with a goal of increasing their comprehension of the literature. There was also a focus on writing to develop students' abilities to express their ideas, rather than grammar skills. By doing so, the program's intent was to both motivate students and increase students' learning and retention of what was taught through the focus on meaningful learning tasks.

Student autonomy was also increased in STRW through the use of cooperative learning structures where peers are used as an instructional resource in the class-room. Cooperative learning give students more responsibility for their own learning and the learning of others (their teammates). As a result, students developed an interdependence that promoted positive social relations in the class and established a climate where students help one another learn. Research by Webb (1985) has shown that when students explain content or skills to one another, both learners benefit in terms of improved performance. The student responsibility for learning in cooperative learning also taps into adolescents drive toward more independence and self-determination, but does so in a way that promotes learning and positive attitudes toward school and academic tasks. When students are given more autonomy and responsibility they are more likely to develop ownership of what they are doing (Maehr & Anderman 1993). Accountability for completion of and performance on those tasks maintains a level of quality in what students do.

Teacher recognition of students' effort and improvement is imbedded in the evaluation methods of the cooperative learning processes. This is an important motivational element, particularly for adolescents. By early adolescence, students have developed a history of success or failure in academic subjects and it has a major influence in their motivation toward and effort in future learning. Those who succeed are motivated and effortful in learning activities, and those who have not succeeded tend to be less motivated and give less effort. In STRW the recognition of improvement, typically resulting from a student's effort, not only changes the goal structure in the classroom, but may affect the goal orientation of the students. Students may begin to recognize that the do not need to be the best in the class. Instead they need to be better than they were before to get recognition. The motivational focus becomes more internal on the part of the students where they look more to master the content than to outperform others. This means that every student has equal potential for recognition and as such all students are more willing to put in the effort to learn. Restructuring the goal structure of the class around recognition for improvement profoundly influences students' motivation and learning behaviors (Maehr & Pintrich 1991).

This project did provide additional resources to the participating schools in part through new materials and in part through staff development for the teachers. For any kind of substantive school reform effort such as this providing adequate resources for teachers as they learn and implement the reform is necessary. Perhaps the most significant of these resource investments was the staff development. In the STRW program staff development for the reading and English teachers was focused and intensive, and directed toward learning and mastery of the instructional processes in the model. For teachers to significantly change their teaching behaviors requires intensity and focus on specific changes with follow-up and coaching them toward mastery. This approach made it clear what the goal of the staff development activity was and provided adequate support for teachers to reach that goal. Of the 20 teachers in the STRW program, all were implementing the program elements at higher than 80%, and they averaged 91% implementation. This high level suggests significant changes in teacher behavior, which is more likely to happen as the result of putting resources into focused and intensive staff development. A second aspect that is likely to have facilitated staff development is that these cooperative learning processes were specific (and specified) to reading and English instruction. They required little interpretation on the part of teachers and resulted in little ambiguity of what was expected. This specificity and clarity is likely to facilitate teachers who attempt to make changes in their classroom practices and behaviors.

Evaluation is an important component of STRW and is central to cooperative learning methods that improve student achievement (Slavin 1990). It gives students the reason to learn. But, as described above, the STRW model in part focuses the evaluation on student improvement as a means to increase motivation for all students and to focus that motivation on effort. The evaluation essentially levels the playing field for all students. Those with more previous success in reading and/or writing have no major advantages in the evaluations.

Finally, STRW restructured the middle school schedule in a way to provide larger blocks of time to allow for more extended learning activities and an integration of reading and English. The double periods allowed teachers to engage students in reading literature and follow-up activities that extended their comprehension of what they read. The double periods also gave students more uninterrupted time to engage in the writing process where they could potentially get feedback on a draft and revise it during the same period. Teachers noted that the extended time also gave them more opportunities to make connections between reading and writing during their instruction.

In conclusion, the Student Team Reading and Writing model used in these middle schools is a multifaceted program for restructuring literacy instruction. The results of this evaluation provide evidence that STRW can be effective in increasing literacy achievement in urban, high-poverty middle schools in high-fidelity and relatively long term implementations. This program also provides evidence in support of the efficacy of using cooperative learning as an instructional and motivational vehicle for teaching early adolescents. Cooperative learning processes increase student achievement through students interacting about the content in a social learning environment. Cooperative learning processes also change the goal structures in the classroom to focus on improvement, resulting in positive motivation for all students. Finally, cooperative learning processes take advantage of the peer orientation of adolescents by constructing a classroom structure where students encourage and support one another in academic work, essentially making it "cool to be good at school."

References

Anderson, R. C., Hiebert, E. H., Scott, J. A., & Wilkinson, I. (1985). *Becoming a nation of readers.* Washington, DC: National Institute of Education.

Anderson, T., & Armbruster, B. (1984). Studying. In P.D. Pearson (Ed.), *Handbook of reading research* (pp. 657–680). New York: Longman.

Beck, I., McKeown, M., McCaslin, E., & Burkes, A. (1979). *Instructional dimensions that may affect reading comprehension: Examples from two commercial reading programs* (Technical Report No. 1979/20). Pittsburgh, PA: University of Pittsburgh, Learning Research and Development Center.

Biancarosa, G., & Snow, C. E. (2004). *Reading nest – A vision for action and research in middle and high school literacy: A report from the Carnegie Corporation of New York.* Washington, DC: Alliance for Excellent Education

Brett, A., Rothlein, L., & Hurley, M. (1996). Vocabulary acquisition from listening to stories and explanations of target words. *Elementary School Journal, 96,* 415–422.

Bridge, C., & Hiebert, E. (1985). A comparison of classroom writing practices, teachers' perceptions of their writing instruction, and textbook recommendations on writing practices. *Elementary School Journal, 86,* 155–172.

DiCintio, M. J., & Stevens, R. J. (1997). Student motivation and cognitive complexity of mathematics instruction in six middle grades classrooms. *Research in Middle Level Education Quarterly, 20,* 27–42.

Doctorow, M., Wittrock, M., & Marks, C. (1978). Generative processes in reading comprehension. *Journal of Educational Psychology, 70,* 109–118.

Eccles, J. S., & Midgley, C. (1989). Stage-environment fit: Developmentally appropriate classrooms for young adolescents. In C. Ames & R. Ames (Eds.), *Research on motivation in education, Vol. 3: Goals and cognitions* (pp. 139–186). New York: Academic Press.

Eldredge, J. L. (1990). Increasing the performance of poor readers in the third grade with a group-assisted strategy. *Journal of Educational Research, 84,* 69–77.

Epstein, J. L., & Mac Iver, D. J. (1992). *Education in the middles grades: National practices and trends.* Columbus, OH: National Middle School Association.

Faulkner, H. J., & Levy, B. A. (1999). Fluent and nonfluent forms of transfer in reading: Words and their message. *Psychonomic Bulletin and Review, 6,* 111–116.

Feldlaufer, H., Midgley, C., & Eccles, J. S. (1988). Student, teacher, and observer perceptions of the classroom environment before and after the transition to junior high school. *Journal of Early Adolescence, 8,* 133–156.

Fitzgerald, J., & Spiegel, D. (1983). Enhancing children's reading comprehension through instruction in narrative structures. *Journal of Reading Behavior, 14,* 1–18.

Flowers, L., & Hayes, J. (1980). The dynamics of composing: Making plans and juggling constraints. In L. Gregg & E. Steinberg (Eds.), *Cognitive processes in writing* (pp. 31–50). Hillsdale, NJ: Erlbaum.

Graham, S., Harris, K., Mason, L. (2005). Improving the writing performance, knowledge, and self-efficacy of struggling young writers: The effects of self-regulated strategy development. *Contemporary Educational Psychology, 30,* 207–241.

Graves, D. (1978). *Balance the basics: Let them write.* New York: Ford Foundation.

Gullickson, A. R. (1985). Student evaluation techniques and their relationship to grade and curriculum. *Journal of Educational Research, 79,* 96–100.

Guthrie, J., & Davis, M. (2003). Motivating struggling readers in middle school through an engagement model of classroom practice. *Reading and Writing Quarterly, 19,* 59–85.

Irvin, J. L. (1990). *Reading and the middle school student: Strategies to enhance literacy.* Needham Heights, MA: Allyn & Bacon.

Irvin, J. L., & Connors, N. A. (1989). Reading instruction in middle level schools: Results from a US survey. *Journal of Reading, 32,* 306–311.

Ivey, G., & Broaddus, K. (2001). Just plain reading: A survey of what makes students want to read in middle school classrooms. *Reading Research Quarterly, 36,* 350–371.

Jenkins, J. R., Heliotis, J., Stein, M. L., & Haynes, M. (1987). Improving reading comprehension by using paragraph restatements. *Exceptional Children, 54,* 54–59.

Johnson, D., & Johnson, R. (1989). *Cooperation and competition: Theory and research.* Edina, MN: Interaction Books.

Maehr, M. L., & Anderman, E. M. (1993). Reinventing the middle schools for early adolescents: Emphasizing task goals. *Elementary School Journal, 93,* 593–610.

Maehr, M. L., & Pintrich, P. R. (Eds.) (1991). *Advances in motivation and achievement, Vol. 7.* Greenwich, CT: JAI Press.

Medo, M. A., & Ryder, R. J. (1993). The effects of vocabulary instruction on readers' ability to make causal connections. *Reading Research and Instruction, 33,* 119–134.

Meece, J. L., Blumenfeld, P. C., & Hoyle, R. H. (1988). Students' goal orientation and cognitive engagement in classroom activities. *Journal of Educational Psychology, 80,* 514–523.

Midgley, C., & Feldlaufer, H. (1987). Students and teachers' decision-making fit before and after the transition to junior high school. *Journal of Early Adolescence, 7,* 225–241.

National Reading Panel. (2000). *Teaching children to read: An evidence-based assessment of the scientific research literature on reading and its implications for reading instruction.* Washington, DC: National Institute of Child Health and Human Development.

Nichols, J. D. (1994). Cooperative learning and student motivation. *Contemporary Educational Psychology, 19,* 167–178.

Nolen, S. (1988). Reasons for studying: Motivational orientation and study strategies. *Cognition and Instruction, 5,* 269–287.

Oldfather, P. (1995). Commentary: What's needed to maintain and extend motivation for literacy in the middle grades. *Journal of Reading, 38,* 420–423.

Osborn, J. (1984). The purposes, uses, and contents of workbooks and guidelines for publishers. In R. Anderson, J. Osborn, & R. Tierney (Eds.), *Learning to read in American schools* (pp. 45–112). Hillsdale, NJ: Erlbaum.

Palincsar, A. S., & Brown, A. L. (1984). Reciprocal teaching of comprehension-fostering and monitoring activities. *Cognition and Instruction, 1,* 117–175.

Paris, S., Wasik, B., & Turner, J. (1991). The development of strategic readers. In R. Barr, M. Kamil, P. Mosenthal, & P. D. Pearson (Eds.), *Handbook of reading research* (*Vol. 2,* pp. 609–640). New York: Longman.

Parker, J. G., & Asher, S. R. (1987). Peer relations and later personal adjustment: Are low-accepted children at risk? *Psychological Bulletin, 102,* 357–389.

Pintrich, P. R., & Schunk, D. H. (1996). *Motivation in education: Theory, research, and applications.* Upper Saddle River, NJ: Prentice Hall.

Pressley, M. (2000). What should comprehension instruction be instruction of? In M. Kamil, P. Mosenthal, D. Pearson, & R. Barr (Eds.), *Handbook of reading research.* (*Vol. 3,* pp. 546–561). Mahwah, NJ: Lawrence Erlbaum Associates.

Rosenshine, B. V., & Stevens, R. J. (1986). Teaching functions. In M. C. Wittrock (Ed.), *Handbook of research on teaching* (pp. 376–391). New York: Macmillan.

Seidman, E., Allen, L., Aber, J. L., Mitchell, C., & Feinman, J. (1994). The impact of school transition in early adolescence on the self-system and perceived social context of poor urban youth. *Child Development, 65,* 507–522.

Slavin, R. (1983). *Cooperative learning.* New York: Longman.

Slavin, R. (1990). *Cooperative learning: Theory, research, and practice*. Upper Saddle River, NJ: Prentice Hall.

Steinberg, L. (1993). *Adolescence*. New York: McGraw-Hill.

Stevens, R. J. (2003). Student team reading and writing: A cooperative learning approach to middle school literacy instruction. *Educational Research and Evaluation, 9,* 137–160.

Stevens, R. J., & Pipich, S. B. (2002). Silent or oral reading: Where is time best spent? *Pennsylvania Education Leadership, 21,* 34–40.

Stevens, R. J., Slavin, R. E., & Farnish, A. M. (1991). The effects of cooperative learning and direct instruction in reading comprehension strategies on main idea identification. *Journal of Educational Psychology, 83,* 8–16.

Strickland, D., Bodino, A., Buchan, K., Jones, K., Nelson, A., Rosen, M. (2001) Teaching writing in a time of reform. *Elementary School Journal, 101,* 385–398.

Thurlow, R., & van den Broek, P. (1997). Automaticity and inference generation. *Reading and Writing Quarterly, 13,* 165–184.

Tomeson, M., & Aarnoutse, C. (1998). Effects of an instructional programme for deriving word meanings. *Educational Studies, 24,* 115–125.

Webb, N. (1985). Student interaction and learning in small groups. In R. Slavin et al. (Eds.), *Learning to cooperate, cooperating to learn* (pp. 147–172). New York: Plenum Press.

Weinstein, C. (1982). Training students to use elaboration learning strategies. *Contemporary Educational Psychology, 7,* 301–311.

Wigfield, A. (2004). Motivation for reading during early adolescent and adolescent years. In D. Stickland, & D. Alvermann (Eds.), *Bridging the literacy achievement gap, grades 4–12*. New York: Teachers College Press.

Wittrock, M. C. (1986). Students' thought processes. In M. C. Wittrock (Ed.), *Handbook of research on teaching* (pp. 297–314). New York: Macmillan.

Chapter 6
Structuring Group Interaction to Promote Thinking and Learning During Small Group Learning in High School Settings

Günter L. Huber and Anne A. Huber

Abstract Reports about success and flaws of cooperative learning in classrooms lead to the conclusion that external structuring of teams and learning tasks is not sufficient, because students often need additional structural support on a level of internal organization of group processes and on the internal level of individual learning orientations. As regards external structuring, the article describes the wide-spread technique of task-specialization in models of cooperative learning as well as its problems, and shows alternative approaches. Support for internal, interactive processes may be achieved by prescribing social roles or even learning, by training relevant competencies before small groups start learning together, by reflecting and evaluating group activities during and after learning, and finally, by modifying how the learners perceive their own and their team-mates' competencies. The optimal approach is to combine these structural supports for small group learning and to complement it with phases of teacher-centered as well as individual learning. Two combinatory models are described, which also have been shown to reduce the uncertainties of small group learning for more certainty-oriented learners, who otherwise liked cooperation less and achieved less than their uncertainty oriented class-mates. Final recommendations include a warning against the exclusive role of individually centered assessment procedures apparently in cooperative environments of teaching and learning.

6.1   Introduction

Social interaction in general is both an effective method and a highly evaluated goal in classroom settings. Social skills are essential parts of self-regulated learning that allow the individual to participate in learning activities in small groups, and to benefit from the opportunities to learn from each other. However, to achieve this goal students and teachers need a learning environment that promotes social-interactive processes of learning, preferably from elementary school on. For example, the school law of Baden-Württemberg (Schulgesetz für das Land Baden-Württemberg 2004) demands that elementary schools support the development of those behaviors and forms of social interaction that are necessary for children to live and learn together, particularly to listen to each other, learn from each other, and interact as partners. In his introduction to the Curriculum 2004 for Baden-Württemberg, von Hentig (2004, p. 11) commented that students have to learn "to do their part in a world characterized by collaboration" as well as learn "to participate actively first in the processes of a smaller, then of the wider community."

This chapter will describe how cooperative situations can be structured to support students not only in their academic learning tasks, but also in acquiring those competencies which they need for efficient social interaction in small groups and for their personal development. Starting out from contradictory results we will describe the necessity for supporting learning in small groups on the external level of task organization, the internal level of structuring social interactions, and at the individual level of learning orientations.

6.2   Contradictory Reports About Learning in Small Groups

Generally, there are positive reports about small group learning from psychological laboratory settings as well as from existing classrooms. Slavin (1995a, b) characterized the findings from numerous studies of cooperative learning as one of the greatest success stories in the history of educational research. In a meta-analysis including 90 field studies comparing cooperative learning and traditional learning, Slavin found that cooperative learning led to higher academic achievement in 64% of the cases. Only in 5% of the cases did traditional learning result in better achievement than cooperative learning, and there were no differences in 31% of the cases. Cooperative learning also showed many positive effects in noncognitive areas, although there were fewer studies that dealt with those effects.

There are, however, also numerous reports from disappointed teachers, who started to implement cooperative learning in their classrooms with great expectations, but gave up after only a short period because of unsettling experiences. Many of their objections centered on three "detaining D's": delays, deficits (in achievement), and disruptions. Therefore, despite theoretical interest in team learning and teachers' generally high appreciation of this didactic arrangement, cooperative learning is a rare event in the average classroom (see e.g., Rotering-Steinberg & von Kügelgen

1986; Rotering-Steinberg 2000). Everyday learning in school seems to be mainly influenced by individualistic and competitive orientations. Teachers again and again complain about negative experiences with learning in small groups.

A closer look at the specific conditions for learning determined by organizational models of group learning shows that beyond the external level of organizing group size, group composition, and distribution of learning tasks two more levels of organization should be taken into account. Depending on age and experience students need support on a level of internal organization of group processes, that is, social interaction between group members, and they need support on the individual level to avoid adverse experiences when they are challenged with controversial suggestions, ideas, and strategies in their learning teams.

6.3   External Organization of Learning in Small Groups

There are two options for organizing learning in small groups on an external level: a product-orientated approach known as collaborative learning and a process-centered approach known as cooperative learning. Both approaches are based on structuring the learning tasks. While collaborating groups try to solve the learning task as a whole, cooperating groups divide the common task into several sub-tasks and merge their results later. Although many publications show that the terms collaboration and cooperation are used synonymously, we want to elaborate on the distinctive use of these terms because this sheds light on the important role of structuring group interactions already on the external level of task organization. According to Roschelle and Teasley (1995), collaborative learning demands joint efforts for coordinated learning activities based on students understanding of collaboration as "a coordinated, synchronous activity that is the result of a continued attempt to construct and maintain a shared conception of a problem" (p. 70).

In this chapter we define Cooperative Learning as a form of interaction in which at least two persons are mutually involved in trying to learn something; groups may only comprise as many members as are still able to interact directly with each other; and, there is no direct supervision by a teacher. The exchange of knowledge and skills must be supported by one or more of the following measures: Task specialization, support of task-specific interactions, support of group processes, and feedback or reward for the learning of the group members (Huber et al. 2001).

Organizing learning in small groups does not necessarily imply that students work together and support each other in mastering their learning tasks. On the contrary, Aronson et al. (2004) noted that traditional learning groups offer opportunities for, or are used by, students to compete with each other. Traditional group work gathers four to six students around one table with a more or less complex task to solve, but usually only with very general advice or rules providing guidance on how they are supposed to interact. Thus, the students meet best conditions for exciting or disappointing experiences in group dynamics, often interfering with subject matter learning. Furthermore, students regularly start to break down their task into less complex parts and to assign them individually to the group members. With this strategy the team makes best use of every team member's specific resources (e.g., reading or arithmetic skills, specific knowledge) for solving the task – but keeps its members from the challenge of learning to cope with less familiar demands, thus enriching their individual resources by learning new skills.

Detrimental effects of learning in small groups are frequently reported when social interaction and interdependency of students are focused on a joint group product, for example, a poster presentation or a filled-in worksheet (see Renkl et al. 1995). In these cases, the success of a team does not depend on the individual learning processes and achievements of its members but on the quality of the one product the team has to present at the end of a learning session. Notorious negative effects of this kind of organization of team learning are "social loafing" (Latané et al. 1979: some team members lean back and let others do the job) and the "sucker effect" (Kerr 1983: those students who believe that they are responsible for the group's task and do the job again and again, will probably experience a decline in motivation).

Illustrative examples of collaborative learning can be found in the literature on joint text production or collaborative writing in classrooms (see Andriessen et al. 1996). A collaborative writing team has to come to a shared understanding of the task and produce together one text as a final product. No doubt this situation offers ample opportunities to learn a lot about the perspectives of other group members as well as about their strategies and skills applied to approach the topic of the writing task, however, not all the participants will necessarily profit from these opportunities. If only the final product counts, that is, if only the quality of the text is evaluated in the end and not the individual progress of each group member in learning to compose a good text, at least some of the participants will soon discover that joint text production leads to acceptable results without too much personal efforts and involvement.

In the context of learning, a conventional understanding of collaboration as working together is highly misleading. The product of learning, that is, the solution of a problem or the completion of a specific task, must not be an end in itself, but just a means to stimulate learning processes. At the end we do not want to show off group products – although joint comparisons and evaluations of these products also offer important learning opportunities, particularly in regard to the promotion of self-evaluation. We want instead to demonstrate that each team member has benefited personally, has gained new experiences, knowledge, and skills as individual products of his or her learning efforts, and is able to contribute individually to the socio cultural dimension of knowing.

Cooperation is usually defined as the activity of the members of a larger group in which more encompassing task or a more complex problem is broken down into parts, which can be mastered individually or in smaller teams. In the end, partial solutions are exchanged and summarized to a final solution. Aronson's et al. (1978) jigsaw puzzle is a fine illustration of this approach to learning in teams. The principle of task specialization in the jigsaw approach generates positive interdependence between learners, who are required to exchange their knowledge and build common understandings (Huber 2006). According to this principle, a more complex learning task is divided optimally into four sub-tasks A, B, C, and D. So called "basic groups" of four members each then decide who will become an expert for which sub-task. Depending on their decision, the members leave their basic groups and form "expert groups" A, B, C, and D, composed only of those class-mates who have opted for the same sub-task. Once they have acquired expert knowledge, the students meet again in their basic groups, to take turns in sharing their expertise with each other. At the end, each team member should know everything about the original learning task as a whole.

6.3.1 Problems of Task Specialization

The jigsaw approach to task specialization has benefits and limitations. Less experienced groups need much support if they are to be prevented from ending up as a pile of puzzle pieces rather than developing a shared understanding of the task at hand. Various ways of providing structural support can be found on the external level of organizing cooperative learning by combining whole class activities, small group activities, and individual activities. In any case, task specialization without other measures to support the interactions between learners is not a very effective way of organizing learning in small groups.

In a meta-analysis of field studies on cooperative learning involving the jigsaw method (i.e., a method of cooperative learning that uses task specialization), Slavin (1995) found that the results were equivocal. Cooperative learning was more effective than traditional learning in 27% of the cases, it was less effective in the same percentage of cases, and in 46% of the cases there were no differences. However, when one takes a closer look at the studies on jigsaw learning, one gets the impression that jigsaw learning is effective if learners are informed about promising learning activities. Learners need at least some help to use effective strategies such as which learning activities should be applied to acquire knowledge, to teach each other, and deepen their individual understanding. Another reason why jigsaw learning is often not as effective as it could be may be the group size. In smaller groups, every member may be more active than in larger groups. Also, loss of motivation should be less a problem in small groups and coordination of activities easier.

6.3.2 Alternative Approaches to External Organization

Huber (2004a) developed the Partner-Puzzle method as a modification of the original jigsaw method. In the Partner-Puzzle method, learners always work together in pairs or dyads. In a first phase they learn a text in pairs. Then they work together with another partner who learned a different text in a different dyad as they teach each other their texts. In a third phase, they deepen their understanding by working on various activities. In all three phases learners are supported by prescribed learning activities. To learn the text in the first phase and to teach it to each other in the second phase, they use index cards with key concepts and they answer questions. In the third phase, they check all cards once more and then spread out their cards to construct a conceptual structure and to cross-link their knowledge (Wahl 2005: methods of card sorting and structuring).

In a study of 7th and 8th grade students studying biology, Huber (2006) demonstrated that structuring the learning using the Partner-Puzzle method was more effective than traditional learning in promoting academic achievement, intrinsic motivation, perceived competence, and self-determination. Moreover, a comparison of the Partner-Puzzle method with and without support of the described learning activities showed that 8th grade students had academic achievement gains and reported strong intrinsic motivation and perceived competence while 7th grade students who received support were also better on some of the achievement measures than those without such support although they did not report better intrinsic motivation or perceived competence. A possible explanation for these differences could be that the 7th grade students whose intellectual abilities are less developed had less cognitive capacity to use the supporting learning activities and, therefore, experienced difficulties. This interpretation is backed by Hoek et al. (1999) who found that low achieving students reach the limits of their cognitive capacity sooner than their more able peers.

The Partner-Puzzle method is one of a number of **WE**chselseitiges **L**ehren und **L**ernen (WELL) methods. WELL stands for Reciprocal Teaching and Learning. WELL methods are based on the assumption that task specialization alone does not guarantee efficient learning and that learners also have to be supported by guidelines or prescriptions of learning activities. We cannot expect that all learners, particularly those who are younger and less experienced begin cooperative learning with efficient strategies in how to acquire knowledge, how to teach each other, and how to deepen their own understanding. For these three learning phases they need support. The learning activities must be prescribed specifically for different goals of cooperative learning, for the knowledge domain, and for learner's competencies. Other WELL methods are the Speed-Duet (Lerntempoduett, Wahl 2004a), the Partner-, Group-or Multi-Interview (Wahl 2004b, c), and Structured Controversy (Huber 2004b; Johnson & Johnson 1994a).

Another very successful way of motivating learners to support each other is to implement group rewards based on the *individual* learning gains of the group members. To be recognized as a successful group, members will do everything to help each other to improve their academic achievement. This is a very effective strategy to promote learning although it is often rejected because it implies competition between groups, therefore, we will concentrate on task specialization.

Task specialization *and* feedback or reward for the learning of the group members are part of the external organization of learning in small groups. These structural supports focus the learners' attention on learning processes instead of caring only for the production of a group result.

6.4   Internal Organization of Learning in Small Groups

Additional support for the interaction of learners is a component of many models or methods of cooperative learning on the level of internal organization. As Kagan (1989) commented, internal structures of cooperative learning prescribe a series of steps together with the appropriate learning behavior and they organize the students' social interaction almost independently of the specific content or domain of subject matter. In addition, these internal structures of cooperation in learning teams provide a divide between product-centered collaboration and process-based cooperation. Kagan (1989/90) proposed that process *structures* may be applied in various learning contexts, while product-oriented learning *activities*, such as designing a team poster, always focus on content.

There are several ways to structure group interactions in cooperative teams. One is to support the task-specific interactions and another to support social interactions or group processes. In cases where the primary goal of cooperative learning is to enhance social competencies, task specific interactions and social interactions are identical.

There are four ways of structuring interactions. First, provide more or less detailed activities for the students. For example, prescribing roles is a less detailed support whereas learning scripts are often very detailed. Second, train students in the relevant competencies before teams start learning together. Third, encourage students to reflect on, and evaluate, learning activities during and after learning. Fourth, help group members modify their perceptions of competence, both of themselves and others, to ensure that all participate equally in the learning process.

Structuring interactions in groups even seems to be helpful when group rewards are applied that are based on criteria of individual learning. Although studies show that group rewards are very effective on their own, there are indications that they could be even more effective if the organizational model provides support for learning activities. It is of interest that Ross and Cousins (1999) found that learning according to the cooperative model "Student-Teams-Achievement Divisions" (Slavin 1986) and its group rewards did *not* promote the learners' competence in giving each other adequate help. In this model students learn cooperatively in teams composed heterogeneously according to individual achievement levels, and the groups receive achievement feedback based on the sum of individual *gain* scores of their members, that is, scores expressing the difference between individual previous knowledge and actual knowledge after cooperation. Theoretically, under these feedback conditions students should be highly motivated to care about each others learning and achievement by asking freely for assistance, giving detailed explanations, testing for understanding, and monitoring each member's learning progress. It is unlikely that groups use elaborated task-specific interactions spontaneously. When teachers do not initiate these kinds of interaction they risk letting learners interact on a rather superficial level (Cohen 1994; Renkl 1997).

6.4.1 Approaches to Structuring Interactions

As already outlined, there are four ways of structuring interactions in small groups:

1. Providing guidelines for specific learning activities;
2. Training in the required competencies;
3. Reflecting on and evaluating available learning activities, and
4. Modifying students' subjective perceptions of competence.

Interventions to support group interactions by implementing specific structures may affect task-specific interactions and/or social interactions. If the members of learning groups do not have a rich repertoire of social competencies at their disposal, it is important to provide support for social interactions. However, smooth social processes in learning groups alone do not guarantee that the team succeeds in its task-specific learning goals. Therefore, we will describe not only ways to structure interactions within small groups, but also outline, in the final section, two models of teaching that combine cooperative learning with other approaches to teaching and learning: the Sandwich approach and the Self-organized learning (SOL) in teams approach.

Providing Guidelines for Learning Activities

These guidelines can be ordered along a dimension of openness versus strictness of prescribing learning activities. A very detailed approach for structuring task-specific interactions is, for example, "scripted cooperation" (O'Donnell & Dansereau 1992) where learners work in dyads with a script on what activities to use at which point of time for learning a text. The prototypical script is the MURDER script, which prescribes activities like reading, summarizing, detecting mistakes and missing information, elaborating, and reviewing the text. Studies show that cooperative learning with this script is more effective than individual learning with and without such a script (Hall et al. 1988, 1989; McDonald et al. 1985; O'Donnell et al. 1986). However, there is only one study that compares cooperative learning with and without a script (McDonald et al. 1985), and in that study, there was no advantage for scripted cooperation (Huber 1999).

A less detailed approach to structuring interactions is built into the WELL methods. WELL methods require task specialization and assume that students should be supported in how to acquire knowledge, how to teach each other, and how to reach deeper understanding of the subject matter. If these activities are not supported, cooperative learning will not be very effective. Most problematic with this approach is that students often assume that their role is finished once they have taught their expert knowledge to the other team members. However, they have to initiate learning activities after teaching so that other members, who are specialized in other aspects of the team's task, get a chance to become experts too.

A rather more open approach is prescribing particular group roles to individual members, for instance, the role of the "listener" or of a "social facilitator." This approach is used within methods of "Learning Together" proposed by Johnson and Johnson (1994b). However, group members' abilities to fill these roles depend on their available competencies or in being able to train them in the necessary competencies before content learning starts.

Competence Training

Competence trainings may be conducted to promote social, methodological, or personal competencies as prerequisites of subject matter learning. It may also be useful to teach students how to implement prescribed learning activities when they lack experience in how to do so.

A meta-analysis by Hattie et al. (1996) shows that strategy training is most effective when it includes reflections on how, when, where, and why to use different strategies. Strategy training is also not very useful unless it is embedded in a real learning context (Reusser 2001) otherwise learners will not apply these strategies when it comes to difficult learning tasks. Cooperative learning methods that contain prescribed learning activities offer relevant learning contexts in which to practice learning strategies. The group members report that guidelines and prescriptions are very useful, and other learners may model how to use the strategies.

Acquisition of knowledge is supported efficiently if learners have opportunities to practice how to give elaborated explanations and how to ask high quality questions. Various studies by King (1989, 1990, 1991) and King and Rosenshine (1993) investigated the effectiveness of training students to ask high quality questions. Learners who received training in how to ask elaborated questions were more effective at asking such questions than control groups. Most important for students' achievement was the quality of the questions as well as the quality of the answers (King 1990).

Within Structured Controversy (Huber 2004c; Johnson & Johnson 1994a) different learning activities are prescribed, however, this may not be sufficient. If learners do not know, for example, how to argue with each other, they need explanations, demonstrations, and training in advance – and only afterwards can they apply this form of activity successfully. Generally, it may be appropriate to train students in the competencies necessary to apply specific learning activities. These competencies then will be differentiated and consolidated by using the prescribed strategies during cooperative learning. Further support comes from reflecting on and evaluating how the learning activities were applied.

Reflection and Evaluation of Learning Activities

Cohen (1994) stated that reflecting on learning processes and the social or methodological competencies involved is highly important for the enhancement of academic achievement. Learning journals or learning diaries, often combined with selected examples of a student's work in a portfolio style, are excellent ways of initiating reflection on one's personal process of learning. They may also lead to deeper processing and longer lasting retention of the content of learning (Renkl et al. 2004). Teachers receive diagnostic information about learning processes, difficulties, and outcomes, which they can use again in their teaching (Uerdingen 2002). Learning processes should not only be reflected individually, but should also be discussed in learning dyads, small groups, and with the whole class to improve learning.

Beck et al. (1997) described an approach that contains different forms of reflection on an individual and a social level. Students first get the chance to observe a model using the strategies that are to be learned. During learning the students write down their reflections related to learning in their journals. They also discuss their experiences in learning dyads and in the whole class. Another fast and easy method is to use rating-scales on which learners assess how they worked together and what they would like to change (Huber 1987). In groups that work together for a longer time it is especially important to use some kind of evaluation to recognize problems early and to support self-regulation of group processes. Reflection and evaluation of learning activities are important components of structuring group interactions. Additionally, these supportive approaches offer rich opportunities for teachers to obtain insight into what is working well and what needs to be changed during learning in small groups.

Modification of Subjective Perceptions of Competence

In small group learning a problem occurs when learners with higher social status participate more frequently in group activities and, thus, have more opportunities to learn. Neglecting lower status members may curb not only their achievement but also the achievement of all members because even potentially important contributions of members with lower status can be lost (Cohen 1993). Therefore, Cohen et al. (1994) introduced exercises to modify perceived competencies by emphasizing that a broad spectrum of competencies (i.e., the contribution of all group members) is necessary to cope with a learning task. Cohen demonstrated that learners with high and low status show comparable amounts of participation after such an intervention, although learners with higher status still offer more help.

6.5 Individual Organization of Learning in Small Groups

Among the unexpected experiences of teachers who implemented cooperative learning at various educational levels are disapproving reactions of at least some of their students. Generally, these students want to know why the teacher does not continue to provide them with the curricular contents but requires that they find out about it in cooperation with some classmates on their own.

These reactions are surprising to many teachers because the organization of learning and instruction is often based on the general hypothesis that all learners are motivated to approach a task if it creates cognitive controversy and gets the learners involved in a process of resolving uncertainties about their environment and/or themselves. Therefore, learning teams should provide excellent conditions for learning, especially if their members are grouped heterogeneously. Sorrentino and Short (1986) showed in their work on uncertainty-versus certainty-orientation that there are indeed persons who are highly motivated to learn from and incorporate new information in situations where uncertainty about the environment and the self is predominant. However, not everyone appreciates controversial social situations as a challenge; there are people who try to avoid the uncertainties of interpersonal controversy that might confront them with new or potentially inconsistent information, even if it is focused on problems of subject matter (see Sorrentino & Hewitt 1984; Sorrentino & Short 1986).

What difference do these differing individual orientations make in cooperative learning? Based on concepts of learning as a social-cognitive process we assume that cooperation in small groups promotes active learning (Stern & Huber 1997) because team members together create and share more ideas and have to consider carefully their various opinions and suggestions to reach a group decision. The greater variety of ideas and suggestions presented as compared to individual learning offers more alternatives in processes of decision-making. Examples include decisions as to what content should be analyzed, which suggested solutions should be tested, or which learning strategies should be applied to solve a given task. More alternatives will also accentuate the impact of individual differences in tolerance of uncertainty on processes and results of learning. Discussion, dispute, and argumentation on the one hand are necessary means of coping with this situation, while on the other hand tolerance of ambiguity is required from each of the members.

In a series of studies, we demonstrated that uncertainty-oriented students' epistemic curiosity is aroused by ambiguous aspects (e.g., opportunities for discovering something new, controversial discussion topics or differing points of view) of instructional settings, while certainty-oriented students are not only not attracted by learning arrangements of the "curiosity" or "debate" type, but also tend to prefer clearly structured situations including guidance by teachers (Huber et al. 1992). Most importantly, we also found that uncertainty-oriented students achieved more during team interactions than their certainty-oriented classmates. Kempas (1994) reported similar findings for teachers of adult learners in an in-service training. However, we should keep in mind that individual uncertainty-versus certainty-orientation will lead to differences in learning behavior and achievement *only* if the learning situation is characterized by uncertainties.

Consequently, differences in individual orientation should not make a difference in situations of individual learning but particularly in situations of cooperative learning. This was shown clearly in a study (Huber et al. 1995) of 209 students of all 8th grade classrooms in two high schools (Gymnasien). Individual uncertainty-orientation versus certainty-orientation was assessed with a 15-item rating scale (Dalbert 1992). Based on these results, we identified in each classroom three clearly uncertainty-oriented students and three clearly certainty-oriented students.

They were confronted individually and in homogeneous groups of three others with the task of preparing an oral presentation about "Our life in 10 years" (subject matter area: German) – first individually, and then they had to compare their ideas and prepare a group presentation. The students' thinking aloud (individual situation) and interactions (team situation) were videotaped and analyzed supported by the software tool AQUAD (Huber & Gürtler 2004). There was no difference in ability between uncertainty-and certainty-oriented students.

Categories of analysis were the numbers of suggested, corrected, repeated, questioned, and finally accepted (i.e., finally written down in a list of possible contents) alternative topics for the oral presentation as well as the frequencies of positive and negative evaluations of alternatives, and the justifications for accepted and rejected alternatives presented. For the analysis of team situations the categories of evaluation and justification were put together into two broader concepts of discussions *in favor of* an alternative and discussions *against* an alternative.

The results showed that except for the number of justifications provided for accepting an alternative there were no significant differences between uncertainty-oriented and certainty-oriented students in the situation of individual learning. However, as soon as the same students had to share their ideas and come to terms with each other in cooperative teams, the picture changed dramatically. Groups of uncertainty-oriented students produced on average 49 independent ideas while groups of certainty-oriented students produced only about 31. Members of uncertainty-oriented groups asked questions – which usually point out unclear or ambiguous aspects in a discussion – about seven times more frequently (arithmetic mean: 8.0 versus 1.2 questions) than members of certainty-oriented groups. In groups composed of uncertainty-oriented members the final list of topics for the presentation was much richer (27 versus 18 ideas) and based on more thorough debates proposing (56 versus 32 arguments) and opposing (40 versus 17 arguments) the suggested alternatives. All of these frequency differences yielded significant Mann-Whitney's U-test results.

In summary, the analysis of decision-making showed almost no differences between uncertainty-oriented and certainty-oriented students when working individually although there were very important differences when working cooperatively. Above all, the groups differed significantly in their discussions about those ideas, which they finally decided to accept. The results show that uncertainty-oriented students profit from opportunities to cooperate, while certainty-oriented students seem to be disadvantaged.

It is of interest that the differences in decision-making between uncertainty-oriented and certainty-oriented students faded with more structured learning tasks – just as the theory of uncertainty tolerance suggests. Thus, we found the most remarkable differences in the unstructured task in German (preparing for an oral presentation) described above, only minor differences in more structured tasks in Social Science, and no differences in highly structured mathematical tasks. This finding suggests that structuring cooperative learning may promote thinking and learning for all students, independent of their individual uncertainty- or certainty-orientation.

6.6   Structuring Interactions by Combining Methods of Teaching/Learning

6.6.1   The Sandwich Principle of Teaching

The Sandwich principle of teaching (Wahl 2005) provides systematically alternative phases of teacher-centered and autonomous learning. During teacher-centered phases teachers provide an overview on how the parts of a specific topic of subject matter are interconnected. These phases are characterized by teacher input on a general level. During the autonomous learning phases, learners get the chance to deal with the learning subject on their own, in pairs or in small groups. The success of autonomous learning phases depends on the mode and degree to which learning is structured.

The approaches to structuring learning must match the demands of the learning goals and the knowledge domain as well as the learners' available competencies. For learners with low previous knowledge, low intellectual abilities, and low competencies the Sandwich layers need to be thinner than for learners with more prerequisites (Gerbig & Gerbig-Calcagni 1998), that is, there must be more and shorter alternations of different phases. The Sandwich principle is a way of reconciling the needs of learners for orientation and structure on the one hand and for active, autonomous construction of their own system of knowledge on the other hand. A detailed example of a Sandwich structure of teaching and learning is shown in the following description of the "self-organized learning in teams."

6.6.2   Self-Organized Learning (SOL) in Teams

Endeavors to promote not only academic learning, but also the development of key qualifications in classrooms—like team competence, communication skills, and personal initiative—have to cope with contradictions between prevailing procedures within the majority of educational institutions on the one hand and the inherent logic of social learning goals on the other. Many schools, particularly at the secondary level "look at the world in 'mono'cultural, egocentric and linear ways," while the social learning perspective in education builds upon "interaction, reciprocity, interdependence, dialogue, and mutual responsibility" (Rey 1996, p. 5). Cooperative learning promises to promote social learning without neglecting academic goals.

Herold and Landherr, at that time Gymnasium teachers in 1995, developed a new organizational framework initially called the "fractal organization of teaching and learning," which promised to meet the demands of modern conceptions of active learning (self-regulatory competencies; Stern & Huber 1997), demands of employers (action competencies), and demands of an information society (media competencies). A general aim was to design a model for implementation in the *gymnasiale Oberstufe* (grades 11–13), but one that was useful also in vocational schools and in adult education (Herold & Landherr 2001; Herold et al. 1997).

To implement this model all students of the same grade (in the case of our study, grade 12) were assigned to three "learning islands." These units contain those subject matter areas, which offer optimal opportunities for creating linkages from the point of view of a particular overlapping theme. In our study, the students learned for six weeks about the topic of Energy on three learning islands for two weeks each under the perspectives of natural sciences/mathematics, languages, and social sciences.

The students took turns as inhabitants of each of the learning islands. In a modified version of Jigsaw learning, each student had to complete the assignments of one of the disciplines represented on the learning island; thus he or she became an expert in this particular subject matter area. Other students on the same learning island acquired expertise for the other subject matter areas. Later, back in their basic teams they shared their expert knowledge, teaching each other and learning from each other with increasing self-responsibility. The teachers were available during this phase of learning as moderators of group dynamics or learning procedures and, if necessary, as the real experts in their particular subject matter domain. This organizational principle was realized on all levels of the teaching/learning system, from structuring a school's complete grade level according to learning islands, breaking them down into expert groups, teams, and finally individual learners (see Fig. 6.1).

Activities in each of the three phases were structured identically: Teachers and students prepared the organization of their activities, that is, students were assigned to learning islands (basic groups) and subject matter domains (expert groups) for the next 10 days. The teachers then started to present an overview on the content of this phase.

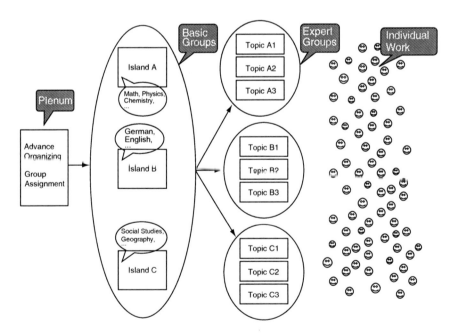

Fig. 6.1 Self-organized learning (SOL; Herold & Landherr 2001)

This introduction served as an advance organizer (Ausubel 1974) and accentuated the linkages between formerly – according to the constraints of traditional teaching and learning in schools – isolated subject matter areas. Afterwards the students met in their expert groups to work together on their assignments and to become experts in their particular field. Next day the students returned to their basic groups and shared their newly acquired knowledge. They applied a variety of communicative techniques to ensure that all group members really understood what they were supposed to learn. This structure was repeated for the following two days with new content. The sixth and seventh day were dedicated to discussion, enrichment and training of what had been learned. The eighth day focused on repetition and clarification of linkages between different aspects of the material and on the ninth day, all students had to pass a test of all aspects and their interrelations learned during the last days. The students and the teachers met the following day (the last of this learning phase) in an "island coffee shop" to share their experiences, problems, achievements, and success. This was an excellent occasion for presentations of all kinds.

For the second and third phase each student moved to another island to master new aspects of the general topic related to other subject matter domains. Over the time of the study, the teachers gave the students increasing degrees of freedom for organizing their work and applying particular learning methods.

Observations during team work and interviews with selected teachers and students as well as standardized self-report instruments show that the model was accepted widely both by students and teachers. For the observation of classroom events during activities in expert groups and base groups we applied a 210-item observation protocol developed for a comparative study of active learning in eight OECD countries (Stern & Huber 1997). Interestingly, the majority of students were enthusiastic about the possibilities of exchanging their ideas independently, mutually tackling problems, and caring for each others' learning. There were some students and some teachers who seemed to be overwhelmed by the complexity of the new learning/teaching situations. They expressed their wish to return to the traditional ways of schooling as soon as possible either overtly by complaining or covertly by not tuning into the needs of other students or teachers.

The approach worked well during the expert phases, that is, when the students met in expert groups dedicated to mastering a particular assignment and working together to become experts in their particular field. They readily gave explanations to each other, and they freely expressed any misunderstandings and asked for more explanations. However, later back in their base groups, students adopted familiar roles – as experts in the teacher's role as well as in the learners' role. More precisely, the experts tried to mediate their knowledge in the familiar style of teacher-centered, frontal lessons, while the other students listened and took notes. Thus, they had only a few chances to experience the challenge of coming to terms with varying understandings and to gain from the opportunity to compare, question, and integrate different perspectives, opinions, and solutions. The difference between these two phases of learning may be due to the fact that the teachers more often stimulated group activities within expert sessions than within base group sessions. In addition, there was a difference in how the model was implemented in the three participating schools. In one school students worked less cooperatively during the base group sessions than students in the other two schools, where the teachers were more in control in these schools.

An initial reaction was to supplement the model with additional layers to the didactic sandwich, which gives more structure to processes of exchanging ideas and sharing knowledge, above all in base groups. Therefore, the teachers received advice on how to differentiate the activities according to different demands of subject matter. For instance, in math, they should take more responsibility for introducing a new topic, but they should delegate the responsibility for applying new knowledge in phases of practice and problem-solving to student teams. Thus, elements of Slavin's (1986) Student Teams – Achievement Divisions were integrated into the current model. Analogically, features of group investigation (Sharan & Sharan 1992) were combined to promote the language parts of the curriculum. Most important, however, was better preparation of students for the challenges waiting for them in the weeks of intervention. Therefore, the students participating in the next school year received specific training in two areas: summarizing their knowledge and presenting it in their own words to their team-mates to prevent traditional lecturing by experts in base groups, and formulating precise questions and giving adequate answers while preventing traditional lecturing.

An evaluation five years later comparing 373 students from 6 schools, where in two schools each teachers had five years of experience with the model, applied it for the first time, or taught in the traditional manner, demonstrated both the advantages over regular classrooms instruction and the importance of teacher experience. As examples we quote here the effects of six weeks of active learning in the intervention environment on availability of learning strategies (see Fig. 6.2) and on achievement pressure (see Fig. 6.3), which the intervention students thought was significantly reduced as compared to students in control schools.

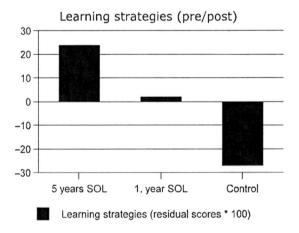

Fig. 6.2 Availability of learning strategies

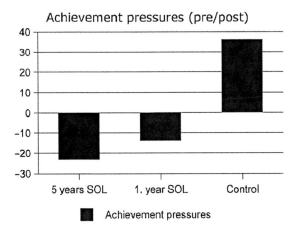

Fig. 6.3 Achievement pressures

Because of differences in the pre-tests we used residual gain scores resulting from pre-to post-test regression analysis as indicators of changes over time. The impact of teachers' experience in structuring the SOL environment for their students is obvious. While the model was a first for all students, the teachers at two schools already had applied this cooperative learning arrangement for five years, whereas the teachers at the other two schools had implemented the intervention for the first time. In regard to the problems with students' individual organization for approaching/avoiding ambiguous situations we found that due to the sandwich structure of the model, certainty-oriented students had ample opportunities to prepare for cooperative interactions and there were no differences in results between uncertainty-oriented and certainty-oriented students.

6.7 Recommendations for Teachers and Researchers

Although we still need to know a lot more about which type of didactical support of learning in small groups is useful for which learning goal, knowledge domain, and individual prerequisites of learners, it is obvious that external, task-centered organization is a necessary, but by no means a sufficient condition for successful cooperative learning. Distinguishing between cooperative and collaborative learning, that is, between breaking down a learning task into different parts for different learners and putting the results together cooperatively versus working together at a common task, may help to draw the attention to interaction processes in small groups. Since differentiating between cooperation and collaboration is linked to distinguishing partial- versus whole-tasks, the predominance of product criteria in school settings may be reinforced.

Therefore, we strongly recommend the underlining of critical aspects of internal organization and individual prerequisites when cooperative learning is implemented. It should be apparent that if we want learners to interact effectively in small groups it is necessary to prescribe appropriate learning activities and in many cases to train students in advance in using those activities adequately. Also in the domain of internal organization we should not debate the advantages of social organization versus task organization or vice versa but conceive of both approaches to structuring learning in small groups as mutually dependent.

If social conditions of learning are neglected, cooperative methods involving task specialization in particular lead only to sub-optimal effects. Task specialization should be complemented by supporting social interaction of group members by prescribing interaction models, by training social interaction in advance, by reflecting on interaction experiences during and/or after group sessions, or by modifying the mutual social perception (in terms of social status, prestige, etc.) of group members. The WELL methods of cooperative learning offer reliable and feasible examples of how to structure group interactions for various situations of learning in small groups.

We want to highlight the importance of reflection processes for cooperative learning. If we intend to find out how effective the learning activities are, it is sensible to implement some routines of reflection and evaluation of these activities. Learners may keep a learning journal or fill in rating-scales about their learning experiences and discuss their opinions or experiences in dyads, small groups or within the whole class. Reflection on individual learning processes takes some time, but it is a very efficient way for teachers to get feedback on what to change in their teaching – and it helps learners to establish competencies of self-regulation. Formulated more concretely, promising environments for learning in small groups should offer structures that not only promote knowledge acquisition but also foster methodological, social, and personal competencies. They provide an environment in which learners can fulfill their basic needs for competence, autonomy, and relatedness (Deci & Ryan 1985, 2002) and lead to intrinsically motivated learning. They allow participants to reduce their prejudices and build friendships across the borders of gender and ethnicity.

These functions of feedback imply, however, that we rethink generally both the role and procedures of assessment in schools, and particularly their impact on cooperative learning environments As long as the prevailing methods of assessment are focused on cognitive achievements, and noncognitive goals like social, methodological and personal competencies as well as process data about learning are ignored, it seems unlikely that teachers and learners will change their habits of teaching and learning.

Implementing learning in small groups needs careful consideration. Not only must consideration be given to how to structure learning tasks but consideration must also be given to how the conditions and processes that enhance social interaction between team mates can be promoted. In addition, the role of the teachers in general and specifically the optimal didactic placement of their activities has to be reconsidered. The "didactical Sandwich" as realized in WELL approaches and the model of teaching and learning appear as promising solutions of this problem.

Finally, the exclusive role of individually centered assessment procedures apparently is obsolete in cooperative environments of teaching and learning. Implementing cooperative learning means more than applying some methods of social interaction in classrooms, but demands instead a comprehensive approach of restructuring routines of teaching and learning in schools.

References

Andriessen, J. E. B., Coirier, P., Roos, L., Passerault, J. M., & Bert-Erboul, J. M. (1996). Thematic and structural planning in constrained argumentative text production. In H. Van den Bergh, G. Rijlaarsdam & M. Couzijn (Eds.), *Theories, models and methodology in writing research* (pp. 237–251). Amsterdam: University Press.

Aronson, E., Blaney, N., Stephan, G., Sikes, J., & Snapp, M. (1978). *The Jigsaw classroom.* Beverly Hills: Sage.

Aronson, E., Wilson, T. D., & Akert, R. M. (2004). *Sozialpsychologie* [Social psychology] (4th revised edn.). München: Pearson Studium.

Ausubel, D. P. (1974). *Psychologie des Unterrichts* [*Psychology of teaching*]. Weinheim: Beltz.

Beck, E., Guldimann, T., & Zutavern, M. (1997). Eigenständiges Lernen verstehen und fördern [Understanding and promoting self-regulated learning]. In K. Reusser & M. Reusser-Weyeneth (Eds.), *Verstehen: psychologischer Prozess und didaktische Aufgabe* [*Understanding: psychological process and didactic task*] (pp. 207–225). Bern: Huber.

Cohen, E. G. (1993). Bedingungen für kooperative Kleingruppen [Conditions for cooperating small groups]. In G. L. Huber (Ed.), *Neue Perspektiven der Kooperation* [*New perspectives of cooperation*] (S. 45–53). Hohengehren: Schneider Verlag.

Cohen, E. G. (1994). Restructuring the classroom: Conditions for productive small groups. *Review of Educational Research, 64,* 1–35.

Cohen, E. G., Lotan, R. A., Whitcomb, J. A., Balderrama, M. V., Cossey, R., & Swanson, P. E. (1994). Complex instruction: Higher-order thinking in heterogeneous classrooms. In S. Sharan (Ed.), *Handbook of cooperative learning methods* (pp. 82–96). Westport, CT: Greenwood Press.

Dalbert, C. (1992). Der Glaube an die gerechte Welt: Differenzierung und Validierung eines Konstrukts [The belief in a Just World: Differentiation and validation of a construct]. *Zeitschrift für Sozialpsychologie, 23,* 268–276.

Deci, E. L. & Ryan, R. M. (1985). *Intrinsic motivation and self-determination in human behavior.* New York: Plenum Press.

Deci, E. L. & Ryan, R. M. (Eds.) (2002). *Handbook of self-determination research* (pp. 3–36). Rochester: The University of Rochester Press.

Hall, R. H., Dansereau, D. F., O'Donnell, A. M., & Skaggs, L. P. (1989). The effect of textual errors on dyadic and individual learning. *Journal of Reading Behavior, 21,* 127–140.

Hall, R. H., Rocklin, T. R., Dansereau, D. F., Skaggs, L. P., O'Donnell, A. M., Lambiotte, J. G., & Young, M. D. (1988). The role of individual differences in the learning of technical material. *Journal of Educational Psychology, 80,* 172–178.

Hattie, J., Biggs, J., & Purdie, N. (1996). Effects of learning skills interventions on student learning: a meta-analysis. *Review of Educational Research, 66,* 99–136.

von Hentig, H. (2004). *Einführung in den Bildungsplan 2004.* [Introduction to the curriculum 2004] Found on Sept. 08, 2005, under http://www.bildung-staerkt-menschen.de/service/downloads/Sonstiges/Einfuehrung_BP.pdf.

Herold, M., & Landherr, B. (2001). SOL Selbstorganisiertes Lernen: ein systemischer Ansatz für Unterricht [SOL Self-organized learning: a systematic approach for the classroom]. Baltmannsweiler: Schneider-Verlag Hohengehren.

Herold, M., Landherr, B., & Huber, G. L. (1997). *Fraktale Lernorganisation in der gymnasialen Oberstufe: Ergebnisse eines Schulversuchs* [*Fractal organisation of learning in the gymnasiale Oberstufe: Results of a study in schools*]. Presentation at the 6th conference of the Fachgruppe Pädagogische Psychologie/Deutsche Gesellschaft für Psychologie, Frankfurt am Main.

Hoek, D., van den Eden, P., & Terwel, J. (1999). The effects of integrated social and cognitive strategy instruction on the mathematics achievement in secondary education. *Learning and Instruction, 9*, 427–448.

Huber, A. (1999). *Bedingungen effektiven Lernens in Kleingruppen unter besonderer Berücksichtigung der Rolle von Lernskripten* [*Conditions of effective learning in small groups in particular consideration of learning scripts*]. Schwangau: Ingeborg Huber Verlag.

Huber, A. A. (2004a). Die Partnerpuzzlemethode [The partner-puzzle method]. In A. A. Huber (Hrsg.), *Kooperatives Lernen – Kein Problem. Effektive Methoden der Partner-und Gruppenarbeit* [*Cooperative learning – no problem. Effective methods of working in pairs and groups*] (S.39–48). Leipzig: Ernst Klett Schulbuchverlag.

Huber, A. A. (2004b). Die Strukturierte Kontroverse [The structured controversy]. In A. A. Huber (Hrsg.), *Kooperatives Lernen – kein Problem. Effektive Methoden der Partner-und Gruppenarbeit* [*Cooperative learning – no problem. Effective methods of working in pairs and groups*] (S.80–85). Leipzig: Ernst Klett Schulbuchverlag.

Huber, A. A., Konrad, K., & Wahl, D. (2001). Lernen durch wechselseitiges Lehren [Learning by mutual teaching]. *Pädagogisches Handeln, 5* (2), 33–46.

Huber, A. A. (2006). *Wechselseitiges Lehren und Lernen als spezielle Form Kooperativen Lernens* [Mutual teaching and learning as special version of cooperative learning]. Unpublished Habilitation thesis. Weingarten: Educational University Weingarten.

Huber, G. L. (1987). Kooperatives Lernen: Theoretische und praktische Herausforderung für die Pädagogische Psychologie [Cooperative learning: Theoretical and practical challenge for Educational Psychology]. *Zeitschrift für Entwicklungspsychologie und Pädagogische Psychologie, 19*, 340–362.

Huber, G. L. (2004). Die Praxis macht den Unterschied. Ergebnisse einer vergleichenden Evaluation [Practice makes a difference. Results of a comparative evaluation]. Presentation in a training course for SOL teachers, Berlin.

Huber, G. L., & Gürtler, L. (2004). AQUAD Six: *Manual for the analysis of qualitative data*. Tübingen: Ingeborg Huber Verlag.

Huber, G. L., Scholz, G., Kahlert, M., Schmidt, M., Standke, C., & Stauche, H. (1995). *Entscheidungsprozesse von Schülern in Lernsituationen* [Decision processes of students in learning situations]. Abschlußbericht für die Deutsche Forschungsgemeinschaft über das Projekt Hu348-8/1 und Scho484-1/1. Universität Tübingen und Universität Jena.

Huber, G. L., Sorrentino, R. M., Davidson, M. A., Eppler, R., & Roth, J. W. H. (1992). Uncertainty orientation and cooperative learning: Individual differences within and across cultures. *Learning and Individual Differences, 4*, 1–24.

Johnson, D. W., & Johnson, R. T. (1994b). Learning together. In S. Sharan (Ed.), *Handbook of cooperative learning methods* (pp. 51–65). Westport, Connecticut: Greenwood Press.

Kagan, S. (1989/90). The structural approach to cooperative learning. *Educational Leadership, 47*, 12–15.

Kempas, G. (1994). *Lehren lernen. Auswirkungen interpersoneller Differenzen auf die Lernprozesse Lehrender* [Learning how to teach. Effects of interpersonal differences on learning processes of teachers]. Unpublished doctoral thesis, University of Tübingen.

King, A. (1989). Effects of self-questioning training on college students' comprehension of lectures. *Contemporary Educational Psychology, 14*, 366–381.

King, A. (1990). Enhancing peer interaction and learning in the classroom through reciprocal questioning. *American Educational Research Journal, 27*, 664–687.

King, A. (1991). Improving lecture conprehension: Effects of a metacognitive stategy. *Applied Cognitive Psychology, 5*, 331–346.

King, A., & Rosenshine, B. (1993). Effects of guided cooperative questioning on childrens knowledge construction. *Journal of Experimental Education, 61*, 127–148.

McDonald, B. A., Larson, C. O., Dansereau, D. F., & Spurlin, J. E. (1985). Cooperative learning: Impact on acquisition of knowledge and skills. *Contemporary Educational Psychology, 10*, 369–377.

O'Donnell, A. M. & Dansereau, D. F. (1992). Scripted cooperation in student dyads: A method for analyzing and enhancing academic learning and performance. In R. Hertz-Lazarowitz & N. Miller (Eds.), *Interaction in cooperative groups: The theoretical anatomy of group learning* (pp. 120–141). New York: Cambridge University Press.

O'Donnell, A. M., Dansereau, D. F., Hythecker, V. I., Larson, C. O., Rocklin, T. R., Lambiotte, J. G., & Young, M. D. (1986). The effects of monitoring on cooperative learning. *Journal of Experimental Education, 54*, 169–173.

Renkl, A., Nückles, M., Schwonke, R., Berthold, K., & Hauser, S. (2004). Lerntagebücher als Medium selbstgesteuerten Lernens: Theoretischer Hintergrund, empirische Befunde, praktische Entwicklungen [Learning diaries as a means of self-regulated learning: Theoretical background, empirical findings, practical developments]. In M. Wosnitza, A. Frey & R. S. Jäger (Eds.), *Lernprozess, Lernumgebung und Lerndiagnostik. Wissenschaftliche Beiträge zum Lernen im 21. Jahrhundert* [Learning process, learning environment, and diagnostics of learning. Scientific contributions to learning in the 21st century] (pp. 101–116). Landau: Verlag Empirische Pädagogik.

Reusser, K. (2001). Unterricht zwischen Wissensvermittlung und Lernen lernen. Alte Sackgassen und neue Wege in der Bearbeitung eines pädagogischen Jahrhundert problems [Teaching between transmission of knowledge and learning to learn. Well-known dead ends and new ways to elaborate on an educational problem of the century]. In C. Finkbeiner & G. W. Schnaitmann (Eds.), *Lehren und Lernen im Kontext empirischer Forschung und Fachdidaktik* [Teaching and learning in the context of empirical research and special didactics] (pp. 106–140). Donauwörth: Auer Verlag.

Rey, M. (1996). Between memory and history. A word about intercultural education. *The European Journal of Intercultural Studies, 7*, 3–10.

Roschelle, J. & Teasley, S. (1995). The construction of shared knowledge in collaborative problem solving. In O'Malley, C. E. (Ed.), *Computer supported collaborative learning* (pp. 69–97). Heidelberg: Springer.

Rotering-Steinberg, S. & von Kügelgen, T. (1986). Ergebnisse einer schriftlichen Befragung zum Gruppenunterricht [Results of a survey on group learning]. *Erziehungswissenschaft - Erziehungspraxis, 2*, 26–91.

Rotering-Steinberg, S. (2000): Untersuchungen zum Sozialen Lernen in Schulen [Studies on social learning in schools]. In C. Dalbert & E. J. Brunner, (Eds.): *Handlungsleitende Kognitionen in der Pädagogischen Praxis* [Action-guiding cognitions in educational practice] (pp. 119–137). Baltmannsweiler: Schneider-Verlag Hohengehren.

Schulgesetz für das Land Baden-Württemberg (Fassung vom 1.4.2004) [School law for the Land Baden-Württemberg]. Found on Sept. 08, 2005, under http://www.leu.bw.schule.de/bild/SchG.pdf

Sharan, Y. & Sharan S. (1992). *Expanding cooperative learning through group investigation.* New York: Teachers' College Press, Columbia University.

Slavin, R. E. (1986). *Using student team learning* (3rd edn.). Baltimore, MD: The Johns Hopkins University.

Slavin, R.E. (1995a). *Cooperative learning: Theory, research, and practice* (2nd edn.). Boston: Allyn & Bacon.

Slavin, R. E. (1995b). *Research on cooperative learning and achievement: What we know, what we need to know?* Baltimore: Center for Research on the Education of Students Placed at Risk, Johns Hopkins University.

Sorrentino, R. M., & Hewitt, E. C. (1984). The uncertainty-reducing properties of achievement tasks revisited. *Journal of Personality and Social Psychology, 47*, 884–899.

Sorrentino, R. M., & Short, J.-A. C. (1986). Uncertainty orientation, motivation, and cognition. In R. M. Sorrentino, & E. C. Higgins (Eds.), *The handbook of motivation and cognition: Foundations of social behavior* (pp. 379–403). New York: Guilford.

Uerdingen, M. (2002). Das Lerntagebuch. Ein Medium zur Begleitung und Unterstützung von Lernprozessen [The learning diary. A medium to accompany and support learning processes]. *Grundschule, 3*, 43–44.

Wahl, D. (2004a). Das Lerntempoduett [The learning speed duet]. In A. A. Huber (Hrsg.), *Kooperatives Lernen—kein Problem. Effektive Methoden der Partner- und Gruppenarbeit [Cooperative learning—no problem. Effective methods of working in pairs and groups]* (S. 58–68). Leipzig: Ernst Klett Schulbuchverlag.

Wahl, D. (2004b). Das Partner-und Gruppeninterview [The partner- and group-interview]. In A. A. Huber (Hrsg.), *Kooperatives Lernen – kein Problem. Effektive Methoden der Partner- und Gruppenarbeit [Cooperative learning—no problem. Effective methods of working in pairs and groups]* (S. 69–75). Leipzig: Ernst Klett Schulbuchverlag.

Wahl, D. (2004c). Das Multiinterview als spezielle Variante des Partner-und Gruppen-interviews [The multi-interview as specific variation of the partner- and group-interview]. In A. A. Huber (Hrsg.), *Kooperatives Lernen – kein Problem. Effektive Methoden der Partner-und Gruppenarbeit [Cooperative learning—no problem. Effective methods of working in pairs and groups]* (S. 76–79). Leipzig: Ernst Klett Schulbuchverlag.

Wahl, D. (2005). *Lernumgebungen erfolgreich gestalten. Wirksame Wege vom trägen Wissen zum kompetenten Handeln in Erwachsenenbildung, Hochschuldidaktik und Unterricht* [Designing learning environments successfully. Effective ways from inert knowledge to competent action in adult education, university didactics, and teaching]. Bad Heilbrunn: Klinkhardt Verlag.

Chapter 7
Feedback and Reflection to Promote Student Participation in Computer Supported Collaborative Learning: A Multiple Case Study

Fleur Prinsen, Jan Terwel, Monique Volman, and Marieke Fakkert

Abstract This chapter describes a multiple case study in Computer Supported Collaborative Learning (CSCL). Feedback and reflection were components in a program in which 5th grade students worked with CSCL in small groups. The feedback and reflection was focused on improving the interaction processes of the students, especially on supporting elaborative contributions in the groups. The interaction processes in two groups were closely followed and analysed, and portrayed through examples. The main research question was: How do interaction processes between students develop within a learning environment in which feedback by the researcher/teacher on elaboration is provided and student reflection on elaboration is encouraged? We expected that feedback and reflection about the quality of the participation, elaboration in particular, would in the initial stages result in better quality participation and more elaborated contributions of the students later on in the process. Looking at the patterns in the interactions over the subsequent lessons, we may conclude that our hypothesis was confirmed. However, the results show significant differences in the quality of participation between individual students and between the two case groups which appear to be related to students' characteristics and group composition, that is, ability and sociocultural background. The implications for teaching are discussed.

7.1   Introduction

Computer Supported Collaborative Learning (CSCL) is aimed at facilitating knowledge sharing and at enhancing the interaction of students engaged in group work. Research shows that CSCL is an activating and motivating arrangement for learning, but an often-heard complaint is that the interactions of students working in CSCL remain shallow (Fischer & Ostwald 2002; Stahl 1999).

In most CSCL designs the teacher plays a central role when it comes to shaping the educational context. The teacher clarifies the learning goals, formulates the task (or helps to formulate it), and suggests what resources can be used to complete the task. The teacher also provides some form of feedback on the process or the completion of the task. Although a great deal of research has focused on the interaction between students, little is known about the effects of teachers' feedback concerning the quality of the interaction in cooperative learning environments (Ross & Rolheiser 2003).

Collaboration in itself is neither effective nor ineffective. It works under certain conditions (Terwel 2003). Theoretical and empirical evidence concerning some of these conditions has led us to design and investigate a learning environment from a sociocultural perspective which will be described later in this chapter.

The main research question was: How do interaction processes between students develop within a learning environment in which feedback by the researcher/teacher is provided and student reflection is fostered? In answering this question we will look, in particular, at the development of the participation of the group and the individuals in the group with respect to:

1. their use of the participation-supporting features of the cscl program (program affordances);
2. their active participation (amount of contributions and number of words per message); and
3. their provision of elaborative contributions.

We will relate these participation measures to student characteristics, the feedback provided, the students' reflections on this feedback and the intentions they express for improving their participation for the upcoming lesson.

This chapter is structured as follows. Firstly, the theoretical background will be described, resulting in the presentation of the basic model guiding the study. Secondly, an outline of the educational program will be presented and the implementation of the program will be described. Thirdly, a section will be devoted to the research design and methods, reporting on the instruments used and the procedure followed. In the results section of the chapter the feedback and interaction processes in the student groups will be described and analysed. The chapter closes with conclusions, discussions, and some suggestions for further research.

7.2   Theoretical Background

CSCL is based on a combination of theoretical notions and strategies developed in the field of cooperative learning and the use of the computer as a medium for supporting communication. Although CSCL may be regarded as a new approach, it is important to recognise the theoretical roots of CSCL and to learn from the vast body of knowledge from theories and research in the field of cooperative learning, in particular, the teacher's role in enhancing active participation of all students (Ross & Rolheiser 2003).

Most cooperative learning theories emphasise the importance of active participation, interdependence, verbalising thoughts, resource sharing, giving and receiving high-level elaborations, and inducing socio-cognitive conflicts as the primary mechanisms for learning and development. In stimulating these processes the role of the teacher in cooperative learning is pivotal. Providing feedback to the students is one of the essentials of cooperative learning and of CSCL. What do we know from the field of cooperative learning about the role of the teacher and more specific about monitoring, feedback, reflection and assessment? In the following we will address four, partly overlapping, theoretical perspectives.

First, we mention the motivational theory of Slavin. In this theory two strategies are central: individual accountability and group reward (Slavin 1995). If both individual students and subgroups are assessed and rewarded, participation and resource sharing within cooperative groups will be fostered and consequently learning will occur. Slavin's motivational theory leans heavily on theories of management and direct instruction in which the reward structure plays a central role.

Second, the interdependence theory of Johnson and Johnson (1994) also contains valuable information about the role of the teacher (see chapter 1). Effective cooperative learning arrangements should make students interdependent through, for example, the provision of assignments and problems that can only be solved when students work together. To reach a good result the students have to be aware that they are dependent on each other. Group evaluation on common group goals can aid the development of interdependence.

The teacher's role in stimulating reflection is another aspect of this theory that warrants attention. Reflection functions to review how well group members are functioning and how to improve the work processes. Only a small number of research studies have been undertaken to examine the importance of the regulation of group processes during group work (Johnson et al. 1990; Yager et al. 1996) and most were conducted in face-to-face contexts. We found two studies only, one by Ulicsak (2004) and one by Dewiyanti (2005), which investigated the issue of regulation within a CSCL environment. There are, however, various researchers who have stressed the importance of reflection in learning processes (Bull et al. 2002; Dillenbourg & Self 1995). Reflection can be described as members' actions that are helpful or unhelpful in making decisions about what actions must be taken to reach the group's goals. These goals may be made explicit or remain implicit in the categories of evaluation.

Third, Cohen's sociological expectation states theory may be mentioned as one theory in which the role of the teacher in enhancing participation of all students is highlighted (Cohen et al. 2004; Cohen & Lotan 1995). This theory explains why some students will dominate group activities and why others are ignored even if their contribution is of value to the group. Central in this theory is the notion of status within the group. Status characteristics can be related to ability, gender, or ethnicity. High-status students will dominate the discussions and teachers can make a difference to group performance by assigning status to students who tend to be ignored and by designing assignments that require multiple abilities. Both strategies can be applied to stimulate participation of all students.

Both Cohen's and Slavin's theories address the important role of the teacher respectively by using a reward structure and by providing feedback on the social processes within the cooperating group. While both theories reveal important social aspects of fostering participation and learning in cooperative groups, they hardly address the question of how the teacher can monitor group discussions strategically aimed at collaborative knowledge building and individual learning.

We now turn to a fourth category of perspectives which may be captured under the term cognitive elaboration. In this category, special attention is given to the role of the teacher in monitoring and scaffolding the cognitive aspects of learning in groups. To put it more specifically, how can the teacher support the construction of concepts and strategies in small group discussions? Within this category of theories, the work of Webb may be mentioned (Webb & Farivar 1999), which stresses the importance of high level elaborations, such as giving and receiving explanations. In addition, Webb investigated how teachers can influence these collaborative processes in small groups.

The work of Brown and Palincsar (1989) must also be mentioned as an important perspective on guided cooperative learning and individual knowledge acquisition. The main concepts in their theory are elaboration in cooperative groups and the guiding role of the teacher. Their theory was applied to their model of *reciprocal teaching*. Under the heading of the role of conflict, Brown and Palincsar gave attention to elaboration as one of the key processes in achieving deeper understanding.

Conflict is another factor that can be seen as a catalyst of change, with explanation, elaboration, justification, warrants, and backing being ingredients in the process. The facilitating effect of cooperative learning depends on a number of key factors: the initial competence of the student, the social status and serious opposition which raises questions about her own view. However, Brown and Palincsar (1989) also mentioned that "Although conflict may be an essential trigger, it has been argued that change is more readily the result of processes of co-elaboration and co-construction"(p. 407).

Crook (1994) took a similar view and saw peer collaboration as having three cognitive benefits: articulation, conflict, and co-construction. Through peer collaboration students are challenged to make their ideas explicit and need to clearly articulate them. When students disagree in their interpretations, conflicts may arise and the students must mutually justify and defend their positions, reflecting on their own (mis)conceptions. Crook's concept of co-construction is based upon Vygotsky's (1978) belief that learning is the sharing of meaning in a social context. Students build upon each others' ideas and, thus, they co-construct (local) knowledge and a shared understanding collaboratively.

The first three perspectives described above address the social participation within cooperative groups, while the fourth category of perspectives focuses on the cognitive (elaboration) aspects of collaboration in small groups. The fifth perspective integrates social and cognitive aspects into a sociocultural theory.

Sociocultural theorists have argued that knowledge construction can be stimulated by offering opportunities to students in a relevant cultural practice. In our sociocultural perspective the notion of guided co-construction has a central place (Van Dijk et al. 2003a,b). From this perspective collaborative, reflective learning under teacher guidance is a basic pattern for the organisation of learning processes. The joint activity can be conceived of as a kind of guided co-construction or guided reinvention in which each participant can profit from cultural resources offered by the others and by materials used in the activity. These resources enable each participant to accomplish more than they could do on their own. In this way, participating in such endeavor can be seen as jointly constructing a zone of proximal development (Van Dijk et al. 2003a,b). In this study co-construction is guided by a teacher providing feedback on the way that students elaborate their contributions.

The sociocultural perspective is the theoretical background for the main concepts in our study: student characteristics, teacher feedback, student reflection, and participation. These concepts and their mutual relationships may be brought together in a model. Fig. 7.1, represents the conceptual model guiding the present study. In this model Participation is taken as the dependent variable.

Fig. 7.1 can be read as follows. Student participation is directly related to students' own resources such as ability level, sociocultural background, and prior knowledge (see the horizontal arrow). However, participation is mediated by (a) teacher's feedback and (b) individual and group reflections on performance. Teacher feedback is given on an individual and group level so that it will be related to the development of the groups' and the individual students' participation.

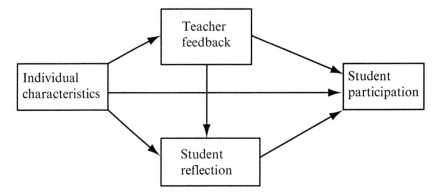

Fig. 7.1 Explanatory model for students' development

7.3 Outline and Implementation of the Program

7.3.1 Outline

Building on this theoretical and empirical evidence for the conditions under which collaboration works, we designed a specific learning environment, which will now be outlined.

We designed an educational program about nutrition and health to be implemented in a CSCL environment: the client version of Web Knowledge Forum (WKF). WKF was developed by Scardamalia and Bereiter of the Ontario Institute for Studies in Education at the University of Toronto. The WKF software provides several facilities to enhance collaboration between the users. Among them, the build-on facility (reacting to a previous note or question by building on it) and the scaffolds (to be used as sentence openers to help students formulate their initial contributions and reactions to each other) are the ones used in this implementation. They help to engage learners in collaboration on one hand and to facilitate knowledge construction on the other (see Fig. 7.2 for an example of how the discussion is displayed on the screen).

While Knowledge Forum facilitated the program by the embedded facilities, the specific curricular content, the guidance and the face-to-face interactions were also essential elements as viewed from our theoretical perspective.

The curriculum content about nutrition and health was situated in a known cultural practice: cooks collaborating in a kitchen to make decisions about what food to buy, what dishes to prepare, and how to prepare the food in a healthy manner, all within the context of a restaurant. The title of the program was "The smart chef."

The researchers conducted all lessons. In doing so they combined the researcher's role with that of developer and teacher. Students in each participating class were divided into heterogeneous groups of four, according to gender, ability, and socio-ethnic background.

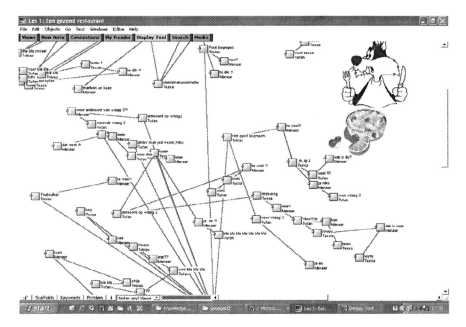

Fig. 7.2 Display of student's contributions (in Dutch language)

The program for the students consisted of an introduction lesson, 3 lessons with discussion questions and two intermediate feedback and reflection lessons. In designing the program we used a combination of face-to-face and computer-supported interaction. The reason for this, in line with the basic concept of guided co-construction, is the importance of including reflection and feedback under the guidance of the teacher that will result in a deeper understanding of the concepts, structures and strategies at stake.

7.3.2   Implementation

The Introduction Lesson

After the teacher introduced the curriculum content and general aim of the lessons to come, the students were given time to practice with the Knowledge Forum program. After this practical introduction, the students received a hand-out with the golden rules (see Table 7.1 below). The students received some time to read these rules, whereupon the teacher explained that the way students react to each other's contributions in the Knowledge Forum is very important.

The golden rules were made to help the students find the answers to the discussion questions together and in a constructive way. It was very important for the students

Table 7.1 The Golden rules

1 When you agree with someone, write down clearly what you agree on precisely
2 Provide clear answers (State why you think this or give a clarifying example)
3 Ask each other (clear) questions
4 Be sure to ask for clarification if you don't understand what is said
5 When asked, provide an explanation and be sure it is helpful to the other
6 It is all right to disagree as long as you explain why you disagree

to be clear on what they were to say to each other (Rule 1 and 2). They were to use as many words as they needed to be precise. Short messages can easily be misunderstood. The students had to make clear what part of the previous message they were reacting to, for instance by repeating the part of the sentence they did not understand (Rule 3). Instead of saying, "I don't understand", the student should say: "I don't understand what you mean by saturated fat." The teacher told the students that it is important to ask each other questions. The teacher stressed the fact that there is no such thing as a stupid question and that it is very smart to ask questions. In fact, the question is already half the answer (Rule 4). The students in the groups were obliged to answer each others questions (Rule 5). They would be evaluated on the help they gave each other. In CSCL environments it is important that students react to each other in agreeable ways, but the teacher should point out to the students that it is also important to disagree with each other sometimes (Rule 6). This is not to be disagreeable, because in providing an explanation or an argument why they disagree, the students can help clear up misunderstandings or even remove incorrect understandings. This is part of learning together. To illustrate the rules the students completed some easy assignments with examples of students reacting to each other.

The teacher explained the function of the sentence openers in the Knowledge Forum program. The ways of reacting to each other in a constructive (and elaborated) manner were scaffolded by the following sentence openers: "I think …"; "My question is …"; "That's right, because …"; "Yes, but …"; "No because …"; "Remark:…"; "Explanation:…" "What do you think?" and "An example:…".

The sentence openers mirror the golden rules in students' support for each other by providing constructive and elaborated reactions to each other. For instance, the sentence opener "No, because …" will remind students that disagreeing is okay as long as you explain why you disagree with somebody else's contribution. In the introduction lesson the teacher also pointed out other procedural tasks that support interactions, such as adding titles to the contributions that cover the domain specific content of the contribution.

The Computer Supported Lesson

In the first lesson the students read a chapter of *The Smart Chef*. This textbook covered some important ideas about nutrition and health. The students tried to imagine that they were the cooks in a particular restaurant. They had to make decisions about the purchase of ingredients, learn to read the labels, decide where to store the food, to compose healthy menus, and to then prepare it in a hygienic manner.

After the students had read a chapter (about six pages), the teacher handed out the discussion questions on paper and the students were given time to prepare the answers on their own. An example discussion question is shown below.

Example Discussion Question

You have read Chapter one of the textbook 'The Smart Chef'. Now you can find the possible answers to the question below. Fill out your answers on this sheet. Make clear sentences and write down everything carefully. Make sure you don't forget anything. After you have found as many possible answers, you go and sit down behind your computer and tell the people in your group what you've found. Perhaps they found different answers to yours. Might they be right too?

Question: Mind the Sugar

Derreck is a new chef in our restaurant. He proposes to put a new recipe on the menu. "Let's make a chocolate pudding!" he says "and then we will add a sugar coating and put a cookie on the top!" Another chef, Mary, says: "Yes, Derreck, that sounds great but it is very unhealthy. There is far too much sugar in it and all sugar is bad for you. Sugar is never good for you." Is Mary right?

The teacher told the students in advance that it is important to first prepare the answers to these questions individually, because it will make the following discussion a lot easier when they come prepared. Before the students sat at their own computers to start the group discussion in the Knowledge Forum, the teacher stressed the point that the students first had to write down their own answers, before reading and reacting to the ideas of the other students in their group. In this way a diversity of ideas would be presented as a starting point for discussion. An average group discussion behind the computer lasted 45 minutes. The students had to discuss two discussion questions in one session.

The Feedback and Reflection Lesson

In the feedback and evaluation lesson the teacher started by reading out loud the group evaluation forms in front of all the participating groups (see Table 7.2). This enabled the teacher to stress the importance of the students performing as groups and introduced a between-groups competition element. It was expected this would support the group members in becoming a real group that would actively collaborate in order to discuss in a constructive and rich manner.

After this teacher-led part of the evaluation, the students joined their group members and each group received a print-out from their own previous week's

Table 7.2 Group evaluation form

1. How was the display of the discussion organised on the screen?
2. How did the group members make use of the sentence openers?
3. Did the contributions concern the content of the assignment?
4. Did the participants give their own answers before reading and reacting to the others?
5. Were there clear titles to the messages?

discussion and a group evaluation form (See Table 7.2). On the discussion printout, the teacher had marked her comments next to the printed contributions. These comments were directed towards the extent to which the contributions were elaborated. Understanding how to improve an interaction process and then applying it is cognitively demanding; providing the feedback comments next to the students' own worked examples might help reduce the cognitive load by demonstrating the principles of elaboration in a concrete and personally relevant way.

When the students had finished reading both the group evaluation form and the discussion printout, the teacher handed out the group assignment. In this assignment the students were asked as a group to think about the things they would like to do differently next time. The answers given formed the group's intentions for the following lesson.

7.4 Research Design

Two cases taken from a more extensive case study (Fakkert 2006) will be presented. The research design was a multiple case study including two collaborative groups from a larger sample.

The educational program was implemented in grade 5 (students 7 years of age) from four elementary schools. To investigate what the students had learned from the group feedback and the individual feedback, two cooperative groups of four students were selected. We chose two groups of students from different primary schools and of different composition (e.g. ability level). Furthermore the two groups showed interesting differences in the development of their participation. In both groups we selected two students from a total of four to describe the individual level in greater depth.

7.4.1 Instruments and Procedures

In this study a combination of quantitative and qualitative measures were used. The interaction processes, in particular concerning teacher feedback, student participation and student reflection, were described and analysed by video footages, observations, interviews along with descriptions of student contributions and teacher's guidance.

In Fig. 7.1 the main concepts are presented. Below the concept-related variables and instruments will be described in the sequence of the model in Fig. 7.1.

7.4.2 Student Characteristics and Prerequisites

Five measures were used to describe the following student characteristics:
(a) gender, (b) socioeconomic (SES) background, (c) IQ percentile scores, (d) reading comprehension, and (e) computer skills. These measures were included because they can be regarded as characteristics and prerequisites that seem to be related to the participation of the students (Prinsen et al. 2006).

Socioeconomic background was determined by using the scores from a National SES scoring system (Esis, 2006).

The Standard Progressive Matrices test (Raven, 1976) was administered to determine general ability (using IQ percentile scores). Scores on a national standardised reading comprehension test (CITO, 1998) were collected to determine student's achievement level in reading comprehension.

Before the lessons started, a questionnaire was administered to determine relevant skills and attitudes. The Computer Skills Scale (CSS) was administered. General computer skills were determined by providing the children with a list on which they could indicate the computer skills they thought they possessed (25 items). A list of general computer skills was taken from a Dutch monitor instrument (Gennip et al. 2002). All instruments proved sufficiently reliable with Cronbach's alpha's of 87 and higher.

7.4.3 Teacher Feedback

Teacher feedback to the group was collected from what the researcher/teacher had written on the group-feedback sheet. This feedback was directed towards the correct use of the participation-supporting features in the computer program (We call these supportive features "participation-supporting" because their use is aimed at improving participation. For instance, a clear organisation of display on the screen makes it easier to follow the thread of the discussion; the use of the sentence openers scaffolds the provision of elaborations; students providing their own answers before reacting to the others, stimulates idea diversity and the provision of clear titles enables fellow students to see at a glance the content of a particular contribution). The group feedback also included an overall assessment of the group being on- or off-topic.

Teacher feedback to the individual students was measured by counting the positive and critical comments written by the researcher/teacher next to the contributions which the students had made to the previous week's lesson. To generate a percentage, the number of comments was divided by the total number of contributions in that particular lesson.

7.4.4   Student Reflection

To determine how the students, as a group and individually, had reflected on their participation and the feedback they had received, a number of measures were used.

Firstly, we videotaped the groups in order to capture the reactions to the feedback the students had received both verbally and on paper and to capture how they cooperatively formulated the group's intentions for the following lesson.

Secondly, we collected and analysed the written responses of the students to the feedback (one week after the first lesson and one week after the second lesson). The group collectively distilled points of improvement or maintenance out of the feedback (intentions for the next lesson) and the group members wrote these down on the assignment form. The extent to which the students wrote down their intentions on the assignment sheet provided an indication of how actively involved the group members were in completing this assignment.

Thirdly, a semi-structured interview was held with the chosen individuals per group in which we asked them what they thought of the feedback and the reflection on it. Did they find it useful and relevant? We also asked them what they would like to do differently the next time you work with Knowledge Forum. Because the implementation of this program was an innovation in the participating classrooms we wanted to know how the students had experienced the lessons. Johnston (1997) has pointed out that there is very little research informing us on how students view educational change, because no one ever asks them. That is why we included some interview questions in our research asking the students what they thought of the program. Because the project included two group reflections, the chosen students were interviewed twice.

7.4.5   Student Participation

Student participation was measured in several ways in each lesson/discussion. The first method involved an evaluation of the way in which the students made use of the participation-supporting features. The evaluation of their correct use of these features was recorded on the group feedback sheets that were read and handed out to the students for later feedback.

The students were also supposed to actively participate in the discussions. Active participation was measured in two ways. First, we counted the number of messages that every student had contributed. We also included another measure of participation, namely the number of words per message. In this research it is assumed that this measure provides an objective measure of determining how elaborated the content of the messages was.

Finally, to determine if student contributions were sufficiently elaborated, we counted the percentage of positive and critical feedback comments on elaboration that the researcher/teacher has written down next to the students' contributions. This count gave us an indication of the quality of student participation.

7.4.6 Analysis

The development in the student participation was analysed in several ways. One way was to examine whether the evaluations made by the researcher/teacher of how the students made use of the participation-supporting features of the program changes over the lessons.

We also considered the improvement in the quality of the messages by looking at the increase in positive feedback comments by the researcher/teacher. These feedback comments were used to evaluate whether the contributions were sufficiently elaborate. The decrease in critical feedback comments was another indicator of quality improvement.

Furthermore, we described how the students adopted the points of improvement indicated in the teacher's feedback and in their own reflections and if and how these were reflected in subsequent actual improvements in their participation. In explaining the changes we took all of the feedback into account as the group members had read both the feedback intended for the whole group and their individual feedback. Furthermore, the students shared their individual feedback with the other group members.

In the analysis we also included an evaluation of the performance in lesson three. With these data, the developments between lessons 2 and 3 are included. However, the evaluations of lesson three were not fed back to the students. Additionally, there was no group reflection and there were no interviews after this third lesson.

Finally, we will relate the student characteristics of the individual cases to the (development in the) different participation measures and we will make a comparison between the two groups in their developments.

7.5 Results (Group A)

The results will be presented as follows. The results section is subdivided into three parts: Description and analysis of group A; description and analysis of group B; and, a comparison between groups A and B.

7.5.1 Description and Analysis of Group A

Group A, consisted of two boys and two girls: Tessa, Tufan, Tobias, and Manaar. To obtain a more in-depth description and analysis of the interaction and responses of the students, Tessa and Tufan were taken as examples. Table 7.3 contains the initial student characteristics of the students in this group.

Table 7.3 shows some differences in student characteristics. Tessa and Tufan differed in their social backgrounds but show the same IQ percentile level, the same reading comprehension level, and the same level of computer skills. Manaar and Tobias both come from a family with average social background.

Table 7.3 Student characteristics for group A

Learner characteristics	Gender	Socio-economic background	IQ percentile	Reading comprehension percentile	Computer skills
Tessa	Girl	1.25 (lower socio-economic)	50th	25% below the national average	33
Tufan	Boy	1.9 (foreign background)	50th	25% below the national average	33
Tobias	Boy	1.0 (average)	95th	25% highest scores	29
Manaar	Girl	1.0 (average)	50th	25% below the national average	30

Manaar's IQ percentile as well as her reading level also matched those of Tessa and Tufan. Only Tobias scored relatively high on general IQ and reading comprehension.

7.5.2   Feedback and Reflection on Lesson 1: Group A

The group was criticised for the way they used the participation-supporting features in the first lesson. The discussion layout on the screen was messy, they did not often use the sentence openers, they strayed from the subject, and their titles were unclear. The group received this critical feedback when the teacher read the evaluation out loud to the class, mentioning the group members' names. The one thing the group had done correctly was provide their own answers to the question before reading and reacting to the answers of the others.

When the group received the reflection task, requiring them to think about the things they could do differently next time, they seemed to be conscious of the fact that they had made incorrect use of the participation-supporting features. On their assignment sheet they collaboratively wrote down that they could improve the group discussion by sticking with the subject and by tidying up the layout of the discussion on the screen.

On the video recording we see the two girls starting to read the comments written next to the printed-out discussion while the boys started to reread the group evaluation. Later on they switched roles. Tessa read the reflection task to the group and wrote down the comments that the group members made. All the members contributed at least one point to improve on, for instance, to remain civil. Tessa contributed some of her own points. She wrote down that they had to use the sentence openers more often and that they had to stay serious and suggest normal titles. Tessa also wrote down on the sheet that they had to provide explanations.

Feedback and Reflection: Tessa and Tufan

Tessa received positive comments from the teacher on the elaborations in her messages. Even though she contributed the fewest number of messages to the discussion, Tessa contributed positively to the group discussion. Tessa not only expressed her agreement with others but also explained why. Another positive aspect which was noted was that she answered all the questions directed to her and she did not react to any contributions that were not serious. Tessa also received the fewest critical comments from the teacher on her use of elaborations (one comment on the fact that she did not explain to her group mate on what point she disagreed with him).

   The following excerpt shows a positive interaction in the group, demonstrating Tessa's ability to integrate two answers and her correct use of the sentence opener "Yes, but...". This was one of the few examples in the discussion where they all used the sentence openers. The titles were unclear and not very serious. The feedback that was given is written next to the contributions.

Excerpt 1: An exemplary interaction with positive teacher comments:

Title: **From?**
By: Tobias
Yes, but... don't you grow fat when you eat fat   *Good explanation, Tobias*
and you don't turn it over into energy?

Title: **Not from???**
By: Tufan
I think: you will become fat especially when you   *Right, Tufan*
eat too much of it.

Title: **blablablabla**
By: Tessa
Yes, but... also when you eat too much fat   *Well done, putting the two*
and you don't do sports or other exercise.   *contributions together,*
                                                     Tessa

   The example above shows the only positive comment that Tufan received. Twenty percent of his contributions received a critical comment, asking him to elaborate on his thoughts. Even though he was the most active participant in his group with 28 contributions, he did not seem to have taken the task too seriously. The following excerpt shows how he did not provide an explanation when asked for one by Manaar.

Excerpt 2: Failure to provide an explanation:

Title: **answer to the second question**
By: Tufan
I would choose this dessert because it tastes better.   *Which dessert, Tufan?*

Title: **for the answer to question 2?**
By: Manaar
… yes but why!!!???

Good thing you are asking for an explanation, Manaar. Try to ask nicely.

Title: **also for question 2**
By: Tufan
I think: just because

Tufan, you have to give an explanation if somebody asks you to explain.

When we asked Tessa what her personal intentions were for the next lesson she commented that she would try to get the others to contribute in a more serious manner. Even though she and the group received some critical comments on the (in) correct use of the supporting features of the computer program and on the provision of elaborations, she did not mention this fact. When asked about the comments she received regarding her elaborations, she said she only remembered about three comments, and that they were all positive. This means that she forgot about the critical comment asking her to explain on what point exactly she disagreed with one of her group mates.

When we asked Tufan what he thought of the feedback he had received he said: "I think I was talking about other things most of the time … more so than the other group members". He compared his performance to the performance of the other group members. By reading the feedback for the group members, he said that he had learned that it was necessary to "stick to the subject." He intended to be more serious.

7.5.3   Feedback and Reflection on Lesson 2: Group A

The overall picture of how the group collaborated in the second lesson is not completely positive. Even though they had written down all the points on which they needed to improve in their reflection after lesson 1, in this particular lesson they did not really improve. The students still did not make correct use of the participation-supporting features of the program. The group seemed to use the sentence openers a bit more often, but now they did not use the correct ones (i.e., the ones to fit with their contribution type). There were fewer distractions from the discussion subject. They still did not always find the possible answers to the questions. The group was encouraged, on the feedback sheet of the second lesson, to try and find more answers next time. The students were also encouraged to provide more explanations to each other, in particular Manaar, who did not perform as well in this respect as she did in the first lesson.

The group did show improvement on the participation measures. On average, the group members contributed fewer messages in comparison with lesson 1 (i.e., lesson 1: 23, lesson 2: 15), but the mean number of words per message was higher: 12 words per message in comparison with nine words before. This might mean that the group sent more content-rich messages. Looking at the number of positive and critical comments made about their elaborations, we see an improvement for the group as a whole. This is encouraging and might also be due to the fact that they tried to stick to the subject this time.

When the group received the reflection task, asking them to think about the things they could do differently in lesson 3, they did not copy all the critical comments they had received from the teacher as they had done in their reflection assignment after the first lesson. Keeping the discussion layout clear and suggesting more suitable titles did not seem to concern them. They did write down their intention to stick to the subject of the lesson and that they would always use the sentence openers. They also repeated their concern with providing explanations.

Feedback and Reflection: Tessa and Tufan

In line with the group's participation in this lesson, Tessa also sent fewer messages, but on average used more words per contribution (i.e., 13). She received a greater percentage of positive comments on her elaborative behaviour than she did in lesson 1, but she also slid back on one point. She did not provide explanations to others when she agreed or disagreed with them, while this was marked as one of her strong points in lesson 1.

Tessa adhered to her intentions for this lesson by providing five comments regulating the group. She told her group mates in these messages that they should stick to the subject more often. She also maintained her positive behaviour of reacting only to messages with serious knowledge and providing an answer for every question directed at her. She did not improve on her use of the procedural aspects, such as suggesting suitable titles and using the sentence openers.

Tufan shows a clear improvement in his participation in this lesson. He made fewer contributions (i.e., 17), but his behaviour improved and he received more positive feedback on his elaborative behaviour. The following excerpt is an example of a clear elaboration Tufan had made. We can also see here that Tufan used the "I think…" sentence opener, while he could more correctly have used "Yes, but …".

Excerpt 3: Tufan making progress in elaborating his answers

Title: **Was not read well**
By: Tobias
Remark: after a week the food had gone bad

Title: **For…**
By: Tufan

| I think: yes but she was talking to her friend for an hour and she was too late, she should have put it in the freezer before. | *Very good, Tufan. Could you add why she should have put it in the freezer sooner?* |

Tufan still showed some diversion from the content of the discussion, even though he intended to change this behaviour. He did start using more diverse sentence openers.

In her reflection, Tessa noticed that there was more use of the sentence openers in the second lesson and that more correct answers were given. Still she intended to make sure that the group kept to the subject and kept using the sentence openers. In the classroom feedback the teacher spent some time explaining the relevance of the different sentence openers and their use in providing the correct type of reactions. Again Tessa did not remember any of the specific feedback comments made next to her contributions. In the interview Tufan, again, showed his intention to stick to the subject next time.

7.5.4   Evaluation of Lesson 3: Group A

In the final lesson the group showed improvement on almost all of the feedback categories, even though they had not shown concern for all of the categories in their group reflection assignment. The group as a whole improved on keeping the discussion display as clear as possible and they all improved on their provision of titles with each contribution. Furthermore, they stuck with the subject this time. The interactions were positive, showing questioning and rebutting of answers by using "Yes, but..." sentences. It has to be noted that a lot of time was spent on contributing regulative messages which were superfluous.

Evaluation of Lesson 3: Tessa and Tufan

Tessa contributed five regulative messages (out of her total of 14 sent messages) telling her group members to use the sentence openers, as she had intended to do. In this lesson, her messages contained more words (i.e., 15) than the averages of her group mates (Table 7.4). She further showed improvement in the use of sentence openers and titles. However, she still forgot to add an explanation when she agreed or disagreed with someone. We found some additional information in the questionnaire the students had filled out before the lessons that might explain the omission. In this questionnaire Tessa reported that she did not like explaining things too much. Tessa consistently reacted only to messages with serious content. This might be a reason for the small number of contributions in the first lesson in comparison to that of her group members. Here we see a sign of negative interdependence: how individual progress can be negatively affected by other members of the group. In contrast, when the discussions on the lessons became more serious, the participation of the group members appeared to be more equitable.

Tufan showed a very positive attitude to the group members this time. He contributed some regulative comments about sticking to the subject. He also asked some clarification questions ("My question is: why did you choose that one, Tobias?") and he corrected Tessa on an important issue in a friendly manner ("Remark: the chicken has to be cooked at 75 degrees, not at 40"). His participation leveled off from 28 contributions in the first to 14 in the third lesson, but in this case the quality of his interactions actually improved despite this decline (Table 7.5). The feedback and group reflections appeared to have made a positive contribution to Tufan's development in this group.

Reflecting in her interview, Tessa told us that she experienced the feedback-method as useful, because it showed her how she and her group members could improve. Still, she showed more concern for the (mal-) adaptive behaviour of her group members, than for her own points of improvement, however, this did not prevent her from showing improvements. She did find it odd that some feedback comments were repeated over and over again. Tessa showed a clear concern for the functioning of the group and a concern for equal participation during the reflection moments. This is a clear sign of positive interdependence.

7.5.5   Overall Developments in Participation and Elaboration in Group A

We now turn to some general trends in the participation and elaboration from lesson 1 through 3 of group A. In the final lesson we can see a clear improvement in most of the feedback categories compared to the earlier lessons. The group members' improvements on elaborative behaviour (Table 7.4) are especially encouraging. It seems that the students became more aware of the expectations and that they tried to improve on several aspects, as they had intended.

The group means in Table 7.4 show that the average total of sent messages declined, but in this last lesson the group averaged 13 words per message (this was 9 in lesson 1). As the group improved on most of the categories, it appears that the decline in contributions does not affect the effectiveness of the collaboration. The contributions made by the group showed improvement in content over the lessons. Teacher feedback and student reflection clearly influenced the interaction pattern from lesson 1 through 3, especially after the feedback on lesson 1.

With reference to the learning characteristics (i.e., their resources as presented in Table 7.3), there are some differences and similarities between the two individual cases. Tessa and Tufan are from different socioeconomic backgrounds (Tufan being from an immigrant background), however, their IQ, reading comprehension score and computer skills are the same. Tufan participates more actively in the first lesson than Tessa but we know from the descriptions that the quality of his participation was low in comparison. Both Tessa and Tufan make gains in the number of words per message. They both contribute 14 messages in the last lesson, with Tessa writing slightly longer messages. Since they are also equally active, it may be concluded that their identical IQ scores, reading comprehension scores, and computer skills have more influence on their active participation than their differences in gender and socioeconomic backgrounds.

We now turn to some trends in the quality of participation and elaboration from lesson 1 to lesson 3. Table 7.5, which concerns the feedback on student's elaborative behaviour, shows that all group members made gains in positive feedback (only Manaar regressed in the second lesson). In the end, it was almost unnecessary to make critical comments on their contributions. They all declined practically to zero percent in the frequency of critical comments on their elaborative behaviour.

By relating Tessa and Tufans' learning characteristics to their elaboration measures in Table 7.5, we draw the following conclusions. Tessa and Tufan show similar patterns in positive and negative comments from the teacher. Tessa starts off more

Table 7.4 Development of individuals and the group on active participation measures for group A

Name	Lesson 1 counts of the participation measures	Lesson 2 counts of the participation measures	Lesson 3 counts of the participation measures
Tessa	18 contributions	17 contributions	14 contributions
	10 words/message	13 words/message	15 words/message
Tufan	28 contributions	17 contributions	14 contributions
	9 words/message	10 words/message	12 words/message
Tobias	17 contributions	12 contributions	16 contributions
	11 words/message	11 words/message	12 words/message
Manaar	30 contributions	13 contributions	10 contributions
	7 words/message	12 words/message	12 words/message
Group mean	23 contributions	15 contributions	14 contributions
	9 words/message	12 words/message	13 words/message

Table 7.5 Development of individuals and the group on elaboration feedback measures: Group A (numerator = N-feedback; denominator = N-contributions)

Criterion	Lesson 1	Lesson 2	Lesson 3
Name	Positive feedback comments on elaboration	Positive feedback comments on elaboration	Positive feedback comments on elaboration
Tessa	3/17 (18%)	4/17 (24%)	4/14 (28%)
Tufan	1/28 (4%)	2/17 (12%)	2/14 (14%)
Tobias	1/18 (6%)	2/12 (16%)	3/16 (21%)
Manaar	2/30 (7%)	0/13 (0%)	4/10 (40%)
Group	7/93 (8%)	6/59 (10%)	13/54 (24%)
Criterion	Lesson 1	Lesson 2	Lesson 3
Name	Critical feedback comments on elaboration	Critical feedback comments on elaboration	Critical feedback comments on elaboration
Tessa	1/17 (6%)	3/17 (18%)	1/14 (7%)
Tufan	5/28 (20%)	1/17 (6%)	0/14 (0%)
Tobias	6/18 (36%)	1/12 (8%)	0/16 (0%)
Manaar	3/30 (11%)	7/13 (56%)	0/10 (0%)
Group	15/93 (16%)	12/59 (20%)	1/54 (2%)

favorably, but they both show an increase in positive feedback and a substantial decrease in critical feedback between lessons 2 and 3. Again we cannot pinpoint a clear influence of the initial differences in socioeconomic background and gender on this development. Teacher interventions, however, seem to be clearly reflected in the developments in participation of all students from lesson 1 to 3.

7.6   Results (Group B)

7.6.1   Description and Analysis of Group B

This group consisted of two boys and two girls: Kristine, Rishi, Kevin, and Yit Man. In the following, Kristine's case is described in greater depth.

Table 7.6 contains the initial student characteristics of the students in this group. All students came from a lower socioeconomic background and Rishi's and

Table 7.6   Student characteristics of group B

Learner characteristics	Gender	Socio-economic background	IQ percentile	Reading compre-hension level	Computer skills
Kristine	Girl	1.25 (lower socio-economic)	25th	10% lowest scores	23/33
Rishi	Boy	1.25 (lower socio-economic)	25th	25% below the national average	33/33
Kevin	Boy	1.25 (lower socio-economic)	25th	15% well below national average	33/33
Yit Man	Girl	1.25 (lower socio-economic)	75th	On the national average	14/33

Kristines' parents were born outside the Netherlands. Except for Yit Man, who had an above average IQ percentile score, the other group members had a below-average score on the IQ test. Only Yit Man had an average score on the reading comprehension test. The others scored below or well below the national average.

With regard to the students' computer skills, Yit Man showed very few computer skills. Rishi and Kevin appeared to be the most skilled users in the group, while Kristine showed average scores on the scale.

7.6.2   Feedback and Reflection Lesson 1: Group B

The group evaluation on their use of the participation-supporting features after the first lesson was not completely positive. The group members stuck to the subject, providing their own answers before reacting to the others, but the discussion layout was messy and the sentence openers were forgotten in most cases (especially by Rishi). The titles did not refer to the subject of the message. The group interacted in a positive way, and was also very active.

In the group reflection, almost all of the critical feedback that the group received on their use of the participation-supporting features was translated by the group into personal improvement points. They wrote the names of each group member followed by a point to improve on. Kevin wrote: "we have to talk about the subject and unravel the lines on the discussion layout." There was no mention of making better titles. Rishi intended to make better use of the sentence openers; a point which was stressed on the group evaluation form.

Feedback and Reflection: Kristine and Rishi

Kristine received some positive feedback comments for contributing questions to this discussion. She was an active participant, contributing 17 messages, almost all of which were questions. Her questions were of good quality, asking for elaboration. The way Kristine was participating is somewhat surprising, taking into account her low computer skills and her low reading comprehension score. The next excerpt provides an example. Kristine makes correct use of the sentence opener 'My question is…'.

Excerpt 4: A question asking for elaboration:

Title: **answer**
By: Rishi
I think: I agree with Derek because he chooses
the fruit dessert.   *Explain why you agree with Derek, Rishi*

Title: **For Rishi**
By: Kristine
My question is: but why?   *Good question! Kristine*

Rishi did not answer Kristine's questions and consequently received a critical comment. The first answer that Kristine contributed to the second discussion was elaborated well. The answer and what followed is shown in the next example:

Excerpt 5: A properly elaborated first answer:

Title: **yoghurt dessert**
By: Kristine
I think: that Mary is right because she says   *Good explanation, Kristine!*
that there is also a lot of sugar (calories) in
fruit, in fruit there are fruit sugars and sugar
makes you grow fat and it's bad for your teeth.

Title: **you can become ill**
By: Rishi
Remark: you can become ill   *What makes you ill, Rishi?*
                                                        You are not being clear

Title: **illness**
By: Kristine
My question is: but how can you become ill?   *Good question! Kristine*

Kristine's question shows that Rishi's answer was not clearly elaborated. Rishi received the most critical comments on his (non)elaborative behaviour. His messages were on average only eight words long. Even though Rishi provided explanations for most of the questions in the discussion, his answers were always short and he never used the explanation sentence opener.

In her reflection Kristine wrote: I'm going to make better questions and I have to give better answers. Rishi intended to make better use of the sentence openers.

7.6.3 Feedback and Reflection Lesson 2: Group B

The overall picture of how the group interacted in the second lesson is a positive one, resulting in positive comments by the teacher. The group kept the layout of the discussion clearer than previously and stuck to the lesson subject, as they had intended. They could still improve on the use of sentence openers. Rishi still failed to use them, even though he intended to do so. When the group evaluations were read to the class, there was some extra attention paid to the subject of asking clear questions. When asking "What do you mean?" it is better to ask "What do you mean *when you say...?*' (repeating the words in the message to which you are reacting). This way there will be less misunderstanding.

The group was, again, actively involved in the lesson, contributing an average of 15 messages per person. For all the participants, the number of words per message went down in comparison to lesson 1. Looking at the number of positive and critical comments made about their elaborations we do not detect any serious improvements either. As the reflection sheet shows, the group focused its attention primarily on improving the procedural aspects of working with the program.

In their reflections it was acknowledged by the students that they did not make correct use of the participation-supporting features of the program. During their reflection on their performance the group was video-taped. The group members first took turns in reading out loud, one by one, the contributions to the previous week's discussion. They also read out loud the feedback comments which were written next to the contributions. Kevin appointed the reader and directed attention to the feedback comments. After they had gone through the whole of the previous week's discussion, Kevin read the assignment to the group and Yit Man wrote down the points of improvement on the sheet. Rishi asked Yit Man to write down "Use more sentence openers." Kevin added "to understand each other better" and "to explain better" and "to give better answers". Rishi said "to make better sentences, to write the answer clearly" and "talk more about the subject."

Feedback and Reflection: Kristine and Rishi

Kristine adhered to her intention to keep asking questions. Seventeen of her twenty-three contributions were questions. It is not really clear if Kristine asked all these questions to get her group members to elaborate or because she really did not understand. Rishi did not make any progress toward contributing more elaborate answers in this lesson. His word count went even further down, to six words per message. He received many critical comments asking him to elaborate. The next excerpt shows how Rishi provides a non-answer to a question which was not directed at him in the first place. When Kristine asks him what he means, Rishi loses track of the conversation completely.

Excerpt 6: Miscommunication

Title: **good opinion**
By: Kevin
That's right, because… you need energy or   *Good explanation, Kevin*
you'll get weak.

Title: **Kevin**
By: Kristine
My question is: but why?   *Good that you ask, Kristine*

Title: **okay**
By: Rishi… Just because   *'just because' is not an*
                                                     explanation, Rishi

Title: **rishi**
By: Kristine
My question is: what… just because?

Title: **just because**
By: Rishi
… Just because, what is the question?

Kristine's original question is not answered. Rishi used many short answers in this discussion. It shows a lack of interest in the discussion, even though his inclination to provide answers generally looked positive. Surprisingly, at some points in the discussion Rishi asks his group members to elaborate ("Remark: because, why?" "just because what?"), even though he does not do it himself.

In the interview, Kristine looked back and told us she had misunderstood the first question "I did not know what a 'TV dinner' was." This might explain her short, initial, answer. Kristine is weak at reading comprehension, so she might internalise fewer answers from reading the text and might sometime not even understand the question. She intended to ask questions in the next lesson. The attention paid to the personal feedback comments on elaboration made Rishi aware of the fact that he had to provide more and better explanations. He intended to do this.

7.6.4   Evaluation for Lesson 3: Group B

In the final lesson the group did not show any further improvements on the procedural aspects, such as the use of sentence openers. The group received fewer positive comments on their elaborative behaviour, but also showed a decline of critical comments. Looking at the quality of the discussion we see the group members showing concern for providing clear answers and understanding what the others are saying. The discussion also showed some clear signs of promotive interaction. They started to ask each other more clarification questions.

Evaluation for Lesson 3: Kristine and Rishi

Kristine contributed a very high number of messages in this lesson (41). Her word count is the same as in the second lesson, with an average of 13 words per message (Table 7.7). Kristine intended to provide good answers and to ask questions, and she did. Sometimes her language use was unclear, but her group members made a point of asking her what she meant to say. Kristine showed that she could ask clear questions (e.g., "My question is: how long can the chicken be kept in the freezer?").

When we look at Rishi's participation in this lesson, not much seems to have changed. One positive aspect is that the percentage of positive feedback comments he receives increases (Table 7.8). In a couple of instances Rishi asked a clarification question in which we see that he did not give up on receiving clarification from Kristine.

Excerpt 7: Rishi keeps asking for clarification

Title: **(untitled)**
By: Kristine
Yes, but... can you put that chicken on the pan in the right way?

Title: **what**
By: Rishi
... what do you mean?

Title: **(untitled)**
By: Kristine
Yes, but... I mean from the chicken

Title: **chicken**
By: Rishi
My question is; what do you mean by chicken?

Rishi also improved his question from asking simply "What do you mean?" to asking more specifically: "My question is: what do you mean by chicken?" In his second message he also made correct use of the sentence opener, "My question is…".

Rishi enjoyed the evaluation lessons. The personal feedback made him realise that he should provide *'longer and better explanations'*. The fact that he realised what his personal points for improvement were did not always translate into a change of behaviour. In the third lesson it seems as though he started to take his responsibility within the group process more seriously.

In her reflection, Kristine told us that she thought the feedback comments were good. She was not very good at formulating to us what exactly she had learned from the evaluation lessons. This seems to be due to her limited language proficiency. All in all we can say that Kristine was a very active participant who made a positive contribution to the group process during the lessons.

7.6.5   Overall Developments in Participation and Elaboration in Group B

The participation measures of group B are presented in Table 7.7.

Looking at the participation measures in Table 7.7, we see that the group is increasingly active with an average of 22 messages per person in lesson 3, but that the word count goes down from 22 words per message in the first lesson to 13 in lesson 3. Their active participation shows a different pattern to the one for group A.

Regarding learner characteristics (i.e., the resources as presented in Table 7.6), there are some differences between the two individual cases. Kristine and Rishi are both from lower socioeconomic backgrounds. Their IQ scores are below average, as are their reading comprehension levels (with Kristine being in the lowest category). However, it appears that the differences between Kirstine and Rishi cannot be explained by their different characteristics as Kirstine does surprisingly well given her scores.

Table 7.7 Development of individuals and the group on active participation measures: group B

Name	Lesson 1 counts of the participation measures	Lesson 2 counts of the participation measures	Lesson 3 counts of the participation measures
Kristine	17 contributions	23 contributions	41 contributions
	16 words/message	13 words/message	13 words/message
Rishi	23 contributions	21 contributions	20 contributions
	8 words/message	6 words/message	7 words/message
Kevin	11 contributions	7 contributions	8 contributions
	31 words/message	30 words/message	21 words/message
Yit Man	2 contributions	8 contributions	19 contributions
	33 words/message	14 words/message	9 words/message
Group mean	13 contributions	15 contributions	22 contributions
	22 words/message	16 words/message	13 words/message

Table 7.8 Development of individuals and the group on elaboration feedback measures: group B (numerator = N-feedback; denominator = N-contributions)

Criterion	Lesson 1	Lesson 2	Lesson 3
Name	Positive feedback comments on elaboration	Positive feedback comments on elaboration	Positive feedback comments on elaboration
Kristine	3/17 (18%)	5/23 (22%)	6/41 (15%)
Rishi	2/23 (9%)	2/21 (10%)	4/20 (20%)
Kevin	6/11 (55%)	4/7 (57%)	2/8 (25%)
Yit Man	1/2 (50%)	2/8 (25%)	4/19 (21%)
Group mean	12/53 (23%)	13/59 (22%)	16/88 (18%)
Criterion	Lesson 1	Lesson 2	Lesson 3
	Critical feedback comments on elaboration	Critical feedback comments on elaboration	Critical feedback comments on elaboration
Kristine	1/17 (6%)	2/23 (8%)	0/41 (0%)
Rishi	8/23 (35%)	8/21 (38%)	1/20 (5%)
Kevin	0/11 (0%)	0/7 (0%)	1/8 (13%)
Yit Man	1/2 (50%)	2/8 (25%)	1/19 (5%)

We now turn to the quality of the elaboration as was measured by positive and negative feedback comments by the teacher on elaborations.

As shown in Table 7.8, the positive feedback comments on elaboration decrease over the lessons, as does the number of words per message. There is, however, some sign of improvement, since the percentage of critical comments decreases greatly in the last lesson.

7.7 Results (Comparison Between Groups A and B)

In this final results section we bring together the group scores from Tables 7.4, 7.5, 7.7, and 7.8 to summarise and compare the patterns between the groups.

In the course of the lessons Group A showed a decline on the average number of contributions, but the content of the contributions was increasingly elaborate as shown by the increase in number of words per message. This was mirrored in the increased positive feedback and the reduction in critical feedback on elaboration by the teacher.

Group B started out with a higher number of words per message and more positive feedback comments on elaboration than group A, but did not show a clear pattern of improvement over the lessons. The mean number of contributions increased from the first to the last lesson while the mean number of words per message decreased. At the same time the group shows a reduction in positive feedback on elaboration.

Even though both groups end up contributing an average of 13 words per message and show a significant reduction in critical feedback in the third lesson, the overall conclusion is that group A seems to outperform group B in their development. We see some positive development in the case description of group B but the differences between the patterns of development between the groups seem to reflect the greater difference in student characteristics and the lower resource level of group B as a whole. Except for one student, all group members of group B showed low scores on general IQ and low to very low reading comprehension scores.

7.8 Conclusion and Discussion

In this chapter we described a program directed at improving the interactions within groups of collaborating students in a CSCL environment. Developments made by two groups of students in two 5th grade classes were described in terms of improvements in their participation. The correct use of the participation-supporting features, their active participation and their provision of elaborative contributions were related to the provided feedback, the students' reflections, students' intentions to improve and student characteristics. In both groups, two case students were followed in their learning processes in order to present examples of development over the lessons.

The main research question was: How do interaction processes between students develop within a CSCL learning environment in which feedback by the researcher/ teacher is provided and student reflection is stimulated? It was expected that feedback and reflection regarding the quality of the participation in the initial stages will result in better quality participation and more elaborated contributions of the students later on in the process. In answering this question we looked, in particular, at the various contributions of the individual students and the groups in relation to the feedback and reflection moments.

Our general conclusion is that the feedback by the researcher/teacher and the reflection moments contributed to the development of the students in terms of participation and elaboration. This positive contribution confirms our expectations. However, it has to be noted that conclusions drawn on the basis of case studies are bound to be tentative. In this exploration we did not compare the groups to groups of students who did not receive feedback on their participation.

The exploration of the two group-cases and the two individual-sub cases show differences between individual students and between groups. In most cases we were able to trace these differences back to student characteristics or resources in the cooperative group and researcher/teacher's feedback and reflections by the students. To substantiate our general conclusions some general patterns and more specific findings, especially concerning the differences between the two case-groups, will be summarised in the remainder of this section.

We detect some general patterns in the cases. The students did not automise the operations of using the sentence openers and adding comprehensive titles to their messages. Even though they keep mentioning this as a point of improvement in their reflections, they did not consistently improve. Perhaps because they worked in small groups and the contributions were read by most of the students anyway, they did not see why adding a clear title matters. It might also be that the students did not adopt the usability of the sentence openers because it seemed unnatural to them and it hindered them in providing quick responses, or it may have been that the students did not want to keep their group members waiting. Synchronous chat programs have a fleeting character (Veerman & Veldhuis-Diermanse 2001). Because students take numerous turns, the pressure to react quickly is high. It has to be noted that multiple occasions were observed whereby students started their sentences with, for instance "Yes but…". Sentence openers might thus be seen as a scaffold to be removed after the students have adopted its use.

A positive aspect was the improvement students showed when it came to sticking to the subject of the lesson. It might be that the focus on providing elaborate contributions helps the students focus on the lesson's content. Again, we did not compare the results with groups that did not focus on providing elaborate contributions. There might therefore be other explanations.

We saw how the groups adopted the idea that they should be providing more explanations to each other. In general, the percentage of critical comments of the researcher/teacher on elaborative behaviour declined over the lessons. Even though the number of critical comments increases slightly in lesson 2, they showed a sharp decline in lesson 3.

The students started asking more clarification questions when the lessons progressed. Clarity and clarifications seemed to have become part of students' ideas of how to reach a positive and effective collaboration. We saw the groups developing a sense of positive interdependence. They did not only focus on their personal points for improvement but also paid attention to the feedback their group members received and the feedback they received as a group. They not only realised they were individually responsible for an effective collaboration but also took responsibility for the achievements of their group mates. This sense of positive interdependence is demonstrated in the regulative comments they made in the different group discussions.

All in all, we believe the results are encouraging, given the short-term nature of the intervention and the great number of matters to which the students had to pay attention. Inconsistency in the progress made might be due to cognitive overload (Bruggen van et al. 2002) in the sense that the students had to split their attention with regard to different aspects of the task. The more limited resources of group B in comparison to group A might explain the differences in their measures of improvement. Additionally transfer from awareness of how a skill is used to the actual use of that skill takes time.

Our method of giving feedback on the students' contributions and encouraging students to reflect on the received feedback appears to be appropriate in that it stimulates both individual accountability in the students, and a sense of positive interdependence within the group. The results of the study support the assumption that group discussion processes can be improved by providing feedback on participation and guiding students towards a more conscious use of the principle of elaboration.

In this study the researchers prepared the feedback. It would be interesting to investigate whether the same results are achieved when the teachers themselves apply this type of learning environment and feedback procedure, or when students rate themselves. We hope to inspire teacher practices with the examples given, while at the same time acknowledging that teachers will always, indeed have to, attach their own interpretations to specific approaches (Leeman & Volman 2001).

We are aware that we have to be careful in generalising the results obtained, given that the study was conducted with a limited population of students. Also, in descriptive studies we have to be attentive to different interpretations. Any reported relations between processes of feedback and reflection on the one hand and developments in student participation on the other have to be treated with care. Further studies will have to substantiate (or reject) the preliminary conclusions from the present study's qualitative analyses.

Our focus was directed towards enhancing student participation. However participation at school is not an end in itself. Schools and classrooms are for learning. The assumption was that promoting participation stimulates learning: those who participate will learn. In this qualitative study, the chain of reasoning, involving student characteristics, student prerequisites, interaction processes, and learning outcomes, is incomplete. This is a limitation that calls for further study into the learning effects of enhancing participation in a CSCL learning environment.

References

Brown, A. L., & Palincsar, A. S. (1989). Guided, cooperative learning and individual knowledge acquisition, In L. B. Resnick (Ed.), *Knowing, Learning and Instruction: Essays in Honor of Robert Glaser* (pp. 393–451). Hillsdale, NJ: Lawrence Erlbaum.

Bruggen van, J. M., Kirschner, P. A., & Jochems, W. (2002). External representations of argumentation in CSCL and the management of cognitive load. *Learning and Instruction, 12*, 121–138.

Bull, S., Dimitrova, V., & Brna, P. (2002). Enhancing reflective modeling through communicative interaction in learning environments. In P. Brna, M. Baker, K. Stenning, & A. Tiberghien (Eds.), *The Role of Communication in Learning to Model* (pp. 183–211). Hillsdale, NJ: Lawrence Erlbaum Associates.

CITO (1998). Toets Begrijpend Lezen (Comprehensive Reading Test), G. Staphorsius, & R. Krom, Centraal Instituut voor Toetsontwikkeling (National Institute for Test Development), Arnhem, The Netherlands.

Cohen, E. G., & Lotan, R. A. (1995). Producing equal-status interaction in the heterogeneous classroom. *American Educational Research Journal, 32*, 99–120.

Cohen, E. G., Brody, C. M., & Sapon-Shevin, M. (2004). *Teaching Cooperative Learning. The Challenge for Teacher Education*. New York: State University of New York.

Crook, C. (1994). *Computers and the Collaborative Experiences of Learning*. London: Routledge.

Dewiyanti, S. (2005). *Learning together: A positive experience. The effect of reflection on group process in an asynchronous computer-supported collaborative learning environment*. Unpublished doctoral dissertation, Open Universiteit, Maastricht, Nederland. http://www.ou.nl/Docs/Expertise/OTEC/Publicaties/sylvia%20dewiyanti/Proefschrift-versie-final_2005.pdf

Dillenbourg, P., & Self, J. A. (1995). Designing human-computer collaborative learning. In C. E. O'Malley (Ed.), *Computer Supported Collaborative Learninig*. Hamburg: Springer-Verlag.

Esis. (2006). *Eniac School Informatie Systeem*, versie 3.40. Rovict, Soest, The Netherlands.

Fakkert, M. C. (2006). *Leerprocessen binnen samenwerkend leren in Knowledge Forum: Multiple case studies naar de effectiviteit van tussentijdse feedback op het leerproces van individuen en de samenwerkende groep.* Unpublished Master of Education thesis, Vrije Universiteit, Amsterdam.

Fischer, G., & Ostwald J. (2002). Transcending the information given: Designing learning environments for informed participation. *Computers in Education, 1,* 378–381.

Gennip, H., van Braam, H., & Poulisse, N. (2002). *Ict-Onderwijsmonitor Basisonderwijs 2000–2001.* Nijmegen: ITS.

Johnson, D. W., & Johnson, R.T. (1994). *Learning Together and Alone: Cooperative, Competitive and Individualistic Learning* (4th ed). Boston: Allyn and Bacon.

Johnson, D. W., Johnson, R. T., Stanne, M. B., & Garibaldi, A. (1990). Impact of group processing on achievement in cooperative groups. *The Journal of Social Psychology, 130,* 507–516.

Johnston, L. D. (1997). *Risking learning? A comparative study of the attitudes and behaviors of some groups of second-year undergraduate students in Information Management seminars, following the introduction of different technologies designed to enhance critical and creative thinking.* Unpublished doctoral dissertation, University of Belfast, Northern Ireland.

Leeman, Y., & Volman, M. (2001). Inclusive education, recipe book or quest. On diversity in the classroom and educational research. *International Journal on Inclusive education, 5,* 267–379.

Prinsen, F. R., Volman, M. L. L., & Terwel, J. (2006). The influence of learner characteristics on degree and type of participation in a CSCL environment. *British Journal of Educational Technology* (Online Early Articles). doi:10.1111/j.1467-8535.2006.00692.x

Raven, J. C. (1976). *Standard Progressive Matrices.* Sets A, B, C, D & E. (ISBN 1856390209). Oxford, England: Oxford Psychologists Press.

Ross, J. A., & Rolheiser, C. (2003). Student assessment practices in cooperative learning, In R. M. Gillies, & A. F. Ashman (Eds.), *Cooperative Learning: The Social and Intellectual Outcomes of Learning in Groups* (pp. 54–68). London: RoutledgeFalmer.

Slavin, R. (1995). *Cooperative Learning: Theory, Research and Practice* (2nd ed). Boston: Allyn and Bacon.

Stahl, G. (1999). Reflections on WebGuide. Seven issues for the next generation of collaborative knowledge building environments, in *Proceedings of CSCL 99*: C. Hoadley (Ed.), *The Third International Conference on Computer Support for Collaborative Learning* (pp. 600–610). Mahwah, NJ: Lawrence Erlbaum.

Terwel, J. (2003). Cooperative learning in secondary education: A curriculum perspective. In R.M. Gillies, & A. F. Ashman (Eds). *Cooperative Learning: The social and Intellectual Outcomes of Learning in Groups* (pp. 54–68). London: RoutledgeFalmer.

Ulicsak, M.H. (2004). 'How did it know we weren't talking?': An investigation into the impact of self-assessments and feedback in a group activity. *Journal of Computer Assisted Learning, 20,* 205–211.

Van Dijk, I. M. A. W., Van Oers, H. J. M., & Terwel, J. (2003a). Providing or designing? Constructing models in primary maths education. *Learning and Instruction, 13,* 53–72.

Van Dijk, I. M. A. W., Van Oers, B.,Terwel, J., & Van den Eeden (2003b). Strategic learning in primary mathematics education: Evaluation of a program in modelling. *Educational Research and Evaluation, 9,* 161–187.

Veerman, A., & Veldhuis-Diermanse, E. (2001). Collaborative learning through computermediated communications in academic education. Proceedings of the International Conference Euro-CSCL'01. The Netherlands.

Vygotsky, L. (1978). *Mind in Society.* London: Harvard University Press.

Webb, N. M., & Farivar, S. (1999). Developing productive group interaction in middle school. In A. M. O'Donnell and A. King, eds, Cognitive Perspectives on Peer Learning pp. 117–149. Mahwah, NJ: Erlbaum.

Yager, S., Johnson, D. W., Johnson, R. T., & Snider, B. (1996). The impact of group processing on achievement in cooperative learning groups. *The Journal of Social Psychology, 126,* 389–397.

Chapter 8
School and Inclusive Practices

Adrian F. Ashman

Abstract Over the past 20 years, there has been an imperative in most Western countries to accommodate students with special learning needs in regular education settings. Inclusion has become the catchword that epitomizes the notion of equality and opportunity in social and scholarly domains. It would seem logical that the adoption of inclusion as a systemic policy would lead to significant changes in classroom teaching and learning practices but this does not appear to be the case. The implementation of new teaching-learning technologies to support inclusive education practices, including peer-mediation, has not kept pace with the acceptance of the rhetoric. In this chapter, I draw a parallel between the evidence supporting the benefits of inclusive education and the data that confirm the value of peer-mediation with students with diverse learning needs.

8.1   Overview

It has been more than 50 years since the focus of attention in education broadened to include students who have problems learning in regular school classrooms. Before that, many of those students attended separate – or special – classes or special schools with peers who had an intellectual disability or one or more other cognitive, physical, or sense impairments. Many of the most impaired students who resided in institutions for people with mental retardation received very little education, if any. In the 1960s, as a reaction to the lack of education apparently being provided in special education settings, there evolved a movement toward providing at least some students with special education needs access to regular education settings (see Dunn 1968).

Mainstreaming, as this movement was called, became an administrative policy that took many students with mild and moderate intellectual disability and many with physical and sense impairments into regular education classes. At that time, mainstreaming involved not much more than the formation of classes (see e.g., Warnock, 1978) that contained students with and without disabilities but there were few adaptations made to either the curriculum or teaching practices that might have produced educational benefits to mainstreamed students. Many teachers and parents were quick to recognise that mainstreaming was little more than maindumping (Chapman 1988; Elkins 1994; Mitler 1988) and there were cynical views expressed that the primary motivation for mainstreaming was simply a cost-saving measure through the reduction in government funding to the special education sector.

Over time, political pressures – largely from parents of students with special learning needs – led to an increase in resources and professional development for teachers aimed at enabling students to take advantage of both the social and scholastic opportunities available in regular classes (see Darling-Hammond 1996). With this development came the demise of the term, mainstreaming, and its replacement by integration and later, by inclusion.

Along with political and administrative directions and mandates came many recommendations for ways in which teaching and learning might occur across education settings to benefit the largest number of students. Curriculum content and classroom practices were scrutinised with a view toward accommodating diverse student learning needs. Teachers were offered professional development opportunities designed to improve their knowledge and skills of disabling conditions and introduce them to inclusive education practices although the requirement for such professional development was voluntary. This meant that there were few significant changes made to the nature of classroom teaching and learning or administrative changes in the host school. Positive exemplars of integration came primarily from highly committed teachers often working in isolation and without much support from either school administration or the school system.

A 40-year history of research on inclusive education should be punctuated with examples of innovative teaching strategies and approaches, such as peer-mediated learning, that enhance the learning experiences of students regardless of ability or impairment. And while any wide-ranging review of inclusive education literature using "inclusive education" or "inclusion" in (for example) the ERIC database will shows a huge range of such initiatives, the conclusion that one might reach is that inclusive education generally has fallen well short of the target. At this point I will make some general observations about the success of inclusion and then move to consider the role of peer-mediated learning in education settings that contain students with diverse learning needs.

In this chapter, I wish to draw a parallel between the histories of inclusive education and peer-mediated learning. The ideals and initiatives associated with inclusion should lead to substantive innovations in teaching and learning practices within regular classes that benefit all students. In similar way, peer-mediated learning offers opportunities to include students with special learning needs in most, if not all, classroom activities with positive outcomes in both social and scholastic domains. The evidence of such effects is, however, far from obvious in the professional literature. I will begin by considering the success of inclusive education and then the outcomes of research relating to peer-mediated learning.

8.2   The Success of Inclusive Education Practices

The professional literature published during the early years of mainstreaming and integration – the 1970s and 1980s – gives the impression of wide-ranging acceptance of the philosophy and subsequent systemic responses based on equity and social justice arguments. Parents of students with special education needs and some teachers applauded the opportunities available to children for increased social engagement and the potential for improved learning outcomes. Reports of successful integration were often limited to anecdotes with some writers drawing attention to the limitations in school schedules, timetables, and teaching practices that restricted opportunities for students to take full advantage of regular classroom activities.

While rarely reported in the professional literature, there was considerable opposition to mainstreaming, integration, and inclusion. Teachers complained that they were not trained to deal with low-functioning students or those presenting very challenging behavior, or students with pronounced physical or sense impairments. Many argued that regular classroom practices were unsuitable or inappropriate and the presence of a student with demanding learning needs – when compared with their peers – reduced the amount of one-to-one teaching contact that could be given to each student in a class (see Nesbit 1994; Vlachou & Barton 1994). Parents of students achieving according to age expectations complained that their children were being disadvantaged educationally, while parents of students with special learning needs also complained that their children were receiving significantly less attention and fewer opportunities than were available in special education settings (see Jenkinson 1997).

By the late 1990s, inclusion had become the accepted educational position with associated rhetoric in most Western countries. Despite this, special education classes and schools continued to exist. Those who more often than not attend regular classes are students with learning difficulties, speech and language difficulties, vision impairment, those thought to be gifted and talented, those with mild intellectual disability, and those with uncomplicated medical conditions.

Over the past two decades a vast professional literature on inclusion has emerged. There are substantial collections relating to the philosophy and values implicit in inclusion. Several writers, for example, have argued that inclusion is a moral imperative that does not require, and cannot wait for, empirical justification (see Biklen 1985; Stainback et al. 1996) while others (e.g., Kauffman et al. 1988) warned about a rush headlong into inclusion because of the lack of support provided by administrators and others responsible for its implementation. In addition to debates about the ethics of inclusion, there are many papers devoted to descriptions and explanations of inclusive processes and practices (see e.g., Baker & Zigmond 1995; Wedell 1995), and there is also a robust collection of commentaries on policy and practice (see e.g., Bricker 1995; Kauffman & Hallahan 1995; Vlachou 2004).

It is curious that the number of empirical studies about the success of inclusive education relative to the vastness of the literature is relatively small and of these, few focus specifically on innovative teaching approaches (e.g., co-teaching, strategy instruction, peer-mediated learning) aimed at improving academic outcomes. In this regard, Mastropieri and Scruggs (2001) argued that highly successful inclusive classrooms are characterized by the effective use of peers for supporting students with special learning needs and reinforcing learning through one-on-one and small group activities. In many cases, journal articles focus on practical issues related to the implementation and structure of inclusive classrooms (see e.g., Forlin 2004). And studies that deal with the success of inclusive practices often are based on small samples, often one or a small number of classrooms. There are also reports of largely unsuccessful attempts to integrate students with acute learning problems, often based upon teacher reports and anecdotes.

Looking broadly at the literature, there is great variability in the results of studies that have evaluated inclusive practices with only modest supporting evidence. Few studies report substantial academic gains by included students and many of these are anecdotal and often emphasise the social aspects of inclusive classrooms (see e.g., Kauffman et al. 1988). Hodges et al. (2006), for example, drew attention generally to the lack of research on academic outcomes for students with special education needs. While their work specifically targeted mathematics and students with emotional and behavioral disorders, their conclusions reflect the general impression that achievement of included students is of modest interest to researchers. While only six of the 13 selected studies were undertaken in inclusive education settings, Hodges et al. drew attention to the paucity of research on academic performance for this group of students. They reported that little attention was given to the development of problem-solving and higher-order thinking skills, suggesting that the lack of research may reflect an emphasis on behavioral issues for this specific student group.

In contrast, there are many reports of positive attitude change toward included children as a result of contact with, and proximity to, good behavior models and also a small number of reports that are less optimistic. Prominent among these are studies involving students with emotional and behavior difficulties who provide significant challenges to classroom harmony. A study by Cook & Semmel (1999) is an excellent example of the difficulties faced by teachers and researchers who aim to improve the classroom social climate. Cook & Semmel reported a low level of social acceptance of students with learning difficulties among their normally achieving peers. They asked students to identify those with whom they would be willing to work, willing to play, and with whom they would spend time in recreation or leisure out of school as everyday playmates. Peer acceptance score for students with mild and severe difficulties in each setting were uniformly low although students with mild disabilities were better accepted in heterogeneous classrooms although they remained low as desirable work mates. This outcome is confirmed by several reports in the literature (see e.g., Pavri & Monda-Amaya 2001).

Gifted and talented students have also come to attention specifically in regard to their involvement in regular education classrooms. Some writers have reported positive outcomes for gifted and talented students in inclusive education settings, especially gains in self-esteem. There are, however, also negative reports. These include lack of flexibility in using the most effective teaching and learning strategies with these students, limitations on the students' curiosity and independent learning. Some writers have claimed that gifted and talented students are readily exploited in regular education classes because they are expected to take on the role of "explainer" (see Braggett & Bailey 2005, for a general review).

I find it curious that there remains a political imperative for inclusive education when the evidence for its success is as equivocal as it is. There is no question in my mind that inclusive education is a prized ideal to which educators and education systems might aspire. I am, however, not at all convinced that every student can benefit from inclusion in a regular education classroom. Students who display dangerous or aggressive behavior and those with a severe mental health condition may put the safety of themselves or others at risk it there is not constant monitoring in regular education classes. Similarly, students with life-threatening medical condition (e.g., severe epilepsy) may also be at risk without regular scrutiny and supervision, at this may be difficult to achieve in regular classes where there is one teacher only. It is also questionable whether students with profound intellectual disability or severe multiple disabilities can be provided with the care, attention, and appropriate educational experiences in regular classes.

For the groups of students mentioned in the preceding paragraph, special schools and special classes seem to be the most suitable education context. In such specifically designed setting, services and resources can be concentrated, there is clear staff commitment to providing the best opportunities for students with high support needs, and there is an appropriate staff:student ratio that is difficult to match in regular schools. This does not mean, of course, that these students should be isolated from their nondisabled peers.

For all students with special education needs, there is an imperative that teaching-learning practices match students' characteristics. And among the repertoire of educational technologies available to support inclusive education practices is peer-mediated learning.

8.3   Peers and Diverse Abilities

The term, mediated learning, comes from the work of Vygotsky who emphasised the role of social interaction in which an expert guides a novice through a task to ensure that the learner acquires the higher-level skills desired. Vygotsky's writings (e.g., Vygotsky 1962, 1978) have had a continuing impact upon the theory and practice of cognitive psychology and its applications to education. One of his primary contentions was that education should be designed to accelerate children's cognitive development rather than provide experiences only at the individual's current level of cognitive maturity. Vygotsky argued that meaning is socially constructed and that learning and cognitive development is affected by the interactions that an individual has with others who are more skilled or knowledgeable.

Like the literature and the anecdotal reports that relate to many (if not most) education innovations and technologies, the literature on peer-mediated learning provides a revealing lesson in contradiction. When asked, many classroom teachers at the elementary and secondary levels claim to use one or a range of peer-mediated learning approaches in their classrooms but few claim that they adhere to complete procedures for any of the well-documented peer-mediated learning programs or conduct formal evaluations of their teaching effectiveness (see e.g., Antil et al. 1998).

In the professional education and psychology literatures one finds numerous applications of peer-mediated learning practices, from preschool (see e.g., Robertson et al. 2003) through elementary/primary (among them Emmer & Gerwels 2002; Fuchs et al. 2002; McMaster et al. 2002), through the secondary education years, (d'Arripe-Longueville et al. 2002; Wolford et al. 2001), into tertiary education (e.g., Darnon et al. 2002; Yetter et al. 2006) and beyond (see e.g., Gardner et al. 2001; Hall et al. 1998; Lazerson 2005).

One might expect comprehensive support for peer-mediated programs and practices thought to enhance the learning outcomes of students with special learning needs, especially in the light of political and administrative mandates for inclusive education. In reality, the literature provides mixed messages of success clouded by an abundance of research methods in which small-group or small-sample studies predominate (see e.g., Baker et al. 2004; Garrison-Harrell et al. 1997; Mortweet et al. 1999; Wolford et al. 2001).

Use of peer-mediated learning strategies has been a feature of formal and informal acculturation processes arguably since before the beginning of recorded history. In modern times, the use of peers to promote effective and efficient learning seems widespread although the exact nature of what constitutes peer-assisted learning varies considerably, ranging from unstructured group work to systematic and structured work programs under various labels such as peer-tutoring and cooperative learning. Many of the chapters in this volume provide strong evidence for the success of cooperative learning approaches. Reviewers of literature collections have claimed that teachers embrace peer-mediated learning because it provides opportunities for feedback by peers to students – including those with special learning needs – via student (rather than teacher) language, because it reduces the demand on the teacher to work on a one-to-one basis with included students during lessons, and because it is thought that there are important gains in students' self-management of learning and metacognitive awareness (see e.g., Bryant & Bryan 1998; Jenkins et al. 2003; Topping 1998).

Advocates of specific peer-mediated learning approaches have amassed impressive collections of support as can be seen in this volume and in some others, demonstrating the effectiveness of a range of peer-mediated learning approaches for students with and without learning difficulties. Some writers claim that their favored approach is the most systematized and well researched (see e.g., Heron et al. 2006) while a more comprehensive synthesis draws attention to the many significant developments including the formulation of integrated theoretical models and program supported by extensive reviews of published work documenting academic and social-emotional gains. These include among many others Topping (2005), a special issue of *Reading & Writing Quarterly: Overcoming Learning Difficulties* (including contributions by Maheady et al. 2006; Morgan 2006), Rohrbeck et al. (2003), and Topping and Ehly (1998).

8.4 Mixed Educational Outcomes

An examination of literature produced over the past 30 years with students with special education needs will, however, reveal a relatively small number of peer-mediated learning studies describing successful interventions in regular education classes. Fuchs et al. (2002) is a good example. This team implemented a dyadic peer-mediated program (Peer-Assisted Learning Strategies, PALS) in 20 class-rooms with a focus on mathematics and reported that teachers were generally supportive of PALS because the intervention benefited students with and without learning disabilities. The same program has been applied to other curriculum areas across the elementary/primary school years (see e.g., Calhoon 2005; Fuchs et al. 2001; McMaster et al. 2002) including considerable work on reading (see e.g., Gardner et al. 2001; Mathes et al. 2003; McMaster et al. 2006; Sáenz et al. 2005; Topping 1998; Topping & Bryce 2004; Wright & Cleary 2006). Despite these reports, there appears to have been relatively little research conducted in inclusive education settings and this has prompted some reviewers to claim that successful peer-mediated learning outcomes must be replicated in public school/general education classrooms for there to be a claim that peer-mediation works successfully in inclusive education settings (Mortweet et al. 1999; Sutherland et al. 2000)

Importantly in recent years, there has also been growth in the number of meta-analytic studies that have sought substantive evidence of the success of various peer-mediated programs and approaches within specific student populations. By carefully selecting studies in which there are comprehensive descriptions of the participants and procedures, meta-analyses have shown favorable peer-mediated intervention outcomes. Rohrbeck et al. (2003), for example, examined 90 studies undertaken with elementary/primary school students drawn from over 4,000 articles and chapters identified in two major databases. Overall, they found statistically significant effect sizes although certain student groups appeared to benefit more than others. For example, students living in urban (rather than suburban or rural) settings showed the greatest achievement gains and students from low-income backgrounds and from minority groups gained more than peers from more favorable socioeconomic backgrounds.

There have, however, also been reviews of peer-mediated learning strategies that have not been as generally supportive as Rohrbeck et al. (2003). Mastropieri and Scruggs (2001), for example, reviewed studies employing peer-assisted learning in secondary school curriculum areas such as Social Studies, English, and Algebra. They concluded that results have been variable with some researchers reporting no statistically significant differences between tutor-supported and independent study conditions. Mastropieri and Scruggs suggested that the social climate of the classroom and various curriculum factors are likely to play an important role in successful learning outcomes.

It would seem useful at this point to overview reports of peer-mediated intervention outcomes for students with a range of specific learning needs. These include students with learning difficulties, emotional and behavior problems, serious intellectual disabilities, students with minority group backgrounds, and finally, gifted and talented students.

8.4.1   Students with Learning Difficulties

Many studies have focused on the use of peer-mediated learning with students with learning disabilities – as defined in the US – although the outcomes appear to have been variable (see e.g., Fuchs et al. 1997; Kuntz et al. 2001). In the light of this, several reviewers have examined collections of published work drawing attention to research methods and analyses that complicate clear views about the success or otherwise of the interventions (e.g., Erlbaum et al. 2000; Maheady et al. 2001; McMaster & Fuchs 2002). McMaster and Fuchs, for example, reviewed research published between 1990 and 2000 and concluded that one of the major complications was researchers' use of peer-mediated learning as one aspect only of multi-component interventions thereby making it difficult to separate the influence of peer mediation from other aspects of the intervention.

In a recent review McMaster et al. (2006) also discussed the limitations of the often-reported successful PALS program. They stated that PALS seems to benefit many students but approximately 20% of low-achieving nondisabled students do not make adequate achievement gains following their involvement in PALS interventions and more than 50% of students with disabilities fail to benefited when assessed on reading achievement tests. They reported that these students generally have low phonological competence, tend to come from low socio-economic areas, have low cognitive competence, and present with attention and behavior difficulties. It is to the credit of this team that they undertook to redress this apparent limitation of the program in a follow-up study but these also proved less than successful.

8.4.2   Students with Emotional and Behavioral Disorders

Social skills and attitudinal outcomes have often been a target of many peer-mediated learning programs. At times, the affective outcomes have been secondary consequences of foci on academic skills, while at other times changes in social interactions have been the researchers' primary concern.

Ryan et al. (2004) examined the outcome of peer-mediated intervention studies (classwide peer tutoring, cooperative learning) on academic achievement of students with emotional and behavior disorders (EMB) based on 14 studies published between 1982 and 2000. They concluded that there were positive academic outcomes across all forms of peer-mediated interventions and reported overall high consumer satisfaction. They noted, however, that the settings in which data had been collected did not reflect the actual placement of students with EMB (only eight studies were conducted in general education classrooms). The reviewers' conclusions do seem overly positive when one examines the summary table of findings for the 14 studies. Eight were uniformly positive. In three studies there were mixed results (gains/no gains), and in three there were marginal or no appreciable gains. Sutherland et al. (2000) reported similar findings in respect of their review of eight cooperative learning studies.

Comparable results to those of Sutherland et al. (2000) were reported recently by Spencer (2006). She reviewed 38 peer tutoring studies undertaken between 1972 and 2002 and considered results according to grade levels. Many of the studies undertaken in elementary classroom showed positive outcomes for tutors and tutees especially in reading, language, and mathematics. Perhaps surprisingly, Spencer reported mixed findings on attitudinal measure although there appeared to be a common increase in positive social interactions between students with and without a disability. Studies undertaken in the middle years of schooling did not appear to be as positive across academic or social-emotional areas as for students in the elementary years and results for secondary school cohorts were mixed across academic and social domains. Despite the variability of outcomes, Spencer still concluded that there is an emerging body of evidence to suggest that students with emotional or behavior disorders may benefit from peer tutoring.

Work by Hodges et al. (2006) might provide some explanation for the mixed research results found with students with EMB. They stated that peer-mediated instruction *may* yield positive social and academic outcomes for students with EMB but because of the difficulties many of these students have in interpersonal relationships, it would seem imperative that peer-mediated interventions include specific training on interpersonal skills to enable the students with EMB to work effectively in dyads or small groups. They cautioned that the lack of research related to academic achievement would suggest that replication and systematic collection of student performance data would be needed before the veracity of any intervention could be assumed.

8.4.3 Students with Disabilities

Several research teams have studied the effects of peer-mediation with students with intellectual disability, acquired brain injury, physical, and sense impairments (see e.g., Liberman et al. 2000; McDonnell et al. 2001; Morgan et al. 1999; Ryan

& Paterna 1997). Consistent with the findings reported in the previous section, not all attempts to improve academic and social outcomes have been successful (see e.g., Brinton et al. 1998, 2000). As has been the case with students with EMB, many studies involving students with severe impairments or disability focus on social-affective issues rather than academic performance.

Notwithstanding the fact that inclusive education policies and practices have been in existence for many years, most studies of peer-mediated learning with students with mental retardation have been conducted in self-contained or other special education settings; few have been undertaken in general education classrooms (Mortweet et al. 1999). In a small New Zealand study, Jacques et al. (1998) examined the effects of interactions between 24 students with mild intellectual disability and their nondisabled peers. All of the students were in regular education settings although half had attended special education classes prior to the intervention. The nondisabled students in the experimental condition demonstrated significant increases in their social acceptance of the children with a disability immediately after the program using a sociometric procedure. There were no changes in the social acceptance of the nondisabled students in the control setting. Of some interest Jacques et al. noted that the teachers ratings of social adjustment of the children in the experimental condition were not significantly different to those of the control children immediately after or at the 5-week follow up (although they indicated that it was *close* at follow up, $p < 0.07$). They suggested that any effects of social learning through participation in the program was likely more likely to be displayed in the children's social behavior in the longer-term than immediately after the intervention.

In a later study, Piercy et al. (2002) again implemented a cooperative learning program to improve the social acceptance of children with moderate to severe intellectual disabilities. The children interacted over 10 weeks in three experimental conditions (cooperative learning, social-contact, and no classroom contact). At the completion of the program, the students without a disability in the cooperative learning groups rated the students with disability more positively on peer acceptance, popularity, and social-distance than children who participated in the two control group settings.

A number of studies have also been conducted on the effectiveness of peer-mediated learning with students with autism. Commonly, the focus of attention has also been either social acceptance by peers or the development of social, cooperative behavior in the student with autism. Weiss and Harris (2001), for example, discussed the importance of the placement of socially competent students with peers displaying autistic behavior, the training of peers to manage autistic behavior, and the initiation of interactions with autistic students. These and other skills such as answering questions, turn taking, and looking at others when they speak are basic skills necessary for the success of cooperative learning activities.

In some studies, researchers have suggested that simply having normally achieving students interact with autistic peers will positively affect both participant groups. However, Weiss and Harris (2001) argued that proximity alone does not bring about enduring social change or the generalisation of social skills beyond the training context. Other writers have expressed similar views. Harrower and Dunlap (2001), for example, drew attention to investigations in which classwide peer tutoring and cooperative learning models were employed successfully. In these, they referred to improvement in targeted academic skills and engagement. There were also increased interactions between children with autism and their classmates who learned to cue and prompt the autistic students successfully to facilitate achievement in the target areas. While these approaches may seem to work effectively in inclusive classrooms, Harrower and Dunlap cautioned that increasing the rate of social interaction among children with disability through peer-mediation might not always lead to enduring changes outside of the program settings (echoing Cook & Semmel 1999). And even within the program itself there is a need to provide specialist support and training in specific strategies such as self-management. A similar suggestion was made by Downs and Smith (2004).

8.5 Students with Minority Group Background

How one learns about the world is influenced by how one is taught and by the readiness to learn. Hence, teaching not only involves providing information but also facilitating the learner's thinking and learning skills and processes through questioning, stimulation, modeling, and supporting the use of appropriate strategies – all of which are common components of successful peer-mediated learning programs. The process of acculturation, however, is not limited to what takes place inside formal education institutions.

In many Indigenous cultures education is an all-of-life experience that is mediated by relationships that exist within a community. In this context, mediation refers to the need for someone other than the learner to translate social and cultural knowledge so that it can be internalised by the learner, in other words, the individual's ownership of concepts and meaning are provided through instruction. Children must comprehend meaning and integrate new knowledge into their own thinking. They must transform external stimuli into internal codes that are consistent with their own knowledge by changing and modifying the original ideas and applying their unique cognitive character to them.

In schools in most Western countries there is an imperative to learn and to demonstrate learning in a clearly hierarchical environment. In many Indigenous communities, however, young people learn from the older members (often the elders) who provide both educational opportunities and experiences and many Indigenous students see no connection between the way in which learning is presented in school and the way in which it occurs within their communities. As a consequence, they often become passive, or even reluctant, learners and their persistence with formal schooling and their level of success can be seriously compromised if judged by Western standards only.

The commitment to social connectedness (communalism) and cooperative learning are often listed among the learning styles that are characteristic of Indigenous cultures, including the African American culture. While Watkins (2002) found that

2–5-year olds in African American communities commonly approached teachers for social help and peers for academic help, older children and youths are often more successful in mediating learning for their peers than are adults. One important reason for this is their use of language that expresses commonly held values, attitudes, beliefs, and shared life experiences. Young people are also often observed to employ a form of apprenticeship with each other that involves coaching, modeling, and observational learning.

Unlike adult apprenticeships during vocational training, peer-mediation among children and adolescents typically operates within a social – rather than instructional – interaction and allows for study, practice, and reflection. Lee (1995) described a learning apprenticeship model for teaching literacy interpretation skills to African American high school students. Two learning environments were created. One involved small work groups, scaffolded learning experiences based on the students' own social discourse, African American literature, and the use of student's social knowledge. The other had a traditional white middle-class orientation typical of high school teaching practices. Not surprisingly, students in the first setting made significant improvements in their independent mastery of problem-solving strategies while those in the traditional setting did not.

Given the background outlined earlier in this section, it is not surprising that peer-mediated learning has been shown to be effective in a number of studies involving minority group students. In their meta-analysis, Rohrbeck et al. (2003), for example, reported that minority students benefited more the PAL interventions in terms of academic outcomes than nonminority students. One explanation for this finding is the establishment of some degree of continuity that PAL creates between home and school. For vulnerable student, Rohrbeck et al. suggested that the messages about academic achievement might be communicated across family, school, and peer group boundaries. The one complication here is the degree to which the results of collaboration endure beyond any intervention or experiment. Samaha and De Lisi (2000) have provided a good example of this.

Samaha and De Lisi (2000) worked with 86 seventh-grade students, 78% of whom were Hispanic and 10% African American. One group worked independently while others worked in mixed- or same-sex small groups on nonverbal reasoning tasks (similar to the Wechsler Nonverbal matrices) that required the students to select correct answers (make judgments) and generate explanation for their solutions. The mixed-gender groups outperformed other groups although the performance of students in all groups declined significantly at the posttest in terms of their judgments when compared with their performance during the experimental phase. Samaha and De Lisi concluded that peer interactions appeared to be beneficial at the time of the collaboration although this did not make the participants more competent to respond correctly to items on their own at a later time. The quality of explanations made by the collaborating students remained high at the posttest and the authors were encouraged by the results of their work with educationally disadvantaged youth. They cautioned, however, that their study was modest, involved only one class period, and dealt with abstract problem-solving rather than typical curriculum tasks.

8.5.1 Gifted and Talented Students

Over a number of years there has been debate in the professional literature about whether peer-mediated learning activities are advantageous or disadvantageous to gifted and talented students. Some writers have argued that peer-mediated learning fails to take the needs of gifted and talented students into consideration, especially flexibility, variety, curiosity, and independent discovery learning (Gallagher & Gallagher 1994; Robinson 1991). The results of several studies have shown mixed outcome in terms of students' achievement, attitudes toward the curriculum and learning, self-efficacy, and learning style, (see e.g., Coleman & Gallagher 1995; Neber et al. 2001; Robinson 2003). Robertson (2003), for example, viewed the role often given to gifted students as the "explainer" and the teacher's helper, and asserted that such a responsibility constitutes exploitation of brighter students, echoing views expressed by Ross and Smyth (1995).

Understandably, supporters of peer-mediated learning do not believe that the interactions and experiences of the brighter students that occur in mixed ability groups are exploitative and, even those who are critical of mixed ability grouping, express at least some support for peer-mediated learning. Melser (1999), for example, found that fourth and fifth grade gifted students gained in self-esteem in heterogeneous groups and lost self-esteem in homogeneous groups although, in both contexts they gained in the targeted academic area, reading. Contrary affective and academic results were reported by Sheppard and Kavevsky (1999) and Ramsay and Richards (1997) who claimed that gifted students were less positive about cooperative learning than their average-ability peers although it appeared as though their attitude toward school subjects was unaffected. More recently, Garduno (2001) found that seventh and eighth grade gifted students made some limited academic gains within cooperative learning settings but lost motivation when they were required to explain content and process to their peers. Overall, participants had a more positive attitude toward mathematics in whole-group, competitive settings than in cooperative settings.

Individual differences among students may account for equivocal results across peer-mediation studies that involve gifted and high-achieving students. In their cluster and factor analytic study, Feldhusen et al. (2000) differentiated students into five relatively homogeneous groups. Some gifted students presented a desire to outperform their peers while others viewed competition as an energizing agent within the classroom learning context. Feldhusen et al. noted that gifted students generally were not negative about competitive *or* cooperative learning conditions. They were able to discriminate between situations in which each was an appropriate learning context and self-aware of their own preferred learning style.

In their meta-analysis of cooperative learning studies involving gifted students, Neber et al. (2001) concluded that cooperative learning approaches can result in small to medium learning gains for gifted and high-achieving students, notably in the low and middle grades. They claimed that there were few studies available that had the methodological precision to enable more robust conclusions to be made about peer-mediated learning, and cooperative learning in particular. Specifically, they stated that there are some studies in which gifted students have been advantaged in mixed ability settings while other researchers have reported gains for these students in homogeneous groups of gifted or high-achieving students only. One of the complications it seems, is the lack of detail in the description of research methods in terms of the accurate application of cooperative learning, and in particular the explicit requirement for goal-interdependency among work group members.

More recently, Patrick et al. (2005) took a slightly different approach to the debate about the efficacy of peer-mediated learning for gifted and talented students. They claimed that the discussion about whether peer-mediation (cooperative learning in this case) is beneficial to high-achieving students should concentrate on the process of task-related interactions. Rather than viewing cooperative learning as a single approach, there should be a more substantive analysis of the similarities and differences in the nature and type of the dialogues that are promoted by different cooperative learning approaches. They concluded that the types of task and the cognitive and interactive processes are important. Formats that emphasize transmission of factual information seem most likely to engender concerns when gifted students' are placed in mixed ability groups because of differences in learning speed between average and gifted students. In contrast, there appear to be benefits for both average and gifted students when higher order thinking and comprehension is required, when students are expected to explain and justify their ideas and reasons.

At this point, it appears that there are situations in which the intellectual needs of gifted students can be accommodated in peer-mediated learning. Patrick et al. (2005), however, have warned that mixed ability grouping and collaborative learning approached do not inevitably benefit those students.

8.6   The Future of Peer-Mediation and Inclusion

In Ashman (2003) I posed the question: Has peer-mediated learning met researchers' and practitioners' expectations? In that context, I observed that we have had more than twenty years of research on, and promotion of, peer-mediation. Moreover, most teachers at the primary/elementary and secondary school levels are familiar with at least the general concepts if not with specifics of any approach. In this chapter I have restricted my review as much as possible to a synthesis of the literature paying particular attention to meta-analytic studies. I might have substantiated by comments by a plethora of references but have included only those that I considered representative.

The evidence suggests that we have not advanced too much further over the last four years to validate the claim that peer-mediated learning is successful in bringing about academic gains and/or social benefits to students in special education or inclusive education settings. Perhaps the best general conclusion would be an adaptation of Patrick et al. (2005): that students with special learning needs *might* benefit from peer-mediating learning experiences but it is not *inevitable* that they will if placed in such a learning context and it is certain that peer mediation is not *necessarily* the most efficient or effective learning strategy for all.

The lessons to be learned from the literature in regard to students with special learning needs seem to be little different to those pertinent to general education settings. There are some positive aspects. For example, there appears to be a leaning toward the development of theories that relate to peer-mediated interventions (see e.g., several chapters in this volume, and also Topping 2005) and fewer reports that offer opinion-rather than empirically supported conclusions about academic and behavior outcomes.

On the negative side of the ledger, while many teachers claim to use peer-mediation as a teaching-learning strategy, they are often not implemented in the manner that their developers and researchers suggest. Antil et al. (1998) conducted follow-up interviews with 21 teachers involved in their study who reported using some form of cooperative learning. Only one of those interviewed reported using the five fundamental components (i.e., positive interdependence, individual accountability, promotive interaction, group processing, development of small group social skills). Five others reported using positive interdependence and individual accountability.

Somewhat bluntly and perhaps over-critically, Walker et al. (1998) stated that many teachers "seem to ignore the concept of best practice and rely upon a hodgepodge of activities, unplanned curricula, and conceptually incompatible interventions to accomplish teaching, learning, and management goals" (p. 8). Rohrbeck et al. (2003) appear to have taken Walker et al. to heart when they stated that at-risk students generally receive instruction marked by poor use of instructional time, lower expectations, and less opportunity for learning and that there is strong evidence for the effectiveness of PAL interventions with these vulnerable students. They concluded that the use of PAL strategies would be a welcome improvement to instructional practices with these students. The comments by Walker et al. and Rohrbeck et al. could be taken in the context of one of the more prominent criticisms of peer-mediated intervention is the failure to apply any chosen approach in accordance with the developers' guidelines.

And while one might pass judgment on teacher adaptations of well-researched programs and approaches, the recommendations offered by researchers to guide the implementation of peer-mediated strategies are often vague and unhelpful. Mortweet et al. (1999), for example, suggested that successful inclusive environments for students with special learning needs should be designed to maximize academic achievement through teacher-directed group activities, high levels of student engagement, student-teacher interactions, appropriate pacing of lessons, questioning and feedback, and the structured use of peers.

Englert et al. (2001) stressed the need for students to participate fully in activities and that it is the teacher's responsibility to ensure that opportunities are provided to enable this to occur. They argued that collaborations must: bring students together in ways that encourage them to learn about the thinking and problem-solving process; encourage mediation so that students' performances reflect the acquisition of skills and lead toward independent learning and problem-solving; and facilitate cultural, historical, and dynamic aspects of the learning environment. These recommendations appear to be slightly less than practical. Others, such as Bryant and Bryant (1998), stated that adaptations are necessary to the teaching-learning environment because students with special education needs do not have the necessary skills to perform appropriately in cooperative activities. These essential adaptations include changes to the teaching procedure, classroom management practices, and the physical environment, plus adaptation of the curriculum and availability of appropriate materials and technology.

At the beginning of this chapter I devoted several pages to inclusive education. In my mind, the histories of inclusive education and of peer-mediated learning have followed parallel pathways. Strong arguments can be made for the promotion and implementation of both notions in our education systems. For inclusion, there are issues of equality of opportunity, for peer-mediated learning there are conceptual bases that have their origins in Vygotsky's writings and in ancient cultural traditions. Practically, both have struggled to find solid ground in regular education classrooms, mainstream schools, and in education systems more generally despite the sparkles of success that are reported in the professional literature.

We know that not all students are advantaged if placed in regular education settings and that others are reluctant or ineffective participants in cooperative learning situations. The academic benefits that might accrue from students' involvement in both contexts are unique to each individual. For students who are progressing satisfactorily through school, the occasional unhelpful experience is unlikely to have serious detrimental consequences. For students who are already disadvantaged by virtue of an intellectual impairment or behavior difficulty, the result of imprudent educational placement can compound their problems and lead to failure. For example, it is likely to be inappropriate, even disadvantageous to involve some students in regular classrooms and in peer collaborations if they do not have the social skills to interact successfully with others in those contexts. Sutherland et al. (2000) and Farrell (2000) made a similar claim when they stated in respect of students with EMB that haphazard placement of these students in groups and expecting them to perform socially and academically is clearly not what cooperative learning advocates would encourage.

Over the years, I have been mindful of the many recommendations that have been made about the importance of ensuring that appropriate preparation is undertaken when students with special learning needs are to be enrolled into regular education classroom. I hold the same views about the involvement of students in peer-mediated learning activities. Most primary/elementary and many secondary classroom teachers have a repertoire of teaching-learning strategies that can accommodate the need for flexibility and facilitate students' academic and social development. It is counterproductive to assume that any approach can satisfy the preferred learning styles and needs of every student.

References

Antil, L. R., Jenkins, J. R., Wayne, S. K., & Vadsy P. F. (1998). Cooperative learning: Prevalence, conceptualizations, and the relation between research and practice. *American Education Research Journal, 35,* 419–454.
Ashman, A. F. (2003). Peer mediation and students with diverse learning needs. In R. M. Gillies & A. F. Ashman (Eds.), *Cooperating learning: The social and intellectual outcomes of learning in groups* (pp. 87–102). London: RoutledgeFalmer.

Baker, J. M. & Zigmond, N. (1995). The meaning and practice of inclusion for students with learning disabilities: Themes and implications from five cases. *Journal of Special Education, 29,* 163–180.

Baker, S., Gersten, R., Dimino, J. A., & Griffiths, R. (2004). The sustained use of research-based instructional practice: A case study of peer-assisted learning strategies in mathematics. *Remedial and Special Education: Special Issue on Sustainability, 25,* 5–24.

Biklen, D. (Ed.). (1985). *Achieving the complete school: Strategies for effective mainstreaming.* New York: Teacher's College, Columbia University.

Braggett, E. & Bailey, S. (2005). Gifted and talented children and their education. In A. Ashman and J. Elkins (Eds.), *Educating children with diverse abilities* (2nd edn.). Frenchs Forest, NSW: Pearson Education.

Bricker, D. (1995). The challenge of inclusion. *Journal of Early Intervention, 19,* 179–194.

Brinton, B., Fujiki, M., & Higbee, L. M. (1998). Participation in cooperative learning activities by children with specific language impairments. *Journal of Speech, Language, and Hearing Research, 41,* 1193–1206.

Brinton, B., Fujiki, M., Montague, E. C., & Hanton, J. L. (2000). Children with language impairment in cooperative work groups: A pilot study. *Language, Speech, and Hearing Services in Schools. Special Issue: Collaboration and inclusion: Multiple perspectives – one focus, 31,* 252–264.

Bryant, D. P. & Bryant, B. R. (1998). Using assistive technology adaptations to include students with learning disabilities in cooperative learning activities. *Journal of Learning Disabilities, 31,* 41–54.

Calhoon, M. B. (2005). Effects of a peer-mediated phonological skill and reading comprehension program on reading skill acquisition for middle school students with reading disabilities. *Journal of Learning Disabilities, 38,* 424–433.

Chapman, J. W. (1988). Special education in the least restrictive environment: Mainstreaming or maindumping? *Journal of Intellectual & Developmental Disabilities, 14,* 123–134.

Coleman, M. R. & Gallagher, J. J. (1995). The successful blending of gifted education with middle school and cooperative learning: Two studies. *Journal for the Education of the Gifted, 18,* 362–384.

Cook, B., & Semmel, M. I. (1999). Peer acceptance of included students with disabilities as a function of severity of disability and classroom composition. *Journal of Special Education, 33,* 50–61.

Darling-Hammond, L. (1996). What matters most: A competent teacher for every child. *Phi Delta Kappan, 78,* 193–200.

Darnon, C., Buchs, C., & Butera, F. (2002). Epistemic and relational conflicts in sharing identical vs complementary information during cooperative learning. *Swiss Journal of Psychology, 61,* 139–151.

d'Arripe-Longueville, F., Gernigon, C., Huet, M-L., Cadopi, M., & Winnykamen, F. (2002). Peer tutoring in a physical education setting: Influence of tutor skill level on novice learners' motivation and performance. *Journal of Teaching in Physical Education, 22,* 105–123.

Downs, A. & Smith, T. (2004). Emotional understanding, cooperation, and social behavior in high-functioning children with autism. *Journal of Autism and Developmental Disorders, 34,* 625–635.

Dunn, L. M. (1968). Special education for the mildly retarded: Is much of it justifiable? *Exceptional Children, 35,* 5–22.

Elkins, J. 1994. The school context. In A. Ashman & J. Elkins (Eds.), *Educating children with special needs* (pp. 71–104). New York: Prentice Hall.

Emmer, E. T. & Gerwels, M. C. (2002). Cooperative learning in elementary classrooms: Teaching practices and lesson characteristics. *Elementary School Journal, 103,* 75–91.

Englert, C. S., Berry, R., & Dunsmore, K. (2001). A case study of the apprenticeship process: Another perspective on the apprentice and the scaffolding metaphor. *Journal of Learning Disabilities, 24,*152–171.

Erlbaum, B., Vaughn, S., Hughes, M. T., Watson Moody, S., & Schumm, J. S. (2000). A meta-analytic review of the effects of instructional grouping format on the reading outcomes of students with disabilities. In R. Gersten, E. Schiller, J. S. Schumm, & S. Vaughn (Eds.), *Issues and research in special education* (pp. 10–135). Hillsdale, NJ: Erlbaum.

Farrell, M. (2000). Educational inclusion and raising standards. *British Journal of Special Education, 27,* 35–38.

Feldhusen, J. F., Dai, D. Y., & Clinkenbeard, P. R. (2000). Dimensions of competitive and cooperative learning among gifted learners. *Journal for the Education of the Gifted, 23,* 328–342.

Forlin, C. (2004). Promoting inclusivity in Western Australian schools. *International Journal of Inclusive Education, 8,* 185–202.

Fuchs, D., Fuchs, L. S., Mathes, P. G., & Simmons, D. C. (1997). Peer-assisted learning strategies: Making classrooms more responsive to diversity. *American Educational Research Journal, 34,* 176–206.

Fuchs, D., Fuchs, L. S., Thompson, A., Svenson, E., Yen, L., Otaiba, S A., Yang, N., McMaster, K. N., Prentice, K., Kazdan, S., & Saenz. L. (2001). Peer-assisted learning strategies in reading: Extensions for kindergarten, first grade, and high school. *Remedial and Special Education, 22,* 15–21.

Fuchs, L. S, Fuchs, D., Yazdian, L., & Powell, S. R. (2002). Enhancing first-grade children's mathematical development with peer-assisted learning strategies. *School Psychology Review, 31,* 569–583.

Gallagher, J. J., & Gallagher, S. A. (1994). *Teaching the gifted child* (4th edn.). Boston: Allyn & Bacon.

Gardner, R., III, Cartledae, G., Seidl, B., Woolsey, M. L., Schiev, G. S., & Utley, C. (2001). *Remedial and Special Education, 22,* 22–23.

Garduno, E. L. H. (2001). The influence of cooperative problem solving on gender differences in achievement, self-efficacy, and attitudes toward mathematics in gifted students. *Gifted Child Quarterly, 45,* 268–282.

Garrison-Harrell, L., Kamps, D., & Kravits, T. (1997). The effects of peer networks on social-communicative behaviors for students with autism. *Focus on Autism and Other Developmental Disabilities, 12,* 241–254.

Hall, S., Gay, B., & Topping, K. (1998). Peer-assisted learning beyond school. In K. Topping & S. Ehly (Eds.), *Peer-assisted learning* (pp. 291–311). Mahwah, NJ: Lawrence Erlbaum Associated Publishers.

Harrower, J. K. & Dunlap, G. (2001). *Behavior Modification. Special Issue: Autism, Part 1, 25,* 762–784.

Heron, T. E., Villareal, D. M., Yao, M., Christianson, R. J., & Heron, K. M. (2006). Peer tutoring systems: Applications in classroom and specialized environments. *Reading & Writing Quarterly: Overcoming Learning Difficulties, 22,* 27–45.

Hodges, J., Riccomini, P. J., Buford, R., & Herbst, M. H. (2006). A review of instructional interventions in mathematics for students with emotional and behavioral disorders. *Behavioral disorders, 31,* 297–311.

Jacques, N., Wilton, K., & Townsend, M. (1998). Cooperative learning and social acceptance of children with mild intellectual disability. *Journal of Intellectual Disability Research, 42,* 29–36.

Jenkins, J. R., Antil, L. R., Wayne, S. K., & Vadasy, P. F. (2003). How cooperative learning works for special education and remedial students. *Exceptional Children, 69,* 279–292.

Jenkinson, J. C. (1997). *Mainstream or special? Educating students with disabilities.* London: Routledge.

Kauffman, J. M., Gerber, M. M., & Semmel, M. I. (1988). Arguable assumptions underlying the Regular Education Initiative. *Journal of Learning Disabilities, 21,* 6–12.

Kauffman, J. M. & Hallahan, D. P. (Eds.) (1995). *The illusion of full inclusion: A comprehensive critique of a current special education bandwagon.* Austin, TX: PRO-ED, Inc.

Kuntz, K. L., McLaughlin, T. F., & Howard, V. F. (2001). A comparison of cooperative learning and small group individualized instruction for math in a self contained classroom for elementary students with disabilities. *Educational Research Quarterly, 24,* 41–56.

Lazerson, D. B. (2005). Detention home teens as tutors: A cooperative cross-age pilot project. *Emotional and Behavioral Difficulties, 10,* 7–15.

Lee, C. D. (1995). A culturally based cognitive apprenticeship: Teaching African American high school students skills in literary interpretation. *Reading Research Quarterly, 30,* 608–630.

Liberman, L. J., Dunn, J. M., van der Mars, H., & McCubbin, J. (2000). Peer tutors' effects on activity levels of deaf students in inclusive elementary physical education. *Adapted Physical Activity Quarterly, 17,* 20–39.

McDonnell, J., Mathot-Buckner, C., Thorson, N., & Fister, S. (2001). Supporting the inclusion of students with moderate and severe disabilities in junior high school general education classes: The effects of classwide peer tutoring, multi-element curriculum, and accommodations. *Education and Treatment of Children, 24,* 141–160.

McMaster, K. N. & Fuchs, D. (2002). Effects of cooperative learning on the academic achievement of students with learning disabilities: An update of Tateyama-Sniezek's review. *Learning Difficulties Research & Practice, 17,* 107–117.

McMaster, K. N., Fuchs, D., & Fuchs, L. S. (2002). Using peer tutoring to present early reading failure. In J. S. Thousand, F. A. Villa, & A. I. Nevin (Eds.), *Creativity and collaborative learning: The practical guide to empowering students, teachers, and families* (2nd edn.) (pp. 235–246). Baltimore, MD: Paul H Brookes Publishing.

McMaster, K. N., Fuchs, D., & Fuchs, L. S. (2006). Research on peer-assisted learning strategies: The promise and limitations of peer-mediated instruction. *Reading and Writing Quarterly: Overcoming Learning Difficulties, 22,* 5–25.

Maheady, L., Mallette, B., & Harper, G. F. (2006). Four classwide peer tutoring models: Similarities, differences, and implications for research and practice. *Reading & Writing Quarterly: Overcoming Learning Difficulties, 22,* 65–89.

Mastropieri, M. A. & Scruggs, T. E. (2001). Promoting inclusion in secondary classrooms. *Learning Disability Quarterly, 24,* 265–274.

Mathes, P. G., Torgesen, J. K., Clancy-Menchetti, J., Santi, K., Nicholsas, K., Robinson, C., & Grek, M. (2003). A comparison of teacher-directed versus peer-assisted instruction to struggling first-grade readers. *Elementary School Journal, 103,* 459–479.

Melser, N. A. (1999). Gifted students and cooperative learning: A study of grouping strategies. *Roeper Review, 21,* 315.

Mitler, P. (1988, September). Intellectual trends in special education of persons with intellectual disabilities. Paper presented at the 16th World Congress of Rehabilitation International, Tokyo, Japan.

Morgan, S. A. (2006). Introduction: Four classwide peer tutoring programs-research, recommendations for implementation, and future directions. *Reading & Writing Quarterly: Overcoming Learning Difficulties, 22,* 1–4.

Morgan, R. L., Whorton, J. E., & Turtle, L. B. (1999). Use of peer tutoring to improve speech skills in a preschooler with a severe hearing impairment. *Educational Research Quarterly, 23,* 44–55.

Mortweet, S. L., Utley, C. A., Walker, D., Dawson, H. L., Delquardri, J. C., Reddy, S. S., Greenwood, C. R., Hamilton, S., & Ledford, D. (1999). Classwide peer tutoring: Teaching students with mild mental retardation in inclusive classrooms. *Exceptional Children, 65,* 524–536.

Neber, H., Finsterwalk, M., & Urban, N. (2001). Cooperative learning with gifted and high-achieving students: A review and meta-analyses of 12 studies. *High Ability Studies, 12,* 199–214.

Nesbit, W. (1994). Inclusive education: Views of a grammarian, not a poet. *Canadian Journal of Special Education, 9,* 119–130.

Patrick, H., Bangel, N. J., Jeon, K-N., & Townsend, M. A. R. (2005). Reconsidering the issues of cooperative learning with gifted students. *Journal for the Education of the Gifted, 29,* 90–110.

Pavri, S. & Monda-Amaya, L. (2001). Social support in inclusive schools: Student and teacher perspectives. *Exceptional Children, 67,* 391–411.

Piercy, M., Wilton, K., & Townsend, M. (2002). Promoting the social acceptance of young children with moderate-severe intellectual disabilities using cooperative-learning techniques. *American Journal on Mental Retardation, 107,* 352–360.

Ramsay, S. G. & Richards H. C. (1997). Cooperative learning environments: Effects on academic attitudes of gifted students. *Gifted Child Quarterly, 41,* 160–168.

Robertson, J., Green, K., Alper, S., Schloss, P. J., & Kohler, F. (2003). Using a peer-mediated intervention to facilitate children's participation in inclusive childcare activities. *Education and Treatment of Children, 26,* 182–197.

Robinson, A. (1991). Cooperation or exploitation? The argument against cooperative learning for talented students. *Journal for the Education of the Gifted, 14*, 9–27.

Robinson, A. (2003). Cooperative learning and high ability students. In N. Colangelo & G. Davis (Eds.), *Handbook of gifted education* (3rd edn., pp. 282–292). Boston: Allyn & Bacon.

Rohrbeck, C. A., Ginsburg-Block, M. D., Fantuzzo, J. W., & Miller, T. R. (2003). Peer-assisted learning interventions with elementary school students: A meta-analytic review. *Journal of Educational Psychology, 95*, 240–257.

Ross, J. A. & Smyth, E. (1995). Thinking skills for gifted students: The case for correlational reasoning. *Roeper Review, 17*, 239–243.

Ryan, S. & Paterna, L. (1997). Junior high can be inclusive: Using natural supports and cooperative learning. *Teaching Exceptional Children, 30*, 36–41.

Ryan, J. B., Reid, R., & Epstein, M. H. (2004). Peer-mediated intervention studies on academic achievement for students with EBD. *Remedial and Special Education, 25*, 330–341.

Sáenz, L. M., Fuchs, L. S., & Fuchs, D. (2005). Peer-assisted learning strategies for English language learners with learning disabilities. *Exceptional Children, 71*, 231–247.

Samaha, N. V. & De Lisi, R. (2000). Peer collaboration on a nonverbal reasoning task by urban, minority students. *Journal of Experimental Education, 69*, 5–21.

Sheppard, S. & Kavevsky, L. S. (1999). Nurturing gifted students' metacognitive awareness: Effects of training in homogeneous and heterogeneous classes. *Roeper Review, 21*, 266–275.

Spencer, V. G. (2006). Peer tutoring and students with emotional or behavioral disorders: A review of the literature. *Behavior Disorders, 31*, 204–222.

Stainback, S., Stainback, W., & Ayres, B. (1996). Schools as inclusive communities. In W. Stainback & S. Stainback (Eds.), *Controversial issues confronting special education: Divergent perspectives* (2nd edn., pp. 31–43). Boston: Allyn & Bacon.

Sutherland, K. S., Wehby, J. H., & Gunter, P. L. (2000). The effectiveness of cooperative learning with students with emotional and behavioural disorders: A literature review. *Behavior Disorders, 25*, 225–238.

Topping K. (1998). Paired learning in literacy. In K. Topping & S. Ehly (Eds.), *Peer-assisted learning* (pp. 87–104). Mahwah, NJ: Lawrence Erlbaum Associated Publishers.

Topping, K. J. (2005). Trends in peer learning. *Educational Psychology. Special Issue: Developments in educational psychology: How far have we come in 25 years? 25*, 631–645.

Topping, K. T. & Bryce, A. (2004). Cross-age peer tutoring of reading and thinking: Influence on thinking skills. *Educational Psychology, 24*, 595–621.

Topping, K. T. & Ehly, S. (Eds.) (1998). *Peer-assisted learning*. Mahwah, NJ: Lawrence Erlbaum Associated Publishers.

Vlachou, A. (2004). Education and inclusive policy-making: Implications for research and practice. *International Journal on Inclusive Education, 8*, 3–21.

Vlachou, A. & Barton, L. (1994). Inclusive education: Teachers and the changing culture of schooling. *British Journal of Special Education, 21*, 105–107.

Vygotsky, L. S. (1962). *Thought and language*. Cambridge, MA: MIT Press.

Vygotsky, L. S. (1978). *Mind in society: The development of higher psychological processes*. Cambridge, MA: Harvard University Press.

Walker, H. M., Forness, S. R. Kauffman, J. M., Epstein, M. H. Gresham, F. M., Nelson, C. M., & Strain, P. S. (1998). Macro-social validation: Referencing outcomes in behavioral disorders to societal issues and problems. *Behavior Disorders, 24*, 7–18.

Warnock, M. (1978). *Special education needs. The report of the committee of enquiry into the education of handicapped children and young people*. London: HSMO.

Watkins, A. F. (2002). Learning styles of African American children: A developmental consideration. *Journal of Black Psychology, 28*, 3–17.

Wedell, K. (1995). Making inclusive education ordinary. *British Journal of Special Education, 22*, 100–104.

Weiss, M. J. & Harris, S. L. (2001). Teaching social skills to people with autism. *Behavior Modification, 25*, 785–802.

Wolford, P. L., Heward, W. L., & Alber, S. R. (2001). Teaching middle school students with learning disabilities to recruit peer assistance during cooperative learning group activities. *Learning Disabilities Research & Practice, 16,* 161–173.

Wright, J. & Cleary, K. S. (2006). Kids in the tutor seat: Building schools' capacity to help struggling readers through a cross-age peer-tutoring program. *Psychology in the Schools, 43,* 99–107.

Yetter, G., Gutkin, T. B., Saunders, A., Galloway, A. M., Sobansky, R. R., & Song, S. Y. (2006). Unstructured collaboration versus individual practice for complex problem solving: A cautionary tale. *Journal of Experimental Education, 74,* 137–159.

Chapter 9
Developing Language and Mastering Content in Heterogeneous Classrooms

Rachel A. Lotan

Abstract In this chapter, I describe what teachers need to do to set up classroom conditions that support development in English, the language of instruction, as well as mastery of subject matter content in academically and linguistically heterogeneous classrooms. To support my argument, I use data from a study conducted in six diverse 7th grade social studies classrooms in California's Central Valley where teachers used complex instruction, a pedagogical approach that supports teaching at a high intellectual level in classrooms with a wide range of previous academic achievement and linguistic proficiency. Students from different language proficiency levels benefited similarly from the intellectually rigorous curriculum and from the quality of interactions with peers during group work. Based on this study, we suggest that schools rethink linguistic segregation and ensure access to challenging and grade-appropriate curricula and equitable instruction for all students. Furthermore, I present to teachers a model of effective, research-based practice that could expand their repertoire of strategies for heterogeneous classrooms.

9.1   Introduction

In many countries, significant proportions of school students are learners of a second, and sometimes third, language. For many of these students, failure to acquire the language of instruction leads to detrimental educational outcomes. This problem turns acute in the middle grades when the development of academic language skills becomes increasingly consequential and knowledge of subject matter content ever more critical.

In the US, most middle school English learners can be found in one of three contexts: newcomer programs, regular mainstream classes, and specially designed programs that combine language and content instruction. Thus, newly-arrived immigrants might be placed in special programs for newcomers only where they receive intensive instruction in English as a Second Language for a semester or for a whole academic year. During this period, they might or might not have access to classes where subject matter is taught in their primary language. Some English learners, though rarely beginners and more often only those who have successfully passed a standardized English language placement test, are allowed to enroll in mainstream classrooms where most students have native or native-like competence in English. In a majority of school districts, however, secondary level English learners are placed in programs that include two or three periods of intensive beginning, intermediate, advanced or transitional ESL instruction, focusing mostly on vocabulary, grammar, and communicative competence. Two or three additional periods are devoted to sheltered subject matter courses. In these classes, instruction is designed to provide English language support for the students as they acquire subject matter content. Often, given that students in these classes have different language backgrounds and different levels of oral and written English proficiency, language and content are simplified, and the pace of instruction slowed down. Because many students stay in this program for the whole period of their middle school and even high school experience, they find themselves in a separate track, effectively a linguistic ghetto (Valdes 1998).

In this chapter, I describe the conditions under which students who are learners of English develop oral and written proficiency in the language and master challenging subject matter content in their academically and linguistically heterogeneous classrooms. To illustrate the argument, I report findings from a study conducted in six 7th grade social studies classrooms in California's Central Valley.[1]

Although development of oral proficiency in second language acquisition is essential for the development of literacy and vocabulary, particularly in the middle grades, these students have few opportunities to interact with peers who are native or native-like speakers of English. Furthermore, because the sheltered subject matter courses include students from different grade levels, they have limited or no access to grade-appropriate subject matter content and, therefore, are unable to complete the course sequences required for graduation or for college entrance. This linguistic tracking, confounded with the academic tracking of secondary students, presents an almost insurmountable obstacle to the educational progress of English learners.

---

[1] The study entitled "Language acquisition and mastery of content for English learners in heterogeneous classrooms" was conducted at the Program for Complex Instruction, Stanford University School of Education. The study was funded by the Spencer Foundation whose generous support is hereby acknowledged.

When middle school administrators and teachers make a commitment to eliminate such academic and linguistic tracking, the results are classrooms where students function at different levels of English language proficiency and where they have a wide range of previous academic achievement. Although educational reformers have proposed cooperative learning as a solution to this instructional and curricular challenge, important issues still remain to be addressed. In these classrooms, where the academic performance and the linguistic proficiency of students might span several grade levels, how can teachers maintain high quality instruction? How can they respond to the pressures of parents who insist on academic rigor and high educational standards for their children? How can students who read well below grade level gain access to age-appropriate learning tasks and curricula? How can students who are still in the process of acquiring the language comprehend and contribute to the verbal interchanges between the teacher and other students in the class, and to the discussions among the students? How can they demonstrate intellectual competence and understanding of content? How can teachers prevent some students from dominating and others from withdrawing from participation and consequently from learning?

If teachers respond to academic and linguistic heterogeneity by watering down the curriculum, then many students will have limited access to instructional experiences that develop conceptual understanding in challenging academic subjects. If, in contrast, teachers respond to diversity by teaching to the academically more advanced students and ignore the needs of those who are not yet proficient in English or those who score well below grade level, many students will fail. To maintain a high level curriculum and to address the needs of a diverse population, teachers must learn how to organize instruction so that students can serve as academic and linguistic resources to one another as they work on intellectually demanding learning tasks.

Providing second language learners in the middle grades with opportunities for English language development and age-appropriate acquisition of content is the topic of serious academic controversy and grave political debate. How do teachers set the stage for creating classrooms that are language-rich and academically vibrant environments, where all students use language actively to communicate with peers and with adults? What kinds of learning tasks and classroom activities are used to promote the development of linguistic proficiency and academic achievement of English learners? How do students serve as linguistic resources for one another and how does the teacher ensure equal participation of students with varying linguistic skills and vastly different academic backgrounds?

9.2 Teaching and Learning in Heterogeneous Classrooms

In previous research, we applied sociological theories and methods to develop and evaluate a set of instructional and curricular strategies intended to produce equitable classrooms, where teachers taught at a high intellectual level while reaching students with a range of previous academic achievement that spanned several grade levels. We called this approach complex instruction. (For more information on the theoretical and empirical bases of complex instruction, see Cohen & Lotan 1997.) We studied the implementation of complex instruction in elementary and middle school classrooms with ethnically, racially, academically, and linguistically diverse student populations. We found that in these classrooms, when teachers successfully delegated authority to manage their groups, students talked and worked together in small groups and served as resources for one another as they completed intellectually challenging learning tasks. In the following, I describe the main features of complex instruction.

Using specially designed activities called skill-builders (Cohen 1994), students learned how to work collaboratively, how to describe and explain accurately, and how to engage in substantive conversations. Students assumed specific procedural roles in their small groups to manage the groups and themselves, taking over some of the traditional responsibilities and duties of the teacher. For example, in each group, the facilitator made sure that all members received a turn and understood the instructions for the task. The reporter presented at the end of groupwork time what the group had found out, introduced and described the group product, and evaluated how the group had worked together. The materials manager collected the manipulatives, props, tools, and supplies needed for the activity and oversaw the clean-up. These roles focused members on the procedural work of the group and did not lead to a division of the intellectual labor of the group. All group members presented their opinions, posed question, clarified their answers, or theorized about the problems to be solved.

The learning tasks assigned to the groups were "group-worthy" tasks addressing essential disciplinary content (Lotan 2003). Different learning tasks of a curricular unit were organized around a central concept, an essential question, or a big idea of the discipline. Successful completion of these tasks relied on creative problem-solving, comprehensive analyses of texts and contexts, systematic interpretation of primary sources, and resourceful argumentation. Tasks were multi-dimensional and required the use of multiple intellectual abilities. Various resource materials such as visuals, audio- or video-recordings, manipulatives, science equipment, costumes and props, graphs, and diagrams served as alternative representations of information and understandings In addition to and in support of textual sources. These resource materials were an integral part of the task and were tightly connected to the assignment posed to the students. By using these resources, students learned how to analyze and extract meaning from visuals, musical compositions or paintings, and how to understand their message thoroughly and deeply. In addition to reading and writing (the traditional academic abilities and skills), students used a host of intellectual abilities as they created three-dimensional models, designed and conducted experiments, located, delved into, and interpreted information from different sources, summarized their data and findings in diagrams, graphs, charts and tables, and used different media to argue their positions persuasively. Through these activities, students could understand what was required to complete the learning task, not only through written or oral instructions, but also through representations and resources other than text. In creating varied and different group products, students benefited from additional opportunities and venues to demonstrate their understanding of the content as well as their intellectual competence.

The learning tasks were open-ended: for some there could be more than one legitimate solution and for others there could be multiple ways of arriving to a solution. As students worked on group-worthy tasks, teachers delegated intellectual authority to the groups and to the individuals. Teachers could often be surprised by the answers or the solutions proposed by the students. Often, they could neither anticipate nor predict students' answers nor could they, under any circumstances, provide scripted responses. Such a situation presupposes deep knowledge of subject matter – a prerequisite for the teacher's ability to respond appropriately to the students' ideas.

In completing the learning task, students were held accountable for their engagement as members of a group and as individuals. Interdependence was strengthened by the requirement for a group product (Johnson, Johnson & Holubek, 1991) and individual accountability was ensured through an individual report to be completed after each group task. Completing these individual reports, students summarized and clarified to themselves what they had learned in their groups. Clear and specific evaluation criteria were embedded both in the group products and in the individual reports. These evaluation criteria provided specific guidelines as to what made for a good product or an acceptable individual report clarifying for the students what they would be evaluated on and how they should evaluate their own efforts. The use of evaluation criteria implied a further transformation of the teacher's traditional role as sole evaluator of students' classroom performances. By giving students the opportunity to evaluate their own performances and those of others, the teacher delegated evaluation rights – formerly the purview of teachers only (Cohen et al. 2002). While the group products and individual reports served as formative assessments of students' knowledge of the content and competent use of language, students demonstrated what they had learned in summative ways through multiple choice unit tests and through writing final unit essays.

When students worked on group-worthy tasks and when the teachers successfully delegated authority for managing the groups, we found that the proportion of students talking and working together was significantly positively related to the average learning gains. At the individual level, we found that the higher the rate of the students' participation in small groups, the higher were their post-test scores when controlling for pre-test scores (Cohen & Lotan 1997). Since rate of participation was a predictor of learning gains, reducing the participation gap among students was imperative. When teachers intervened to create equal-status interactions in small groups, the gap between previously high- and low-achieving students decreased. Cohen (1994) proposed specific interventions to equalize participation in small groups: the multiple ability orientation and assigning competence to low status students. The implementation of these interventions narrowed the participation gap by eliminating students' academic and social status as a predictor of participation and thus of learning gains (see Cohen & Lotan 1995).

Clearly, none of the implementation of these different elements of complex instruction was possible without the intensive use of language. Oral and written language was constantly used by the students and by the teachers in the classrooms. The structure of small groups and the use of resource-rich curricular materials provided more students with opportunities for active participation, for producing language in meaningful contexts, and for authentic communication with peers and with the teacher. Native speakers and English learners were in classrooms that had the following critical features: teachers organized the classroom to maximize student interaction in small groups; they worked to equalize rates of participation of students of different academic and social status; curricula were intellectually demanding and rich in resources. Teachers delegated *procedural* authority to students to manage their groups; they delegated *intellectual* authority by assigning group-worthy learning tasks; and they delegated *evaluation rights* by empowering students to assess their own and their peers' engagement and performances. Data collected through classroom observations confirmed the high quality of implementation of complex instruction.

9.3 Language Acquisition in Linguistically Heterogeneous Classrooms

How do aspects of complex instruction further the acquisition of English in academically and linguistically heterogeneous classrooms? To address this question, I will briefly connect two fields of research: one on language acquisition and the other on teaching and learning in heterogeneous classrooms discussed earlier.

Firth and Wagner (1997) argued that traditionally "the predominant view within second language acquisition (SLA) research ... is individualistic and mechanistic and fails to account in a satisfactory way for interactional and socio-linguistic dimensions of language" (p. 285). They called for an urgent reconceptualization of SLA to enlarge the theoretical as well as methodological parameters of the field by conducting classroom-based, socio-linguistic research with particular attention to the interactions of second language learners. In the same issue of the journal, Hall (1997) strengthened their argument and proposed to "reconfigure theoretical and pedagogical concerns with language and language learning" (p. 301). She argued that first, by adding a socio-linguistic dimension to the more prevalent psycho-linguistic approach to the study of SLA, attention would be shifted from the traditionally narrow view of language learning as an individual's mastery of phonological, morphological, syntactic, and pragmatic systems in largely context-free settings, to language learning as a process of acquiring socially constituted communicative practices of the target language community. Second, although currently infrequent in SLA research, a careful examination of how second language is learned through the learners' active involvement in the communicative practices of the classroom (i.e., their interactions with the teacher and with peers), might "lead us to contemplate new issues, develop new questions, and thus engage in explorations of both theoretical and empirical regions that to date have gone largely unnoticed... in the SLA field" (p. 306). This socio-linguistic perspective of language acquisition parallels a view of the classroom as a social system (Lotan 2006), where features of the learning task, teacher's delegation of authority and orchestration of participation structures, patterns of interaction, and expectations for intellectual competence and performance are conceptualized using central sociological principles.

Some researchers of SLA agree that second language learners must be exposed to linguistically rich environments where they can engage in conversational exchanges and negotiations that are the basis for second language acquisition (Ellis 1984; Genesee et al. 2005; Long & Porter 1985). Learners must be exposed to linguistic input from peers as well as from adults. Input refers to elements of the linguistic environment from phonological and morphological features and syntactic structures to correction and feedback that guide learners to more accurate production. Input also includes elaborations, questions, and prompts to aid the learner's comprehension, on one hand, and responses to requests from the learner for clarification, reformulation, or further explanation, on the other. Researchers further differentiate between situations that include input from native speakers as opposed to settings where interaction is among nonnative speakers exclusively. In her work, Wong Filmore (1985, 1989) emphasized the crucial importance of native language models for nonnative speakers. In addition, Wong Filmore described how teachers affect language learning by presenting their materials, by structuring their lessons to provide opportunities for students to practice the target language, and by explicitly calling attention to features and uses of the language. The quality and quantity of the input and that of students' intake can influence the kind of language acquired and the speed with which it is acquired.

In addition to linguistic input and intake, language learners benefit from repeated opportunities for important as well as linguistically accurate output, as they struggle to produce understandable communication and demonstrate their knowledge and understanding. Swain (1985) showed how lack of opportunities for interaction in a classroom dominated by teacher lecturing prevented students from developing strategies for getting meaning across successfully. Wong Filmore (1989) concluded that one of the features of effective language instruction is supported practice in the Vygotskyian sense; "It is when learners put what they have learned of the new language to use in trying to communicate with others that they discover whether or not it works, and what they have yet to learn. The best practice in the new language is the supported production that learners get from speakers who know the language better than they do and who can assist the learners by helping them go beyond their productive means in the new language" (p. 137).

Student-student interaction is the cornerstone of complex instruction and the main precursor of student learning. Through the teacher's delegation of authority and students' increased level of participation, opportunities for linguistic input as well as output are abundant. Furthermore, the emphasis on securing equal-status interactions among native, native-like speakers and English learners increases the probability of significant participation of all students in the learning process.

The structure of the learning task can support active negotiation and increase both the quality and the quantity of children's use of language. For example, Cazden (2001) suggested that the optimal environment for language learning might be one in which students engage in problem-solving, interdependent tasks, manipulate objects and talk about them, and are exposed to clear referents for the nouns and the verbs of the classroom discourse.

Brown (1991) distinguished between procedural and interpretive decision making tasks. He found that interpretive tasks are cognitively more demanding and require more intricate negotiating and more detailed deliberating. He proposed that the more challenging the task, the more opportunities for students to develop their linguistic competencies. Engaging in such tasks would result not only in language practice but also in further language learning. Group-worthy tasks, as used in complex instruction and as described above, are good examples of such tasks.

Thus, this literature on second language acquisition has clear implications for the social context conducive to second language acquisition in schools. Classrooms need to be language-rich environments where students can interact with adults and with peers who include both native and nonnative speakers. Students need to use language actively and frequently to communicate on consequential, interdependent tasks embedded in the disciplines and that require the use of real objects, manipulatives, and varied representations of the information. When teachers pay particular attention to the linguistic features of their talk, they are able to facilitate and scaffold students' comprehension. When they provide feedback to students' output and organize the classroom to foster student interaction, they create conditions that support extensive and productive language use. Classrooms where complex instruction is used to promote talk are settings that incorporate these prerequisites for language acquisition.

While the second language acquisition literature points us to some important cognitive, linguistic, and social processes that contribute to language learning, it does not distinguish between acquisition of basic communicative skills and the kind of language or discourse necessary for successful academic functioning in mainstream classrooms. Increasingly, researchers who study the schooling of second language learners advocate developing competence in academic English, and describe what such language might look or sound like.

In early conceptualizations, Cummins (1981, 1989) and others (Chamot & O'Malley 1994; Collier 1987) described some differences between conversational language (basic, interpersonal communication skills) and cognitive, academic language proficiency. Cummins argued that while the former is context-embedded, allowing learners to draw on paralinguistic clues and shared frames of references, the latter is often less contextualized in classroom settings and therefore learners must rely almost exclusively on language for comprehension. Although initially a useful distinction, Cummins' definition is too broad and focuses mainly on the learner's cognitive role in acquiring academic language, neglecting important socio-linguistic aspects, such as register for example.

Valdes and Geoffrion-Vinci (1998) used the term register to refer to language varieties associated with situational uses. Based on a relative distribution of particular linguistic features, they describe a continuum of registers from very high levels (such as those used in formal lectures) in academic articles, or arguments in court, to mid-level (used in newspaper reports, popular novels, or interviews), and low-level registers (used in intimate and casual conversations). Furthermore, they argued that because high status groups have access to language use in contexts (e.g., academic, religious, administrative) where the high/formal varieties are used narrowly and in strictly prescribed ways, these varieties come to characterize the written and, as a reflection of their hyperliteracy, the oral language of high status groups as well. In a parallel argument, Valdés and Geoffrion-Vinci (1998) posited that lower-ranked groups with limited access to the same contexts, tend to develop repertoires that include lower registers in both the oral and the written modes. Furthermore, high-status, dominant groups use their high-level repertoire of linguistic markers to deliberately distance themselves from lower-status groups in society, while members of nonelite groups must consciously work to acquire ways of speaking that characterize the high-status groups to which they aspire to belong. Based on their research on the proficiency of Spanish by Chicano college students, the authors concluded that students might benefit from classroom activities that expose them to the high-level registers they would be expected to produce in authentic academic contexts. This research implies that exposing second language learners to an academic register as early as possible could be of great benefit. Not only would they acquire the language formally associated with the academic context, but also the language associated with the academic content of a discipline, thereby gaining greater access to such content.

Cognitive scientists are exploring learning and thinking in subject matter domains, but little explicit attention is being paid to the implications of such learning and thinking by second language learners. While knowledge structures and linguistic practices of the various disciplines are different in many ways and similar in others, appropriation of academic discourse and deep understanding of content are as important for mathematics and for language arts, as they are for science and for social studies. Language interactions such as questioning and explaining, deliberating and justifying, discussing problematic situations and weighing possible solutions, reasoning and analyzing, summarizing and interpreting – in short, negotiating meaning, are indispensable for understanding complex subject matter content. Spanos et al. (1988) described particular syntactic constructions, logical connectors, and various semantic features associated with mathematics language. Furthermore, Lemke (1990) identified the linguistic characteristics of classroom science talk and writing, noting a heavy reliance on passive voice, technical vocabulary, and syntactic ambiguity and Short (1994) investigated the nature of language in social studies classrooms. The social studies register seems to reflect linguistic features similar to those used in the humanities as well as nontechnical aspects of the language in mathematics and science classrooms. The language functions and skills of the discourse in social studies classrooms are similar to the higher-literacy demands of other content areas in terms of defining, describing, sequencing, giving examples, explaining, justifying, comparing and contrasting, establishing cause and effect, or evaluating. Thus, the mastery of such a register is important for the academic achievement and success of second language learners.

Scholars of the development of students' cognition seem to agree that learning and thinking in the subject matter come about through socially situated negotiations of meaning and active construction of knowledge. However, researchers such as Heath (1983), Gee (1990), and Michaels (1981) have demonstrated that such negotiations of meaning and construction of knowledge are influenced by the children's cultural backgrounds and their own forms of discourse and repertoire.

In addition to learning the general rules for acceptable classroom talk, the social practices of how to discuss subject matter in routine, predictable ways are negotiated with, and by, participants. For that purpose, students need to be exposed to, and become familiar with, central concepts and epistemological queries of the discipline and its linguistic genre. To develop such academic and linguistic competence, however, students need to understand the learning task and to be able to contribute to the conversation about it in substantial ways.

Teachers play an important role in structuring opportunities for the development of such discourse. First and foremost, they use academically challenging, rigorous, and content-based curricula. Second, they model discipline-specific lexical items and syntactic structures. Third, they monitor students' oral and written output, and provide specific feedback. In general, teachers orchestrate high-level classroom discourse in whole class as well as in small group settings.

Arellano (2003) conducted a study investigating the processes by which bilingual students acquired academic English and learned social studies content in a classroom using complex instruction. She found that the students she observed showed significant growth in two domains: (a) in the knowledge about social studies content they studied as measured by gain scores on multiple choice unit tests; and (b) in the oral and written language skills in English they needed to demonstrate that knowledge. Arellano analyzed student talk during small group interactions and found that over time, English learners increased the use of complex language functions such as explanations and justification. As these students practiced making presentations, they developed discourse strategies that made their language more explicit and increasingly appropriate for formal audiences. In examining the students' written products, Arellano found significant growth in their writing ability both as they completed their individual reports and as they composed the final unit essays. They focused on central ideas, included supporting details and evidence, and showed development in their use of organizational patterns of the essays. In her final discussion, Arellano emphasized the crucial role of the teacher in creating a classroom environment where she was able to challenge her students cognitively and linguistically.

9.4   Acquiring Language and Mastering Content in Complex Instruction Classrooms

In this section, I report on a study conducted under the auspices of the Program for Complex Instruction at the Stanford University School of Education. This study documented how students who are intermediate English learners in mainstream classrooms can achieve academically by both developing discipline-specific discourse in oral and written performance and achieving mastery in subject matter content. As originally proposed, the study described and tested the classroom conditions that support and enhance student growth and development in the language of instruction as well as in knowledge of content. We argued that students in general and English learners in particular strengthen their language skills and learn content when they have opportunities to carry out intellectually challenging tasks and actively use English to communicate in meaningful situations. Such opportunities are available in classrooms where teachers use resource- and language-rich materials, academically rigorous curricula, and instructional practices that maximize peer interaction; where they model and monitor academic discourse and make explicit strategies for learning language; and where they work to equalize participation among students of different academic and social status. With complex instruction, teachers create such opportunities for the students in their classrooms.

We collaborated with a team of teachers from Gerona Middle School in California's central valley and supported them in the use of complex instruction in their linguistically and academically heterogeneous mainstream classrooms. We chose to conduct our study in 7th grade middle school classrooms because this is when the development and use of academic English and mastery of content knowledge become particularly critical. Although Gerona was located in the midst of a middle class neighborhood, at the time of this study, children from the newly built, relatively large homes of the area were not attending this middle school but rather where bussed to a newly-built school in a different part of town.

At the time of the study, 76% of the students at Gerona were designated as English learners and 95% of those reported Spanish as their home language. Over 15% of English learners were in beginning and early intermediate level ESL programs (transitional ESL programs, ESL 1, and ESL 2) as determined by testing in the spring of their 6th grade. As a year-round school, Gerona Middle School was divided into four tracks. Beginning and intermediate level (including transitional) ESL students were grouped in one track and were taught using a combination of English and Spanish instruction.

We began our study with an intervention following negotiations with the principal of the school, district officials, the instructional resource team, and a team of teachers. We requested that a significant proportion of students designated by the school as "Transitional Limited English Proficient" be placed into mainstream social studies classrooms where the teachers used strategies of complex instruction. As mentioned above, in the past, these students had been separated from their mainstream peers and placed in sheltered ESL content area classrooms. As our request was granted, we further collaborated with the teachers and administrators at the school to ensure that the classrooms included about 15–20% "Transitional" students, with the remainder consisting of "English Only" students (those whose families reported using no other language at home), "Fluent English Proficient" students (previously labeled Limited English Proficient but now exited from all English language support), and "Mainstream Limited English Proficient" students (still officially labeled as Limited English Proficient, but deemed ready for mainstream classes). Students in our sample were designated by the school as belonging to one of four language proficiency groups: English Only (EO), Fluent English Proficient (FEP), Limited English Proficient (Mainstream LEP), and Transitional (TR). Among the 214 students, a total of 63.6% were second language learners at various levels of English proficiency: FEP: 17.2%; LEP: 26.1% and Transitional 18.2%. Despite expressed doubts and hesitations by the principal and the teachers, we insisted that the classrooms in our sample receive textbooks that included adequate curricular resources and grade-appropriate academic language. These textbooks had been deemed as too difficult in the past and had not been used at the school. Furthermore, we conducted a week-long professional development institute, additional follow up days during the academic year, and provided consistent feedback to the teachers on their use of complex instruction strategies.

Ms. B. and Mr. E., two social studies teachers, taught in the classrooms included in our study. Ms. B's class was in the A Track (the track that included mostly students in ESL) and Mr. E's classes were on the C Track. Both teachers attempted to coordinate their curriculum and instruction with the English Language Arts teachers in their respective tracks. These teachers also used complex instruction strategies in their courses. Students in Ms. B's classroom were most evenly distributed among the different language groups. This classroom was the only mainstream classroom taught by this teacher during the academic year while her other classrooms were sheltered social studies classrooms. Although she used the same curriculum and instructional strategies as the classrooms included in our study (even with her 8th grade classes), we did not collect data in her sheltered classrooms. The design of this study required that we collect data in mainstream classrooms only. All of Teacher E's classrooms were considered mainstream classrooms.

In addition to the language proficiency designation, we recorded data on student scores on the standardized SAT-9 tests (reading, language, mathematics, and spelling) administered in 6th grade. On all four subscales about two thirds of the students scored in the first and second quartiles; very few students (e.g., less than 1% reading and just under 4% in mathematics) scored in the fourth quartile on these tests. The average GPA for the 181 students in the sample who had recorded grades was 2.1 (SD = 1.1). A little over a tenth of the students (11.6% of the sample) had GPA of 4 and 31.5% had GPAs below 2. According to these measures, many students in our sample were significantly underprepared academically. Many students also needed significant language supports to access the curriculum. One of these supports was the availability of curricular materials in Spanish. There were slightly more male students than female students in the sample: 54.7% and 45.3%, respectively.

9.4.1 Student Achievement Data

We collected student achievement data in six social studies classrooms across four thematic units that address the 7th grade social studies framework. The four units used in the classrooms in order of implementation were: (1) Shaping the Mosaic of Islam; (2) How do Historians know about the Crusades; (3) Taking your

Proper Station: Life in Tokugawa Japan;(4) Challenging the Authority of Institutions: The Reformation. For each of these four units, we administered a multiple choice pretest before the introduction of the material related to the unit. At the conclusion of each unit, students took a multiple-choice post-test and wrote a final unit essay. For all four units, the post-test scores were statistically significantly higher for the sample as a whole and for the students in all four language designation categories. Furthermore, by the fourth and last unit, students designated as Transitional made greater gains and scored on the average as high as students designated Limited English Proficient, despite the fact that if we had not intervened, these students would have been in segregated ESL classes.

For our more detailed analyses, we focused on the essay for the fourth unit, implemented at the end of the academic year: *Challenging the authority of institutions: The Reformation*. In addition to the multiple choice test, for the final assessment of the unit, students were asked to write a persuasive essay calling their friends and family members to join or not to join Martin Luther in his challenge to the authority of the church. This essay reflects the big idea of the unit. Students were prompted to state their argument or thesis (for or against joining Martin Luther), state a counter-argument, and provide at least three items of evidence to support their original argument.

We scored the essays in two phases. In the first phase, we were looking for ways in which students used elements of the genre of a persuasive essay, how they organized their essays, how they used linguistic features and writing conventions, and finally how they used vocabulary related to the unit in particular and to social studies in general. The quality and accuracy of the subject matter content were addressed in the second phase.

Our analysis of the data from the initial phase showed that the first two categories (Statement of Position and Support for Position) had minimal variation since a significant majority of students across language groups received high scores on these two categories. Although differences were small and all means for all categories were still above 2.0 (range 1–3), there were significant differences among Transitional and LEPs on three of the ten categories: Providing Evidence and Reasons, Organization, and Vocabulary. Data analysis from the second phase showed that on Understanding the Big Idea of the Unit, the mean score was 2.38 ($SD = 0.59$), with no difference among students from different language designations. The mean number of Items of Content was 10.66 ($SD = 3.78$) and again, no statistically significant differences among students from different language designation groups.

9.4.2 Classroom Experiences

At the end of each rotation in each of the four units, students were required to complete individual reports. The average number of individual reports completed in each classrooms was both an indicator of the quality of implementation of complex instruction as well as a measure of accountability for the individual student. For the

Reformation Unit, the average number of IRs turned in was 3.14 ($SD = 1.71$) and the range was from 0–5. Fifty-five percent of the students turned in 4 or 5 IRs, while 22% did not turn in any or just one. We found that the number of Individual Reports completed was a significant predictor of the achievement measures for individual students.

To rate the quality of talk in the small groups, we recorded students as they worked in their small groups. We scored a total of 93 tapes and captured student talk in English and Spanish in the following categories: reading texts, interpreting texts, defining and assigning terms, describing, justifying with reasons/evidence, stating cause and effect, making connections to other activities, units or everyday life, other content talk, talking about spelling and pronunciation, paraphrasing or repeating, presentational talk, evaluative talk, facilitator talk, and off-task talk. In additional analyses, we recorded the proportion of on-task talk for all students to obtain a measure of their individual "air-time" within the small group. These tapes are a rare and rich database for group interactions and individual talk in a real classroom setting.

9.4.3 Major Findings

First, there were significant learning gains for students from all four language groups in both content knowledge and use of English language for academic purposes as measured by the different types of assessments. For all four units, the post-test scores were significantly higher than the pre-test scores for the sample as a whole and for the students in all four language designation categories. The analyses of the final unit essays showed that students understood the big idea of the unit, had mastered the content, and used persuasive strategies and the language of the discipline to communicate in English about their academic tasks.

Second, the school's designation of English learners as transitional underestimated their linguistic and academic achievements as indicated by their performances in the mainstream classroom. On the various outcome measures developed for purposes of this study (a measure of academic oral proficiency; multiple choice unit tests; final unit essay), on the average, students designated as Transitional English Learners performed just as well as students designated as Limited English Proficient. Transitional students, by making significant gains, were able to first narrow and then close the achievement gap between them and the rest of the students in these mainstream classes. These findings lead us to question the school's designations as well as the basis for these designations since they don't seem to be sensitive enough to capture the students' academic performances and achievements in the mainstream classroom.

Bunch (2006) conducted a study in the classrooms described here. He found that students in these classrooms, while designated as being fluent in conversational English, yet classified as lacking academic English, were able to participate fully in challenging academic tasks in English. They engaged productively in the groupwork tasks, they were able to conduct multiple kinds of linguistic transactions, they demonstrated awareness of varied audiences as they presented reports and they talked about their ideas with great energy and enthusiasm.

Third, we were able to develop assessments sensitive enough to capture what English learners know and are able to do regarding subject matter content in English. A careful examination of student work allowed us to develop scoring categories and scoring guides that reflect students' use of oral and written language for academic purposes. Focusing on language and content separately allowed us to document students' understanding of the big idea of the unit, their ability to explain and to persuade orally and in writing, to talk and write about abstract concepts, and to use different modes of communication and specific genre or register to address different audiences for different tasks.

Fourth, the quality and the quantity of the interaction in small groups are related to students' performances in English at both the individual and the group levels. Our data reflect significant and sustained interaction related to subject matter in both English and Spanish. Students took advantage of opportunities to engage in social studies talk in English, learned and used vocabulary and specific "terms of art" related to the discipline, and rehearsed and practiced oral presentations by using presentational language. The group interaction also served as the bridge from oral to written language as students were preparing their individual reports as well as their group presentations. For example, we found that the proportion of presentational talk in the small group was a predictor of the student's use of persuasive strategies in their individual essays. Students used Spanish mostly to reinforce meanings, negotiate procedures, to move the group along and to make sure that everyone was on board.

Fifth, the quality of the implementation of complex instruction was related to student outcomes. From previous research on complex instruction, we were assured that to support positive learning gains, in addition to the rigorous curriculum and the attention to equal participation, the interaction in the small groups needed to be at a certain level. Our classroom observation measures reflect the fact that this interaction level was maintained throughout the four units in all classrooms of the study. Furthermore, the number of individual reports completed (an additional measure of the quality of implementation), was related to all individual achievement measures. We also found that Mr. E, one of the teachers in our study, needed significant assistance while implementing complex instruction in five classrooms on a single day. The two research assistants present consistently helped the teachers with both the logistics and the actual set up of the lessons.

9.5 Conclusion

Providing English learners with opportunities for language development and age-appropriate acquisition of content is a primary concern for researchers, policy makers and practitioners interested in equitable educational outcomes. How to proceed is a timely and highly contested political issue.

The material presented in this chapter suggests that working with students who are learning content while still developing proficiency in the language of instruction requires a comprehensive approach to changing their educational experiences in academically and linguistically heterogeneous classrooms. By using challenging curricula and meaningful assessments, by strengthening the teacher's instructional practices to include strategies for supporting second language acquisition and for treating problems of unequal participation in small groups, and by educating students to serve as academic and linguistic resources for one another, we can assist schools in effectively preparing diverse populations to meet high standards for knowledge, skills, and productivity.

References

Arellano, A. D. (2003). Bilingual students' acquisition of academic language: A study of the language processes and products in a complex instruction classroom. Unpublished dissertation, Stanford University.

Brown, R. (1991). Group work, task difference, and second language acquisition. Applied Linguistics, 12 (1), 1–12.

Bunch, G. (2006). "Academic English" in the 7th grade: Broadening the lens, expanding access, Journal of English for Academic Purposes, 5, 284–301. doi:10.1016/j/jeap.2006.08.007.

Cazden, C. (2001). Classroom discourse: The language of teaching and learning. Portsmouth, NH: Heinemann.

Chamot, A. U. & O'Malley, J. M. (1994). The CALLA handbook: Implementing the congnitive academic language learning approach. Reading, MA: Addison-Wesley Publishing.

Cohen, E. G. (1994). Designing groupwork: Strategies for the heterogeneous classroom. New York and London: Teachers College Press.

Cohen, E. G. & Lotan, R. A. (1995). Producing Equal Status Interaction in Heterogeneous Classrooms. American Educational Research Journal, 32, 99–120.

Cohen, E.G. & Lotan, R.A. (Eds.) (1997). Working for Equity in Heterogeneous Classrooms: Sociological Theory in Action. New York: Teachers College Press.

Cohen, E. G., Lotan, R. A., Abram, P. L., Scarloss, B. A. & Schultz, S. E. (2002). Can groups learn? Teacher's College Record, 104, 1045–1068.

Collier, V. (1987). Age and rate of acquisition of second language for academic purposes. TESOL Quarterly, 21, 617–641.

Cummins, J. (1981). The role of primary language development in promoting educational success for language minority students. Schooling and language minority students: A theoretical framework. Los Angeles: California State University.

Cummins, J. (1989). Empowering minority students. Sacramento: CABE.

Ellis, R. (1984). Classroom second language development. Oxford: Pergamon Press.

Gee, J. (1990). Social linguistics and literacies: Ideologies in discourses. London: Falmer.

Genesee, F., Lindholm-Leary, K., Saunders, W. & Christian, D. (2005). English language learners in U.S. schools: An overview of research findings, Journal of Education for Students Placed at Risk, 10, 363–385.

Hall, J. K. (1997). A consideration of SLA as a theory of practice: A response to Firth and Wagner. The Modern Language Journal, 81, 301–306.

Heath, S. B. (1983). Ways with words. Cambridge: Cambridge University Press.

Johnson, D., Johnson, R. T., & Holubek, E. J. (1991). Cooperation in the classroom. Edina, MN: Interaction Book.

Lemke, J. L. (1990). Talking science: Language, learning and values. Norwood, NJ: Ablex Publishing.

Long, M. & Porter, P. (1985). Group work, interlanguage talk, and second language acquisition. TESOL Quarterly, 19, 207–225.

Lotan, R. A. (2003). Group-worthy tasks. Educational Leadership, 6, 72–75.

Lotan, R. A. (2006). Managing groupwork. In C. Evertson & C. Weinstein (Eds.), Handbook of Classroom Management: Research, Practice, and Contemporary Issues (pp. 525–539). Mahwah, NJ: Lawrence Erlbaum Associates.

Michaels, S. (1981). "Sharing time": Children's narrative styles and differential access in literacy. Language in Society, 10, 423–442.

Short, D. J. (1994). Expanding middle school horizons: Integrating language, culture, and social studies. TESOL Quarterly, 28, 581–608.

Spanos, G., Rhodes, N., Dale, T. C. & Crandall, J. (1988). Linguistic features of mathematical problem-solving: Insights and applications. In R. Cocking & J. Maestre (Eds.), Linguistic and Cultural Influences on Mathematical Learning (pp. 221–240). Hillsdale, NJ: Lawrence Erlbaum Associates.

Swain, M. (1985). Communicative competence: Some roles of comprehensible input and comprehensible output in its development. In S. M. Gass & C.G. Madden (Eds.), Input in Second Language Acquisition (pp. 235–253). Rowley, MA: Newbury House Publishers.

Valdés, G. (1998). The world outside and inside schools: Language and immigrant children. Educational Researcher, 27, 4–18.

Valdés, G. & Geoffrion-Vinci, M. (1998). Chicano Spanish: The problem of the "underdeveloped" code in bilingual repertoires. Modern Language Journal, 82, 473–501.

Wong Filmore, L. (1985). When does teacher talk work as input? In S. M. Gass & C. G. Madden (Eds.), Input in Second Language Acquisition (pp. 17–50). Rowley, MA: Newbury House Publishers.

Wong Filmore, L. (1989). Teaching English through content: Instructional reform in programs for minority students. In J. Esling (Ed.) Multicultural Education and Policy: ESL in the 1990's. A Tribute to Mary Ashworth (pp. 125–143). Toronto, Ontario: Ontario Institute for Studies in Education.

Chapter 10
Teacher Practices and Small-Group Dynamics in Cooperative Learning Classrooms

Noreen M. Webb

Abstract Collaborative peer learning environments have received increasing attention in classrooms due to the potential for improving learning and achievement. Prior research on small-group collaboration identifies several behaviors that significantly predict student learning, such as exchanging explanations and applying help received. Less often studied are the effects that teacher practices have on student interaction in collaborative groups, especially how teacher discourse in the classroom influences the degree to which students carry out help-related behavior when working with other students. This chapter reviews the functioning and responsibilities of students as help-seekers and help-givers, and then contrasts the results of two studies to investigate how teacher practices may influence help-related behavior in collaborative groups. The findings suggest that productive group collaboration—especially exchanging explanations—may follow from classroom instruction in which teachers hold students accountable for playing an active role in generating problem-solving approaches and for explaining their thinking.

10.1 Introduction

Due to the potential for collaborative peer learning environments to improve student learning and achievement, school districts, state departments of education, national research organizations, and curriculum specialists in the U.S. recommend, or even mandate, the use of peer-based learning (California State Department of Education, 1985, 1992; National Council of Teachers of Mathematics, 1989, 1991; National Research Council, 1989, 1995). A principal way in which students can learn from collaborative work is to engage in help-related behavior, both giving help and receiving help. As discussed below, not every kind of help is equally beneficial for learning. Exchanging explanations is more productive than exchanging other kinds of information, such as answers to problems.

Researchers have studied a wide range of activities designed to promote explaining in collaborative groups, including:

(a) instruction in specific explaining skills (Fuchs et al. 1999; Gillies & Ashman 1996, 1998; Swing & Peterson 1982);
(b) assigning students to roles of summarizer (also called learning leader or recaller) and listener – also called active listener, learning listener, or listener/facilitator (Hythecker et al. 1988; O'Donnell 1999; Yager et al. 1985);
(c) requiring students to ask each other specific high-level questions about the material (often called reciprocal questioning, Fantuzzo et al. 1989; King 1989, 1990, 1992, 1999);
(d) prompting students to give elaborated explanations, explain material in their own words, and explain why they believe their answers are correct or incorrect (Coleman 1998; Palincsar et al. 1993);
(e) instruction in giving conceptual rather than algorithmic explanations (Fuchs et al. 1997); and
(f) using specific metacognitive prompts to promote comprehension monitoring and explanations of student reasoning (Mevarech & Kramarski 1997).

These approaches, which have proven to be successful in raising the level of discourse in group discussions, focus on instructions and activities for students and groups. Less often studied are the effects that teacher practices have on student interaction in collaborative groups. In particular, little is known about how teacher discourse in the classroom influences the degree to which students carry out help-related behavior when working with other students. This paper, then, reviews the functioning and responsibilities of students as help-seekers and help-givers, and then investigates how teacher practices may influence help-related behavior in collaborative groups.

10.2   Help-Related Behavior: Theoretical Perspectives and Empirical Results

From a theoretical perspective, both the help-giver and the help-receiver may benefit from sharing information, especially explanations or detailed descriptions of how to solve problems or carry out tasks. Giving explanations may help the explainer to reorganize and clarify material, recognize misconceptions, fill in gaps in his or her own understanding, internalize and acquire new strategies and knowledge, and develop new perspectives and understanding (Bargh & Schul 1980; King 1992; Peterson et al. 1981; Rogoff 1991; Saxe et al. 1993; Valsiner 1987; Webb 1991). In the course of explaining, students think about the salient features of the problem and develop a metacognitive awareness of what they do and do not understand (Cooper 1999). Receiving explanations may help students correct misconceptions, fill in gaps in understanding, and strengthen connections between new information and knowledge previously learned (Mayer 1984; Rogoff 1990; Sweller 1989; Wittrock 1990). Exchanging help that involves less elaboration than explanations (e.g., answers or calculations) may also have fewer benefits for learning because it may involve less cognitive restructuring on the part of the help-giver and may not enable help-receivers to correct their misconceptions or lack of understanding.

Many researchers have explored the power of giving and receiving explanations in peer-directed small groups (Brown & Palincsar 1989; Fuchs et al. 1997; King 1992; Nattiv 1994; Peterson et al. 1981; Saxe et al. 1993; Slavin 1987; Webb 1991; Yackel et al. 1990). Most researchers have found that giving explanations relates positively to achievement (see Webb & Palincsar 1996). That is, when a student gives an explanation in order to help someone else, this action also benefits her own understanding and achievement.

Conversely, the empirical results on the relationship between receiving explanations and learning outcomes are often weak or inconsistent (see Webb & Palincsar 1996). Previous research consistently shows that receiving no response to questions negatively relates to achievement, as does receiving only the answer without an explanation. However, receiving explanations does not usually significantly relate to achievement (Hooper 1992; Nattiv 1994; Ross & Cousins 1995a; see also reviews by Webb 1989, 1991; Webb & Palincsar 1996).

Effective explanations require several conditions. Explanations received must be relevant to the target student's need for help, timely, correct, sufficiently elaborated to enable the target student to correct his or her misconception or lack of understanding, and comprehensible (Webb 1989). Even if explanations adequately meet all of these dimensions, Vedder (1985) proposed that effective explanations require two additional conditions. First, the student receiving help must have the opportunity to use explanations to solve the problem or carry out the task for herself. Second, the student must use that opportunity for practice by attempting to apply the explanations received to the problem at hand. That is, the student must both have and take advantage of the opportunity to apply the information contained in the explanation.

Empirical work has confirmed Vedder's (1985) predictions that students are most likely to benefit from receiving explanations when they also attempt to apply the explanations received to solve the problems at hand (Webb & Farivar 1999; Webb et al. 1995). For example, Webb and Mastergeorge (2003a) found that 76% of students who both received explanations after requesting help and applied the explanations to solve groupwork problems by themselves without assistance from their groupmates succeeded on analogous problems on the achievement posttest. Of the students who engaged in one of the behaviors (receiving explanations or applying explanations to the problem at hand) but not both, or who engaged in neither behavior, none succeeded on the achievement posttest.

Whether students give explanations and whether students who seek help apply it to the task at hand depends on a complex interplay of small-group and whole-class dynamics. The remaining sections explore these dynamics, describing the small-group interactions that may shape the behavior of help-seekers and help-givers, and the variety of teacher practices that may influence how students interact in collaborative groups.

10.3   Small-Group Dynamics that Shape Help-Related Behavior

Not only are help-seeking and help-giving behaviors related to student learning, but the behaviors relate to each other. This section explores how different kinds of help-seeking behavior may lead to different kinds of help received, and how the nature of help received may impact the subsequent behavior of help seekers.

10.3.1   The Relationship Between Help-Seeking Behavior and Help Received

When students have trouble understanding the material or don't know what to do, they may ask for help in various ways. They may ask for the answer instead of an explanation ("What did you get for number 3?"), may ask a specific question about part of a problem ("Why did you have to subtract 1 from 30"?), or may ask a general, unfocused question ("How do you do it?" or "I don't understand it."). Previous research shows that specific questions targeting a particular aspect of the problem are more likely to elicit explanations or in-depth procedural descriptions than other types of questions (Webb et al. 1995; Webb & Mastergeorge 2003a; Webb et al. 2006). For example, Webb et al. (2006) found that as many as 75% of students who asked specific questions obtained high-level help (descriptions of the problem-solving procedures) whereas no more than 44% of students who asked only general questions successfully obtained high-level help. Students who only asked general questions or gave general statements of confusion largely received low-level help, such as the answer or calculations to write down, received offers to copy other students' work, or were completely ignored when they asked for help.

Several factors may account for the relative success of specific questions in eliciting explanations. First, specific requests make it easier for groups to understand the nature of a student's confusion or uncertainty and to formulate an appropriate and precise response (e.g., "Why did you move the decimal point two places?").

Second, specific requests may signal to the group that the help seeker wants to learn how to solve the problem, has sufficient understanding of the problem to be able to pinpoint a specific area of uncertainty, and will profit from the explanations provided. Groups' attributions of students who ask specific questions as motivated to learn may be strengthened by the fact that these help seekers frequently show persistence in seeking help (e.g., repeating their questions) and make changes in their questioning strategies, such as making their questions increasingly focused on what they do not understand (e.g., "Why is it 6.4?", "No, why is the decimal point there?"). Groups' perceptions of these help seekers' level of understanding may be accurate. One study showed that although students who asked specific questions were not more knowledgeable about the content than students who asked only general questions as indicated by pretest scores, they did show greater knowledge about the task on the days they were observed to ask questions (Webb et al. 2006). Most of the students who asked specific questions solved at least part of the problem correctly before they asked questions or they exhibited some content knowledge within the context of their questions. For example, some students correctly obtained a common denominator for two fractions (e.g., $1/2 + 2/3$) even though they did not understand how to add the fractions otherwise (converting them to the equivalent fractions $3/6 + 4/6$: "For number 11, I got the bottom number but I don't know how to do it.").

When students ask general questions or admit general confusion without identifying a particular area of difficulty, in contrast, groups may not know where to begin to formulate an explanation. Groups may also believe that students asking general questions are too confused about the problem to benefit from explanations and, consequently, may believe that the most efficient response is to provide or dictate numerical procedures and answers. Confirming this perception, Webb et al. (2006) found that students who asked only general questions were typically unable to solve any part of the problem before they asked for help, and indicated major misunderstandings or lack of understanding in the context of their questions (e.g., "Do you just add the denominators?"). Even when students who asked only general questions did receive explanations, they often gave evidence of not understanding the explanations by admitting outright that "they didn't get it," by asking questions that showed their continued confusion, or by echoing elements of explanations (e.g., repeating some numbers mentioned) without any apparent attempt to understand the explanations received (Webb & Mastergeorge 2003a).

Groups may also be reluctant to provide detailed help in response to general questions if they perceive these help seekers as trying to depend on others to do the work. That is, other group members may view these help seekers as social loafers or free riders (Kerr & Bruun 1983; Salomon & Globerson 1989). The tendency of some students to immediately ask general questions before attempting any work on a problem (Webb & Mastergeorge 2003b) could easily reinforce both perceptions. Such students may not only be too confused or unmotivated to ask specific questions, they may also be afraid to attempt work on the problem and fail, at risk of looking stupid and threatening their self worth (Butler & Neuman 1995; Covington 1984; Middleton & Midgley 1997; Newman 1991, 1994, 1998).

A further contributing factor to the relative failure of general questions to elicit high-level explanations may be the negative socio-emotional behaviors sometimes linked to asking general questions. First, Webb et al. (2006) found that students who asked general questions—but not students who asked specific questions—received negative socio-emotional responses that may have suppressed their further attempts to seek help or actively work on problems. Some groups insulted students when they asked for help (e.g., calling them stupid). Students outright dismissed other general attempts to seek help ("Ask someone else") or ignored them completely. Students who received insults in response to their help seeking rarely persisted in seeking help and often passively withdrew from group work. These behaviors are consistent with previous research showing that rudeness reduces participation in group discussions (Chiu & Khoo 2003; Mulryan 1992; Salomon & Globerson 1989). Second, students who asked general questions—but not students who asked specific questions—sometimes initiated negative socio-emotional behavior such as insulting their teammates, which almost guaranteed that groups would not respond when these students sought help (Webb et al. 2006). Engaging in such behavior may serve to confirm groups' perceptions that students who only ask general questions (especially before attempting work on the problem) are unable or unmotivated to do the work.

10.3.2 Relationship Between Help Received and Carrying out Further Work

Several studies have shown that receiving explanations is more likely than receiving low-level help (or receiving no help) to make it possible for help seekers to carry out subsequent problem solving without assistance from others. Again, Webb et al. (2006) found that as many as 50% of students who received high-level help (descriptions of how to solve problems) went on to solve problems without assistance whereas only 29% of students who received only low-level help (e.g., answers, calculations) then solved problems without assistance. Even controlling for prior achievement, receiving high-level help predicts students' abilities to carry out further work on problems (Webb & Farivar 1999). These findings suggest that students learn more from receiving high-level help than from receiving low-level help such as answers without supporting details.

The level of help received may also have motivational effects on help seekers. Receiving high-level help may make students feel supported and encouraged by their group and feel that their efforts are worthwhile. Receiving low-level or no help, on the other hand, may discourage students from expending further effort. Receiving low-level help may frustrate help seekers because they cannot use the help to learn how to solve the problems or even to gain enough knowledge to phrase specific questions. And low-level responses, even neutral responses such as "Let me think about that for a moment," may be interpreted as criticisms, which may hinder further participation (Chiu 2000). In line with these expectations, Webb and Mastergeorge (2003a) found that a number of students who received low-level or no help seemed to give up trying to understand and resorted to copying or asking for answers, or simply stopped working altogether.

10.4 The Role of the Teacher: Two Studies

The previous sections showed that students' experiences in small groups shape their interactions with teammates in complex, reciprocal ways. Adding to these peer influences on group functioning are teacher practices. This section examines teacher practices in two studies that showed quite different patterns of student collaborative-group interactions. In Study 1, students rarely engaged in interaction shown to be predictive of learning (especially engaging in high-level helping behavior). In contrast, in Study 2 students frequently explained their problem-solving strategies. The sections below describe in detail some of the differences in student interaction between the two studies and highlight the role of the teacher in bringing about such variation.

10.4.1 Description of the Two Studies

In Study 1, the researchers investigated student interaction and learning in a semester-long cooperative learning program implemented in four 7th-grade mathematics classrooms. The program used multiple sets of activities designed to develop students' ability to work effectively in small groups, including activities to develop basic communication skills, feelings of inclusiveness, helping skills, and the ability to give explanations (see Farivar & Webb 1998, for details). During mathematics instruction, teachers gave a whole-class introduction to the day's material and then students worked in heterogeneous groups on the assigned mathematics problems for the rest of the class period. The teacher circulated among groups, watching groups work and answering questions when necessary. Observers audiotaped all classroom and small-group interaction during three curriculum units (decimal operations, fractions, percentages). Because student and teacher behavior was similar across the curriculum units and across teachers, findings described below are averaged across both teachers and curriculum units (the findings described here are drawn from data and results reported in Webb & Mastergeorge 2003a; Webb et al. 2006; Webb et al. 2006).

In Study 2, researchers investigated student and teacher discourse and student learning in three 2nd- and 3rd-grade classrooms whose teachers had participated in a professional development program specifically designed to help them engage their students in algebraic thinking (Carpenter et al. 2003; Jacobs et al. 2005). Unlike Study 1, teachers in this study received instruction and practice in posing mathematics problems designed to stimulate student thinking, asking questions to elicit student descriptions of their thinking, and setting up whole-class and small-group contexts in which students could converse with one another and with the teacher about their thinking and in which teachers expected and encouraged students to share answers, ideas and strategies. During each class, teachers introduced a problem, asked pairs to work together to solve the problem and share their thinking, and then brought the class together for selected students to share their answers and strategies with the whole class (usually at the board). Observers videotaped or audiotaped all whole-class interaction and more than half of the pairs in each classroom as they solved problems on equality and relational thinking (e.g., $10 + 10 - 10 = 5 + \_\_$). As in Study 1, the findings are averaged across teachers (the findings described here are drawn from data and results reported in Webb & Ing 2006; see also Franke et al. 2006).

10.4.2   Student Behavior in the Two Studies

In Study 1, students engaged in mostly low-level help-seeking and help-giving behavior. First, help seekers more often asked general questions than specific questions: 80% of help-seeking questions were general. Second, students rarely gave explanations: students gave high-level help on only 10% of groupwork problems. The researchers in Study 1 defined high-level help as a procedural description of how to solve a problem (or part of it) that included verbal labeling of at least one quantity, as illustrated in the following explanation of how to add $\frac{2}{3} + \frac{3}{4}$ (Webb et al. 2006, p. 74):

> You see how it has different denominators, so what you have to do is do the common multiples. Go, like, 4, then put 8 then 12 then 16. Then the same for 3, 6, 9, 12. When you do that, the lowest one that you have in common is 12.

On the remaining 90% of group-work problems, students gave either answers ("6.4%") or unlabeled calculations ("It's 4 times 12."). Moreover, even when students asked for assistance, they rarely received high-level help: only 25% of requests for help elicited a high-level response. Third, when students did receive help, they infrequently used it to solve problems unassisted. When help seekers asked questions, they applied the help received to carry out unassisted work on only 37% of the problems. On the remaining problems, the help seekers acknowledged the help received or claimed to understand how to solve the problem without providing any concrete evidence of understanding ("Oh, OK", "OK. I get it."), carried out the calculations that other students had set up ("29 times 13?"), wrote work down that other students dictated ("It equals 1 and $\frac{6}{12}$ ... $\frac{7}{12}$ plus $\frac{11}{12}$, you get $\frac{18}{12}$. And then you divide 12 into 18. [It's] 6. You divide it by 2."), or simply requested the answer ("Just give me the answer, people.").

The students in Study 2 gave explanations far more often than students in Study 1. In Study 2, students gave explanations on 50% of problems. For example, for the problem "Is the number sentence 10 + 20 = 20 + 10 true or false?", a student explained: "I knew that 10 and 10 are the same, and I knew that 20 and 20 have to be there. So it's like a mirror. 10 and 10 are the same, and 20 and 20 are the same, so they're equal." Not only did students often explain or describe their thinking, on more than 40% of problems they engaged with their partner about the work, sometimes giving explanations to each other as in the following example for the problem 11 + 2 = 10 + __:

> Student 1: I just added 11 plus 2, and then I...saw it was 13, huh. So then I added 10 plus 3, and I saw it was 13 too. So I pull down a number and I put 13, huh. And then suddenly I, look at, they just did one up. Goes from 10, next is 11...it goes from 2, next is 3.
> Student 2: Yeah. So you know why I put the lines? It's 'cause if this is a higher number and this is a lower number, and the next one is 2 plus 3, this is 11. 'Cause 11, this is higher, this is lower, this is higher, this is lower. So 2...it doesn't care if it's switched. But 3 plus, I put this 'cause this number is lower and this number...is higher. And then I say that if this is higher, the next one has to be lower. And if this is lower...

> Student 1: 11 plus 2 equals 10 plus 3.
> Student 2: And if this is lower, this had to be higher.

> Student 1: ...I saw that too. 'Cause 11 is higher than 10...this one's gotta be higher than this one. So this one's lower and this one's higher. And this one's lower and this one's higher. Get it?

The students in Study 2 more often responded to requests for help with explanations than the students in Study 1: about half of questions in Study 2 elicited an explanation. As in Study 1, however, Study 2 students did not often apply the explanations they received to the problem at hand. Study 2 students applied the help they received on 38% of the problems (e.g., carrying out the problem for themselves, paraphrasing the explanation, disagreeing with the explanation). On the remaining problems, Study 2 students echoed the numbers that other students dictated, acknowledged the help without doing further work ("I got it"), or did not pay further attention to the problem.

Not only did the students in the two studies interact quite differently, but the teachers also behaved differently. The following sections describe differences in teacher behavior between the two studies and how these differences may have translated into differences in between-student interaction.

10.4.3 Promoting Active Help Seeking

Before students can be expected to pose specific questions to their groupmates, they must feel that it is permissible to ask questions. In the two studies, teachers differed in the extent to which they signaled the desirability of asking questions. In Study 1, teachers gave mixed signals about the appropriateness of question asking.

On the one hand, teachers instructed students to ask questions of each other during group work and encouraged them to ask each other before seeking outside assistance ("Did you ask your group first?"). Moreover, on the few occasions in which teachers did respond to student questions during group work, they helped quite willingly. On the other hand, during whole class instruction these same Study 1 teachers rarely invited students to ask questions or seek help in any way (or to contribute in ways other than providing calculations and answers to problems), possibly undermining other messages about the propriety to student questions.

Although Study 2 did not focus on student questioning, teachers showed a receptiveness to help seeking in several ways. First, teachers responded positively to students' questions during small group work. Second, teachers sometimes invited questions ("Does anybody else have a question about that?", "Does everyone understand that?", "So do you understand why [Student] thinks it's false?", "Is there anyone who does not understand this problem?") and reinforced student questions ("So why did you do that? That's what she's asking."). Furthermore, teachers sometimes invited students to respond to other students' suggestions ("Do you agree with [Student]?", "Is there anyone who disagrees with [Students'] explanation on how they solved number one?").

10.5 Promoting Explanation-Giving

10.5.1 Directing Students to Explain to each other

Teachers in Studies 1 and 2 reminded students of the importance of giving explanations rather than answers ("If they explain it, that means don't give them the answer, right? Explain it", Study 1), or asking students to share their thinking and explain to each other ("Share with your table partner what you did. What kind of thinking went on? How did you solve it?", Study 2).

How teachers followed up on these general directives, however, varied. In Study 1, when teachers visited small groups they asked students to help each other on 3% to 20% of their visits, across the three curriculum units in the study. In only a few cases did the teacher explicitly ask students to *explain* to each other. Most of the time, they gave more general instructions about helping ("You are supposed to help each other out here," "You have to check with each other," "Show him what to do."). In Study 2, in contrast, teachers reminded students to explain to each other during nearly all group visits. Sometimes teachers gave general reminders ("Did you explain to your partner what you did?), while others targeted specific students ("Can you explain it to her because she thinks it's 12.") or situations ("You think it's false. She thinks it's true. So can you explain to him why you think it's true? And then you explain to her why you think it's false.").

10.5.2 *Requesting Explanations*

Teachers often encourage their students to give explanations by requesting them. In Study 1, however, teachers generally asked low-level questions, such as asking students to provide a single-word or single-number answer. Low-level questions represented 74% of teacher questions during whole-class instruction and 84% of teacher questions during visits with small groups. Most of the remaining teacher questions requested student responses that contained somewhat more elaboration than a single word or number, such as a calculation ("What do I subtract?") or a description of a procedure ("What is the first thing to do when we add fractions?").

Only rarely did teachers in Study 1 ask students to explain how to solve a problem. On average, they asked students to give an explanation (e.g., "If you have 67 cents, you have the correct answer. Who would like to explain it?") once only during whole-class instruction (representing about 2% of teacher questions), and never during interaction with small groups. Similarly, after students gave an answer, teachers rarely asked them to explain how they obtained their answers, regardless of the answer's correctness. During whole-class instruction, on average, teachers asked students to explain how they obtained their correct answer only once and asked students to explain how they obtained their incorrect answer less than once. Of all student answers suggested, teachers asked for an explanation on only about 3% of them. The infrequency with which Study 1 teachers asked students to explain or describe how they arrived at their answers was at odds with the primary focus of the cooperative learning program on giving explanations rather than answers. This likely sent students a mixed message about the importance of giving elaborated responses to each other.

In contrast, in Study 2 the teachers frequently asked students to give an explanation. During whole-class instruction, teachers typically called students to the board to explain how they solved the problem. Teachers requested both the answer and an explanation as well as reminded students to explain if they didn't immediately volunteer an explanation (e.g., "You think 200. Why do you think that?"). After students gave an explanation or described their strategy (or a portion of it), teachers very frequently asked students to explain their thinking, as demonstrated in the following examples of teacher questioning:

What has a partner? What are you talking about?
It doesn't need to have a pattern? What do you mean?
OK, you are using the tally strategy. Why do you have 14 tallies?
How does it help you knowing that 14 divided by 2 is 7?
Why did you choose to write two times a number is 14?
Why did you minus 10? And where did you get that 10 from?
Why did you put take away zero?
What do you mean if it's take away or plus?

During their interactions with groups, Study 2 teachers asked similar questions to those asked during whole-class interactions, prompting students to explain how they obtained both their correct answers ("Can you explain to me what you did here?", "Why do you think 25?") and their incorrect answers ("No, don't erase it. Tell me what you are doing right here," "Why do you think it's 1?").

Teachers in Study 2 encouraged students to give explanations in two additional ways. First, Study 2 teachers asked for explanations of alternative strategies or answers. When students voiced incorrect answers in Study 1, the teachers often immediately called on other students to provide a different answer. In Study 2, in contrast, the teachers invited additional explanations whether the students provided correct suggestions ("Is there someone else who has a different way?") or incorrect suggestions ("Did someone else think differently?"). Second, Study 2 teachers provided positive reinforcement for students who struggled with giving explanations. They did this by giving students ample time to explain their thinking and called for the rest of the class to do the same ("I like how most of us are patiently waiting for these two ladies to share with us what they are working on," "Let's give him a minute, OK?", "Thank you for giving her some think time"). They also encouraged students who had difficulties ("Explain your thinking. You're on the right track.").

10.5.3 Responding to Student Explanations

Teachers can reinforce student explanation giving in multiple ways, such as explicitly calling to attention the fact that a student gave an explanation, asking further questions about the explanation, repeating or rephrasing it, adding details to it, or inviting other students to react to it. All of these behaviors highlight the value of giving explanations. In Study 1, although teachers seldom asked students to provide explanations, teachers did respond to the few explanations given, usually by repeating them or paraphrasing them, and occasionally asking questions about them. The following example shows a Study 1 teacher carrying out several of these behaviors, including asking the student to clarify part of his description, to explain why he chose that procedure, and summarizing and elaborating the student's explanation.

> Teacher: We want to figure out how much a 4-minute phone call will cost. The first minute is 19 cents. ... and each additional minute is going to cost ... 12 cents. So how are we going to figure out how much that costs?
> Student: Add, ah, 19 and three twelve, and it's 55.
>
> Teacher: Ok, you said three twelve. What do you mean by three twelve?
> Student: Three 12's. Like three 12's.
>
> Teacher: Ok, so you are saying multiply 12 cents by three. Why'd you get that?
> Student: Because 19 is one, and then there is ... three more other ones.
>
> Teacher: Ok, there are four minutes total. One of the minutes costs 19 cents, and the other three cost 12 cents each. So we are going to multiply three times 12 to find how much those three minutes cost.

In Study 2, because teachers frequently asked students to explain their thinking, they had many opportunities to respond to students' explanations. As described above, teachers frequently asked students to provide further elaboration on or clarification of their explanations. In addition, teachers revoiced students' explanations by repeating them, paraphrasing them, elaborating upon them, or summarizing them. Sometimes teachers revoiced steps in students' explanations ("So you're telling me thirty plus zero is thirty and thirty minus zero is thirty?", "So he said 4 plus 9 is 13. Five times 3 is 15. That's not the same number, so it's false. Okay, I can agree with that") or provided summaries of students' explanations that served as conclusions to a problem:

> I see what you are saying. So the 200 and the 200 are partners, and the one and the one are partners. ...So it doesn't matter which way. These ones are still partners. They are the same. These 200's are partners. They are still the same. So either way we do it, it's still the same on both sides.

In some cases, teachers' responses served to highlight particular ideas in a student's explanation:

> So what I see [Student] did here is she actually thought of 14 divided by two and for some reason she made a connection to multiplication because she understands that division and multiplication are opposites.

> Ok, so [Student] was looking at a lower number on one side and a higher number and he was trying to see where they met.

When teachers responded to students' explanations, they reinforced the importance of providing them, something that likely carried over into students' group work.

10.5.4 Modeling Explanations in Other Ways

As explained above, Study 2 teachers often took advantage of students' explanations to further explain class content. In Study 1, because the students did not frequently give explanations, the teachers did not have the same opportunities. However, Study 1 teachers had other opportunities to model giving explanations, such as explaining in the context of their instruction or by responding to students' answers with explanations. However, these teacher behaviors rarely occurred. Only 11%, on average, of Study 1 teachers' instructional statements during whole-class instruction went beyond answers and unlabeled descriptions of calculations; in teachers' interaction with small groups, only 10% of statements went beyond answers and numbers. Commonly, teachers described calculations without explaining what the numbers referred to ("Take away the first three, you have two left") or answers without any calculations ("If you know how to do it, you can just write $\frac{6}{9}$ equals $\frac{2}{3}$ ").

Further, Study 1 teachers' feedback to students' suggested answers rarely included explanations. During whole-class instruction, teachers gave justifications of why a student's response was correct less than 2% of the time ("77%. That means you moved it [the decimal point] over once, you gained a dot, and you moved it over again, you gained another dot, like that."), and gave justification of why a student's response was incorrect less than 8% of the time ("You have to move the decimal point two places to the right and stop."). For the vast majority of student suggestions, teachers confirmed or rejected the student's response "Alright," "No. Can't be."), repeated their responses ("22 cents."), or called on other students without elaborating upon the student's suggestion. During group work, teachers' responded similarly to students' suggestions: *no* correct suggestion elicited a teacher explanation, and less than 10% of incorrect suggestions elicited explanations.

The following example shows the teacher responding to a student's incorrect procedure with calculations. Here, the student proposed to reduce the fraction $\frac{8}{16}$ by dividing the numerator by 2 twice and dividing the denominator by 2 once, thereby obtaining $\frac{2}{8}$ instead of $\frac{1}{2}$ (Webb et al. 2006, p. 99). The teacher did not explain the correct procedure for reducing fractions nor did she explain why the student's strategy was incorrect.

> Student: Can I just go to $\frac{2}{8}$?
> Teacher: Ok, what did you divide by to get that?
>
> Student: Huh?
> Teacher: T: What did you divide? You had to divide by something. Did you divide by 4 and 4... Is 16 divided by 4...8? Huh-uh.
>
> Student: What do you mean 16 divided by 4, oh, 2?
> Teacher: You have to divide them both by the same number.
>
> Student: Ok. But, is what I do, half of 8 is 4, then half of 4 is 2.
> Teacher: Oh, but you can't do that.
>
> Student: I can't?
> Teacher: Well, why don't you divide by 8? Does 8 go into 8? Does 8 go into 16?
>
> Student: Yes.
> Teacher: Ok, try that.

When teachers responded to students' work with calculations and answers rather than explanations, they provided an example that students were likely to follow in group work. Moreover, teachers communicated that correcting students' answers was more important than helping students correct their misconceptions.

10.5.5 Exploring Students' Conceptions and Misconceptions

To understand which type of help would most benefit students, teachers must understand students' conceptions (or misconceptions) about the problems they need to solve (Carpenter et al. 1989). As described above, Study 1 teachers rarely asked students to explain how they solved a problem. Only within small groups did teachers even try to diagnose students' errors, and these few attempts met with limited success. Typically, Study 1 teachers asked a small number of questions ("How did you get this?", "Where did you get the 30, though?") before giving up, proceeding to set up the problem for the student, and leading the student through the problem step by step.

In Study 2, teachers more often pushed students to articulate their thinking until their strategies (whether correct or incorrect) became clear. Study 2 teachers engaged in repeated the questioning noted earlier in order to uncover details of correct strategies (e.g., the precise computational strategy used to solve the number sentence $11 + 2 = 10 + \underline{\quad}$) or incorrect strategies (e.g., proposing the answer 50 for the number sentence $50 + 50 = 25 + \underline{\quad} + 50$ in the belief that 50 must have an identical partner on each side of the number sentence).

10.5.6 Encouraging Students' Active Participation

The behaviors predictive of help seekers' learning—asking specific rather than general questions and applying help received to the problem at hand—portray the help seeker as an active learner both when formulating questions and after receiving help. How teachers engage with students during instruction conveys much information to the students about whether teachers expect them, as learners, to play active or passive roles. Study 1 teachers generally used a recitation style of instruction in which they assumed responsibility for setting up the steps in the problem and asked students to fill in the calculations:

Teacher: Number 3 is $\frac{1}{6}$ plus $\frac{2}{3}$. We have to find the common denominator. For both fractions. Does anyone have an idea what that common denominator would be?
Student: Six.

Teacher: Okay, how do we find out? Remember? You have to find the multiples? Least common multiple? Name me the multiples of 6.
Student: Six, 12, 18, 24.

Teacher: Name three multiples of 3.
Student: Three, 6, 9.

Teacher: Does any one see a multiple that they have in common?
Student: Six.

Teacher: That's going to be our common denominator. Ok?

In some cases, the teacher gave students more responsibility for identifying steps in the problem, but still maintained control over guiding students through the problem:

Teacher: $\frac{1}{6}$ plus $\frac{2}{3}$, I see some trouble. What is it?
Student: The denominators are not the same.

Teacher: Alright, you've got [to find] the least common denominator. The least common multiple, and what would the least common multiple be?
Student: Six.

Teacher: Six. Six goes into six and three goes into six. What do I have to do now?
Student: Three times 2 is 6. Now on top it will be 2 plus 2 equals 4.

> Teacher: Alright, these are called equivalent fractions, don't forget that. Alright this stays
> the same. What do I do now? Now you add 4 plus 1.
> Student: Five.
>
> Teacher: Can I reduce that?
> Student: No.

These patterns of interaction signaled that the "teacher" (help-giver) plays the active role in problem solving and the "student" (help-seeker) carries out the steps or calculations identified. Groups usually followed these roles, with help givers doing most of the work and help receivers either carrying out calculations set up by others or copying entire problems.

Study 2 teachers, in contrast, gave students complete control over solving the problems:

> Teacher: Do you want to come up and tell us how you solved number one? ($14/2 = (3* \_\_) + 1$)
> Student: Because two....because 7 times 2 is 14, so if that [side] equals 7 this side has to equal 7. So 3 times a number plus 1. So, 3 times 2 equals 6, plus 1 equals 7.

Sometimes, when students had trouble formulating an explanation, Study 2 teachers prompted the students to go in a particular direction and provided hints to help them explain how to solve the problem, for example:

> But how does it help you knowing that 14 divided by 2 is 7? Now you solved the left hand side of that problem. Now you know that the left side is 7. The answer to, the quotient, on the left hand side is 7 and how does that help you with the right and side, with the missing number that you are looking for?

In rare cases only did Study 2 teachers lead a student through the calculations in a problem and this guidance occurred only after a student had explained his or her strategy and the teacher had already uncovered a specific misconception. In contrast to the Study 1 teachers, Study 2 teachers' step-by-step guidance came after student proffered explanations and served the purpose of reviewing the problem and helping the class solidify the correct approach (e.g., carrying out multiplication before addition in a sequence of operations).

10.6   Conclusion

This paper showed that both help seekers and help givers play important roles in collaborative learning. To maximize achievement, help seekers should ask specific, rather than general, questions about what they do not understand and should actively apply, rather than passively acknowledge, the help they receive. Help givers should provide explanations rather than answers and should give help seekers opportunities to carry out unassisted problem solving.

Our examination of student and teacher behavior in two studies of collaborative learning suggests, further, that teacher practices in the classroom have an important influence on students' help-related behavior. Although teachers in both studies provided general instructions for students to explain to each other, the teachers in the two studies engaged in very different instructional practices. Study 1 teachers assumed responsibility for setting up the steps in the problems and tended to lead the whole class through the problems step by step. Most teacher questions required the students to provide the answer to a calculation or offer the next step in the problem. Rarely did Study 1 teachers ask students to explain or describe how they arrived at their answers. When interacting with small groups, Study 1 teachers sometimes asked students to describe the procedures they used for solving problems (especially when they offered incorrect answers), but these episodes occurred infrequently. Through their practices, these teachers modeled the role of "teacher" (help giver) as the active participant and the role of "student" (help seeker) as relatively passive. In group work, Study 1 students tended to adopt these roles. Typically, help givers solved problems and gave or dictated calculations or procedures (but not explanations) to help seekers. Help seekers, in turn, accepted help without testing their own understanding by attempting to solve the problems without assistance.

Study 2 teachers held students responsible for explaining their thinking, or at least describing the strategies they used for solving problems. Teachers rarely accepted answers without requesting justifications. Moreover, Study 2 teachers frequently asked questions about students' explanations, requesting further clarification of students' procedures and reasons for using them. When students had difficulty, teachers generally played the role of coach rather than taking over the problem solving for the student. When interacting with small groups, Study 2 teachers frequently prompted students to explain to each other. Corresponding to teachers' emphasis on students explaining their thinking, when working in groups Study 2 students tended to give each other more explanations than Study 1 students. Overall, Study 2 students participated more actively in group collaboration.

These findings suggest that productive group collaboration—especially exchanging explanations—may follow from classroom instruction in which teachers hold students accountable for playing an active role and for explaining their thinking. Study 2 teachers used practices found in other research to raise the level of discourse in classrooms, such as asking students to justify, clarify, and reflect on their ideas (Hogan & Pressley 1997), use questions to elicit student thinking (Carpenter et al. 1989; Carpenter et al. 1999; Carpenter et al. 1996), having students generate their own problem-solving approaches, and listening to students without evaluating their approaches (Wood et al. 1991, 1995; Yackel et al. 1991). Changing classroom practices from the teacher-centered instruction seen in Study 1 to the more student-centered instruction seen in Study 2 may require radical shifts in teachers' beliefs about teaching and learning (Franke et al. 1997) and may need to occur over a long period of time (Wood et al. 1991). Meeting this challenge, however, will likely lead to more effective group collaboration.

Acknowledgement   This work was supported in part by a grant from the Academic Senate on Research, Los Angeles Division, University of California; by grant number 1093264 from WestED to the Center for the Study of Evaluation/CRESST (funding to WestED was provided by

grant number ESI-0119790 from the National Science Foundation; and by the National Science Foundation under Grant No. ESI-0119732 to the Diversity in Mathematics Education Center for Learning and Teaching. However, all opinions, findings, and conclusions and recommendations are mine.
I would like to acknowledge the contributions of Megan Franke, Angela Chan, Dan Battey, Julie Kern Schwerdtfeger, Deanna Freund, and John Iwanaga to the collection and coding of data for Study 2, and the contributions of Marsha Ing to both Studies 1 and 2. I would also like to thank Kariane Mari Nemer for her helpful suggestions on an earlier draft of this paper.

References

Bargh, J. A., & Schul, Y. (1980). On the cognitive benefit of teaching. *Journal of Educational Psychology, 72,* 593–604.

Brown, A. L., & Palinscar, A. S. (1989). Guided, cooperative learning, and individual knowledge acquisition. In L.B. Resnick (Ed.) *Knowing, learning, and instruction: Essays in honor of Robert Glaser* (pp. 393–451). Hillsdale, NJ: Lawrence Erlbaum Associates.

Butler, R., & Neuman, O. (1995). Effects of task and ego achievement goals on help-seeking behaviors and attitudes. *Journal of Educational Psychology, 87,* 261–271.

California State Department of Education. (1985). *Mathematics framework for California public schools, kindergarten through grade twelve.* Sacramento, CA: California Department of Education.

California State Department of Education. (1992). *Mathematics framework for California public schools, kindergarten through grade twelve.* Sacramento, CA: California Department of Education.

Carpenter, T. P., Fennema, E., Franke, M. L., Levi, L., & Empson, S. B. (1999). *Children's mathematics: Cognitively guided instruction.* Portsmouth, NH: Heinemann.

Carpenter, T. P., Fennema, E., Peterson, P. L., Chiang, C. P., & Loef, M. (1989). Using knowledge of children's mathematics thinking in classroom teaching: An experimental study. *American Educational Research Journal, 26,* 499–531.

Carpenter, T. P., Franke, M. L., & Levi, L. (2003). *Thinking mathematically: Integrating algebra and arithmetic in elementary school.* Portsmouth, NH: Heinemann.

Chiu, M. M. (2000). Group problem-solving processes: Social interactions and individual actions. *Journal for the Theory of Social Behavior, 30,* 27–49.

Chiu, M. M., & Khoo, L. (2003). Rudeness and status effects during group problem solving: Do they bias evaluations and reduce the likelihood of correct solutions? *Journal of Educational Psychology, 95,* 506–523.

Coleman, E. B. (1998). Using explanatory knowledge during collaborative problem solving in science. *Journal of the Learning Sciences, 7,* 387–427.

Cooper, M. A. (1999). Classroom choices from a cognitive perspective on peer learning. In A. M. O'Donnell & A. King (Eds.) *Cognitive perspectives on peer learning* (pp. 215–234). Hillsdale, NJ: Lawrence Erlbaum Associates.

Covington, M. V. (1984). The self-worth theory of achievement motivation: Findings and implications. *Elementary School Journal, 85,* 5–20.

Fantuzzo, J. W., Riggio, R. E., Connelly, S., & Dimeff, L. A. (1989). Effects of reciprocal peer tutoring on academic achievement and psychological adjustment: A component analysis. *Journal of Educational Psychology, 81,* 173–177.

Farivar, S., & Webb, N. M. (1998). Preparing teachers and students for cooperative work: Building communication and helping skills. In C. M. Brody & N. Davidson (Eds.), *Professional development for cooperative learning: Issues and approaches* (pp. 169–188). Albany, NY: State University of New York.

Franke, M. L., Fennema, E., & Carpenter, T. (1997). Teachers creating change: Examining evolving beliefs and classroom practice. In E. Fennema & B. S. Nelson (Eds.), *Mathematics teachers in transition* (pp. 255–282). Mahway, NJ: Lawrence Erlbaum Associates.

Franke, M. L., Freund, D., Iwanaga, J., & Schwerdtfeger, J. K. (2006). *Exploring the impact of large-scale professional development focused on children's algebraic reasoning.* Paper presented at the annual meeting of the American Educational Research Association, San Francisco.

Fuchs, L. S., Fuchs, D., Hamlett, C. L., Phillips, N. B., Karns, K., & Dutka, S. (1997). Enhancing students' helping behavior during peer-mediated instruction with conceptual mathematical explanations. *Elementary School Journal, 97*, 223–249.

Fuchs, L.S., Fuchs, D., Kazdan, S., & Allen, S. (1999). Effects of peer-assisted learning strategies in reading with and without training in elaborated help giving. *Elementary School Journal, 99*, 201–219.

Gillies, R. M., & Ashman, A. F. (1996). Teaching collaborative skills in primary school children in classroom-based work groups. *Learning and Instruction, 6*, 187–200.

Gillies, R. M., & Ashman, A. F. (1998). Behavior and interactions of children in cooperative groups in lower and middle elementary grades. *Journal of Educational Psychology, 90*, 746–757.

Hooper, S. (1992). Effects of peer interaction during computer-based mathematics instruction. *Journal of Educational Research, 85*, 180–189.

Hythecker, V. I., Dansereau, D. F., & Rocklin, T. R. (1988). An analysis of the processes influencing the structured dyadic learning environment. *Educational Psychologist, 23*, 23–27.

Jacobs, V. R., Franke, M. L., Carpenter, T. P., Levi, L., Battey, D., & Chan, A. (2005). *Exploring the impact of large-scale professional development focused on children's algebraic reasoning.* Paper presented at the annual meeting of the American Educational Research Association, Montreal.

Kerr, N. L., & Bruun, S. E. (1983). Dispensability of member effort and group motivation losses: Free-rider effects. *Journal of Personality & Social Psychology, 44*, 78–94.

King, A. (1989). Effects of self-questioning training on college students' comprehension of lectures. *Contemporary Educational Psychology, 14*, 366–381.

King, A. (1990). Enhancing peer interaction and learning in the classroom through reciprocal questioning. *American Educational Research Journal, 27*, 664–687.

King, A. (1992). Facilitating elaborative learning through guided student-generated questioning. *Educational Psychologist, 27*, 111–126.

King, A. (1999). Discourse patterns for mediating peer learning. In A. M. O'Donnell & A. King (Eds.) *Cognitive perspectives on peer learning* (pp. 87–116). Hillsdale, NJ: Lawrence Erlbaum Associates.

Mayer, R. E. (1984). Aids to prose comprehension. *Educational Psychologist, 19*, 30–42.

Mevarech, Z. R., & Kramarski, B. (1997). IMPROVE: A multidimensional method for teaching mathematics in heterogeneous classrooms. *American Educational Research Journal, 34*, 365–394.

Middleton, M. J., & Midgley, C. (1997). Avoiding the demonstration of lack of ability: An under-explored aspect of goal theory. *Journal of Educational Psychology, 89*, 710–718.

Mulryan, C. M. (1992). Student passivity during cooperative small groups in mathematics. *Journal of Educational Research, 85*, 261–273.

National Council of Teachers of Mathematics. (1989). *Curriculum and evaluation standards for school mathematics.* Reston, VA: The National Council of Teachers of Mathematics.

National Council of Teachers of Mathematics. (1991). *Professional Standards for Teaching Mathematics.* Reston, VA: The National Council of Teachers of Mathematics.

National Research Council. (1989). *Everybody counts: A report to the nation of the future of mathematics education.* Mathematical Sciences Education Board, Washington, DC: National Academy Press.

National Research Council. (1995). *National science education standards.* Washington, DC: National Academy Press.

Nattiv, A. (1994). Helping behaviors and math achievement gain of students using cooperative learning. *Elementary School Journal, 94*, 285–297.

Newman, R. S. (1991). Goals and self-regulated learning: What motivates children to seek academic help? In M. L. Maehr & P. R. Pintrich (Eds.), *Advances in motivation and achievement.* (pp. 151–183). Greenwich, CT: JAI Press.

Newman, R. S. (1994). Adaptive help seeking: A strategy of self-regulated learning. In D. H. Schunk & B. J. Zimmerman (Eds.), *Self-regulation of learning and performance: Issues and educational applications.* (pp. 283–301). Hillsdale, NJ: Lawrence Erlbaum Associates.

Newman, R. S. (1998). Students' help seeking during problem solving: Influences of personal and contextual achievement goals. *Journal of Educational Psychology, 90*, 644–658.

O'Donnell, A. M. (1999). Structuring dyadic interaction through scripted cooperation. In A. M. O'Donnell & A. King (Eds.) *Cognitive perspectives on peer learning* (pp. 179–196). Hillsdale, NJ: Lawrence Erlbaum Associates.

Palincsar, A. S., Anderson, C., & David, Y. M. (1993). Pursuing scientific literacy in the middle grades through collaborative problem solving. *Elementary School Journal, 93*, 643–658.

Peterson, P. L., Janicki, T. C., & Swing, S. R. (1981). Ability x treatment interaction effects on children's learning in large-group and small-group approaches. *American Educational Research Journal, 18*, 453–473.

Rogoff, B. (1991). Guidance and participation in spatial planning. In L. Resnick, J. Levine & S. Teasley (Eds.), *Perspectives on socially shared cognition* (pp. 349–383). Washington, DC: American Psychological Association.

Rogoff, N. (1990). *Apprenticeship in thinking: Cognitive development in social context.* Oxford, UK: Oxford University Press.

Ross, J. A., & Cousins, J. B. (1995). Impact of explanation seeking on student achievement and attitudes. *Journal of Educational Research, 89*, 109–117.

Salomon, G., & Globerson, T. (1989). When teams do not function the way they ought to. *International Journal of Educational Research, 13*, 89–99.

Saxe, G. B., Gearhart, M., Note, M., & Paduano, P. (1993). Peer interaction and the development of mathematical understanding. In H. Daniels (Ed.) *Charting the agenda: Educational activity after Vygotsky* (pp. 107–144)). London: Routledge.

Slavin, R.E. (1987). Ability grouping and student achievement in elementary schools: A best-evidence synthesis. *Review of Educational Research, 57*, 293–336.

Sweller, J. (1989). Cognitive technology: Some procedures for facilitating learning and problem solving in mathematics and science. *Journal of Educational Psychology, 81*, 457–466.

Swing, S. R., & Peterson, P. L. (1982). The relationship of student ability and small-group interaction to student achievement. *American Educational Research Journal, 19*, 259–274.

Valsiner, J. (1987). *Culture and the development of children's action.* New York, NY: John Wiley.

Vedder, P. (1985). *Cooperative learning. A study on processes and effects of cooperation between primary school children.* Westerhaven Groningen, Netherlands: Rijkuniversiteit Groningen.

Webb, N. M. (1989). Peer interaction and learning in small groups. *International Journal of Educational Research, 13*, 21–40.

Webb, N. M. (1991). Task-related verbal interaction and mathematics learning in small groups. *Journal for Research in Mathematics Education, 22*, 366–389.

Webb, N. M., &. Farivar, S. (1999). Developing productive group interaction in middle school mathematics. In A. M. O'Donnell & A. King (Eds.) *Cognitive perspectives on peer learning* (pp. 117–150). Hillsdale, NJ: Lawrence Erlbaum Associates.

Webb, N. M., & Ing, M. (2006). *Student discourse and learning in elementary school mathematics classrooms.* Paper presented at the annual meeting of the American Educational Research Association, San Francisco.

Webb, N. M., Ing, M., Nemer, K. M., & Kersting, N. (2006). Help seeking in cooperative learning groups. In R. S. Newman & S. A. Karabenick (Eds.), *Help Seeking in academic settings: Goals, groups and contexts* (pp. 45–88). Lawrence Erlbaum Associates.

Webb, N. M., & Mastergeorge, A. M. (2003a). The development of students' learning in peer-directed small groups. *Cognition and Instruction, 21*, 361–428.

Webb, N. M., & Mastergeorge, A. M. (2003b). Promoting effective helping behavior in peer-directed groups. *International Journal of Educational Research, 39*, 73–97.

Webb, N. M., Nemer, K. M., & Ing, M. (2006). Small-group reflections: Parallels between teacher discourse and student behavior in peer-directed groups. *Journal of the Learning Sciences, 15(1)*, 63–119.

Webb, N. M., & Palincsar, A. S. (1996). Group processes in the classroom. In D. Berliner & R. Calfee (Eds.) *Handbook of educational psychology* (pp. 841–873). New York, NY: Macmillan.

Webb, N. M., Troper, J. D., & Fall, R. (1995). Constructive activity and learning in collaborative small groups. *Journal of Educational Psychology, 87*, 406–423.

Wittrock, M. C. (1990). Generative processes of comprehension. *Educational Psychologist, 24*, 345–376.

Wood, T., Cobb, P., & Yackel. E. (1991). Change in teaching mathematics: A case study. *American Educational Research Journal, 28*, 587–616.

Wood, T., Cobb, P., & Yackel, E. (1995). Reflections on learning and teaching mathematics in elementary school. In L. P. Steffe & J. E. Gale (Eds.), *Constructivism in education* (pp. 401–422). Hillsdale, NJ: Lawrence Erlbaum Associates.

Yackel, E., Cobb, P., & Wood, T. (1991). Small-group interactions as a source of learning opportunities in second-grade mathematics. *Journal for Research in Mathematics Education, 22*, 390–408.

Yackel, E., Cobb, P., Wood, T., Wheatley, G., & Merkel, G. (1990). The importance of social interaction in children's construction of mathematical knowledge. In T. J. Cooney & C. R. Hirsch (Eds.), *Teaching and learning mathematics in the 1990s* (pp. 12–21). Reston, VA: National Council of Teachers of Mathematics.

Yager, S., Johnson, D. W., & Johnson, R. T. (1985). Oral discussion, group-to-individual transfer, and achievement in cooperative learning groups. *Journal of Educational Psychology, 77*, 60–66.

Chapter 11
Explanation Giving and Receiving in Cooperative Learning Groups[1]

John A. Ross

Abstract Students who give explanations to their peers learn more from small group discussions than students who do not. In this chapter, I will identify four instructional challenges posed by this finding: (a) explanation giving is rare; (b) usually upper ability students only offer explanations of their thinking, meaning that the students who could most benefit from this powerful learning strategy are least likely to engage in it; (c) asking for an explanation may not contribute to the learning of the explanation seeker; and (d) the quality of explanations provided by even the most able students tends to be poor. In this chapter I will describe four practical classroom strategies for improving the quality and frequency of explanations in cooperative learning groups. These strategies include direct teaching of help giving and help seeking, improving the social climate of the classroom, improving teacher interventions in small group activities, and implementing reciprocal roles.

[1]Send comments on the chapter to Dr. John A. Ross, Professor of Curriculum, Teaching and Learning, University of Toronto, PO Box 719, 1994 Fisher Drive, Peterborough, ON K9J7A1 Canada. Preparation of the chapter was funded by the Social Sciences and Humanities Research Council of Canada. The views expressed in the chapter do not necessarily represent the views of the Council.

11.1   Cooperative Learning Research:
Practical Benefits for Teachers

Two clusters of cooperative learning research have immediate practical value to teachers. The first cluster consists of evaluations in which cooperative learning is compared to credible alternatives, such as well-designed whole class instruction. These studies demonstrate that cooperative instructional methods lead to cognitive and affective gains for students from kindergarten to graduate school (e.g., Johnson et al. 2000). Equally important, they demonstrate to teachers that specific structures have differential effects. For example, Group Investigation (GI) is superior to Student Teams–Achievement Divisions (STAD) in reaching high level language objectives (such as comprehension) but GI is less effective than STAD in achieving recall type language objectives (such as language conventions) (Sharan et al. 1985; Sharan & Shachar 1988). Teachers also find helpful the many studies in this cluster that identify moderators, that is, factors that amplify or depress the effects of cooperative learning, such as Terwel's (2003) demonstration that low ability secondary school students do not benefit from cooperative learning unless given special training.

The second cluster of cooperative learning research useful to teachers focuses on mediators, that is, mechanisms that explain why cooperative learning is effective. The most practical findings focus on what students say to each other when working on joint tasks: their implicit and explicit requests for help and the contributions, solicited or spontaneous, that students make to the construction of a joint product or shared understanding. The key finding is that all forms of help giving, especially giving explanations, contribute to student learning (Nattiv 1994; Ross & Raphael 1990; Veenman et al. 2005; Webb 1989; Webb et al. 1996, 2002, 2003; Webb & Farivar 1994; Webb & Ing 2006). A quality explanation is one that supplies sufficient guidance to enable the recipient to generate a specific answer for the immediate task while providing the receiver of the help with procedural and/or conceptual knowledge to solve future problems of a similar type on his or her own. In practice, researchers code as explanations virtually any kind of elaboration that goes beyond answer giving.

Explanations are more frequently given when students are in structured cooperative groups than when working in unstructured settings (Gillies 2004a, b; Gillies & Ashman 1998). Explanation exchanges are more frequent in cooperative learning classrooms because cooperative learning discourages students from ridiculing others (a major impediment to help seeking), eliminates competitive reward structures that penalize help givers, and establish norms of mutual sharing. Even though adoption of the leading cooperative learning methods leads to greater helpfulness, maximum benefits are likely to accrue only if teachers overcome substantial instructional challenges.

11.2   Instructional Challenges

11.2.1   *Infrequent Occurrence of the Most Beneficial Talk*

The most powerful form of discourse, asking for an explanation and getting one, seldom occurs. For example, Ross and Cousins (1995b) found that explanations were infrequently requested and given even in a cooperative condition in which explanation sharing was required. The typical grade 7–8 student asked for an explanation once per 35-min period and received an explanation twice. Across three studies involving grade 7–10 students who were working cooperatively on complex open ended tasks, 64% never asked for an explanation, and of those that did, more than half did not receive an explanation in response. The instructional challenge is finding ways to increase the frequency of high quality explanations that students give and receive.

11.2.2   *Unequal Participation in Knowledge Construction*

Instrumental or mastery-oriented help seeking is characterized by students alternating between giving help and receiving it (Nelson-Le Gall 1992). But student conversations in naturally occurring and structured settings are more like tutoring sessions than symmetrical information exchanges. Webb (1989) reported six studies in which giving explanations correlated strongly with ability. The more able students explained and the less able listened. Lower ability student passivity and upper ability student dominance in student groups has been often observed (Good et al. 1992; Mulryan 1994, 1995), even in cooperative learning classrooms (King 1993). The dominance of cooperative group work by more capable students is particularly strong when the goal is required to produce a single product. Pressure from high-ability students to complete tasks quickly creates a helper/helpee caste system that reduces participation by the less able because they slow the group down. In these circumstances, students who believe their offerings are of little value respond by withdrawing from the task (Karau & Williams 1993). The instructional challenge here is how to ensure that lower ability students give as well as receive explanations.

11.2.3   *Asking for Explanations May Not Contribute to Learning*

Asking for explanations might contribute to achievement in several ways. Asking for an explanation and receiving one gives students the opportunity to observe and model the understanding of more able group members. In addition, framing a request may trigger self-appraisal and reorganization of current knowledge. Asking for explanations may stimulate cognitive conflict with other students but such interactions can also lead to cognitive restructuring as the help seeker recognize gaps in his/her understanding and fills them with ideas provided by peers. Finally, a request can be a strategy for sharing information processing demands that frees mental space, enabling the help seeker to focus on the acquisition of new ideas. Despite these potential benefits, the evidence in support of asking for explanations is very mixed, with as many studies showing no effects as positive outcomes (see e.g., Ross & Cousins 1995b).

Students have to be skillful to get good help. Effective requests are explicit, focused, repeated and directed toward an individual who is willing and able to provide the help (Wilkinson & Spinelli 1983). In addition, asking for help entails costs. Excessive help seeking reduces peer esteem—such students are perceived to be free-loaders rather than contributors to group efforts (Nelson-Le Gall & Glor-Scheib 1986). Ross and Cousins (1994) found that students who were more aware of the costs of seeking help were less likely to seek it. The same study also found that students who were most in need of help (based on teacher identified rank in class and pretest scores) did not seek it because they were not able to employ their competence on the task. Other studies have found that help seekers frequently utter vague requests such as "What are you doing?" (Ross & Cousins 1995a, p. 110). The instructional challenge for teachers is to ensure that students ask for help when they need it and formulate their requests effectively.

11.2.4   The Quality of Explanations Given by Students Is Poor

The explanations that students give to each other are often far below the quality needed to support knowledge construction. Consider this typical example provided by a high ability student in a grade 6 classroom in which students were required to explain their solutions and help other group members understand them (Ross 1995b).

When asked to calculate the number of rabbits in a store when there were 10 more legs than ears, Dave computed the answer out loud, but his words omitted much of his thinking.

> Dave: Okay, 2 ears to a rabbit. So 4, 8, 10, no, 4, 8, 12, and 16. That's 4 rabbits. 2, 4, 6, 8; 5 times 4 is 20, so there's 2, 4, 6, 8, 10. There's 5 rabbits in the store.

Embedded in Dave's brief explanation were four steps:

- He identified required knowledge not stated in the problem: Rabbits have two ears ("2 ears to a rabbit") and four legs (not spoken).
- Although he began by talking about ears, he first counted legs aloud ("4, 8, 10"), making a self-corrected error ("no 4, 8, 12, and 16"). After calculating legs for four rabbits he repeated the series for ears ("2, 4, 6, 8").
- He intuited that the solution was five (not spoken immediately) and stated a partial procedure: number of rabbits multiplied by four gives number of legs ("5 times 4 is 20").

- He verified his solution by counting aloud the number of ears for five rabbits ("so there's 2, 4, 6, 8, 10").

In describing his solution Dave moved rapidly between ears and legs with no conversational markers to signify changes. Dave's account of his solution gave listeners an incomplete model of problem-solving. When prodded to explain, he told how his answer met the conditions of the problem, but never described how he came up with it. His explanation evoked confusion and Dave became increasingly exasperated:

> Dave: There's 5 rabbits in the store. It's so simple. There's 5 rabbits times 4 legs equals 20 right?
> Bobby: Wrong.
>
> Dave: Unless you're some kind of weirdo. And there's 5 times 2 ears is 10. That's 10 difference. Now was that hard?
> Carole: Offer to explain to the rest of the group.
>
> Dave: I did. I just did.
> Donna: Ask for help.
>
> Bobby: He said something about 5 times 4 and all this. And then 5 times 2 and then this and that.
> Dave: Well it can't be 4 times 5 because there is not 5 legs on a rabbit. (Ross, 1995b, p. 413)

Other group members began to parrot Dave's explanation, repeating it to each other and to the teacher when she visited the group. In this study the same pattern of justifying a solution rather than explaining how it was produced occurred in all groups, as did repetition of answers generated by others.

Explanation givers in this study acted as mini-teachers: The student who solved the problem earned the right to question others in the group, calling on each group member to repeat the correct solution, rather than eliciting alternate solutions or alternate explanations for a particular solution. There was no monitoring of the accuracy of these recited solutions. If students said they did not understand the solution, the explanation giver repeated it verbatim. Explanation exchanges were contrived. There was routine compliance with the requirement to explain rather than authentic dialogue. In these episodes, students were rehearsing content but not constructing understanding.

Many student explanations, 30% in Ross and Cousins (1995a), contain errors and misconceptions. In the following example, Nate explained how to distinguish between a negative and a positive correlation between two variables in a scatterplot graph. He shrouded the correct core of his explanation with additional thoughts that were incorrect and confusing.

> Nate: That's positive [correlation]. You know you can tell? This way. As the graph goes up, as these numbers go up, these numbers go up too [accurate description of a positive correlation]. If it was going like this, as these numbers go up, these number would go [down – accurate description of a negative correlation]. You know, how like, two positives make a ...
> Valerie: Negative.
>
> Nate: Yes.
> Valerie: Two positives make a negative.

Nate: Yes.
Valerie: Two negatives make a positive.

Nate: And a positive plus a negative makes a negative … as you are going up this way, both of these are going up, so it's positive [accurate description of a positive correlation]. If you are going down that way, as this number goes up, this one would get lower, on here [accurate description of a negative correlation]. See? So, a negative plus a positive times a positive will make a negative.
Valerie: Oh (Ross & Cousins, 1995a, p. 111)

In addition to problems related to explanation quality, students rarely monitor the effects of their explanations (Ross 1995b; Ross & Cousins 1995a; Ross et al. 1996; Webb et al. 2006), even though explanation use is a strong predictor of student learning (Webb & Mastergeorge 2003; Webb et al. 1995). The quality of help provided affects students' willingness to seek it. For example, Ross and Cousins (1995b) found that students who asked for and received an explanation became more conscious of the cost of help seeking than students who asked for help but did not receive an explanation. The instructional challenge for teachers is how to ensure that students are able as well as willing to give high quality help.

11.3   Promising Instructional Strategies

Researchers and cooperative learning trainers have suggested a number of strategies for improving the frequency and quality of high-level help given to students. Although the techniques are well described in the literature and procedural manuals such as Farivar and Webb (1991) are available, it is not always possible to disentangle the effects of specific training from other cooperative learning elements. These strategies can be organized in different ways, including the four categories suggested below.

Direct Teaching of Help Seeking/Giving. Several studies have demonstrated that teaching students how to ask for and give help has a positive effect on the frequency and quality of help given and received. For example, Ross (1995a) examined the effects of a treatment in which students were given feedback on their inter-group communication and taught how to self-evaluate group processes. Grade 7 students were given edited transcripts of their small group discussions of mathematics problems. Instances of help seeking, help giving, and on-task behaviour were coded. In addition, students performed a brief skit (designed by Swing and Peterson 1982) to distinguish high-level from low-level help. Students used the coded transcripts to assign their group a score on each of the three categories. Feedback on their group appraisals was provided. Students designed an improvement plan to increase the frequency of the three categories. Student names were replaced with colours to reduce the costs of social comparison. Students used a self-assessment target to monitor their group processes one to two times per week for eight weeks. After four weeks they received two new sets of coded transcripts in order to contrast the performance before and after they began monitoring their communications. In these transcripts requests for explanations and explanations were highlighted. Teacher probes assisted interpretation of the transcripts. Group monitoring continued for another four weeks.

Teaching students how to self-evaluate their group processes had significant positive effects on help seeking. After training, lower ability students were more willing to seek explanations, suggesting there was a change to group norms that help should be sought and given when needed. There were fewer unnecessary requests for help. Explanation seekers became more persistent and used better request strategies. For example, when Sandi had difficulty drawing a geometric figure her requests were more persistent and precise than they had been before the training.

> Sandi: Dominique, you know how to do this?
> Dominique: [no response]
>
> Sandi: You know how to do this thing?
> Dominique: [no response]
>
> Sandi: Do you change this to bigger?
> Dominique: [no response]
>
> Sandi: Do you make your compass bigger when you do the two little arches?
> Dominique: [explains how to construct the figure] (Ross 1995a, p. 134)

There was greater student recognition that high-level help was more valuable than giving low-level help. As one student stated: "I have to understand it. Not just say the answer." (Ross 1995a, p. 134).

The training also had significant positive effects on all types of help giving, including giving of explanations. For example, a student who prior to the treatment had explained on only one occasion (when the teacher explicitly asked him to explain his solution) became eager to do so after the group began to monitor its processes, saying "Do you notice I'm being a lot nicer?" (Ross 1995a, p. 134). There was less exclusion of lower ability students who could not keep up. For example, prior to the training Sharon was often left behind.

> Sharon: Hey what about me?
> Curtis: You're not in it.
>
> Sharon: Hey you guys, what about me? How come you guys won't let me do none?
> Gwen: Because you are not even here yet.
>
> Sharon: I'm on number 15.
> Gwen: Yeah, I know, but we're on number 16.

After the training her group continued to treat her rather roughly but they now acknowledged their obligation to help her.

> Curtis: We have to wait for her. We have to wait for her.
> Gwen: Come on, Sharon. You know we are waiting.
>
> Sharon: You guys were going and you weren't supposed to.
> Gwen: I know; we won't. We won't do the answers.
> Curtis: We won't look at the answers. We'll wait for you. (Ross 1995a, p. 135).

There was also evidence that after the training high ability students adjusted their language to meet lower ability student needs (e.g., using "timesing" rather than multiplication).

Finally, the self-assessment training had a positive effect on monitoring of explanations. We found all types of monitoring increased after feedback: diagnostic monitoring (i.e., students reviewing the written work of a peer to locate errors), decomposing steps in a problem and checking for understanding of each step, and explanation monitoring. In the weak form of the latter, a high ability student asked a help seeker if they understood the solution or gave them a quick quiz that required the rehearsal of a solution strategy. The more powerful form of explanation monitoring was very rare. In the few instances observed (all were after the training) the explainer asked the target student to do the next problem or solve one of the same type out loud. However, the explainers did not give up control as they continued to decompose the task into small components and prompt the help recipient on each step.

Veenman et al. (2005) developed a treatment that combined direct teaching of a model of help seeking, charting productive help giving behaviours (both from Farivar & Webb 1998) and explanation prompts (from King 1994). The treatment produced large effect sizes. Trained grade 6 students generated more high level elaborations then either of two control groups: one control had experienced two years of cooperative learning without helpfulness training; the other control had experienced neither cooperative learning nor helpfulness training.

Webb and Farivar (1994) also generated positive results for a five-week initiative that trained grade 7 students in help giving and receiving. The procedures (described in Farivar & Webb, 1991) combined training in specific skills with self-assessment of their use. Students in the experimental condition gave and received more elaborated help than controls and had higher achievement. However, the findings were significant for African-American and Hispanic students only. There were no effects for white students. In addition, the effects were larger for one teacher than the other, which the researchers attributed to the effect of teacher modeling. Finally, the treatment contributed to achievement on complex outcomes, not on low-level tasks. Fuchs et al. (1999) also reported effects for help giving training that were limited to a particular group. The training increased the frequency of elaborated help given for grade 4 students but grade 2–3 students did not benefit because they were not developmentally ready.

The limits of direct teaching of help seeking and help giving behaviours were visible in a study that used strategies from several successful programs to train grade 5 students. The training program (Ross et al. 1996) included the Swing & Peterson (1982) skits, activities selected from Farivar & Webb (1991), activities in which students generated strategies for giving help (based on examples from Ross & Raphael, 1990 videotapes) and checklists in which students recorded instances of effective helping (from Ross, 1995a). The treatment had a negligible effect on student communication—explanations actually declined in one class, although the frequency returned to original levels over time (Ross et al. 1996). The ineffectiveness of the treatment was attributed to a program factor (the examples of good and poor help were too subtle for the cognitive levels of the students), an implementation factor (the instructional decisions made by the program conflicted with the preferred teaching styles of the two teachers who enacted the treatment), and a research partnership issue (the researchers failed to recognize early enough in the program that the surface problems reported by teachers were symptomatic of fundamental disagreements with program intentions).

These findings suggest that direct teaching of helpfulness is a fruitful strategy for increasing explanation exchanges. But the mixed results suggest that the strategy is a demanding one for both teachers and students. For students, the role of effective help giver requires the adoption of sophisticated teaching skills that may not be modeled in their classrooms. Students used a "teacher as teller" style of instruction that consisted of repeating instructional explanations provided by teachers, even when recipients of the explanation explicitly stated they did not understand the teacher's lesson (see for example, "Wanda" in Ross & Cousins, 1995b. p.112). Students also repeated the I-R-E model (teacher initiates question, student responds, teacher evaluates) which is a weak generator of knowledge construction. McMahon & Goatley (1995) found that the I-R-E pattern persisted in student-led discussions, even after attempts to introduce richer discourse patterns.

11.3.1 Improving the Social Climate of the Classroom

Several cooperative learning developers have argued that creating classroom structures that promote interdependence and provide explicit training in prosocial skills is prerequisite to student willingness to help each other. This approach is especially central to Group Investigation (Sharan & Sharan 1976) and Learning Together (Johnson & Johnson 1987). Particular strategies for developing a positive climate are described in Abrami et al. (1994), Cuseo (2006), Johnson and Johnson (1987), and Kagan and Kagan (1994).

Although there is extensive evidence about the positive effects of cooperative learning methods that include social climate development, there is little research that focuses exclusively on the effects of climate building on students' help seeking and help giving behaviour. Gillies & Ashman (1996) produced very positive results with two, short training sessions for grade 6 students. Students practiced small group skills, such as listening to each other, giving constructive feedback on ideas, sharing tasks fairly, clarifying differences of opinion, trying to understand perspectives of others, and monitoring group progress. Student practice was supported with recording sheets for each of the target behaviours. Gillies and Ashman found that trained students scored higher than students in the control condition on interaction patterns and on student achievement. The trained students were more responsive to peers who asked for explanations; they gave more task-related help and used more inclusive language. In addition, trained students perceived their groups differently: they were more likely than control students to report that students in their group expanded on points made by peers, shared ideas, were sensitive to others, made joint decisions, and took responsibility for group management.

In a follow up study, Gillies & Ashman (1998) trained grade 1 and grade 3 students in a simpler set of skills than was provided to grade 6 students. Training for these younger students focused on social skills such as listening to each other, providing constructive feedback, sharing tasks fairly, resolving differences amicably, trying to understand another's perspective, and monitoring progress. Gillies and Ashman found that trained students in both grades provided more explanations than controls, including complex elaborations such as explanations with evidence.

However, Webb & Farivar (1994) found that social skills training was more effective when it was combined with helpfulness training. The social skills alone condition in their study consisted of inclusion activities such as learning class-mates' names and interests and basic communication skills such as attentive listening, no put downs, and equal participation. Webb and Farivar found that when helpfulness training was added to the social skills approach, students gave and received more elaborated help than students in the social skills alone condition.

Cohen & Lotan (1995) demonstrated that status-equalizing treatments could increase participation by low status groups. Such treatments include setting norms about asking for help, telling students that group tasks require multiple abilities possessed by different group members, and assigning competence to low status individuals (e.g., through public praise of low status students when they demonstrate skills required by the task). However, research using Cohen's approach (Complex Instruction) has not addressed the effects on explanation exchanges and challenges in implementing it have been reported (Cohen 1998; Cohen et al. 1994).

In summary, support for social skills training has been widely advocated as a technique for improving student helpfulness. There are persuasive theoretical rationales behind the recommendation. Improving the social climate is likely to reduce student fear of ridicule that impedes help seeking (Newman & Goldin 1990) and students are more likely to help each other when they have strong feelings of commitment to their peers. The evidence in support of social skills training on explanation exchanges is consistently positive, although limited, and social skills training is more likely to have positive effects when it is combined with direct teaching of helpfulness skills.

11.3.2   Strengthen Teacher Interventions

Explanation exchanges are more likely to develop if teachers model the interaction processes they want students to adopt. For example, a grade 7 mathematics teacher used her visits to student groups to reinforce a model of explanation giving in which the help seeker provided as much of the solution as she could. The teacher gave feedback to the help seeker, shouldered some of the burden of the task (by filling in missing steps and recording the help seeker's thinking), developed a problem-solving heuristic from the example, and assigned a practice task that required the help seeker to recapitulate the steps (Ross 1995a). For example,

Heather: First, you have to find the common denominator.
Teacher: OK

Heather: And then you have to change it to an improper fraction. No, regroup first.
Teacher: Regroup. You don't change to an improper fraction for subtraction or addition…
So there's your common denominator, which is 15-8 over 12. Is that what you got? …
I don't understand what you've done. Here, let me write it out for you…OK, so common
denominator is…right…now, Heather, where do you regroup from? …OK, what do we
have to do to the 6? …Good girl, that's right.

Louise: What do you do with the 3 though?
Teacher: Well, what do you think you should do with the 3? …That's right…yeah, you're
OK. I think what you have to do with questions like that, is that you have to take it step by
step…you can't jump…otherwise you're going to get confused, and when you go back to
see what you did, you're not going to know what you've done because you skipped a step…
Now you're going to have to share your knowledge with these two because I don't know it
they know (Ross 1995a, p. 137).

In contrast, Ross (1995b) found that teacher interventions conflicted with the directions given to groups. The teacher in this study, as in Ross (1995a), gave explicit instructions that explanations should be sought and given and that the purpose of the group activities was to understand mathematical ideas. She told students that clues, rather than a complete solution, should be offered and that talk should focus on strategies and not just calculations. But when the teacher visited groups she accepted rapid-fire recitations that were justifications of why the final answer to the problem was correct, instead of requiring explanations of how problems were solved. In doing so, the teacher reinforced group practices in which requests for explanation were monitoring moves made by group leaders. That is, the most knowledgeable person in the group solved the problem and then called on others to explain (recite) the solution that the original problem solver had devised. In this study the teacher's interventions conflicted with her espoused intentions. Students imitated the teacher's behaviour rather than her statement of task requirements.

Webb & Ing (2006) found substantial differences among three teachers when they visited student pairs. Only one of the three teachers in the study engaged students in discussions of mathematical ideas regardless of whether their work was correct or incorrect. This teacher drew attention to discrepant answers given by the pair and asked them to resolve discrepancies. Webb et al. (2006) found that teacher interventions were generally ineffective in promoting explanation exchanges because the model of explanation giving encouraged a focus on procedural correctness rather than on understanding mathematical concepts. They also found that in the few instances in which a teacher provided higher-level help to a group, students raised the level of their help giving after the teacher left. There was also evidence that teacher interventions depressed the depth of student help if the teacher provided lower-level help than what the group had been providing prior to her visit.

Much of the research on promoting student helpfulness has been conducted in mathematics, in part because student exchanges of appropriate explanations are a key component of the current wave of mathematics reform. But many of the studies have focused on tasks that provide for a single correct solution to a routine problem. In contrast, Brodie (2000) observed a grade 9 teacher intervening in small group deliberations around a rich task (measuring the area of complex shapes represented in a geoboard). Brodie demonstrated that this teacher's interventions supported the view that mathematical reasoning develops through conjectures, attempts at proof, and refutations through counter examples. The teacher provided examples that challenged the assumptions of the group, asked the group to be more precise about their theory, record instances that supported and disconfirmed their theory, and figure out why their theory was only partially successful. She argued for a view of mathematics as a dynamic rather than fixed body of knowledge and attended to student motivation by getting students to realize that a failed strategy has value when problem solvers recognize its limitations. At no point did the teacher provide direct instruction on how to measure the area of complex shapes.

An important component of teacher interventions is modeling how to monitor help use. Several studies (Ross 1995b; Webb & Mastergeorge 2003; Webb et al. 1995, 2006) have reported that students rarely monitor how their help is used. In addition, students who receive help tend to be overly optimistic about their grasp of it. Webb et al. (1995) found that constructive use of help on the same problem was infrequent: in most cases students who were given help did no further work on that problem or copied the answer they were given. However, the higher the use of the help on a subsequent problem (e.g., working through the next problem independently as opposed to finishing calculations started by another student or doing no work at all), the higher the achievement in the unit.

In summary, teacher interventions have an impact on student ability and willingness to give high-level help. The most productive strategies for strengthening the effects of teacher interventions are to model help giving and monitoring of help use. Improving teacher interventions is, however, likely to be challenging. They need to allocate their time among multiple groups, deciding which groups they should spend more time with. They also need to balance between focusing on the group's process needs and their need for support on content issues. For example, Chiu (2004) found greater content help depressed performance if the group was on track but there was no negative effect if the group did not understand the problem. A central challenge is that teachers may not be aware of key events in the group's deliberations that occurred when the teacher was not present. Brodie (2004) suggested that for teachers to intervene effectively they need to train students how to report their group's progress so that teachers can intervene knowledgeably.

11.3.3 Implement Reciprocal Roles

Advocated of cooperative learning models, especially Learning Together, have long advocated the assignment of learning roles within groups. To be effective role assignments need to meet certain conditions:

1 The roles need to be meaningful. Roles such as "summarizer" contribute more to group knowledge construction than roles such as "source searcher" because the

former requires the synthesis of diverse ideas into a coherent structure (Schellens et al. 2006a).

2 Student roles need to rotate to ensure that lower status students participate equally in group deliberations, including giving explanations. Duran & Monereo (2005) found that alternating from tutor to tutee reduced the dominance of high ability students and increased participation by the less able.

3 Teachers need to support role implementation, especially of lower ability students. King (1993) found that when low-ability students were assigned leadership positions, more able group members usurped their roles. Teachers can give less able students supplementary training in advance of group work to provide prerequisite knowledge and/or special information not known to other group members. The status equalizing strategies recommended by Cohen et al. (1994) are also useful. In addition, teachers can alleviate some of the difficulty in providing high level help by supplying detailed role directions, including generic prompts, to elicit and structure explanations. For example, King (1994) demonstrated positive effects on student discourse by giving students generic question stems to produce their own elaborative questions for thinking skills ("Explain how…"), applications ("How would you… to… ?"), develop examples ("What is a new example of… ?"), analyze relationships ("How does… affect… ?"), make predictions ("What do you think would happen if… ?"), synthesize ideas ("What are some possible solutions for the problem of… ?") and evaluate ("Why is… better than… ?"). Other successful strategies for supporting explanation exchanges have been demonstrated for learner and teacher roles in paired reading (O'Donnell & Dansereau 1992), for structured partnerships (Fuchs et al. 1999), and for metacognitive prompts (Kramarski & Mevarech 2003).

4 The extent to which the teacher structures student interactions through role assignments should be appropriate for the age of the students. Joung (2004) found that high structure (students were required to identify the argumentation categories enacted in their posts to an online group) contributed to higher interaction among university students. However, Ross & Raphael (1990) found that grade 4 students were more likely to ask for and receive high-level help in a low structure condition (i.e., simple roles developed by students) than in a high structure condition (detailed roles assigned by the teacher).

5 The roles should be nonhierarchical. Roles such as "group leader" encourage control of group deliberations through authority rather than on evidence based argument.

11.4 Implications for Teachers

Research has much to offer teachers struggling with the four instructional challenges of group work identified earlier in this chapter. Researchers have developed practical classroom strategies, and persuasive evidence about their effectiveness, that increase the frequency of high quality help giving, equalize student participation in group deliberations, increase the likelihood that asking for explanations will be a functional help seeking strategy, and improve the quality of student explanations. Adoption of the strategies reviewed in this chapter (direct teaching of helpfulness, improving the social climate of the classroom, strengthening teacher interventions, and implementing reciprocal roles) will amplify the positive effects of cooperative learning.

But where to start? I suggest that teachers begin by rethinking how they use roles in cooperative groups. This familiar strategy can be made more powerful by providing greater support for the implementation of roles that generate high quality explanations. The most accessible of methods for doing so is to provide students with generic prompts (e.g., King 1994). These prompts force students to think of the material to be learned in different ways. They provide a structure to guide deeper processing that is more effective than nonelaborative questions like who, what, where, and so on (King & Rosenshine 1993) and questions generated by students without the guidance of elaborative prompts (King 1990). In addition to enhancing student discourse in small groups, these prompts can be used to structure teacher interventions in small group deliberations and to move whole class discussions to deeper understanding.

References

Abrami, P., Chambers, B., Poulsen, C., & Kouros, C. (1994). Positive social interdependence and classroom climate. Genetic, Social, and General Psychology Monographs, 120, 327–346.

Brodie, K. (2000). Teacher intervention in small-group work. *For the Learning of Mathematics, 20*(1), 9–16.

Chiu, M. M. (2004). Adapting teacher interventions to student needs during cooperative learning: How to improve student problem solving and time on-task? *American Educational Research Journal, 41*, 365–400.

Cohen, E. G. (1998, April). *Beyond the buzzwords: Equity and cooperative learning.* Paper presented at the annual meeting of the American Educational Research Association, San Diego, CA.

Cohen, E. G., & Lotan, R. (1995). Producing equal-status interaction in the heterogeneous classroom. *American Educational Research Journal, 32*, 99–120.

Cohen, E. G., Lotan, R., Whitcomb, J., Balderrama, M., Cossey, R., & Swanson, P. (1994). Complex instruction: Higher order thinking in heterogeneous classrooms. In S. Sharan (Ed.), *Handbook of cooperative learning methods* (pp. 82–96). Westport, Connecticut: Greenwood Press.

Cuseo, J. (2006). *Cooperative collaborative structures explicitly designed to promote positive interdependence among group members* [Web Page]. URL http://www.cat.ilstu.edu/additional/tips/coopStruct.php [2006, June 29].

Duran, D., & Monereo, C. (2005). Styles and sequences of cooperative interaction in fixed and reciprocal peer tutoring. *Learning and Instruction, 15*, 179–199.

Farivar, S., & Webb, N. (1991). *Helping behavior activities handbook.* Los Angeles, CA: University of California at Los Angeles.

Farivar, S., & Webb, N. (1998). Preparing teachers and students for cooperative work: Building communication and helping skills. In C. M. Brody, & M. Davidson (Eds.), *Professional development for cooperative learning: Issues and approaches* (pp. 169–187). Albany, NY: State University of New York.

Fuchs, L. S., Fuchs, D., Kazdan, S., & Allen, S. (1999). Effects of peer-assisted learning strategies in reading with and without training in elaborated help giving. *Elementary School Journal, 99*, 201–220.

Gillies, R. (2004a). The effects of cooperative learning on junior high school students during small group learning. *Learning and Instruction, 14*, 197–213.

Gillies, R. (2004b, April). *Teachers' and students' interactions during cooperative and small-group learning*. Paper presented at the annual meeting of the American Educational Research Association, San Diego, CA.

Gillies, R., & Ashman, A. (1996). Teaching collaborative skills to primary school children in classroom-based work groups. *Learning and Instruction, 6,* 187–200.

Gillies, R., & Ashman, A. (1998). Behavior and interactions of children in cooperative groups in lower and middle elementary. *Journal of Educational Psychology, 90,* 746–757.

Good, T., McCaslin, M., & Reys, B. (1992). Investigating work groups to promote problem solving in mathematics. In J. Brophy (Ed.), *Advances in research on teaching, Vol. 3* (pp. 115–160). Greenwich, CT: JAI Press.

Johnson, D., & Johnson, R. (1987). *Learning together and alone: Cooperative, competitive, and individualistic learning*. Englewood Cliffs, NJ: Prentice-Hall.

Johnson, D. W., Johnson R. T., & Stanne, M. B. (2000). *Cooperative Learning Methods: A Meta-Analysis*. [Web Page]. URL http://www.co-operation.org/pages/cl-methods.html [16 January 2006].

Joung, S. (2004, April). *The effects of high-structure cooperative versus low-structure collaborative design on online debates in terms of decision change, critical thinking, and interaction pattern*. Paper presented at the annual meeting of the American Educational Research Association, San Diego, CA.

Kagan, S., & Kagan, M. (1994). The structural approach: Six keys to cooperative learning. In S. Sharan (Ed.), *Handbook of cooperative learning methods* (pp. 115–133). Westport, CN: Greenwood Press.

Karau, S., & Williams, K. (1993). Social loafing: A meta-analytic review and theoretical integration. *Journal of Personality and Social Psychology, 65,* 681–706.

King, A. (1990). Enhancing peer interaction and learning in the classroom through reciprocal questioning. *American Educational Research Journal, 27,* 664–687.

King, A. (1994). Guiding knowledge construction in the classroom: Effects of teaching children how to question and how to explain. *American Educational Research Journal, 31,* 338–368.

King, A., & Rosenshine, B. (1993). Effects of guided cooperative questioning on children's knowledge construction. *Journal of Experimental Education, 6,* 127–148.

King, L. (1993). High and low achievers' perceptions and cooperative learning in two small groups. *Elementary School Journal, 93,* 399–416.

Kramarski, B., & Mevarech, Z. R. (2003). Enhancing mathematical reasoning in the classroom: The effects of cooperative learning and metacognitive training. *American Educational Research Journal, 40,* 281–310.

McMahon, S., & Goatley, V. (1995). Fifth graders helping peers discuss texts in student-led groups. *Journal of Educational Research, 89,* 23–34.

Mulryan, C. (1994). Perceptions of intermediate students' cooperative small-group work in mathematics. *Journal of Educational Research, 87,* 280–291.

Mulryan, C. (1995). Fifth and sixth graders' involvement and participation in cooperative small groups in mathematics. *Elementary School Journal, 95,* 297–310.

Nattiv, A. (1994). Helping behaviors and math achievement gain of students using cooperative learning. *Elementary School Journal, 94,* 285–297.

Nelson-Le Gall, S. (1992). Children's instrumental help-seeking: Its role in the social acquisition and construction of knowledge. In R. Hertz-Lazarowitz & N. Miller (Eds.), *Interaction in cooperative groups: The theoretical anatomy of group learning* (pp. 49–68). Cambridge, UK: Cambridge University Press.

Nelson-Le Gall, S., & Glor-Scheib, S. (1986). Academic help-seeking and peer relations in school. *Contemporary Educational Psychology, 11,* 187–193.

O'Donnell, A., & Dansereau, D. (1992). Scripted cooperation in student dyads: A method for analyzing and enhancing academic learning and performance. In R. Hertz-Lazarowitz & N. Miller (Eds.), *Interaction in cooperative groups: The theoretical anatomy of group learning* (pp. 120–141). Cambridge, UK: Cambridge University Press.

Ross, J. A. (1995a). Effects of feedback on student behavior in cooperative learning groups in a grade 7 math class. *Elementary School Journal, 96,* 125–143.

Ross, J. A. (1995b). Students explaining solutions in student-directed groups: Cooperative learning and reform in mathematics education. *School Science and Mathematics, 95,* 411–416.

Ross, J. A., & Cousins, J. B. (1994). Intentions to seek and give help and behavior in cooperative learning groups. *Contemporary Educational Psychology, 19,* 476–482.

Ross, J. A., & Cousins, J. B. (1995a). Giving and receiving explanations in cooperative learning groups. *Alberta Journal of Educational Research, 41,* 104–122.

Ross, J. A., & Cousins, J. B. (1995b). Impact of explanation seeking on student achievement and attitudes. *Journal of Educational Research, 89,* 109–117.

Ross, J. A., Haimes, D., & Hogaboam-Gray, A. (1996). Improving student helpfulness in cooperative learning groups. *Journal of Classroom Interaction, 31*(2), 13–24.

Ross, J. A., & Raphael, D. (1990). Communication and problem solving achievement in cooperative learning groups. *Journal of Curriculum Studies, 22,* 149–164.

Schellens, T., Van Keer, H., De Wever, B., & Valcke, M. (2006a, April). *Comparing knowledge construction in two cohorts of asynchronous discussion groups with and without scripting.* Paper presented at the annual meeting of the American Educational Research Association, San Franciso.

Sharan, S., Kussell, P. H.-L. R., Bejarano, Y., Raviv, S., & Sharan, Y. (1985). Cooperative learning effects on ethnic relations and achievement in Israeli junior-high school classrooms. In R. Slavin, S. Sharan, S. Kagan, R. Hertz-Lazarowitz, C. Webb, & R. Schmuck (Eds.), *Learning to cooperate, cooperating to learn* (pp. 313–344). New York, NY: Plenum Press.

Sharan, S., & Shachar, H. (1988). *Language and learning in the cooperative classroom.* New York: Springer, Verlag.

Sharan, S., & Sharan, Y. (1976). *Small group teaching.* Englewood Cliffs, NJ: Educational Technology Publishers.

Swing, S., & Peterson, P. (1982). The relationship of student ability and small-group interaction to student achievement. *American Educational Research Journal, 19,* 259–274.

Terwel, J. (2003). Co-operative learning in secondary education: A curriculum perspective. In R. M. Gillies, & A. F. Ashman (Eds.), *Co-operative learning: The social and intellectual outcomes of learning in groups* (pp. 54–68). London: Routledge/Farmer.

Veenman, S., Denesen, E., van den Akker, A., & van der Rijt, F. (2005). Effects of a cooperative learning program on the elaborations of students during help seeking and help giving. *American Educational Research Journal, 42,* 115–152.

Webb, N. M. (1989). Peer interaction and learning in small groups. *International Journal of Educational Research, 13,* 21–39.

Webb, N. M., Chizhik, A. W., Nemer, K. M., & Sugrue, B. (1996). *Equity issues in collaborative group assessment: Group composition and performance.* Paper presented at the annual meeting of the American Educational Research Association, New York.

Webb, N. M., & Farivar, S. (1994). Promoting helping behavior in cooperative small groups in middle school mathematics. *American Educational Research Journal, 31,* 369–396.

Webb, N. M., & Ing, M. (2006, April). *Student discourse and learning in elementary school mathematics classrooms.* Paper presented at the annual meeting of the American Educational Research Association, San Francisco.

Webb, N. M., Kersting, N., Ing, M., Nemer, K., & Forrest, J. (2003, April). *The evolution of group dynamics and learning in peer-directed groups.* Paper presented at the annual meeting of the American Educational Research Association, Chicago.

Webb, N. M., & Mastergeorge, A. (2003). Promoting effective helping behavior in peer-directed groups. *International Journal of Educational Research, 39,* 73–97.

Webb, N. M., Nemer, K. M., & Ing, M. (2006). Small-group reflections: Parallels between teacher discourse and student behavior in peer-directed groups. *The Journal of the Learning Sciences, 15,* 63–115.

Webb, N. M., Troper, J., & Fall, R. (1995). Constructive activity and learning in collaborative small groups. *Journal of Educational Psychology, 87,* 406–423.

Wilkinson, L. C., & Spinelli, F. (1983). Using requests effectively in peer-directed instructional groups. *American Educational Research Journal, 20,* 479–501.

Chapter 12
Teachers' and Students' Verbal Behaviours During Cooperative Learning

Robyn M. Gillies

Abstract While much is known about how teachers can promote discourse among students and how students, in turn, help each other, little is know about how teachers' verbal behaviours affect students' discourse and learning during cooperative learning. This chapter builds on research undertaken by Hertz-Lazarowitz and Shachar (1990) that identified the differences in teachers' verbal behaviours during cooperative and whole-class instruction. Two studies undertaken by the author are presented. The first study examines the difference in teachers' verbal behaviours during cooperative and small-group instruction while the second study discusses the additive benefits derived from training teachers to use specific communication skills to enhance students' thinking and learning during cooperative learning. The chapter also discusses how students model many of the verbal behaviours their teachers use in their own discourse with their peers to promote thinking and learning.

Cooperative learning is widely accepted as a pedagogical practice that can be employed in classrooms to stimulate students' interest in learning through involvement with their peers. When children interact cooperatively they learn to listen to what others have to say, give and receive information, discuss differing perspectives and, in so doing, develop mutual understandings of the topic at hand. In fact, talk is so important that it is now recognised as more than a means of sharing thoughts. It is also a social mode of thinking and a tool for the joint construction of knowledge by teachers and learners (Mercer 1996). Students who cooperate show increased participation in group discussions, engage in more useful help-giving behaviours, and demonstrate more sophisticated levels of discourse than students who do not cooperate with their peers (Gillies and Ashman 1998; Shachar and Sharan 1994).

While cooperative learning provides opportunities for students to dialogue, concern has been expressed about the quality of the discourse that often emerges if children are left to engage in discussions without any training in how to interact with others. Meloth and Deering (1999) found that task-related talk about facts, concepts, strategies, and thinking is very important to students' learning yet such high-level cognitive talk only appear with low frequency when left to emerge as a by-product of cooperative learning. In a study of the discourse structures of fifth-grade students who worked on science experiments in small groups, Chinn et al. (2000) reported that children used high quality discourse only when they were required to discuss reasons for their solutions. Moreover, when they did, it predicted the learning that occurred. Mercer et al. (1999) also maintained that children need to be taught how to engage in group discussions if they are to use language effectively to think and reason together. Similarly, Rojas-Drummond et al. (2003) found that children do not initially use exploratory talk to think and reason together but can be taught to do so. In short, Meloth and Deering, Chinn et al., Mercer et al., and Rojas-Drummond et al. believe that direct intervention by teachers to facilitate discussions is warranted if children are to learn to dialogue effectively with each other.

Teachers play a critical role in promoting interactions among students and cooperative learning provides opportunities for these interactions to be encouraged. However, although much is known about how teachers can promote discourse among students and how students, in turn, help each other, little is know about teachers' verbal behaviours during cooperative learning. This chapter builds on research undertaken by Hertz-Lazarowitz and Shachar (1990) that identified the differences in teachers' verbal behaviours during cooperative and whole-class instruction. It does this by discussing two studies undertaken by the author that examined the difference in teachers' verbal behaviours during cooperative and small-group instruction in high schools and the additive benefits derived from training teachers to use specific communication skills to enhance children's thinking and learning during cooperative learning in elementary schools. The chapter will also discuss how students model many of the verbal behaviours their teachers use in their own discourse with others to promote thinking and learning. Finally, the theoretical implications of the role teachers play in the social construction of knowledge, both at the interpersonal (Vygotsky 1978) and intrapersonal levels

(Piaget 1950), will be discussed with particular emphasis on specific strategies teachers use to scaffold children's learning. This is particularly important given that both Vygotsky and Piaget acknowledge the importance of interactions with others in the development of social reasoning and cognition.

12.1 The Teacher's Role in Promoting Students' Discourse

Teachers induct students into ways of thinking and learning by making explicit how to express ideas, seek help, contest opposing positions, and reason cogently and, in so doing, help them to generate new ways of thinking and doing (Meloth and Deering 1999; Mercer et al. 1999). Students are sensitive to teachers' discourse as it affects how they react to learning and the perceptions they form of their learning environment (Patrick et al. 2001).

In a study that investigated the relationship between learning environment and students' reported use of avoidance strategies during mathematics among sixth-grade students, Turner et al. (2002) found that teachers who emphasised the relevance of learning and encouraged students to be active learners, stressed mastery-goals for personal competence, used language that expressed strong positive affect about learning, and conveyed positive expectations to their students (i.e., teachers used highly motivational language). Students in these classrooms understood that learning was valued and success was accompanied by effort and indicated by personal improvement as opposed to comparison with others.

In contrast, teachers who focused on directing and assessing students used language that tended to be more directive and authoritarian which often limited student opportunities to act autonomously (i.e., teachers stressed performance goals). In these classrooms, students understood that learning is predominantly a means of achieving recognition, and their success is gauged by outperforming others, surpassing class or grade standards, or looking smart. Interestingly, Turner et al. (2002) found that students in these latter classrooms had higher rates of cheating, disruptive behaviour, and self-handicapping and avoidance behaviours than students in classrooms where teachers used supportive instructional and motivational discourse.

In a follow-up in-depth study that examined the classroom participation of two students in mathematics lessons during sixth- and seventh-grades, Turner and Patrick (2004) found that despite students' achievement goals being consistent across the two years, both students' patterns of participation changed markedly from one year to the next, depending on the encouragement and support they received from their teachers. The authors concluded that teachers' communicative behaviours do affect students' engagement behaviours and they can have measurable effects on students' work habits.

There is no doubt that patterns of classroom instruction are related to students' achievement-related behaviours and affect. Teachers who are encouraging and supportive of students' endeavours are more likely to provide students with opportunities to act autonomously as learners than teachers who are more focused on performance outcomes and test results. It is interesting to note that although the teachers in the Turner et al. (2002) and Turner and Patrick (2004) studies did not specifically identify cooperative learning as a pedagogical practice in their classrooms, many of the activities the students undertook did involve students working cooperatively on complex, open-ended problem-solving activities with other students. This grouping arrangement is particularly interesting because Hertz-Lazarowitz and Shachar (1990) found when they investigated the discourse of 27 elementary teachers in Israel who alternatively implemented whole-class and small-group instruction in their classrooms that their discourse was affected by the organisational structure of the classroom.

During whole-class instruction, Hertz-Lazarowitz and Shachar (1990) reported that teachers' discourse could be categorised as lecturing, giving instructions, using short-answer questions, administering collective discipline, and giving general praise. In contrast, during small-group learning (i.e., cooperative learning), teachers' discourse could be categorised as encouraging students' initiatives, helping students with their learning, facilitating communication among students, providing feedback on task performance, and praising individual student's efforts. In fact, during whole class instruction over 90% of teachers' discourse involved the use of formal communication categories that were highly structured and addressed a collective audience, whereas during cooperative learning, 75% of their discourse involved informal communication categories or ways of communicating that are seen as more intimate, personal, and supportive of students' endeavours. In effect, the study demonstrated that when the teachers implemented cooperative learning, they changed the way they taught and this affected the way they interacted with their students. This finding was particularly interesting, given that the same teachers taught whole-class and small-group instructional lessons interchangeably. Moreover, all teachers had received extensive training over a full school year in how to implement cooperative learning in their classrooms prior to the commencement of the study.

12.2   Using Cooperative Learning in Classrooms

Despite the benefits widely attributed to cooperative learning, teachers are often reluctant to implement this pedagogical practice in their classrooms. In a study of classroom grouping practices in the UK, Baines et al. (2003) reported that elementary students rarely worked cooperatively in small groups, despite being seated in small groups. Most children worked individually or under the direction of an adult attached to their group. By secondary school, students either worked in dyads or in groups of 11 or more members with little autonomy over the size of the group, the task they were to complete, and how they were to interact. Grouping practices were aimed at maintaining control, keeping students focused and on-task, and maximising teacher-directed learning. In short, Baines et al. (2003) suggested that small group work does not appear to be widely endorsed as a practice that promotes students' interaction and learning.

In a study that examined the prevalence, conceptualisation, and form of cooperative learning used by elementary teachers in the US, Antil et al. (1998), found that few teachers were employing recognised forms of cooperative learning in their classrooms even though all had indicated they employed this pedagogical practice daily in different subjects. Similar observations have been made by Gillies (2003a) about teachers' grouping practices in Australian schools.

A reluctance to embrace cooperative learning may be due, in part, to the challenge it poses to teachers' control of instruction, the demands it places on classroom organisational changes, and the personal commitment teachers need to make to sustain their efforts (Kohn 1992). It may also be due to a lack of understanding of how to embed cooperative learning into the classroom curricula to foster open communication and engagement between teachers and students, promote cooperative investigation and problem-solving, and provide students with environments where they feel supported and emotionally secure (Johnson and Johnson 2003; Sharan et al. 1999).

This dilemma was recognised by Blatchford et al. (2003) who argued strongly for the development of a social pedagogical approach to implementing group work in classrooms. This includes helping teachers to prepare the classrooms for group work so that consideration is given to the size and composition of groups, seating arrangements, and the number of groups and their stability over time. It also includes ensuring that students are taught how to interact appropriately so they learn to trust and respect each other as well as how to plan and organise their group tasks. Additionally, the authors believed that teachers need to ensure that group work is fun so that students do not feel threatened by it. Finally, teachers play a role in adapting and structuring the group context and task and making sure that it is integrated into the curricula (see Baines et al. (2003) in this volume for an elaborated discussion on developing a social pedagogy of the classroom).

Ensuring that teachers structure group work experiences so that students will derive maximum benefits from student interaction is crucial, given that teachers have a propensity to talk and students to listen. In such instances, as Galton et al. (1999) found, teachers' talk in elementary classrooms consists mainly of teachers making statements and asking factual or closed questions which require minimal responses from students. In fact, Galton et al. observed that 75% of teachers' interactions involve teachers telling students facts and ideas or giving them directions and this percentage held whether teachers were interacting with a class, a group or an individual. Children are rarely asked cognitively challenging questions where they are required to think about issues and justify their responses. Galton et al. attributed this finding to the introduction of the National Curriculum that places a heavy burden on teachers to cut down on students' participation to get through the content. In such classrooms, the channel of communication tends to be one-way as teachers talk at students who are required to listen and respond, often reiterating information provided earlier by the teacher.

There is no doubt that whole-class instruction affects the way teachers interact with their students as Hertz-Lazarowitz and Shachar (1990) demonstrated in their study of teachers who used both cooperative learning and whole-class instruction interchangeably in their classrooms. During cooperative learning when teachers interact with students in small groups, they use more pro-social and positive verbal behaviours and interacted in a more informal and friendly manner than when they use whole-class instruction. The change in teachers' verbal behaviours was so marked that Hertz-Lazarowitz and Shachar argue that "when teachers change their instructional style to cooperative learning they become involved in a complex process of linguistic change as well" (p. 89). Given this finding it is particularly important that teachers' discourse during small group activities is investigated to determine not only what small grouping practices influence teachers' discourse but also how teachers' discourse may enhance student discussion, social reasoning, and the construction of knowledge. This is especially important given the key role teachers play in promoting student interaction and engaging them in the learning process.

12.3   Teachers' Discourse During Cooperative Learning: A Review of Two Studies

In the first study, Gillies (2006) sought to determine if teachers who implement cooperative learning in their classrooms engage in more facilitative, learning interactions than teachers who implement group-work only and whether students, in turn, model their teachers' verbal behaviours and engage in more positive helping interactions than their peers in the group-work only groups. This distinction between cooperative groups and group-work only groups is necessary because many teachers group students for convenience and do not ensure that the key elements that identify cooperative learning are present (Johnson and Johnson 1990). Moreover, it has been argued that group-work only groups have many of the characteristics of the traditional whole-class setting where groups are not established so students are required to work together (i.e., no goal interdependence) and children work individually on tasks for their own ends as they do when their success is gauged by outperforming others (Turner et al. 2002). Consequently, there is no motivation to act as a group or exercise joint efficacy to solve a problem or accomplish a task (Johnson and Johnson 2003).

In the second study, Gillies (2004) sought to determine if teachers who implement cooperative learning can also be trained to use specific communication skills to facilitate thinking and learning in their students during cooperative group work. In this study, the teachers in both conditions were taught to embed cooperative learning strategies into the classroom curricula, however, only one cohort of teachers received additional training in the specific communication skills that are designed to enhance teacher-student interactions during cooperative learning.

12.4   Study One: Discourses During Cooperative and Small-Group Learning

Background to the study. This study (Gillies 2006) was implemented in four large high schools in Brisbane, Australia. The study aimed to compare two types of grouping practices that teachers commonly use in classrooms; cooperative learning and group-work only groups. In the cooperative learning groups (cooperative condition) teachers systematically implemented the key elements of cooperative learning as defined by Johnson and Johnson (1990) whereas in the group-work only groups (small-group condition), there was no systematic implementation of these elements.

Twenty-six teachers from grades 8 to 10 volunteered to participate in the study and agreed to embed cooperative learning activities into a unit of work (4–6 weeks) once a term for three terms. All the teachers were highly regarded by their respective principals for their commitment to enhancing their professional skills and their willingness to implement new and innovative practices in their classrooms. Their teaching experience ranged from 5–25 years; four teachers were male and 22 were female which is roughly indicative of the ratio of male to female teachers in Australian schools at that grade level. The teachers taught a range of subjects from those in the core curriculum (e.g., mathematics, English, and science) to those with a vocational orientation (i.e., manual arts and technology, hospitality, and art).

Two groups of students from each of the above teachers' classrooms participated in the audio-taping of the group discussions. While 208 students participated in these groups, the final data set was 104 students because of teacher or student absences on the day the research team visited the school. Although the attrition rate was somewhat disappointing, observations of the remaining students' groups indicated that the data obtained were reflective of the groups' in the various classrooms.

12.5   Training in Cooperative Learning Pedagogy

All teachers participated in a two-day workshop to provide them with the background knowledge and skills required to implement cooperative learning in their classrooms. This included information on the key elements required to establish cooperative learning proposed by Johnson and Johnson (1990) and included how to:

- establish positive task interdependence (regarded as critical for the activities the students were to undertake);
- teach the small group and interpersonal skills (i.e., actively listening, considering the perspective of others, stating ideas assertively but appropriately, resolving conflicts, and democratic decision-making);
- ensure individual accountability (i.e., ensuring that all students contribute to the group's task and were accountable for their contributions);
- promote student interaction (i.e., students work in small groups with members facing each other and all were expected to offer help to each other); and,
- provide opportunities for students to reflect on their group's achievements (i.e., what has the group achieved and what do they still need to accomplish).

Additionally, the teachers were asked to ensure that they negotiated the following ground rules with their students to encourage group discussion. These included making sure that students understood that all information was to be shared, the group was to work to reach agreement, reasons needed to be presented, challenges were to be accepted, alternative ideas were to be discussed, and everyone was encouraged to participate in the discussion (Wegerif et al. 1999).

As part of the process of embedding cooperative learning strategies into their curriculum units, teachers were expected to also consider the following four organisational dimensions of the classroom proposed by Blatchford et al. (2003, p. 162): (a) the classroom context – preparing the classroom and the groups; (b) interactions between children – preparing and developing pupil skills; (c) the teacher's role – preparing adults (i.e., the class teacher) for working with groups; and (d) tasks – preparing the lessons and group activities.

12.6 Measures

Teachers' verbal behaviours. The observation schedule that was used in this study was originally developed by Hertz-Lazarowitz and Shachar (1990) but modified for purposes of this study, based on trialling in classrooms where teachers used cooperative learning. The six categories of verbal behaviours that were identified included: Teacher control (i.e., broadly defined as teachers giving instructions); questions (i.e., questions where responses were pre-determined and based on information students had previously learned); discipline (i.e., reprimanding students); mediated-learning (i.e., scaffolds, prompts, and challenges students' thinking); encourages (i.e., praises students' efforts); maintenance (i.e., language designed to help maintain the activity). Teachers' verbal behaviours were coded according to the frequency over each observed lesson.

Students' verbal behaviours. The students' verbal behaviours were grouped into six categories, based on observations of students' verbal behaviours in classrooms where cooperative learning had been implemented. The categories of verbal behaviour that were identified included: elaborations (i.e., provided detailed help); questions (i.e., open and closed questions); short responses (i.e., responses that are not elaborated); engages (i.e., statements or discussion that holds the attention of other students); interrupts (i.e., negative disruption to the discussion); and directions (i.e., instructs others). These verbal behaviours were coded according to frequency across each observed lesson.

12.7 Observation Schedule of the Teachers' Application of Cooperative Learning

An observation schedule of the teachers' application of a cooperative learning approach was developed (i.e., after trialling) and the following five dimensions, informed by the key elements of cooperative learning (Johnson and Johnson 1990), were observed: (a) uses a range of cooperative learning strategies, (b) uses language that reflects the fact that cooperative learning strategies are being employed, (c) facilitates the students use of cooperative learning, (d) reinforces students use of learning strategies, and (e) develops interdependence in the students. Each dimension was rated on a Likert scale from 1 to 5 to indicate whether the behaviour was not observed (1) to whether it was almost always observed (5). Finally, an overall rating of 1–5 was made on the implementation of a cooperative learning approach in the observed lessons. Teachers who obtained a rating of 4–5 were observed to have implemented cooperative learning with high fidelity (cooperative learning condition) whereas teachers who obtained a score of 1–3 were observed to have implemented cooperative learning with low fidelity (small-group condition).

12.8   Procedure

Teachers were audiotaped twice across the three units of work in which they used cooperative, small group activities. This audio-taping usually occurred in the final 2 weeks of the 6 week work unit to give the students time to adjust to working together on the task. Each teacher and two groups of students were taped simultaneously during the observed lessons.

During the audio-taping, teachers wore a microphone while an audiocassette with a directional microphone was used to tape the students' group discussions. Additionally, an observer sat at the back of the classroom and completed an observational schedule on the application of the cooperative learning framework used to identify the extent to which teachers had implemented the key components of cooperative learning in the lesson that was observed.

12.9   Results

Teachers' verbal behaviours. The data collected on the teachers' verbal behaviours were analysed to determine if there were differences between the teachers in the cooperative and small-group conditions. Significant differences were found with teachers in the cooperative condition asking more *questions* (effect size = + 0.26, or more than a quarter of a standard deviation) and using more *mediated-learning* behaviours (effect size = + 0.52, or more than half a standard deviation) than their group-work only peers.

Students' verbal behaviours. Similarly, data collected on the students' verbal behaviours were analysed to determine if there were differences between the two conditions. Significant differences were found with students in the cooperative condition recording more elaborative responses (effect size = + 0.65 or nearly two-thirds of a standard deviation), more short responses (effect size = + 0.34 or over a third of a standard deviation), and more engaging behaviours (effect size = + 0.30 or over a quarter of a standard deviation) than their group-work only peers.

12.10 Discussion

This study was designed to test the thesis proposed by Hertz-Lazarowitz and Shachar (1990) that when teachers implement cooperative learning, as opposed to whole-class teaching, the organisational structure of the classroom affects the way teachers interact with students. It did this by investigating whether teachers who implemented cooperative learning engage in more facilitative, learning interactions than teachers who implement group work only. The study also sought to determine if students in the cooperative groups model their teachers' verbal behaviours and engage in more helping behaviours than their peers in the small-group only groups.

The results show that teachers who implement cooperative learning asked more questions and engaged in more mediated-learning behaviours than teachers who implement group-work only. While the questions tended to follow the predicted closed question format that Galton et al. (1999) identified as typical of the types of questions teachers tend to ask that have the potential to limit learning, the mediated-learning behaviours were, in contrast, designed to challenge children's understanding and thinking of the problem-solving activities the children were working on in their groups.

The following examples are typical of the mediated-learning behaviours that the teachers in the cooperative learning condition tended to ask: "Perhaps you could consider using this … and seeing if it can be reconciled with what you have here (information)?" (Tentative question designed to prompt students' thinking); "I'm not sure I understand what you're trying to achieve. Perhaps you can clarify it for me?" (Challenges students' to justify their decision); and "I'd suggest that you try and consider John's perspective on this own because he seems to understand how these elements can be synthesised" (Scaffolding learning by suggesting that the group consider John's response). There is no doubt that these types of verbal behaviours promote positive interactions among students as they listened intently to what their teachers said and then responded to the challenges they posed.

An examination of the students' verbal behaviours at the end of the study showed that the children in the cooperative learning condition recorded nearly three times as many elaborations, twice as many short responses, and half again as many engagement behaviours as students in the group-work only groups. This is interesting because Cohen (1994) and Cohen et al. (2002) argued it is the frequency of task-related interactions that are important for group productivity and learning and it was clear from the pattern of interactions that emerged that the students in the cooperative groups engaged in more verbal behaviours that are regarded as helpful and supportive of group endeavours than their peers in the group-work only groups.

It appeared that these verbal behaviours might have emerged, partially, from the dialogic exchanges the students participated in with their teachers where they were alternatively challenged and prompted to think more deeply and clearly about the issues under discussion. Brown and Palincsar (1988) and Palincsar and Herrenkohl (2002) proposed that when teachers use these strategies in very explicit ways to enhance children's comprehension of text, children begin to anticipate what they may encounter, integrate the new information with prior knowledge, and develop new understandings. The teachers' mediated-learning interactions may have triggered an expectation in the students that sensitised them to the need to provide more explanations and detailed responses to other students' requests for help or perceived need for help.

The multidirectional dialogic exchanges that occurred in the cooperative groups among the students and with their teachers may also have occurred because students understood how they were to negotiate the group task. While the group tasks tended to be open and discovery-based in both conditions, the students in the cooperative groups had a clear understanding of the expectations that they were required to exchange information and ideas and work constructively together to find a solution to the problem at hand. In these groups, students demonstrated high levels of participation as they interacted in an environment that encouraged their contributions and validated their efforts (Gillies 2003b; Turner et al. 2002). In contrast, expectations for the group task were not as clearly defined in the group-work only groups where members often functioned independently of others because their groups lacked the structure and direction of their cooperative counterparts.

It is clear that when teachers establish cooperative learning in their classrooms they create well-structured and self-directed groups and it is this organisational feature that affects the way they interact with their students. In these groups, students are task-focused so the interactions with their teachers are designed to assist and promote their understanding of the task. This contrasts to the group-work only condition where teachers may establish similar small groups but they appear to lack the structure and direction of their cooperative counterparts. In these groups, teachers and students do not engage as often in the reciprocal dialogues that are evident in the cooperative groups and students are less interactive with each other than their cooperative peers.

12.11   Conclusion

The study showed that teachers who establish cooperative learning in their classrooms engage in more mediated-learning behaviours than teachers who establish small group-work only groups. Moreover, when students work in cooperative groups where teachers use more facilitative, learning behaviours, they too are more helpful and facilitative of each other's learning than students who work in groups where cooperative learning is not widely endorsed. The study provides strong support for the thesis that the organisational structure of the classroom affects the way teachers interact with their students.

12.12   Study Two: Teachers' and Students' Discourse During Cooperative Learning

Background to the study. This study (Gillies 2004) built on earlier work by seeking to determine if teachers who implemented cooperative learning could be trained to use specific communication skills to facilitate teachers' and students' discourses during cooperative learning. Although there is a wealth of research that demonstrates that children can be taught various dialoguing scripts and questioning techniques to promote thinking and understanding during peer learning (see Fuchs et al. 1997; King 1999; O'Donnell 1999; Palincsar 1999), there is less information available on how these skills are employed by teachers during cooperative learning. Moreover, although the role of high-quality interactions (i.e., giving explanations) in enhancing learning in cooperative groups is widely acknowledged (Webb and Farivar 1999; Webb and Mastergeorge 2003), documenting the role teachers play in challenging children's thinking and scaffolding their learning has been somewhat neglected. This is quite surprising given that Schulz et al. (2000) found that when teachers were required to use specific evaluation criteria that specified how students were to engage in subject matter investigations and integrate different intellectual skills into the task, they focused on more academic-content talk, gave more specific feedback, and were more likely to elicit more evaluative comments from their students than teachers who were not given the evaluation criteria. In short, the evaluation criteria changed the way teachers talked to their students which, in turn, helped students to provide more well-reasoned responses.

Although this study did not investigate the effects of teacher talk on student interactions or learning, it does provide some interesting insights into the potential for teacher discourse to mediate students' interactions during cooperative learning. Given that more able others (i.e., children or adults) scaffold children's learning through social interaction (Vygotsky 1978), it seems logical to assume that teachers are also likely to do so when they are involved in implementing cooperative learning where they have been found to engage in more facilitative interactions with their students than teachers in whole-class settings (Hertz-Lazarowitz and Shachar 1990).

This study aimed to compare teachers' and students' discourse in classrooms where teachers had been trained to implement cooperative learning in addition to specific communication strategies (cooperative-interactional condition) to classrooms where teachers had been trained to implement cooperative learning only (cooperative condition). Eleven elementary schools in Brisbane, Australia, participated in the study. All the schools had a similar socio-demographic profile so they were randomly allocated to one of two conditions; the cooperative-interactional condition (six schools) or the cooperative condition (five schools) so all teachers in the one school were in the same condition.

Thirty teachers from grades 4 to 6 in the above schools agreed to participate in the study and to embed cooperative learning into one unit of their social science curriculum (i.e., 4–6 weeks) once a term for two terms. All teachers were respected and experienced by their colleagues for their classroom organisational skills, their commitment to enhancing their professional skills, and their willingness to trial new pedagogical practices in their classrooms. Both the cooperative-interactional and the cooperative conditions had a similar mix of experienced and less experienced teachers.

Two hundred and forty students from the above teachers' classrooms agreed to participate in the study and have their group discussions audiotaped. However, because of absences on the day the research team visited the schools, the final data set was 208 students. Stratified random assignment of students to groups within classes was used ensure that all groups consisted on one high-ability student, two medium-ability students, and one low-ability student. While there is evidence that no one form of grouping is more advantageous than others, low-ability students do benefit from interacting with higher ability children and high-ability students are not disadvantaged by working in mixed-ability groups (Lou et al. 1996).

12.13   Training in Communication Skills

Although teachers in both the cooperative-interactional and cooperative conditions received training in how to establish cooperative learning in their classrooms (discussed previously in Study 1), only the teachers in the cooperative-interactional condition received additional training in the communication skills designed to challenge children's thinking and promote learning. These included the skills of reflecting meaning (e.g., "It sounds as if …"), validating efforts and focusing on key issues (i.e., "You've worked well together. I wonder what you may need to do now to find a solution?"), reframing statements to help students consider an alternative perspective (i.e., "You're saying that it's far too difficult, yet I notice that you've already recorded one possible solution"), and tentatively offering suggestions (i.e., "I wonder if you've considered … ?"). These skills, which are commonly used in counselling, are designed to challenge students' understandings and perspectives with the intention of helping them to focus more clearly on the problem at hand (Egan 2002). It has been argued that teachers need to model the use of questioning, reasoning, and problem-solving strategies if students are to learn how to engage in high-level discussions during small-group work (King 1999).

Teachers' verbal behaviours. The observation schedule used in this study is described previously in Study 1. Once again, teachers' verbal behaviours were coded according to frequency across each recorded class session which lasted 45 minutes.

Students' verbal behaviours. The observation schedule used in this study is described previously in Study 1. Verbal behaviours were coded according to frequency across each observed lesson.

Learning outcomes questionnaire. The learning outcomes questionnaire enabled teachers to gauge the extent to which the children were building understandings and making connections between information discussed during their cooperative learning experiences. It consisted of a set of generic questions stems, based on Bloom's (1956) taxonomy that was originally developed by King (1991) and modified by

Gillies and Ashman (1996, 1998). The questions stems were arranged according to level of complexity from those that asked children to recall basic factual details through to those that required children to analyse and integrate information or propose solutions.

Questions that tapped basic recall of facts generally began with the following sentence stems: "What is … ?" "How many … ?" In contrast, questions that were highly complex and required students to evaluate multiple sources of information usually began with the following sentence stems: "Discuss the pros and cons of …" or "Select and justify …." Students were assigned a learning outcomes score of 1–6 depending on the highest level of response they were able to successfully complete.

The advantage of using this type of measure to tap children's learning was that it allowed teachers to construct a learning outcomes measure that was authentic and relevant to the unit of work the children had completed. That is, the questionnaire covered equivalent content and an appropriate range of material within the work unit and it accurately reflected all six response levels.

12.14   Procedure

As with the first study described earlier, the teachers were audiotaped once during each of the two social science curriculum units in which cooperative learning strategies were embedded. Once again, the audiotaping occurred in the last 2 weeks of each unit of work and the teachers wore an audio-microphone and were taped for the full class period. Two student groups were also identified and taped during these class periods by placing a cassette player with a directional microphone on the table to capture the students' discussions. Additionally, ten learning outcomes questionnaires were collected from each class at the completion of the second work unit.

12.15   Results

Teachers' verbal behaviours. The data collected on the teachers' verbal behaviours were analysed and significant differences were found with teachers in the cooperative-interactional condition recording more questions (effect size = + 0.57) and mediated-learning behaviours (effect size = + 0.50) than their cooperative peers. In contrast, teachers in the cooperative condition recorded more of the following behaviours: control behaviours (effect size = + 0.22), disciplinary comments (effect size = 0.62), encouraging behaviours (effect size = + 0.16), and maintenance behaviours (effect size = + 0.56).

Students' verbal behaviours. Similarly, data collected on the students' verbal behaviours were analysed and significant differences were found with children in the cooperative-interactional condition recording more elaborations (effect size = + 0.23), questions (effect size = + 0.23), and short answer responses (effect size = + 0.69) than their peers in the cooperative condition. In contrast, the children in the cooperative condition recorded more engaging behaviour (effect size = + 0.65).

Learning outcomes questionnaire. The students' scores on the learning outcome questionnaire were analysed and while there were significant differences between the two conditions, with children in the cooperative-interactional condition obtaining higher learning outcomes, the effect size (+0.02) was very small, limiting the educational significance of the result.

12.16   Discussion

This study sought to compare the effects of the two conditions on teachers' verbal behaviours during cooperative learning. It also sought to compare the verbal behaviours of the students in the two conditions. The study ran over two school terms and teachers were required to embed cooperative learning into one unit of work for each term. The results show that the teachers in the cooperative-interactional condition who had been trained to implement specific communication strategies that were designed to challenge children's thinking and scaffold their learning asked more questions and used more mediated-learning behaviours than their peers in the cooperative condition. In contrast, the teachers in the cooperative condition engaged in more disciplinary comments and used more maintenance language than the teachers in the cooperative-interactional condition.

Although the teachers in the cooperative-interactional condition not only asked more questions than their cooperative peers, they also increased their questioning behaviour over the study which was somewhat surprising, given the emphasis that had been placed on asking questions that probed and challenged children's thinking rather than those that elicited short and unelaborated responses. However, Turner et al. (2002) argued that this type of verbal behaviour can be effective if used in combination with instructional scaffolding such as occurred in this study when teachers engaged in mediated-learning behaviours.

This type of questioning, in conjunction with instructional scaffolding, is demonstrated in the following teacher-student dialogue where the teacher asked a closed question (one that elicited a short answer response) that was followed by a probe, designed to help the students focus more intently on the issue at hand:

1. Teacher: *What have you got here?* (referring to the work the students are doing)
2. Students: *Our diorama* (short answer response)
3. Teacher: *I wonder if you've considered including this information as part of your presentation?* (Teacher posing a tentative question to help students consider additional information needed)

4. Student: *We though of that and we were going to try and put it in here 'cause we though it would fit better. We think it's better to show it here with this* (pointing to picture of graph) *so people can understand what it means.*

In the above dialogue, the teacher begins by asking a closed question (Turn 1) to which the students respond with a short answer (Turn 2). The teacher then probes the children's thinking by asking a tentative question to see if they had considered all the information (Turn 3). This question stimulates a detailed and well-reasoned response that demonstrates that the students had considered alternative ways of presenting the information.

It appeared that the mediated-learning behaviour that the teacher used helped to set up a sequence of reciprocal interactions between the teacher and her students that stimulated their thinking and problem-solving strategies. Interestingly, teachers in the cooperative-interactional condition engaged in over 30% more interactions with their student groups than the teachers in the cooperative condition. It may be that training teachers to use specific communication skills heightened their sensitivity to the way they interacted with their students so they realised the importance of probing, scaffolding, and challenging children's thinking.

The frequency of the dialogic exchange that occurred between the teachers and students in the cooperative-interactional condition appeared to make students acutely perceptive of the importance of being more responsive to other group members needs and, in so doing, they modelled many of the verbal behaviours they had heard their teachers demonstrate in their interactions with them.

This modelling is illustrated in the following dialogue that is a small part of a continuous discussion that occurred in one of the small groups in the cooperative-interactional condition. In the exchange reported below, the students are discussing an information report they are writing on king penguins:

Student 1: What do you think about this? I wrote down ...
Student 2: That's pretty good (Encouragement by student of another's efforts). What are you going to write down? (Challenge to another student to identify what he is going to contribute)

Student 1: What are you doing? (Student challenges another student's contribution to the group)
Student 3: I found (king penguins) go further north – north of Antarctica. Enemies would be? What do you reckon enemies would be? (Challenge to group's thinking) (Response is not clear)
Student 4: Yeah! That's what I'm thinking (validation of idea). It has many enemies. Put many enemies (All students engage in a vibrant discussion about predators)
Student 1: Was any other features? Yeah! Any other features? What do you reckon? (Seeks group's opinion on other information to be included)

In the above dialogue, the students used a number of verbal behaviours that their teacher had demonstrated in her interactions with them. For example, they sought each other's opinion on ideas or information: *What do you think about this?* and encouraged each other: *That's pretty good*; and challenged the group's thinking: *What do you reckon enemies would be?* These types of interactions occurred many times over as the students challenged each others' perspectives, validated and acknowledged each other's efforts, and actively sought the ideas of others – models of interacting that their teachers had demonstrated with them.

It has been suggested that children probably learn new ways of thinking and talking by listening to teachers' model these types of verbal behaviours in their interactions with students (Cohen et al. 2002). Moreover, when teachers are explicit in the types of thinking they want children to engage in, it encourages students, in turn, to be more explicit in the types of help they provide to each other during group discussions. This is particularly important because it is the quality of the talk that students generate that is a significant predictor of student learning (King 2002; Webb and Farivar 1999). This certainly happened in this study with the students in the cooperative-interactional condition obtaining higher learning outcome scores than their peers in the cooperative condition, and although the small effect size limits the interpretation placed on the result, the trend was positive.

12.17   Theoretical and Practical Implications

The major theoretical and practical implications that emerged from the two studies were evident in the effect cooperative learning has on teachers' and students' discourse and in the role that teachers play in the social construction of knowledge at both the intra- and inter-personal level for the students they teach.

The first study demonstrated support for Hertz-Lazarowitz's and Shachar's (1990) thesis that the organisational structure of the classroom affects the way teachers interact with their students. This is not surprising given that those authors argued that there are four inter-dependent dimensions in the classroom, the organisational structure, the learning task, the students' academic and social skills, and the teacher's instructional style, so that changes in one dimension are likely to affect changes in other dimensions simultaneously. Hence, in classrooms where cooperative learning is endorsed, students work in small groups on complex tasks that require them to exchange ideas and share information and resources as they work on solving the problem at hand. When this happens, the centrality of the teacher is reduced as students become more personally active in their dialogic exchanges which are more intimate, spontaneous, and creative as they work to socially construct joint understandings and learning.

In this type of classroom, Hertz-Lazarowitz and Shachar (1990) found that teachers act as facilitators of learning rather than dispensers of knowledge so when they encounter small, cooperative groups rather than whole classes or large groups, they radically increase their prosocial instructional behaviours and drastically decrease their negative ones. Interestingly, Study 1 found that when teachers engage in dialogic exchanges with students in cooperative groups, they engage in more mediated-learning and questioning behaviours designed to challenge and scaffold students' thinking and learning and students, in turn, model many of these behaviours in their interactions with each other, providing more elaborations, directions, and short answer responses, or verbal behaviours that are generally regarded as more helpful and supportive of group endeavours.

There is no doubt that teachers play a key role in the social construction of knowledge at both the inter-personal (Vygotsky 1978) and intra-personal level (Piaget 1950) and while teachers did this in both studies reported here, it was more apparent in the second study that had a learning outcomes measure. The mediated-learning interactions that the teachers used were designed to not only scaffold students' learning but also to prompt meaningful cognitive and metacognitive thinking about their problem-solving activities. Moreover, because the teachers used language that was tentative and inviting, they were able to scaffold or mediate potential learning while also challenging students' thinking and encouraging them to consider alternative perspectives (King 2002). When teachers interact in this way, they not only introduce students to new patterns of thought but also new ways of resolving perturbations and making decisions. It has been suggested that children probably learn new ways of thinking and talking by listening to teachers model these behaviours in their interactions with students (Cohen et al. 2002; see King, this volume). Moreover, Rojas-Drummond et al. (2003) were able to demonstrate that children obtain particular benefits in reasoning and learning from dialoguing when there is careful integration of teacher-led discourse and peer interaction. Furthermore, this is something teachers must be willing to do if they are to ensure that the social pedagogic potential of classroom group work is to be fully realised (Blatchford et al. 2003).

In summary, there is no doubt that cooperative learning positively affects how teachers interact with their students and how students, in turn, interact with each other. In such classrooms, teachers are more friendly and intimate and are more likely to engage in mediated-learning and questioning behaviours than teachers who work in classrooms where cooperative learning is not established. Furthermore, teachers' discourse is enhanced when they are taught specific communication skills designed to scaffold and challenge students' thinking and learning.

References

Antil, L., Jenkins, J., Wayne, S., & Vadasy, P. (1998). Cooperative learning: Prevalence, conceptualizations, and the relation between research and practice. *American Educational Research Journal, 35*, 419–454.

Baines, E., Blatchford, P., & Kutnick, P. (2003). Changes in grouping practices over primary and secondary school. *International Journal of Educational Research, 39*, 9–34.

Blatchford, P., Kutnick, P., & Galton, M. (2003). Towards a social pedagogy of classroom group. *International Journal of Educational Research, 39*, 153–172.

Bloom, B., Engelhart, M., Furst, E., Hill, W., & Krathwohl, D. (1956). *Taxonomy of educational objectives: The classification of educational goals. Handbook 1: Cognitive domain.* New York: David Mckay.

Brown, A., & Palincsar, A. (1988). Guided, cooperative learning and individual knowledge acquisition. In L. Resnick (Ed.), *Cognition and instruction: Issues and agendas.* Hillsdale, NJ: Lawrence Erlbaum.

Cohen, E. (1994). Restructuring the classroom: Conditions for productive small groups. *Review of Educational Research, 64*, 1–35.

Cohen, E., Lotan, R., Abram, P., Scarloss, B., & Schultz, S. (2002). Can groups learn? *Teachers College Record, 104*, 1045–1068.

Chinn, C., O'Donnell, A., & Jinks, T. (2000). The structure of discourse in collaborative learning. *The Journal of Experimental Education, 69*, 77–89.

Egan, G. (2002). *The skilled helper: A problem-management and opportunity-development approach to helping* (7th edn.). Pacific Grove, CA: Brooks/Cole.

Fuchs, L., Fuchs, D., Hamlett, C., Phillips, N., Karns, K., & Dutka, S. (1997). Enhancing students' helping behavior with conceptual mathematical explanations. *The Elementary School Journal, 97*, 223–249.

Galton, M., Hargreves, L., Comber, C., Wall, D., & Pell, T. (1999). Changes in patterns of teacher interaction in primary classrooms: 1976–1996. *British Educational Research Journal, 25*, 23–37.

Gillies, R. (2003a). Structuring cooperative group work in classrooms. *International Journal of Educational Research, 39*, 35–49.

Gillies, R. (2003b). The behaviours, interactions, and perceptions of junior high school students during small-group learning. *Journal of Educational Psychology, 95*, 137–147.

Gillies, R. (2004). The effects of communication training on teachers' and students' verbal behaviours during cooperative learning. *International Journal of Educational Research, 41*, 257–279.

Gillies, R. (2006). Teachers' and students' verbal behaviours during cooperative and small-group learning. *British Journal of Educational Psychology, 76*, 271–287.

Gillies, R., & Ashman, A. (1996). Teaching collaborative skills to primary school children in classroom-based work groups. *Learning and Instruction, 6*, 187–200.

Gillies, R., & Ashman, A. (1998). Behavior and interactions of children in cooperative groups in lower and middle elementary grades. *Journal of Educational Psychology, 90*, 746–757.

Hertz-Lazarowitz, R., & Shachar, H. (1990). Teachers' verbal behaviour in cooperative and whole-class instruction. In S. Sharan (Ed.), *Cooperative learning: Theory and research* (pp. 77–94). New York: Praeger.

Johnson, D., & Johnson, R. (2003). Student motivation in cooperative groups: Social interdependence theory. In R. Gillies & A. Ashman (Eds.), *Cooperative learning: The social and intellectual outcomes of learning in groups* (pp. 136–176). London: RoutledgeFalmer.

Johnson, D., & Johnson, R. (1990). Cooperative learning and achievement. In S. Sharan (Ed.), *Cooperative learning: Theory and research* (pp. 23–37). New York: Praeger.

King, A. (1991). Improving lecture comprehension: Effects of a metacognitive strategy. Applied Cognitive Psychology, 5, 331–346.

King, A. (1999). Discourse patterns for mediating peer learning. In A. O'Donnell & A. King (Eds.), *Cognitive perspectives on peer learning* (pp. 87–115). Mahwah, NJ: Lawrence Erlbaum.

King, A. (2002). Structuring peer interaction to promote high-level cognitive processing. Theory into Practice, 41, 33–40.

Kohn, A. (1992). Resistance to cooperative learning: Making sense of its deletion and dilution. *Journal of Education, 174*, 38–55.

Meloth, M., & Deering, P. (1999). The role of the teacher in promoting cognitive processing during collaborative learning. In A. O'Donnell & A. King (Eds.), *Cognitive perspectives on peer learning* (pp. 235–255). Mahwah, NJ: Lawrence Erlbaum.

Mercer, N. (1996). The quality of talk in children'collaborative activity in the classroom. *Learning and Instruction, 6*, 359–377.

Mercer, N., Wegerif, R., & Dawes, L. (1999). Children's talk and the development of reasoning in the classroom. *British Educational Research Journal, 25*, 95–111.

Lou, Y., Abrami, P., Spence, J., Poulsen, C., Chambers, B., & d'Apollonia, S. (1996). Within-class grouping: A meta-analysis. *Review of Educational Research, 66*, 423–458.

O'Donnell, A. (1999). Structuring dyadic interaction through scripted cooperation. In A. O'Donnell & A. King (Eds.), *Cognitive perspectives on peer learning* (pp. 179–196). Mahwah, NJ: Lawrence Erlbaum.

Palincsar, A. (1999). Designing collaborative contexts: lessons from three research programs. In A. O'Donnell & A. King (Eds.), *Cognitive perspectives on peer learning* (pp. 151–177). Mahwah, NJ: Lawrence Erlbaum.

Palinscar, A., & Herrenkohl, L. (2002). Designing collaborative contexts. *Theory into Practice, 41*, 26–35.

Patrick, H., Anderman, L., Ryan, A., Edelin, K., & Midgley, C. (2001). Teachers' communication of goal orientation in four fifth-grade classrooms. *The Elementary School Journal, 102*, 35–58.

Piaget, J. (1950). *The psychology of intelligence*. London: Routledge & Kegan.

Rojas-Drummond, S., Perez, V., Velez, M., Gomez, L., & Mendoza, A. (2003). Talking for reasoning among Mexican primary school children. *Learning and Instruction, 13*, 653–670.

Schulz, S., Scarloss, B., Lotan, R., Abram, P., Cohen, E., & Holthuis, N. (2000). *Let's give 'em somethin' to talk about: Teachers talk to students in open-ended group tasks*. Paper presented at AERA Annual Meeting, New Orleans, LA.

Shachar, H., & Sharan, S. (1994). Talking, relating, and achieving: Effects of cooperative learning and whole-class instruction. *Cognition and Instruction, 12*, 313–353.

Sharan, S., Shachar, H., Levine, T. (1999). *The innovative school: Organization and instruction*. Westport, CT: Bergin & Garvey.

Turner, J., Midgley, C., Meyer, D., Gheen, M., Anderman, E., & Kang, Y. (2002). The classroom environment and students' reports of avoidance strategies in mathematics: A multimethod study. *Journal of Educational Psychology, 94*, 88–106.

Turner, J., & Patrick, H. (2004). Motivational influences on student participation in classroom learning activities. *Teachers College record, 106*, 1759–1785.

Vygotsky, L. (1978). *Mind in society: The development of higher psychological processes*. Cambridge, MA: Harvard University Press.

Webb, N., & Farivar, S. (1999). Developing productive group interaction in middle school mathematics. In A. O'Donnell & A. King (Eds.), *Cognitive perspectives on peer learning* (pp. 117–150). Mahwah, NJ: Lawrence Erlbaum.

Webb, N., & Mastergeorge, A. (2003). Promoting effective helping in peer-directed groups. *International Journal of Educational Research, 39*, 73–97.

Wegerif, R., Mercer, N., & Dawes, L. (1999). From social interaction to individual reasoning: An empirical investigation of a possible socio-cultural model of cognitive development. *Learning and Instruction, 9*, 493–516.

Concluding Remarks

Robyn M. Gillies, Adrian F. Ashman, and Jan Terwel

There is a large body of research literature that provides substantial evidence of the effectiveness of cooperative learning as a pedagogical practice that promotes socialization and learning in students with diverse learning and adjustment needs across different age levels. While much of the research has focused on the benefits students derive from participating in cooperative activities, scant mention has been made of the key role that teachers play in implementing cooperative pedagogy in their classrooms. The purpose of the chapters in this volume has been to address this omission by highlighting what teachers need to know and do to ensure that cooperative learning is implemented effectively in their classrooms. The chapters were grouped so that those which addressed theoretical perspectives of how students learn in groups were presented first (Chap. 1–3) followed by those that highlighted the different ways in which teachers can structure interactions among group members (Chap. 4–9). Finally, the remaining chapters focused on the role that teachers play in facilitating students' interactions (Chap. 10–12).

Understanding the key role theory plays in helping to explain how and why students cooperate in small groups is crucial for guiding research and practice. To date, among the most prominent theoretical perspectives already mentioned in the Introduction of this book and elaborated in subsequent chapters, Moreton Deutsch's Social Interdependence theory is significant (see chapter by Johnson & Johnson). This theory not only offers explanations of why students are motivated to work together but also identifies the benefits they derive from cooperative experiences, including greater efforts to achieve, improved social relationships, and an enhanced sense of competence.

Although Social Interdependence theory underpins much of the research on cooperative learning, two other perspectives have been proposed in this volume that contributes to our theoretical understanding of how students learn and construct knowledge together. The first is the critical pedagogical perspective which Hertz-Lazarowitz argues has the potential to change how teachers teach and children learn. The second is the social pedagogic approach of Baines and colleagues that examines the relationship among group size, composition, learning tasks, supportive interactions with peers and teachers, and the training students undertake to work effectively in groups. Understanding the contributions that these theoretical perspectives make are critical for helping to extend our knowledge of how classroom social contexts may promote or inhibit social interaction and learning.

Having students work successfully in groups is also very dependent on how teachers structure the interactions that occur within classrooms and in other teaching-learning contexts. A number of chapters in this volume propose different ways in which these interactions can be facilitated by providing children with examples of questions that encourage them to probe and interrogate information, link previous understandings to new information, and use these new understandings to co-construct new knowledge and solve problems (see chapters by King, Webb, & Ross).

In other chapters, authors highlight how specific interrogation strategies can be embedded in curriculum content to enhance students' understanding and learning (see chapters by Stevens, Huber & Huber, & Prinsen et al.). Emphasis is placed on the role that teachers play in this process, including ways in which they can facilitate learning through the provision of opportunities for students to work on complex, relevant, open-ended tasks that promote discussion and challenge students' thinking. At this point, it is important to realize that curriculum domains (e.g., mathematics or world orientation) have their own, unique possibilities for cooperative learning. For instance, cooperative learning in mathematics provides new ways to adapt teaching and learning to individual differences among students. The work of the Dutch mathematician, Hans Freudenthal, inspired many researchers to design and investigate cooperative learning in heterogeneous groups of four. His work is an example of how to look at individual differences as a resource instead of a hindrance for teachers of mathematics (Gravemeijer & Terwel 2000; Terwel 1990, 2003). Hence, it is argued that cooperative learning approaches cannot simply be applied in whatever domain of study. In designing cooperative learning environments the small group interaction needs always to be viewed in relation to the curricular content and the specific classroom context. Attention is also directed at the importance of ensuring that teachers provide engaging and responsive instruction that addresses the personal and social needs of the students in their classrooms.

This is no more apparent than in the chapter by Ashman who recounts the difficulties that students with high support needs often face when they are included in regular classes where they are often provided with few supports to assist their learning. Students with high support needs include those who have severe emotional or behavioural difficulties, life-threatening medical conditions, and those with severe and profound intellectual disabilities. Ashman argues that for these children, special classes or special educational programs are often more appropriate for their specific needs, given that the research on the achievements of children with high support needs with peer-mediated learning experiences is equivocal.

Of particular note, teachers should be aware that the research on the effects of peer-mediated learning on students with high support needs has been less extensive than for normally achieving students and often investigators have employed small samples. In addition, interventions have been relatively short. These factors often contribute to perceptions of the limited educational significance and generalization of peer-mediated interventions. Being aware of the limitations of the research on peer-mediated learning, especially for students with high support needs, is important when teachers are determining how and when these students can best be supported in a range of teaching-learning environments.

Although there are limitations on the use of peer-mediated learning with some groups of students with high support needs, this does not appear to be the case with minority group students for whom English is a second language. Lotan clearly demonstrated how students can develop oral and written proficiency in academic and linguistically heterogeneous classrooms where they are able to interact with others. She argues that exposing students to linguistically rich environments where they can participate in discussions and negotiations with peers and teachers is critical for developing language proficiency. Moreover, she argues that teachers need to provide students with opportunities to use language actively and frequently as they work interdependently on tasks with others. Furthermore, teachers must be mindful of the importance of monitoring students' discussions, facilitating and scaffolding their learning. In effect, Lotan argues that the classroom social context is critically important for promoting second language learning.

There is no doubt that students learn from interacting with their peers. Webb drew attention to the need for students to understand not only how to provide quality help but also ensure that it is provided it in a way that students perceive as being relevant and timely. Research clearly indicates that the benefits of receiving help are maximized when students requesting help receive explanations that are appropriately detailed, salient to the context, and applicable to the problems they are confronting.

While learning to give explanations in response to requests for help is important if learning is to occur, Ross argued that children rarely give explanations and when they do, the quality of the explanation often does not contribute to the help seeker's learning. The challenge for teachers is to find ways of helping students to increase the frequency of high quality explanations. Suggestions for how this can be achieved are documented in his chapter.

Finally, Gillies reminds us of the important role that teachers play in the cooperative learning process. While it has often been assumed that the teacher should adopt a non-interventionist role, research reported in her chapter clearly demonstrates that cooperative learning provides teachers with many opportunities to model appropriate helping behaviors that students, in turn, will model and use in their interactions with each other to facilitate discussion and learning.

While the contributors to this volume have provided some explanations on how students learn when they cooperate and how teachers play a key role in promoting this learning, there are still many unanswered questions that need further investigation if these issues are to be fully explicated. This includes additional research on both the critical and social pedagogical perspectives that are informing the development of theory, ways in which cooperative learning can be designed for different curricula content and classroom contexts, including how it can be used for students with high support needs, and the issues teachers confront, both personally and pragmatically, when they adopt a cooperative learning approach to meet the personal and social needs of students in their classrooms. Such research will make invaluable contributions to informing teachers' professional practices in schools.

References

Gravemeijer, K. & Terwel, J. (2000) Hans Freudenthal: A mathematician on didactics and curriculum theory. *Journal of Curriculum Studies, 32,* 777–796.

Terwel, J. (1990). Real maths in cooperative groups in secondary education. In N. Davidson (Ed.), *Cooperative learning in mathematics* (pp. 228–264). Menlo Park: Addison-Wesley.

Terwel, J. (2003). Cooperative learning in secondary education: A curriculum perspective. In R. M. Gillies & A. F. Ashman (Eds.). *Cooperative learning: The social and intellectual outcomes of learning in groups* (pp. 54–68). London: RoutledgeFalmer.

Index

COMPUTER-SUPPORTED COLLABORATIVE LEARNING

Printed in the United States
146964LV00003B/27/A

9 780387 708911